ELUSIVE REFORM

ELUSIVE REFORM

Democracy and the Rule of Law in Latin America

MARK UNGAR

LYNNE
RIENNER
PUBLISHERS

BOULDER
LONDON

Published in the United States of America in 2002 by
Lynne Rienner Publishers, Inc.
1800 30th Street, Boulder, Colorado 80301
www.rienner.com

and in the United Kingdom by
Lynne Rienner Publishers, Inc.
3 Henrietta Street, Covent Garden, London WC2E 8LU

Library of Congress Cataloging-in-Publication Data
Ungar, Mark.
   Elusive reform :   democracy and the rule of law in Latin America   /   Mark Ungar.
      p.   cm.
   Includes bibliographical references and index.
   ISBN 1-58826-035-6
   1. Rule of law—Latin America.   2. Democracy—Latin America.   3. Political
stability—Latin America.   4. Latin America—Politics and government—1980–   I. Title.
KG552.U558   2001
321.8'098—dc21

                                                                        2001034950

British Cataloguing in Publication Data
A Cataloguing in Publication record for this book
is available from the British Library.

Printed and bound in the United States of America

The paper used in this publication meets the requirements
of the American National Standard for Permanence of
Paper for Printed Library Materials Z39.48-1984.

5   4   3   2   1

CONTENTS

TABLES

ACKNOWLEDGMENTS

MANY PEOPLE AND ORGANIZATIONS helped make this book possible. For their academic support and insight, I want to thank Margaret Crahan, Douglas Chalmers, Consuelo Cruz, Robert Kaufman, Stephen Marks, Guillermo O'Donnell, Alfred Stepan, Leopoldo Schiffrin, Paulo Sérgio Pinheiro, Anthony Pereira, Martín Abregú, Julio Borges, Vladimir Villegas, Rafael Bielsa, Luis Paravicini, and the late Carlos Nino.

For their generous financial backing, I am grateful to the National Security Education Project of the U.S. Congress, the Department of Political Science and the Institute of Latin American Studies of Columbia University, and the Research Foundation of the City University of New York. Many organizations in Latin America also gave a great deal of help and information. In Venezuela, these organizations include La Red de Apoyo por la Justicia y la Paz, the Judicial Council, the Supreme Court of Justice, the Presidential Commission for State Reform, the Ministry of Justice, the Public Ministry, the Judicial Police, and many members of Congress. In Argentina, they include the Centro de Estudios Legales y Sociales, the Justice Ministry, the Instituto de Estudios Comparados en Ciencias Penales y Sociales, Poder Ciudadano, the Bar Associations of the Federal Capital and of La Plata, the Human Rights Office of the Interior Ministry, and the Argentine Federal Police. In Bolivia, I was helped by the Ministry of Justice and Human Rights, the Defensoría del Pueblo, the Public Defense Office, the Permanent Assembly of Human Rights of Bolivia, the Judicial Council, and the Judicial Police.

Lynne Rienner Publishers provided an exceptional level of support and assistance throughout the editorial and publication process. All of my friends, my family, and my partner, Bob, provided an endless supply of encouragement, humor, and love. I also want to thank my colleagues and students at Brooklyn College, my fellow committee members at Amnesty International, and the courageous human rights defenders with whom I have had the privilege of working. My friends in Caracas have been an example of how to fight injustice with humanity. And the memory of my mother, Carol, has been a reminder of how to really give of yourself.

—*Mark Ungar*

1

INTRODUCTION

DEMOCRACY CANNOT EXIST without the rule of law. A constitution is useless without a judiciary that supports it, a law is ineffective without officials who uphold it, and an election is empty if the winners do not respect the rights of all citizens. In Latin America—as in Europe, Africa, and Asia—the ability to create a rule of law helps determine democracy's character and future prospects. This book defines the *rule of law* as comprising an independent effective judiciary, state accountability to the law, and citizen accessibility to conflict-resolution mechanisms. The rule of law makes constitutional rights a daily reality, and adopting measures to create it is therefore one of the biggest steps toward democratic consolidation. Without such *rule of law reforms*, nondemocratic patterns rooted in history will thrive under the cover of democratic institutions and, eventually, undermine them. This book explains when democratic regimes are able to enact such measures and, once enacted, the limits of their effectiveness. I contend that executive dominance and judicial disarray lead to rule of law reforms but that these two conditions return to threaten those very changes.

Even with a growing recognition of the importance of the rule of law, there has been very little analysis of why reform does or does not work. Most generally, the sheer extent of needed changes is a barrier to their enactment. Most countries emerging from long authoritarian eras are ill-equipped to build a new constitutional order; their judiciaries and state agencies are paralyzed by corruption, infrastructural disabilities, questionable jurisprudence, incomplete legislation, and political interference. Incremental policy adjustments and personnel changes do not begin to resolve such problems. The extent of the undertaking becomes even clearer when unpacking the definition of a rule of law into its three main elements: (1) an *accountable, law-abiding state* whose agencies cooperate with judicial procedures, carry out court rulings, and follow constitutional norms in good faith; (2) *independent judicial functioning*, where judges and judicial

1

officials make binding decisions on cases and interpretations of the law, with necessary logistical and material support and without undue interference by governmental or private interests; and (3) *judicial access*, which is the availability of impartial mechanisms of conflict and grievance resolution, primarily but not exclusively in the judiciary, to all individuals.

Weakness in these elements has two general causes. First, the executive branch is either too repressive and/or too unresponsive. Institutionalized practices of the agencies of Latin America's executives slow down reform after democratic transitions, whereas short-term politics often make elected presidents unresponsive to long-term needs. In most new democracies, executives also strong-arm judicial nominations, manipulate the law, and meddle in cases affecting basic rights. The second overarching cause is judiciaries wherein bias, delays, corruption, and various forms of bureaucracy prevent them from meeting their own procedural standards and constitutional obligations. Even if they are efficient, in addition, those judiciaries may be inaccessible to the vast majority of citizens, discriminatory against certain social sectors, or lacking rudimentary channels such as notification of defendants' families. In both the executive and judicial branches, moreover, political parties and economic actors wield tremendous influence through unwritten agreements, pacts, patronage, financial incentives, and threats.

At face value, these two conditions—*executive power* and *judicial disarray*—are broad enough to explain any kind of reform and, consequently, no particular kind of reform at all. They also risk confusing the problem with the solution by casting the executive and the judiciary in both roles. But only such an approach can show why the rule of law is elusive, because those responsible for creating it are also responsible for enforcing it. Presidents are necessary for developing and approving reform measures in response to long-term needs, but they may end up ignoring or undermining those measures that even they initially supported. Judges usually want more powers and clearer procedures but may be too compromised, overwhelmed, or suspicious to handle them responsibly. A democracy working to create a rule of law is trying to pull itself up by its own bootstraps: the same officials and institutions it relies on are the same ones that obstruct needed change.

Because the executive and judicial branches employ a wide range of officials that interact in many ways, executive power and judicial disarray describe certain power dynamics involving all those responsible for a rule of law. Executive power is not simply the traditional, heavy-handed repressive power of a president but also the many uses of executive authority at the national, provincial, and local levels. It is domination of political agendas and of the legislatures that turn them into law. It is the excessive use of constitutional executive authorities such as appointment, the exploitation of informal instruments such as state monies, and usurpation of legislative and judicial authorities, such as administrative oversight. It is also, even in a democracy, the many uses of undemocratic practices by officials within the executive branch. Even in countries with a history of short-lived presidencies, such as Bolivia, the executive historically has overshadowed the other branches of government. The judicial branch in particular has been politically and institutionally subservient. So even though most barriers to rule of law occur within the judiciary, the ability to overcome them depends on the will of an authoritative president to get reforms enacted and make sure that they are enforced. But with the decline of the state-run economies, and growing disillusion with party politics that now weaken the executive branch, executive power needs to be reexamined. One of the best ways to do so is through an executive's responses to the rule of law reforms intended to limit its power. Such responses are thus critical not only to the effectiveness of those reforms but also to democratization in general.

Similarly, judicial disarray means more than an exasperated dismissal of the judiciary's obvious chaos. It is about specific procedures within each judicial agency, the actual uses of judicial authority, and the financial and logistical supports that courts require. It means both the judiciary's responsibility to defend human rights as well as its need to ensure a juridical security, in which economic and political conflicts are resolved through the law. Fully grasping the nature and extent of such disarray, therefore, means disentangling a country's numerous judicial functions—from public-order policies to the conflicts between judges and the police—to see how they affect individual rights and democratic governance.

Most rule of law reforms are motivated from the repercussions of executive power and judicial disarray as well as the interaction between them. In particular, elected officials enact measures when they realize that an institution no longer functions and that they may be blamed for it, fairly or unfairly. The benefits to political officials of a pliant judiciary diminish when it can no longer carry out basic functions like conducting trials and protecting international capital. To improve state administration and the confidence in the courts needed for investor confidence and popular support, presidents might even take measures that limit their own power. The attempts by former Mexico President Ernesto Zedillo to reduce his party's stranglehold over the state in the late 1990s; the limits enacted in the mid-1980s by former Argentina President Raúl Alfonsín in the wake of a dictatorship; and the last-ditch efforts of Venezuela's dying parties to streamline the judiciary in the late 1990s—all attest to the executive's sway over reform.

But these instances are the exception. When it comes to putting together actual proposals, it may dawn on political officials that the change might impinge upon them in more ways than anticipated. Measures that at first are promoted as sensible may suddenly be attacked as reckless. Conveniently, each reform stage—formulation, revision, implementation— is filled with opportunities to destroy or dilute it. The final product is thus often poorly conceived reform lacking enforcement mechanisms, ignoring root causes, or generating more problems than it solves. It is a tall order, after all, to create an independent, uncorrupt judiciary that holds the state accountable and brings in all sectors of society. To fill it, rule of law reform must cast a wide net, from the courts to Congress to the police—catching many powerful people in the process. Such politics shows how a democratic regime itself can slow movement toward a rule of law by allowing only certain reforms, at certain times, to be enacted. This hesitation is part of the larger weakness of Latin America's democracies. A reluctance to touch military law may reflect manipulation by the armed forces, for example, and a closed privatization scheme may reveal an overly intimate relationship between Congress and big business.

But shared understandings of how the executive and the judiciary have harmed the country in the past, and growing consensus on how they will affect its future, can overcome such political impediments. Each democracy's own priorities and assessments, in turn, will then give it a certain path of reform. In countries emerging from a long period of military rule, such as Chile, Argentina, and El Salvador, most proposals have focused on checking presidential power and making the judiciary accessible to pent-up grievances. In countries where the executive branch is criticized more for being unresponsive than repressive and the judiciary more for being inefficient than inaccessible, such as Colombia, Venezuela, and Ecuador, reforms have been geared toward improving policy and administrative efficiency. Executives can be both unresponsive and repressive, of course, and judiciaries both inaccessible and inefficient. In such cases, reform will be a mix reflecting the political urgency and institutional capacity associated with each condition.

Once in place, though, reforms must then confront the same conditions that gave rise to them: a repressive or unresponsive executive power, and an inefficient or inaccessible judiciary. Additional support is rarely forthcoming, as the window of opportunity for enactment usually closes after only a limited number of measures are approved. An executive that has regained its political footing with an improving economy or new elections may shake off reforms foisted upon it; worsening economic problems reorder civil society's priorities; and new institutions and officials created through reform may acquire their own patterns of abuse and inefficiency.[1] Reforms may also be further impaired by what they don't address. Measures to check the executive's repressive tendencies, for example, may fall victim to new crime-fighting policies. Reforms that improve the judiciary's efficiency may be limited in the long run because they ignore accessibility, and those dealing with accessibility will mean little if the judiciary itself remains inefficient.

Executive power and judicial disarray also fuel one another, as executives weaken the judiciary's attempts to strengthen itself and as judicial disarray encourages extensions of executive power. Reforms are thus ineffective unless they deal with both politics and bureaucracy. Checks on power can be run aground by bureaucracy, and as those trying to reduce bureaucracy can be circumvented by unaccountable officials. No matter what happens along the way, reforms eventually need to deal with the deeper, intangible attitudes beneath the bureaucratic surface. Even after a transition from authoritarianism, many Latin American polities are pervaded by attitudes that view compromise as weakness and laws as nonbinding guidelines. Because the judiciary is dominated by the executive, is structurally weak, and enjoys few working channels to citizens, it is also imbued with such nondemocratic views and practices. The resulting "legal culture" of "prevailing perceptions of what the legal system stands for together with actual practices and custom that have become ingrained in the profession," Joseph Thome (2000: 8) states, "can vitally affect its accessibility and effectiveness." If unaltered by reform, such a culture will curtail democracy's ability to build a rule of law.

As a result, the changes made amid such politics and attitudes will often be hollow. Most dangerously, they can cause a split between *authority*—which is the legitimate legal backing to carry out a function—and *power*—which is simply the physical means to carry out a function, with or without legal support. The judiciary may end up with the authority but not the power to carry out criminal investigations, and police agencies may acquire the power without the authority to do so. Such divergence is what allows undemocratic practices to flourish within democratic institutions. Under these conditions, officials who propose reform proposals without sufficient political and material backing might simply inoculate institutions from real progress.

A New Framework of Understanding

Each chapter in this book describes how executive power and judicial disarray hinder reforms' effectiveness and how some measures are able to withstand the political interests and corrosive attitudes involved. A new state agency may build its own political base, a new process may be a magnet for citizen action, or decentralization may create agencies out of an overbearing executive's reach. The ability of reforms to get past these barriers affects the consolidation of democracy, the focus of the final chapter (Chapter 8).

To paint such a broad picture, the book goes beyond existing studies of judicial reform. It views current conditions not only through contemporary democratic standards but also through practices that come from the past and will extend into the future. Most of Latin America's original nation-builders—including Simón Bolívar, Antonio José de Sucre, Mariano Moreno, Mariano Gálvez, Simón Carreño, and Dionisio Herrera—were concerned about the rule of law and institution-building (Sucre 1918; Moreno 1918; Tudela y Bueso 1998). But historical patterns of conflict overwhelmed these early ideals, leaving most Latin American republics with little more than a constitutional shell. The democratization era that began in the early 1980s—a reaction in part to the worst of history's repression—marks a return to the original questions of how to implement democratic standards. This new beginning has brought many promising changes. But more than a decade later, these democracies are entering the more difficult phase of delivering on popular expectations, which means that reforms are expected to show results. New due process rights, new oversight agencies, and other changes must be seen to have concrete impacts on the corruption, inefficiency, and other problems for which they were created.

To understand the extent of these expectations, this book focuses on the rule of law rather than on the judiciary. Most studies recognize that reform is political, but their focus on the judiciary often misses the wider context that determines reforms' effectiveness. This book, therefore, goes beyond formal judicial agencies to critically look at other parts of the state, such as the ombudsmen, and at trends within society, such as vigilante violence. The state's role is not limited to its enactment of judicial reforms but to the many ways its institutions and policies affect the rule of law. Similarly, society's role is about not only its relations with the judiciary but also its actual ability to resolve its grievances and demands for "justice." This broad approach helps uncover and highlight some of the deeper characteristics of democracy. In particular, the limits on state reform reveal weak accountability, the limits on judicial reforms demonstrate politicization, and the limits on judicial access show tensions in state-society relations. These are characteristics that make a democracy's routine practices undemocratic.

With a case-study focus on Argentina and Venezuela, I try to explain when and why democracies' rule of law reforms are effective or ineffective, devoting two chapters to each of the three basic elements of the rule of law. Chapters 2–7 are organized in a similar fashion. The first section of each of those chapters reconceptualizes one element by examining the actors, structures, and functions that it comprises. This approach explains the legal background and political development of each element, identifying the long-term interactions that reforms try to alter.

The second section in Chapters 2–7 then traces the element's historical roots, explaining through path dependency how executive power and judicial disarray from the past create obstacles to the element's realization in the present. This second section covers five periods in Latin American history: the colonial period, when the foundations of Latin American law were laid; independence to the 1850s, a time of civil war and *caudillismo*; the era of oligarchic stability of the latter 1800s; the state-building and violence at the turn of the century; and the period of democratic promise and reversal, from the 1920s through the 1980s.

Building on these conceptual and historical analyses, the third section of Chapters 2–7 looks at rule of law reform in the contemporary democratic period. Comparatively examining the entire region but focusing on post-1983 Argentina and post-1958 Venezuela, it explains how the enactment and implementation of specific reforms are shaped by executive power and judiciary disarray. This approach brings out specific challenges to the rule of law, such as politicization in judicial independence reforms and accountability to the law in police reforms.

Chapter Summaries and Organization

Chapters 2 and 3 examine the state. Chapter 2 disentangles the complex relationship between the state and the judiciary in order to explain why state agencies are crucial to the rule of law, as well as why rule of law reforms involving the state are difficult to establish during times of democratic transition or instability. The state and the rule of law affect each other in innumerable ways. Inadequate cooperation, organization, and accountability prevent the judiciary from receiving the support and information it needs from the state, and governments' emphasis on controlling crime and social unrest often interfere with rule of law functions. The first two sections analyze the historical relationship between the state and the rule of law, the development of state agencies with rule of law functions, and the judiciary's ability to hold those agencies accountable to the law.[2] How much a state is "law-abiding" is evaluated by state agencies' respect for constitutional due process guarantees, by their implementation of relevant judicial rulings, and by their cooperation in giving information to the judiciary and of investigating charges against state officials.

The final section in Chapter 2 examines the principal contemporary reforms within the state. The first kind of reform aims to improve the administration of state agencies involved with the rule of law—particularly penitentiary systems—by quickening criminal investigations, improving cooperation among ministries, opening up the formulation of executive policies, improving congressional oversight, decentralizing national agencies, and strengthening the Ministerio Público (Public Ministry/Attorney General's Office), *fiscales* (public prosecutors—officials of the Public

Ministry/Attorney General's Office), and public defenders. The second major kind of state rule of law reform focuses on improving agencies' accountability to the law. The main measure utilizing this approach has been the creation of national ombudsmen (usually, the Defensoría del Pueblo), institutionally independent agencies that receive citizen complaints and supervise their progress through the appropriate channels.

Chapter 3 expands on this analysis by examining the state agency responsible for daily enforcement of the rule of law: the police. Looking at the roles and the history of policing in Latin America, this chapter describes the breadth of police reform and its importance to the rule of law. Because the police is a major outlet of executive policy, as well as a major actor in judicial processes, police reforms are linked to both executive power and judicial disarray. The three main police reforms, discussed in the third section, are institutional restructuring, changes in the police's judicial role, and improvement in its relations with society.

Chapters 4 and 5 focus on the judiciary. Chapter 4 examines judicial independence and functioning, first by reconceptualizing the concept of judicial independence itself. It then looks at the development of judicial administration and independence through Latin American history, focusing on courts' efficiency and their deflection of interference on key matters like court jurisdiction and government decrees. The third section looks at attempts to reclaim the judiciary's authority through four main areas of judicial reform: more open and rigorous selection of judges; personnel training; court discipline; and resource management. Specific measures include stricter court standards; a more detailed set of infractions and punishments; and a requirement for a two-thirds majority of Congress, rather than a simple plurality, for approval of Supreme Court *magistrados* (judges).[3] The need to improve the quality of judges and judicial personnel has led to proposals for training schools, increases in salaries, and limits on court caseloads, as well as specialized courts and *salas* (chambers) for specific issues like sentencing and constitutionality. There also are efforts to reverse the centralization of Latin American judiciaries, which has curtailed judicial access, distanced officials from societal problems, and fell far from its goal to reduce corruption and favoritism. Finally, the corruption, red tape, inadequate staffs, and poor planning in the judiciary have prompted efforts to better manage resources, modernize the courts, and secure bigger budgets for them.

Chapter 5 discusses how all these problems are being tackled at once by one of the most important judicial independence reforms: judicial councils (most often called the Consejo de la Judicatura or Consejo de la Magistratura). Usually having constitutional ranking and always sparking political controversy, these councils are intended to zero in on the executive powers and judicial inefficiencies that are the main causes of low judicial independence and effectiveness. In particular, the councils select the initial nominees for the courts, directly cutting off the executive's biggest influence over the judiciary; and most councils have disciplinary and budgetary authority within the judiciary itself, allowing them to get at the source of internal inefficiency. Examining the actual experiences of these councils, however, I show in Chapter 5 how they are both motivated and weakened by executive power and judicial disarray. When created through a broad consensus beyond the executive, judicial councils have more potential to reduce executive power; and when created at a time of minimal judicial problems, they have more potential to really address them. But when rushed through by a domineering executive or amid high judicial disarray, these councils are less likely to be effective—or even to survive.

Chapters 6 and 7 turn to the third main element of the rule of law—judicial access—which in a democracy must go beyond formal accessibility of the courts. In particular, it should include access to other forms of conflict resolution as well as the political use of the law by society in general. In Chapter 6, the first two sections outline the concept of judicial access and its role through history, measuring it by the lack of popular channels to the courts as well as by trends in "legal mobilization," in which the citizenry "invoke[s] legal norms" and judicial channels "as a form of political activity by which [it] uses public authority on its own behalf" (Zemans 1983). The third section then looks at three of the three main kinds of reforms to improve judicial access: improvements in legal defense; the establishment and improvement of legal aid centers; and the use of alternative dispute resolution (ADR) mechanisms.

Chapter 7 focuses on a fourth and more significant reform, which is the creation of community justice forums to peacefully resolve disputes that never reach the courts. Unlike the other measures, community justice operates outside the judicial system, which alone makes it the most promising, uncertain, and politically threatening change. The law often encourages forum members to be "unjudges": nonlawyers unaffiliated with political parties and creative in their rulings. Once in place, community justice forms avoid judicial disarray and executive power by circumventing the judiciary and executive. As with other reforms, however, executive power as well as judicial disarray still loom. Forums must first dodge the many means of executive influence, such as financial incentives and party controls. Even more difficult to avoid, however, is the judiciary. Many forum cases wind up in the courts, their rulings often clash with national law, they by necessity refer to court rulings, and problems they confront, such as crime, are affected by the judiciary's functioning.

As discussed throughout the chapters, reforms in each element of the rule of law can get caught in such a cycle. Table 1.1 outlines the conditions that lead to reforms while also endangering their effectiveness.

Table 1.1   Causes and Obstacles of Rule of Law Reforms

PROBLEMS:

(1) The Executive: (2) The Judiciary:
    Unresponsive and/or repressive   Inefficient and/or inaccessible

MOTIVATE but then HINDER:

(1) The State:	(2) The Judiciary:	(3) Judicial Access:
Accountability	Independent Functioning	Citizen Participation
Principal Reform Areas:	*Principal Reform Areas:*	*Principal Reform Areas:*
• Improved administration	• Selection of judges	• Legal defense
• Accountability to the law	• Personnel training	• Support centers
• Better criminal policy	• Discipline	• Alternative dispute
• Decentralization	• Resource management	resolution
• Police forces		• Community justice

Case Studies

To bring out the dynamics of rule of law reform, this book focuses on the cases of Argentina and Venezuela. These countries are chosen for three basic reasons. First, they have initiated two of contemporary Latin America's broadest rule of law reform efforts, incorporating the whole spectrum of judicial actors, structures, and functions. These two cases thus have stronger explanatory power than such countries as Chile and Costa Rica, which have more cautious proposals and less divisive politics. Argentina and Venezuela also reveal more about reform than countries like Peru, Colombia, Paraguay, and Nicaragua, where executive power and domestic turbulence have been far and away the largest obstacles to change. In Argentina and Venezuela, presidents and political parties have not been quite strong enough to stop public pressure and institutional mal-functioning from being translated into reform proposals. Instead, the fluid politics in these countries shows how the characteristics and priorities of a democratic regime influence the types and effectiveness of enacted meas-ures. In Argentina, an authoritarian past and the post-1989 neoliberal eco-nomic policies have given priority to reforms that address the repressive nature of the executive and the inefficiency of the judiciary. Emphasis was put on individual guarantees and selection of judges in the wake of the dic-tatorship, and then, with the move toward neoliberalism, on making courts more effective with changes such as introducing ADR. In Venezuela, in contrast, growing disillusion with a corrupt political elite and institutional malfunctioning put priority on reforms to improve the responsiveness of the executive and the accessibility of the judiciary. The result was a push for stricter court discipline, better government policies, and community justice systems.

Second, the transitions undertaken by Argentina and Venezuela represent two basic paths of democratization that help to define the connection between democratization and reform. Like Argentina, many countries have endured histories of domineering executives and fluctuating economies. Other democracies like Venezuela enjoy steady constitutionalism, economic growth, and strong party control but are hit by crises that expose the weakness of their democratic institutions. Rule of law reform, shaped by both historical practices and contemporary politics, is part of these divergent paths. In Argentina, the brutality and collapse of the 1976–1983 dictatorship created a strong popular momentum for a rule of law as well as a political break that allowed reforms to be less hindered by partisan interests. In Venezuela, in contrast, the corruption, inefficiency, and partisanship of its democracy led to support for a different kind of change. Whereas Argentina and other new democracies are gradually moving toward consolidation—with new constitutions to strengthen existing democratic institutions—Venezuela is an older democracy moving in a less certain direction, with a constitution attempting to redefine democratic institutions. Because the majority of democracies follow one of these two patterns, but not as clearly or strongly, Argentina and Venezuela best demonstrate the importance of the rule of law in Latin America's democratic consolidation.

Third, these two cases also highlight international and regions patterns of reform. Since the late 1980s, Latin America has experienced a momentum for measures such as new penal codes, judicial councils, and ombudsmen. Many of these changes have been promoted by judicial specialists, lawmakers, and nongovernmental organizations (NGOs). Much of the funding has come from international financial institutions (IFIs) such as the World Bank and the Inter-American Development Bank (IDB), as well as government agencies such as the U.S. Agency for International Development (USAID).[4] The World Bank, for instance, has been involved in about forty reform projects, ranging from sweeping overhauls to limited pilot projects. But the lack of significant progress and government cooperation on many projects has led many IFIs to curtail or reevaluate their projects in the region. In Bolivia, the World Bank froze a judicial restructuring program because of the government's delays in enacting implementing laws. Because they were the scenes of two of the original and largest externally funded projects, Argentina and Venezuela most clearly show the influences of external involvement. Venezuela had the region's first World Bank plan, "'marketed' as the Bank's flagship involvement" in judicial reform around the world (Lawyers Committee 1996: 1), and Argentina had both one of the largest planned projects (IDB) and one of the first to be canceled (a World Bank project).

The Rule of Law in Democracy

Chapter 8 applies the issues laid out in the book to the question of democratic consolidation. By helping reconcile constitutional guarantees with everyday practices, the rule of law sheds light on the more elusive characteristics of consolidation, such as accountability, participation, and security. Accountability of state agencies is ultimately monitored through legal processes, for example, and citizens' long-term economic security depends on a wide range of laws. By showing how progress on the rule of law can support democratic consolidation, Chapter 8 projects the book's original question—When are democracies able to enact effective reforms?—into the future.

Writings on democratic theory and democratic consolidation do mention rule of law components, such as judicial independence, as part of the arrangements that sustain democracy.[5] But the literature is generally limited to individual measures or case studies that do not apply rule of law reform to the larger processes of democratization and the daily administration of justice. This shortcoming contributes to the poor understanding of the gap between democratic transition and consolidation. Stuck between the *first transition* to a democratically elected government and the *second transition* to "an institutionalized, consolidated democratic regime,"[6] many democracies are "of a type not yet theorized," as Guillermo O'Donnell asserts (1993: 1355–1356). Although much of the literature looks at the most recent authoritarian regime or the "birth defects" of the transition from it, just as important are the prior historical and current political processes that weaken democratic standards even within institutions created expressly to promote them. Rule of law reform exposes this understudied dimension of democratization, making it a necessary addition to the literature. If the first stage of reform is coming to grips with the rule of law's complexity (Binder 1993), this book moves into the second and far more difficult stage of implementing reforms amid complex political conditions. With this approach, the book shows why the link between reform and democratization is an intrinsic, "internal relation, and not simply a historically contingent association" (Habermas 1996: 454).

One way it gives substance to this link is through vague but critical elements of democracy, whose existence is difficult to prove but whose absence is obvious. One of those concepts is accountability. Many studies (Schedler et al. 1999) define accountability as involving both answerability to and enforceability of legal norms, and others outline the institutional reforms designed to enhance it. But such analyses need to go one step farther into the regular uses of the law. No matter how broad the mechanisms of accountability, they still cover only a small percentage of actions and will never touch the majority of daily activities. Public scandals and indictments of top officials are usually only the tip of the iceberg. Beneath the surface, accountability is compromised by embedded abuses, exploitative relations, and politicization. Such use of power and resources for political ends is often taken for granted, but it still reflects weak accountability to constitutional and administrative standards. The politicization of the many small but critical steps in judicial processes—which broad legal and constitutional analyses often miss—represents one of the many links between accountability and politicization. A bribe here and a phone call there may not account for much on their own, but together they erode the foundations of democratic rule. The accountability needed for democracy, in short, is about the wider set of attitudes, relations, and decisions that compose the rule of law. Although most studies recognize and study the politicization and accountability of state agencies, this book focuses on how and if reform addresses its many causes and consequences. It shows, for example, how attempts to improve relations between courts and legislatures are often more effective when they account for institutional competition as well as for bureaucratic inefficiency.

Along these lines, rule of law reform also helps identify officials complicit in harmful processes. Presidents, for example, have the most power but the least incentive for promoting judicial independence. But if the "executive does nothing to strengthen the judiciary," and Congress does not take up the mantle, "the resulting dearth of effective and autonomous institutions" may destroy the separation of powers, "without which there is no ... protection for the rights of citizens" (Valenzuela 1992: 61). A democratic regime is consolidated when no significant actor "spends significant resources attempting to achieve their objectives by creating a non-democratic regime" and when all actors "become habituated to the resolution of conflict within the specific laws, procedures and institutions sanctioned by the new democratic process" (Linz and Stepan 1996: 8). But what if democratically sanctioned laws and institutions start to function with semi- or undemocratic processes? What if political actors such as parties can achieve their objectives through such processes, gravitating toward and finding refuge in the formally democratic institutions that carry out the law and protect their interests? The administration of justice itself becomes a collective reserve domain of power and, as in earlier eras, forms around benefits to certain actors rather than those to society. The book shows how this occurs by exposing the practices that block the accountability and accessibility essential to democracy.

Such an approach helps widen understanding of other areas of state-society relations. One key to democracy's survival is its ability to provide a certain level of economic security in which citizens and businesses can plan and invest. Without such security, the lower classes that form the majority will have little stake in a democratic regime and will likely be attracted to its alternatives. The middle and upper classes will be likely to move their money and themselves out of the country—which itself hinders economic development and makes it more difficult to provide security for the poor. Since Hugo Chávez's 1998 presidential victory in Venezuela, for example, the uncertainty of economic policy has accelerated emigration rates.[7] For the rest of Latin America, the massive economic restructuring that has accompanied democratization poses a challenge for governments on how to use the law for both microeconomic security and macroeconomic progress.

Focusing on undemocratic actions also reveals differences between state and societal legal practices. Neighborhood vigilantism, indigenous traditions, grassroots mobilization, and a lack of confidence in the courts all demonstrate an irrelevance of state laws and procedures within society. By the time officials recognize this irrelevance, conventional reform is unlikely to be very effective. Instead, new measures must work to challenge the judicial disarray and executive politics that are partly responsible for fomenting public suspicion in the first place. Vocal ombudsmen, independent judicial councils, and community justice forums are the kinds of changes best able to escape the typical reform trap. Even in these cases, however, bridging the distance between state and society is a long-term endeavor. And it must begin with a return to the basics of the rule of law.

A Look Ahead

Because the story of any reform does not end with its formal adoption, this book is about reforms' success as proposals and, for those enacted, their success as laws. Despite these measures' diversity, the book demonstrates how they are first motivated by, and then slowed down by, the excesses of executive power and judicial disarray. When only some reforms are enacted or when enacted reforms are weak, the institutions that uphold a rule of law have difficulty in altering undemocratic policies and behaviors. Such inability, in turn, undermines foundations of democracy such as accountability and security. The lack of a rule of law drains legitimacy from democracy's institutions by narrowing the realm of contestation over policy, cutting off channels of citizen participation, and stoking undemocratic behavior within state institutions. "One of the most erosive courses of action a democratic government can follow is one where they demonstrate their ambivalence about the system of law. Such ambivalence undermines their very claim to democratic obedience"; in fact, when "the judiciary is contaminated there is no more hope.... It is then that a crisis of legitimacy can be anticipated" (Dogan 1995).

Just as previous scholarship on political change in other eras looked at revolution and democratic breakdown, the current focus should be on explaining how democracies make changes necessary for their future. This book uses this approach through three steps. It first "unpacks" each element of a rule of law to reveal the actors, structures, and functions that compose it—and that often are also the obstacles to lasting change. It then analyzes the historical background of each rule of law element in order to bring out the long-term patterns that reforms try to alter. Finally, it develops a theoretical model that explains the actual enactment and effectiveness of specific proposals in a democratic regime. Concerns over executive power and judicial disarray—expressed through various means, such as politicians' fear of being blamed for failing institutions—lead to rule of law reform proposals. The proposals that become laws, however, must then reconfront executive power and judicial disarray. This hypothesis, and the conceptual and historical analyses on which it is based, is applied in the following chapters to each of the elements that together compose the rule of law.

Notes

1. For purposes of definition, *civil society* "is composed of those more or less spontaneously emergent associations, organizations, and movements that, attuned to how societal problems resonate in the private life spheres, distill and transmit such reactions in amplified form to the public sphere" (Habermas 1996: 366–367). *Political society* is "that arena in which" political parties, interest groups, and other associations organize "to gain control over public power and the state apparatus" (Stepan 1988: 3–4).

2. The state agencies most responsible for *judicial functions* are the Ministry of Justice, the Ministry of the Interior, the Public Ministry and/or Ombudsman, the judicial council, public defenders, and the police.

3. In most Latin American countries, members of the supreme court and of the judicial council are called *magistrados* (magistrates), whereas those in superior and appellate courts are referred to as judges.

4. According to the World Bank and the Inter-American Development Bank, the countries, international financial institutions, and loans/total projected amounts (in millions of U.S. dollars) break down as follows: Argentina (WB, approx $50; IDB, $100/200); Costa Rica (IDB, $11.2/16); Honduras (IDB, $7.2/8); Peru (WB, $21/29; IDB, $5/7); Bolivia (WB, $25/50); Ecuador (WB, $10.7/14.3); Nicaragua (IDB, $1.7/1.925); Paraguay (IDB, $12/33.9); Colombia (WB, $9.4/15.7); El Salvador (IDB, $22.2/27.3); Panama (IDB, approx $7), and Venezuela (WB, $30/60).

5. See O'Donnell et al. 1986; Rustow 1970; Karl 1990; Dahl 1971; Aristotle 1984; Schumpeter 1950. Democracy's most commonly cited components include citizen participation in public affairs; freedom of association and expression; free and fair elections; civilian rule over nonelected institutions such as the military; separation of powers; elites' ability to transcend social cleavages (Lijphart 1968); regime efficacy and efficiency (Linz 1978b); overlapping memberships with a strong middle class; and the accepted validity of the law.

6. *Government* is the set of elected officials in charge of state agencies for a mandated period of time. *Regime* is the "ensemble of patterns, explicit or not, that

determines the forms and channels of access to principal governmental positions, the characteristics of the actors who are admitted and excluded from such access, and the resources [and] strategies that they can use to gain access" (O'Donnell et al. 1986: 73).

7. According to the U.S. Immigration and Naturalization Service, the number of Venezuelans entering the United States jumped from 460,457 in 1996 to 535,355 in 1998 to nearly 600,000 in 2000. See Ketty Rodríguez and Daniel Shoer Roth, "Los venezolanos: Un éxodo hacia Miami," *El Nuevo Herald*, February 18, 2001.

2

THE STATE AND THE RULE OF LAW

You know what we do here with things that aren't working? Blow them
up. The central bus terminal is a mess? Blow it up. Catia prison beyond
salvation? Blow it up. The constitution no longer appropriate? Blow it up!
—Beatriz Valdez, legislative aide,
Venezuelan House of Representatives

RULE OF LAW REFORM'S BIGGEST HURDLE is also its most important
instrument: the state. Many studies assume that a division of government
powers means a division of functions as well. The rule of law depends not
only on the judicial branch, however, but also on a range of nonjudicial
state agencies, from the Justice Ministry to local police forces.[1] Although
the judiciary holds state officials accountable to constitutional standards
and laws, the network of state agencies is responsible for implementing
those standards and laws into daily governance. Many state agencies also
use the law as an instrument of power, as when a party expands its patronage through a particular ministry or when the police discriminate against a
certain population. The routine actions and problems within state agencies
also have a daily impact on the judiciary, as when delays within state
bureaucracies cause backlogs in the courts. A rule of law, in short, requires
a law-abiding state. Reforms should not simply be policy options used at
the discretion of state officials but also an evaluation of those officials and
policies themselves.

A state that adheres to the law is especially important during democratization. Its agencies need to help uphold a constitution, establish administrative regulations, and respond to citizen demands. In this role, the state's
executive, legislative, and independent agencies carry out many specific
functions needed for a rule of law, such as arrest, investigation, arbitration,
and incarceration. Citizens come into contact with state administrators far
more than with judges or elected officials, and whether those administrators

17

deal with citizens in a law-abiding way is central to popular perceptions and support for democracy. Reforms of state agencies regarding the rule of law—*state rule of law reforms*—are thus critical for democracies working to establish a rule of law.

There are two main areas of such reforms: those to improve the administration of state institutions, such as prisons, that involve the rule of law; and those to make those institutions accountable to constitutional guarantees. These two areas—administration and accountability—are especially important in Latin American democracies. Political instability and deadlock hinder adequate policy formation, forcing many state agencies to work out their administrative approaches on the spot. Many government ministers are in office too briefly to alter this pattern or too long to have an incentive to do so.

Along with the judiciary, responsibility for these areas in most modern states falls on executive, legislative, and independent agencies. The primary function of many of these nonjudicial state agencies, such as the Public Ministry (MP, for Ministerio Público), are judicial. The rest have judicial functions as secondary obligations. The bulk of the state is located within the executive branch, comprising a "public administration" responsible for the daily implementation of policies and laws. Within the executive branch, the agencies that often have the most responsibility over rule of law functions are the Justice and Interior Ministries, commonly responsible for formulating national policies, overseeing most police forces, and running the penitentiary systems.

Within the legislative branch, committees and personnel who oversee state agencies or formulate bills also have rule of law functions. In Venezuela, for example, the lower house of Congress has a Justice Subcommission and a Human Rights Subcommission, which draft legislation; and the Regional Development Commission handled the debate in the early 1990s on the legislation to create neighborhood *jueces de paz* (justices of the peace). In Argentina, the Commission on Human Rights receives reports on rights abuses, a bicameral noninvestigatory monitoring commission deals with denunciations of state officials, and special commissions handle new laws or agencies. Legislatures throughout Latin America, in addition, have temporary committees on special issues such as constitutional reform.

Finally, four main independent agencies have the role of overseeing the state's institutional administration and its protection of constitutional rights. The newest among them are the Defensorías del Pueblo, which investigate complaints against state agencies. The *Defensorías* are an offshoot of the MP, which prosecutes criminal, civil, and commercial offenses on behalf of the state and, in many countries, also investigates abuses by state officials.[2] Latin America's MPs historically have been part of the executive branch but continue to be part of the executive in only seven countries.[3] Third, a separate public defenders' agency provides legal representation to indigent detainees and is connected to the MP, judiciary, or Justice Ministry (see Chapter 7). Finally, the independent Judicial Council handles judicial nominations, discipline, and budgets (see Chapter 5).

Most state rule of law reforms are a reaction to executive power and judicial weakness. A transition to democracy itself motivates better policies, cooperation, and vigilance on constitutional rights, often through bolstering agencies that can be a check on the president. Although countries' reform projects differ widely, they usually include establishing *Defensorías* and judicial councils. In some countries, such as Argentina, such reforms grew out of the historical experience of repression; in other countries, such as Venezuela, they came from a push to make the executive more effective.

Many presume that a democratic transition itself would gradually allow such changes to occur. But they are often blocked through the exercise of executive power by presidents, governors, mayors, and the network of state agencies that they head. The powers and structures of the state long precede and regularly frustrate those of the regime. Many government and party officials have patronage networks rooted in state agencies, find it easier to influence civil servants who are not accountable to the law, and certainly do not want courts second-guessing their actions. In Latin America, state agencies are also more resistant to reform because of their long-standing centralization. Decentralization can break national agencies' administrative monopoly, but because of the responsibilities involved—such as respect for constitutional rights in judicial processes—decentralization may only lead to a weaker and less consistent national rule of law. Along with such executive-branch power, disarray in the judiciary also motivates state rule of law reform. In particular, the courts' limited capacity to keep track of the impacts of both public and private actors on constitutional rights has increased support for establishing or strengthening oversight agencies like the *Defensoría* and the MP. But even when such impetus overcomes the political opposition to enactment, a lack of cooperation among policymakers can hinder the actual enforcement and utility of these reforms later on.

This chapter's first section explains the importance of the state and the rule of law to each other by reexamining the state through its rule of law functions; the second section traces the historical patterns of those functions in the Argentine and Venezuelan states; and the third section then uses these conceptual and historical analyses to examine state rule of law reforms under democratic regimes, focusing on accountability and administration. I contend that reforms' effectiveness depends on their ability to roll back long-standing practices of state agencies that are part of executive power and judicial disarray.

The State's Role in the Rule of Law

The state and rule of law are connected because state agencies carry out much of the law and because the law is the primary basis for state action. Because of this mutual dependence, government policy matters little if the state does not act democratically.[4] More than trust in specific leaders or governments, enforcement of the law—by and even against state agencies—captures the essence of democracy's legitimacy. With political and civil-society organizations in many democracies lacking strong allegiance, state bodies become the primary link between citizens and governments. Biased or uneven application of the law by those agencies affects the state's administrative effectiveness as well as its popular legitimacy. But if state agencies enforce the constitution and if citizens have adequate access to them, the ability of both the state and society to act in a consistent, predictable manner would be far stronger, as, by extension, would the democracy. As democracies juggle multiplying demands, the way state agencies create, undermine, or substitute for a rule of law is an intrinsic part of democratization.

But what determines how the state uses the law? As in the past, state agencies are affected by their relations with each other and with the government. In a democracy, they must also respond to new and often contradictory societal demands and legal guidelines. In states with histories of severe repression, all of these influences are colored by a need to curtail the state's coercive power. Along with such a history, the individual guarantees of a democracy push the state to be *self-restraining* in its actions. This dilemma between restraints and requirements permeates all of the state's relationships—with itself, with the government, with the law, and with society. Resulting pressures can cause agencies to cut legal corners and resort to undemocratic practices.

The state's rule of law responsibilities are most directly affected by the relationships among the many differentiated, coordinated institutions that make up the state. In contrast to arguments that the state is molded by external interests, Weberian conceptions regard the modern state as having its own independent interests. And because state agencies have different powers and objectives, they pursue these interests in ways that are more competitive than cooperative. A centralized judicial body that has always carried out policies from the capital, for example, may "discover" too many "problems" in any plan involving relinquishment of its power to other bodies. The expanding size and patronage of Latin American states in the course of the twentieth century, in addition, forced state agencies to devote increasing resources to processing information, keeping up with basic tasks, and maintaining watch over rival agencies. When the legal guidelines and greater professional insecurity of contemporary democracies were added on, most agencies responded with undemocratic practices such as intimidation and restricted access.

The state is also shaped by its relations with the government. Whereas the state comprises administrative agencies under executive authority, the government is the set of top executive and legislative officials who run the state, elected for discrete periods of time. Although ministers and other top state officials are government appointees, the state and government do not always share the same interests, and most governments manipulate state agencies to boost their own power and weaken rivals. A change in regime makes this relationship more tense, as a new government is both dependent on and distrustful of state agencies formed under previous regimes. Some new leaders may see the only recourse as the outright liquidation of certain agencies, as President Vicente Fox is attempting to do with some of Mexico's law-enforcement bodies. Even with less drastic approaches, the greater instability of government policy in any democracy foments confusion and suspicion within the state. Along with the economic and political pressures transmitted down on them by the government, state agencies are also likely to resist the citizen demands transmitted upward through channels set up by the new regime.

Although state agencies must deal with each other and with the government in any regime, in a democracy they must also deal with a wider set of laws. Creating a legally *binding authority* in a modern democracy requires a set of operating laws that must be applied consistently and in accordance with individual rights. In addition to carrying out the law, therefore, state agencies are bound by it. They derive strength from the efficiency and coordination that law engenders yet are limited by the oversight and accountability it demands. But the state's attitude to new laws may or may not change along with changes in policy, personnel, or regime. Most democratic regimes abide by a constitution, for example, but state operations are often better suited and more accustomed to less democratic but more efficient approaches like arbitrary decisionmaking. The law, however, is still the only legitimate basis of state action. Even if a prohibition against arbitrary arrests is ignored by a state agency, in a democracy that prohibition remains *the* point of reference, whether or not respected in practice. As such, state agencies have no choice but to respond to the law and in most cases attempt to justify their actions with it. Such tensions often lead not only to undemocratic practices but also to a greater aptitude for hiding them.

Most of all, the state responds to society. Even institutional conceptions of the state explain its development through its efforts to control, shape, help, and gain support from societal groups through means such as taxation, communications, and force. Marxists see the capitalist state as captured by the bourgeois elite, despite having "relative autonomy"

(Poulantzas 1968) on certain occasions. During many times of crisis since independence, for example, Argentine state officials were able to play industry and labor against the other. Pluralism, in contrast, views the state as a space where competing interests act out differences through such means as elections and bargaining, with gradually shifting balances of political power shaping state institutions (Truman 1951). In either conception, state agencies gain strength and autonomy when they are able to form their own interests, act upon them, and use society's needs to acquire power. This tack is easier under authoritarianism than under democracy, where more policymakers must respond to more demands through more channels and under more legal controls. For many democracies, the policies that result are incoherent, tentative, and contradictory. To sidestep or minimize this confusion, state agencies develop their own independent links with different social sectors. This alternative base of support further encourages the state's disassociation with the government and the law.

In historical perspective, all of these pressures are part of the process of *state formation*, a term that describes "the creation, consolidation, and extension of" the state over society through instruments of coercion and organization (Callaghy 1984: 81). These processes usually emerge out of political and economic imbalances, such as postfeudal needs for more efficient administration, military mobilization, or export promotion. When one or more of these objectives take priority, the state forms around structures that promote it. In Western Europe, for example, modern laws were formed to ensure property and economic transactions as trade and industry expanded, as well as to delineate citizen rights and responsibilities as societies developed. But those facing serious security threats had to invest more in military structures than in economic ones. So while countries such as Holland that depended on trade developed into states geared toward economic development, countries like Russia with greater security needs developed states based more on coercive capacities (Tilly 1992). Formation patterns do not stop even in highly developed states, such as when Woodrow Wilson prior to World War I and Dwight Eisenhower during the Cold War warned that a growing military would reshape the American state. In the undeveloped regions of Latin America, Africa, and Asia, most states were born into war-ridden, economically unstable conditions. For them, internal order took precedence over other needs and functions, turning the law into a handmaiden for structures of repression and surveillance.

Even when external threats peter out, most states keep the physical and legal powers they developed, which are usually in the hands of centralized institutions with wide discretion. New democratic regimes are thus attempting to impose rules on agencies not designed or accustomed to follow them. Studies of state formation focus on the strengthening of state agencies, but "formation" during democratization can mean the trickier task of dismantling coercive or unaccountable ones. The poor coordination and high turnover of officials characteristic of new democracies make this task particularly difficult. Normal democratic politics means that more ideas are discussed than enacted, turning the state into a "subjective realm of plans, programs, or ideas" rather than of concrete action (Deutsch 1981: 337). Actual implementation of state rule of law reforms is thus a real accomplishment. But assessing its likelihood must begin with examination of how the state itself was formed.

The Rule of Law in Latin American State Formation

In Latin America, the most significant impacts on early state formation were civil wars, economic underdevelopment, and external influence. More so than the successor states of French and British colonialism, those ruled by Spain were characterized by an anemic infrastructure, lack of coordination, unaccountable local rule, personalistic government, and mercantilist economics. In the first decades of independence, as a result, state formation was focused on keeping large territories and diverse populations together. Leaders attempted to do this with overly centralized governments. Castile itself was highly centralized, especially during the reigns of Philip III (1556–1598) and of the Bourbons (1700s), and the government applied this approach in its colonialist endeavor. One body, the Europe-based Consejo de Indias, was responsible for all colonial administration. In the colonies themselves, the main political division was of the four viceroyalties. Regional centers called *audiencias*, which had legislative powers and were the highest judicial agencies, served as the link between local settlements and the viceroyalties. *Cabildos* were the governments of the local settlements. In isolated regions such as the southern cone, they developed with little outside influence under officials with strong local followings. To dilute some of their power, Castile created *intendencias* between the *cabildos* and the *audiencias*, establishing new ones as settlement expanded. The crown's consuming suspicion of its colonial representatives led to governing structures characterized less by rational administration than by bureaucracy and back-stabbing.

Upon independence, this administrative inefficiency and geographic separation led to the first obstacles to state formation: civil war and *caudillismo*. Peru, Mexico, and Argentina were rent by internal conflict during their first years, and Venezuela, Ecuador, Chile, and Central America became regional centers breaking away from larger nations. And everywhere, provincial caudillos carved out personalistic regimes with separate armies and governments, engaging in continual conflict with one another and with weak central states based in and often limited to distant capitals.

The short-term response from those capitals was compromise and cease-fires. But as national governments gained strength, their longer-term response was centralization and coercion, based on the Spanish model. As set in motion by early leaders such as Bolívar in Gran Colombia and José de San Martín in Argentina, the Enlightenment in Latin America was closer to paternalism than to liberalism, leading to states whose "behaviour stems more closely from the earlier enlightened despotism than from revolutionary ideology" (Griffin 1992: 138). Latin America thus experienced a damaging convergence of militarization and centralized administration: instead of at least leading to an efficient state structure, centralization only antagonized regional powers and stimulated coercive capacities.

Political leaders also attempted to rally the population around ideals, needs, and identities that make nationhood seem necessary and natural. What "had been merely geographic areas of the Spanish Empire suddenly had to understand and define their destiny as autonomous units; they had to create guiding fictions of peoplehood and 'nationness' in order to approach the ideological consensus that underlay stable societies in other parts of the world" (Shumway 1991: 3–4). Most of those "guiding fictions" revolved around strong executives and discretionary power. Elite, educated Creole bureaucrats—most of them trained in the law—managed the early state reforms and administration. Most of these officials who legislated the constitutional reforms during the first years of New Granada's independence, for instance, served in the colonial government and "impressed" on their societies "the centralist arrangements they knew how to handle and for which no adequate substitute was found during the upheavals of the age" (Veliz 1978: 150).

By the late nineteenth century, new and more practical constitutions helped extinguish civil wars and unify countries. But coercive practices were firmly in place, with new constitutional standards struggling to catch up. And the renovated republics were headed by political and economic oligarchies that, as before, did not hesitate to alter those constitutional orders to deal with provincial restlessness and economic weakness.

Argentina

Argentina's early history revolved around the determination of Buenos Aires province to preserve its political and economic dominance. The *primera junta*, the nation's first independent government, was formed during Napoleon's control of Spain and comprised Buenos Aires elites who designed policy for their province at the expense of others. Later, in 1811, the ruling *junta grande* and the provincial level *juntas provinciales* were replaced by a three-person Buenos Aires Triumvirate that called for constraining "popular arbitrariness" in the provinces and establishing a "rule of law" (Busaniche 1965: 323–324) on its own terms. The Triumvirate organized supposedly "national" assemblies that were dominated by handpicked, pro–Buenos Aires Unitarians. When these assemblies entertained Federalist proposals for a looser federation, they were promptly shut down by police.

The irreconcilable split between Unitarians and Federalists gave the country sixty years of civil war. At the 1816 Congress of Tucumán, where Argentina formally declared independence, the Federalists succeeding in creating a powerful executive, the so-called Supreme Director, elected by a Congress based on provincial population instead of equal representation. Provincial opposition to the plan was crushed by Buenos Aires troops. But the Tucumán federation collapsed after four years, and in 1820 Buenos Aires was forced to give the provinces more autonomy.[5] But the tide again shifted to Buenos Aires, which imposed constitutions without proper ratification in 1819 and 1827. Although the era's legal structures were continually changing, one of the few consistent characteristics was a high level of national and discretionary power by Buenos Aires governors.[6] In this position, the province of Buenos Aires went ahead and developed its own state. Between 1821 and 1827, it borrowed money to bankroll a "Happy Experience" that professionalized much of the public administration, abolished the Catholic Church's courts, improved physical infrastructure, and established educational institutions such as the University of Buenos Aires.

Juan Manuel de Rosas took power as the Buenos Aires governor in 1829 on a Federalist program supported by the provinces, the urban poor, poor rural *gauchos* (cowboys), and some large landowners.[7] In an approach adopted by strongmen that followed him, he used populist appeal to create an expansive, highly centralized, and paternalistic state in the name of federalism. As the "Restorer of Laws," Rosas was also given near-dictatorial powers, which he used to restrict basic freedoms. He often devised punishments personally, and his secret security force, the Mazorca, carried out systemic human rights violations. As with his predecessors, Rosas's state-building depended more on its leader's personality and policies than on input from other officials or citizens groups. So despite its unique impact, Rosas's rule did not expand Argentina's political choices beyond *caudillismo* and elite democracy, both of which were based on a discretionary executive.

After ousting Rosas in 1852, Entre Rios provincial caudillo Justo José de Urquiza began the first true federation with the Pact of San Nicolás, which granted him wide-ranging powers up until the ratification of the 1853 constitution. Buenos Aires rejected the pact, but the rest of the provinces ratified it and remained under Urquiza until 1859, when he retired after the one presidential term that the constitution allowed. Inspired by the balance of powers and individual protections in the U.S. Constitution, Argentina's 1853 version marked a turning point for the country. Above all, it institutionalized federalism and granted provinces "all power not delegated...to the federal government," including the authority to choose their governors and run most administrative functions (articles 104–105). Pressed to resolve the disorder around it, however, the government's short-term approach was based on laws that were more repressive and a state structure that was more centralized than the constitution would suggest. The constitution's article 6 gave the president authority to "intervene" in any province, for example, which was employed liberally to deal with upstart provinces and undesirable election results. Only such discretionary extrainstitutional solutions seemed able to meld the elites' formal support for democracy and their distrust of the popular channels that democracy involved.

After becoming president in 1862, former Buenos Aires chief Bartolomé Mitre established banking structures, transportation and communications networks, and, most important for the rule of law, commercial and civil codes along with new courts. But this enlarged state was staffed primarily by natives of Buenos Aires city, whereas both elections and economic development in the provinces were commandeered by the president's allies. The state continued to expand under the 1868–1874 Domingo Sarmiento presidency, which built more educational institutions and transportation networks and updated the military and commercial codes. Like Mitre, though, Sarmiento centralized power and intervened at will in the provinces.

With its nationalist, statist ideology, the Argentine leadership also set its sights on the country's sprawling territory, which had just 500,000 people at the time of independence. Visions of Gran Argentina as an outpost of European civilization fired up ambitious campaigns such as the "Conquest of the Desert" in the 1870s, which settled more than 14 million hectares. Despite the construction of railways and ports and the promotion of European immigration, the huge geographic distances and economic disparities among the provinces made this expansion uneven. Foreign investments helped build infrastructure, but most of it remained within a small elite. Immigrants swelled to 20 percent of the population (compared to less than 15 percent in the United States at the time), but most of the recent arrivals did not have the capital to buy land or were prevented from doing so. This led to severe urban growth and its resultant problems. The population of Buenos Aires skyrocketed from 40,000 in 1800 to 774,000 in 1895. The city of Córdoba quadrupled in size over the same period; Rosario, the capital of the confederation, grew from 1,000 in 1800 to 93,000 in 1895 (Sargent 1994). As crime and insecurity rose along with the population, the state expanded and strengthened its police and military forces.

After the turn of the century, liberalization spearheaded by the recently formed Radical Party (UCR, for Unión Cívica Radical) began to counteract state strength by promoting greater citizen participation. Expanded suffrage under the 1912 Sáenz Peña Law and Radicals' electoral victories allowed the country's liberal tendencies to rise to the surface, aided by increasing rates of voting. But the change was still led by the executive, and the governments of Hipólito Yrigoyen (1916–1922 and 1928–1930) were, like their predecessors, largely personalistic. Unable to push reforms through Congress and losing popular support amid falling wages, the government intervened in the provinces twenty times—fifteen by decree—to break Conservative opponents' political hold. But these were only stopgap measures. As it caved under pressure from the oligarchy and the extreme left, the regime retreated into the security of a "partyocracy" (see Iñigo Carrera 1985). In a pattern that continues to be repeated throughout Latin America, a government with progressive reforms failed to create functioning institutions to carry forward those changes beyond its own stay in power.

The 1930 coup that toppled Yrigoyen then placed coercion at the center of the state's ongoing formation. Determined to extinguish social violence, and borne of a violent act itself, the military regime turned to repressive law enforcement and individual rights restrictions. Police agencies grew so much in the 1930s that their power, unlike the liberal reforms of earlier periods, extended beyond the military regime of the time. Elected President Juan Perón also used coercive power to crush the opposition during the 1940s and 1950s, as did his military successors up until the 1983 democratic transition.

Venezuela

As in Argentina, war set Venezuela off on its historical path. After its particularly violent 1810–1821 struggle against Spain, Venezuela became a part of Gran Colombia along with Ecuador and Colombia under the authoritarian rule of revolutionary leader Simon Bolívar. The new nation, however, fell apart after five years because it could not wrest sufficient power from officials in Caracas, Bogotá, and Quito. In the successor republic, Caracas reassumed its place as the administrative and political center even as it adopted a formally federal system. As all "Venezuelans know only too well," the autonomy of the country's states "has never been practiced, but it is a myth written in all the constitutions" (Sagárzazu 1904:13), making federalism one of the country's guiding fictions from the beginning.

Like most of the region, nineteenth-century Venezuela was characterized by slow development and interprovincial conflict, with a concentration of economic power by large landowners and political power by central and provincial executives. Much of the conflict at the time was fought by assorted caudillos under the banners of the Liberal Party and the Conservative Party. The so-called Conservative Oligarchy ran the government from 1830 until 1848 but was weakened by the infrastructural destruction of the independence wars, as well as by the country's dependence on agricultural products prone to large price fluctuations. A liberal coalition that took power in 1848 instituted reforms like debt relief and the abolition of slavery, which only reignited conflicts that culminated in the 1859–1863 Federal Wars. Under Antonio Guzmán Blanco, order was restored and a new political arrangement was introduced by the 1864 constitution. Ushering in the country's first extended period of relative peace, the constitution gave formal autonomy to the twenty states while maintaining a highly centralized federal government. The only two actual authorities given to the Venezuelan states, in fact, were to be "independent" and to combine with each other (articles 1 and 4). As in other federal republics, peace and politics required formal provincial autonomy, but long-term stability was assumed to require centralized and discretionary executive control.

Stable constitutionalism began to allow the development of state structures of oversight, albeit with little political weight. One of them was the MP, whose services began in 1826 with municipal *procuradores* who assisted judges on court cases. An 1847 law allowed the executive to name and remove *fiscales* (public prosecutors) in the Superior Courts (but not the Supreme Court), and between 1836 and 1863 *fiscales* were established in each state. Their roles were broadened by successive criminal codes into nearly all public cases before the courts, and the 1897 penal code created the Public Ministry in permanent form.

Dominating national politics for eighteen years, Guzmán pulled a far-flung and sparsely populated country closer together after the 1870s. The central state expanded exponentially, from the establishment of the Corte de Casación (Appeals Court) in the 1881 constitution to the formation of seven new ministries between the 1860s and 1890s. National armed forces gradually replaced those of the states. But the federal system functioned primarily as a patronage network in which Caracas distributed material benefits to regional caudillos through the regional development *juntas*, who "elected" the president through the Federal Council. Guzmán's 1881 constitution replaced direct popular elections with indirect votes and reduced the number of states from twenty to nine, maximizing the president's control over them. Under Guzmán's tutelage, Joaquín Crespo took power in the mid-1880s. Through the 1892 Legal Revolution, he reversed the changes of the 1881 constitution by reinstating the secret direct vote and the twenty-state composition, playing caudillos against each other and drumming up popular support. But such actions eventually led to armed opposition against Crespo. The resulting power vacuum was filled by Táchira strongman Cipriano Castro, who took power in 1899. Castro consolidated his power by continuing Guzmán's centralization, disempowering caudillos and traditional parties by appointing governors and local officials, and increasing executive power in the 1901 and 1904 constitutions.

But such policies were no match for the underlying conflicts they tried to squelch. In 1908, an anti-Castro revolt brought Juan Vicente Gómez to power; the following year he promulgated a constitution that restored the twenty-state system, this time administered through the Council of Government (whose usefulness had run its course by 1914 and was duly eliminated from that year's constitution).[8] Gómez accelerated Castro's modernization by centralizing taxation, initiating huge public works projects, and building up a military to support his regime and its control over the states. He kept the legislative and judicial branches on a tight leash and swiftly put down all opposition, with "workers' feeble protests evok[ing] no response but police violence and long prison terms" (Ewell 1984: 59).

Gómez's laissez-faire economic policies left little funding for social services, education, and agricultural development. But when oil was discovered in the 1920s, state expansion accelerated anew. The executive branch sprouted new ministries, financial institutions, and aid programs for the states. The oil industry also turned a fragmented and primarily rural society into a highly mobile and rapidly urbanizing one. Workers organized a strong labor movement, and organizing in the cities culminated in protests by students, military officials, and city residents in 1928 and 1929. These growing political movements eventually coalesced into the Acción Democrática (AD) political party, which was formally founded in 1941 and went on to dominate post-Gómez politics.

After Gómez's death in 1935, the stage was set for either conflict or liberalization. Most transitions to democracy include a phase of liberalization in which an authoritarian executive allows some new political and legal freedoms. This opening was made in Venezuela by Gómez's successors, who found themselves dependent on AD for popular acceptance and civil peace. Eleazar López Contreras, Gómez's minister of war, succeeded him in the presidency from 1936 to 1941. Walking a fine line between the popular movement and *gomecistas* (Gómez's appointees and cronies), he instituted the so-called February Program of new social and educational services as well as an attack on state corruption while maintaining the prohibition on rival political groups. López was succeeded by his own minister of war, Isaías Medina Angarita, whose 1945 constitution nationalized the judiciary by giving the federal government control of the administration of justice throughout the country. He also expanded political freedom, which allowed for union, peasant, and professional organizing. Medina's combination of continuity and liberalization served as a controlled transition from the Gómez clique to a new elite with more democratic ideals and more structured links to the population. AD was the biggest proponent and beneficiary of this change. The party rapidly grew during the Medina period, achieving political domination by putting into practice its slogan—"not a single district nor single municipality without a party organization"—and increasing the number of party members from around 75,000 in 1941 to nearly 500,000 in 1948 (Martz 1966: 77–78).

This steady passage out of *gomecismo* was interrupted in 1945 when the illness of Medina's handpicked successor, who was acceptable to AD, led to a succession crisis. In alliance with AD, the military, eager to shed Gómez's generals, took over in a coup led by junior officer Marcos Pérez Jiménez. This led to the three years of AD government known as the *Trienio*. After the initial takeover, AD leader Rómulo Betancourt served as provisional president, ruling primarily by decree and hurrying in poorly drafted reforms. Following the trend of using specialized institutions to handle justice issues, for example, he created in 1946 the Tribunals of Administrative Responsibility to prosecute officials for illicit enrichment. But the retroactive power of the courts caused a backlash, prompting reexamination of their rulings and passage of the more moderate Law Against Illicit Enrichment.

In December 1947, the country's first-ever universal elections brought the other main AD leader, Rómulo Gallegos, to power. Gallegos established seven more state institutions, which tightened government control of the economy and expanded AD patronage. A new constitution limited the president to one term, established universal suffrage, and ensured citizen welfare, labor rights, and Supreme Court review of laws' constitutionality. Another constitutional clause, however, allowed the president to detain any person suspected of antigovernment conspiracy. But all of these measures, along with AD organizing that brought in sectors such as *campesinos* (peasants), threatened the Catholic Church, large landowners, and the military. This opposition culminated in a 1948 military coup.

The 1948–1958 military regime of Marcos Pérez Jiménez continued state growth—including the establishment of twenty-two state institutions—which increased citizens' economic dependence on the government. The junta used the main police force, the Seguridad Nacional, to repress the population and to keep state agencies in line. In 1950, it created the Ministry of Justice and gave it ultimate authority over the judiciary, including the power to appoint all judges.

As in Argentina, the main thread of continuity in predemocratic Venezuela was of increasingly controlling executives who dominated the judicial and legislative branches and bound the state together with guiding fictions of national destiny. Both states also became militarized from ongoing armed conflicts between the center and the provinces, as well as with neighboring countries. Nonmilitary state functions lagged behind raw material exporting, which, along with foreign borrowing, concentrated resources in the hands of political and economic elites. Labor organizing during industrialization, educational advances during times of state expansion, and political organizing during liberalization often triggered stronger counterreactions from those elites. But even popular movements, such as *justicialismo* (Peronism) in Argentina and AD in Venezuela, mimicked historically "effective" models of personalistic rule.

State Rule of Law Reforms and Democracy

Because history had carried Latin American states beyond the rule of law, contemporary democratic regimes have worked to bring them back to it through administrative and accountability reforms. Administrative measures aim to improve state agencies' functioning so that they better uphold the law in their daily actions, and accountability measures monitor these agencies' protection of constitutional rights. We can outline the most significant administrative reforms, which include improving government policies and decentralizing national government responsibilities to provincial and local governments that can better administer them. Accountability measures include strengthening of the Ministerio Público, which traditionally has been Latin America's main oversight body; improving cooperation between state agencies; and incorporating constitutional rights in decentralization projects.

The main state rule of law reforms on the administration of state agencies are:

- Effective criminal, penitentiary, and judicial policies;
- Well-planned decentralization; and
- Effective Defensoría del Pueblo.

The main state rule of law reforms on the accountability of state agencies are:

- Effective MP;
- Effective Defensoría del Pueblo;
- Intra-agency cooperation in judicial processes; and
- Decentralization with national standards.

For both administration and accountability, however, the most significant reforms have been penitentiary measures and the creation of the Defensoría del Pueblo. As crime and arrests increase, first of all, prisons are now where the rule of law is at its most vulnerable. Murder, rape, drug-trafficking, malnutrition, the spread of disease, neglect, and due process violations all take place under the state's twenty-four-hour watch. Such abuses make prisons the ultimate test of the state's rule of law functions. Measures to improve conditions include strengthening legal protections, training personnel, improving cooperation in judicial procedures, and operational decentralization. But such proposals face huge political and financial hurdles, turning the status quo into a coexistence of criticisms and tolerance. As with other state functions, running the prisons has become a balancing act between individual rights and administrative responsibility.

The *Defensoría*, secondly, oversees rights protection in the practices of all state agencies, including prisons. It also criticizes and helps formulate government policy and monitors private businesses, like electricity companies, with impacts on the law and citizen rights. The breadth of this mandate has brought the agency more than its share of political controversy, highlighting the politics of enacting and implementing effective reform. So while prison reform reveals the extent to which the state violates the rule of law, the *Defensoría* shows what officials are really willing to do about it.

The momentum of democratization itself opens up opportunities for state rule of law reforms as the new regime works to make the state more accountable, efficient, and accessible. But this goes only so far: governments are often reluctant to initiate changes that may build a rule of law in the long run but affect political interests in the short run. Such calculations are part of the relationship between a new democratic government and the state it inherits. Because the state helps ensure stability, and because many of its most capable officials are tainted by authoritarianism, measures to reduce state discretion are often avoided. The government will often justify this stance by associating abusive state practices with the past or by disassociating such practices from the state agencies that carried them out. Obstacles to the rule of law are thus created less by the mode of transition than by unaltered processes, less by the transition's "birth defects" (Karl and Schmitter 1991) than by its inheritance. The *government* may now be held accountable through elections, but the *state* is unlikely to be more accountable than the government is willing and able to make it.

Above all, new democratic regimes want to keep a lid on society, and the most readily available instrument to do so is excessive and discretionary executive power. Ministers are given broader roles in an elected administration but within the president's strict policy confines, for example, and independent agencies are granted new authorities without the support to carry them out. Political parties, similarly, often balk at measures deemed to reduce the patronage they have cultivated in state agencies, unless necessary to defuse politically destabilizing pressures. The level of party strength can directly affect the state. Venezuela's main parties had become the primary source of organization outside the authoritarian regime, and with the end of that regime were able to dominate state agencies. In Argentina, in contrast, more fluid political alliances and direct repression prevented the country's parties from attaining comparable influence, and so reforms supporting neutral institutions were proposed more quickly during the democratic transition. The effectiveness of state rule of law reforms is also weakened by disarray in the judiciary. Chronic delay, bureaucracy, and corruption blunt state reforms designed to improve policy formulation or oversight of rights protections. Judges' authority to inspect prisons is limited by a lack of personnel, for example, and the MP's call for a trial against a state official may mean little if it takes the judiciary six years to conduct it.

Such limits have helped make criminal and judicial policies inconsistent and ineffective. The political will of executive ministers and top policymakers is rarely strong enough, and their tenure rarely long enough, to see through policies from formulation to implementation. A typical example of the resulting frustration occurred in Bolivia over the government's delayed response to the increase in crime during the 1990s, despite developed measures such as the Plan of Citizen Security.[9] Even though crime quadrupled between 1993 and 1999, the plan was not enacted until 1999 and was limited primarily to purveyance of police equipment.

To reverse or at least make up for these trends, state reform's best hopes lay in improving administration and accountability. Because of the severe administrative needs and the level and the obscurity of abuse, reforms of the penitentiary system represent the ultimate challenge for administration. Because it is a national agency trying to oversee the entire state, the *Defensoría* is the ultimate test for accountability.

The biggest consequence of a lack of coherent government policy is a shift of burden to state agencies, whose day-to-day acts replace long-term plans. Nowhere is this more evident than with criminal policy. Confronting a crime rate more than twice the world average, Latin America's anxious governments have reacted with tough policies such as new public-order laws. But such policies have not addressed the socioeconomic instability that has fueled crime or the policing approaches that have been unable to stem it. With the exception of Paraguay, every country experienced a surge in crime throughout the 1990s. In 1990, the region's homicide rate was 22.9 for every 100,000 inhabitants; the world average was 10.7 (Búvinic and Morrison 1999). After 1995, most studies estimate that the regional rate has jumped to nearly 29 per 100,000. About 68 percent of South America's population has been victimized by crime, above the world average of 61 percent, and 31 percent reports being assaulted, above the global average of 19 percent.

Prison administration.   Governments' ineffective policy response has allowed mounting crime, public pressure, and slow judicial processes to fill

Latin America's prisons way beyond capacity—turning them into one of the state's biggest administrative headaches as well the its biggest rights violator. With arrest and incarceration rates reaching unprecedented levels (in the 1980s, the number of prisoners shot up 65 percent in Chile and 200 percent in Venezuela), overcrowding has increased in every Latin American country during the 1990s. Most inmates have not been tried, with about a third of those waiting for trial already completing the maximum sentence for the accused crime. These delays do not even include the huge numbers in police jails and lockups, which in many countries even exceed the population of the prisons. As such crowding increased, so has (with the exception of Chile and Mexico) prison violence. In Brazil's São Paulo state alone, the annual number of prison riots jumped from a few dozen in the early 1990s to nearly 200 by 1997.[10] In most countries, prisons have gotten so violent that guards leave many parts of them unpatrolled, and even postriot crackdowns and shifts of prisoners have scant impact.

Inhumane conditions characterize prisons of all sizes and security levels. In Bolivia's San Pedro Prison, one of the country's largest, those with resources can buy their own cells, but most are crammed into tiny spaces and sleep in stairways and hallways. The children of inmates living in the prison ferry weapons and drugs in and out, and many of the patients in the facility's medicine-free clinic lie on the floor. The main prison of the national drug police force (FELCN, for Fuerza Especial en la Lucha Contra el Narcotráfico), in contrast, is a small, high-security facility. But it is also overcrowded, with an average of four inmates squeezed into nearly airless cells of about six by ten feet.[11]

Between 1992 and 1999, national prison populations rose an average of 57 percent in Latin America, with Nicaragua, Panama, Costa Rica, Argentina, and Honduras having the biggest increases. Estimated percentages of overcapacity are generally reliable, but national averages of such overcapacity obscure differences between facilities with intended population levels and those way beyond them. In some individual prisons, overcrowding reaches up to 400 percent. Table 2.1 reports the most recent estimates of prison capacity. In countries with unreliable or highly divergent statistics, overcapacity can only be estimated as "moderate," between 100 and 130 percent, or "severe," above 130 percent. Reported percentages of unsentenced prisoners vary more, with estimates in countries such as Peru and Uruguay ranging from 60 to 90 percent. In countries that calculate these numbers, reliable statistics are averaged in Table 2.1 to the most conservative percentage or range. In countries without reliable reports, the percentage of unsentenced prisoners is estimated as "moderate," which is under 50 percent, or "severe," above 50 percent. Spending is perhaps the least indicative number but nevertheless shows a serious lack of financial commitment to the prisons. Most reports provide an estimate of spending on food and health, which are the most important expenditures. But even in

Table 2.1   **Latin American Prisons: Capacity, Sentencing, and Spending[a]**

Country	% Above Intended Capacity	% Unsentenced	Spending per Prisoner
Argentina	provincial average 140	average 77	varies by province
Bolivia	162	60+	n/a
Brazil	state average 157	45	varies by state
Chile	moderate	51	n/a
Colombia	137	42	$1.44 (food only)
Costa Rica	167	moderate	n/a
Cuba	approx. 175	moderate	n/a
Dominican Republic	215	74	n/a
Ecuador	143	severe	n/a
El Salvador	135	75+	n/a
Guatemala	101	62	n/a
Honduras	severe	90	$0.40 (food and health)
Mexico	state average 150	varies by state	varies by state
Nicaragua	wide range	moderate	$0.58 (food only)
Paraguay	212	80–90	n/a
Panama	126	severe	n/a
Peru	severe	65+	$0.75 (food only)
Uruguay	moderate	70+	n/a
Venezuela	160	70+	$1.86 (total prison costs)[b]

Source: Observatoire International des Prisons, 1995; Bolivia Minister of Justice and Human Rights; the National Penitentiary and Jail Institute, which runs Colombia's prison system; Reuters, "Peru Admits Jails Packed with Unsentenced Inmates," April 24, 1996 (Peru's vice-minister of justice said the rate of unsentenced inmates in his country was around 90 percent); Chile's numbers from Jiménez A., 1992. Spending per prisoner is $2,835 in the United States.

Notes: a. In Guatemala, there are 8,460 inmates in a system of 8,373 capacity, but many prisons are over 70 percent of capacity. In Honduras, the average wait for trial is twenty-two months. In Brazil, there are about 220,000 prisoners in a system built for 145,000 (*The Economist,* February 24, 2001, p. 37).

b. *El Universal,* March 21, 1995, p. B1. At Eldorado Prison in Bolívar state, spending is around $0.18 per prisoner per day. There is one bed for every four inmates, cells are infested with vermin, and inmates go without shoes, clean bathing water, and eating utensils.

the best of these cases, prisoners still lack medicines and depend on family for food. In countries that report overall spending and divide it by the number of prisoners, as in Venezuela, the number is particularly deceptive because most spending is administrative.

Such overcrowding and underspending have not been much of an incentive for reform. But an increase in riots and escapes, along with mounting international criticism, has finally pushed governments to take more than ad hoc measures. A 1997 law passed by Colombia's legislature freed inmates who had served 60 percent of their prison terms unless they were charged with serious crimes such as terrorism and drug-trafficking. Ecuador adopted a similar plan, releasing the 40 percent of inmates charged with use or possession of small amounts of drugs. A provision in the country's new constitution also allows judges to release unconvicted prisoners imprisoned for more than a year, which, by the end of 1999, led to the freedom of about 600 of the 2,100 entitled prisoners. In Bolivia, the justice minister introduced new bail laws, hired more public defenders, and released thousands of debtors from prison. A 1996 law allows the release of prisoners if no charges are brought for eighteen months. Brazil increased its prison budget from $4 million in 1994 to $110 million in 1997 and has enacted bills to replace incarceration with community service for some first-time offenders.

Throughout the region, new penal and penal process codes will also help relieve overcrowding by speeding up judicial processes with such changes as emphasizing the presumption of innocence, introducing oral trials, strengthening the MP, clarifying the police's criminal investigation role, and providing language assistance.[12] Peru added prohibitions of disappearance and torture to its code, and Colombia's code was supplemented with proscriptions of disappearance and massacre.

Lasting improvements, however, will depend on greater commitments by the executive agencies and increased order in the judiciary. A 1998 Brazilian law authorizes alternative sentencing for nonviolent offenders, for example, but in São Paulo state only a fraction of eligible prisoners has been put on the program. More prisons and better administration are needed in order to impose rules, control violence, seize weapons and cellular phones, and break up gangs and drug-trafficking. But in most countries the plans for such change get mired in politics. Colombia announced plans to build 40 new prisons in February 1999 but has not approved the funds. In Panama, a lack of a central archive of inmates has hampered programs to reduce prison overcrowding. And even with better facilities and administration, the rule of law will not improve without training prison police officers to carry out these tasks in a law-abiding way, as abuses only increase violence and inmate organizing. In the judiciary, speedier trials will not reduce prison populations if the police continue to arrest people in large numbers but the courts do not process them and the executive does not promote probation and parole laws. Brazil's prison population has risen 50 percent since 1995, yet only 2 percent of homicides lead to convictions.

The Defensoría del Pueblo.   With administrative improvements slow at best, more attention has been given to accountability. State agencies must not only be run well but also be accountable to the law in doing so. To increase accountability, one of Latin America's most promising rule of law reforms is the Defensoría del Pueblo, an independent national ombudsman agency mandated to investigate rights abuses, field complaints from citizens, initiate legal recourses, and formulate policy. It is an offshoot of the Ministerio Público, which helps protect constitutional guarantees in the judicial process by overseeing court functioning, public administrators, detainee treatment, and requesting prosecutions. The MP is one of Latin

America's earliest oversight agencies. An MP prototype may have existed for fiscal matters in the Roman Empire, but the first clear reference to one was by Castile's King Pedro I in 1351 (Ruiz Gutiérrez, 1952: 417). Formed as a legal support for the monarch (Zafra 1961: 42), it gradually expanded into public affairs and after the French Revolution was, in most countries, almost exclusively for the public interest.

Despite their early origins, Latin America's MPs were gradually undermined by politics, obligations, and expectations. Above all, there are far too many jobs involved in the dual role of prosecuting crimes and overseeing the state. The fundamental "problematic," according to Peru's top *fiscal* (prosecutor), is that the agency "is put in charge of so many tasks, so many functions and is given only one structure" (Catacora 1991: 132). In most of the region, the *fiscales* (the prosecutors that compose the MP) are overworked, underpaid, and rotated within jurisdictions with a frequency that disrupts judicial processes. They also complain of confusing rules, unclear relations with other agencies, and controls by Congress. Explaining his government's failure to pass a law regulating the MP, for example, Bolivia's *fiscal general* said that the constitution is being interpreted in a way that "makes Congress appear as the MP's boss" and allows for constant interference in the MP's work by outside officials.[13] The MP's yearly reports to Congress, in fact, complain that external interference, unclear guidelines, and weak functional autonomy prevent it from carrying out its constitutional obligations (Ministerio Público de la Nación 1996: 56).

The *Defensorías* grew out of the increasingly recognized need to supplement the MPs with a more focused agency. As Table 2.2 shows, governments throughout Latin America created *Defensorías* in the 1990s. Some of those governments may be gambling that the *Defensoría* will relieve political pressure and improve state functioning without threatening real interests. But *Defensorías* can become more powerful than expected as they grow adept at nurturing allies and publicizing abuses. The agency already enjoys high levels of public popularity and credibility as a new and politically untainted institution, and its ability to collect information has given it a vocal advocacy role. With its mandate over the full range of human rights, it also makes politically potent links between the human rights that most officials prefer to approach separately, such as when the *Defensorías* of Colombia and Peru blame political conflict for the economic suffering of women and indigenous people.

Often given constitutional ranking, the *Defensoría* has a defined set of formal powers but a wide range of informal ones. It is not a judge or prosecutor and cannot detain individuals, pass rulings, or impose punishments. But it can formulate legislative bills and administrative reforms, mediate conflicts, and promote adhesion to international agreements. It speaks on behalf of marginalized populations, and promotes resolutions to problems with public services such as water, electricity, transportation, and agricul-

Table 2.2   Defensorías del Pueblo[a]

Country	Year Formed	Authorities	Obstacles/Challenges
Argentina	1993	1. Investigate abuses in the	1. Extrajudicial violence
Bolivia	1997	courts, police, public	2. High expectations
Brazil	Municipal:	administration, prisons,	3. Society's "intuitive" legal
	various years	public and private services	norms
Colombia	1992	2. Issue reports	4. Political uncertainty
Ecuador	1997	3. Formulate policy, legislation	5. Executive manipulation
Guatemala	1994	4. Utilize legal recourses:	6. Police violence
Mexico	State level:	*amparo,* habeas corpus, etc.	7. Judicial inefficiency
	various years	5. Advocate for societal groups	8. Violence in society
Panama	1977		9. International problems:
Paraguay	1992		narco-trafficking
Peru	1996		
Venezuela	1999		

Note: a. Countries outside Latin America with ombudsmen in the legislative branch, executive branch, or in individual states or specialties (such as consumer protection): Sweden (the first one, in 1809), Finland, Denmark, New Zealand, Holland, Norway, Spain (1978), Portugal, Liechtenstein, Austria, United Kingdom, Germany, Italy, France, Mauritius, Israel, Tanzania, Zambia, India, Philippines, Papua New Guinea, Australia, United States, Canada, Guyana, and Trinidad and Tobago.

ture. Either on its own initiative or on behalf of an aggrieved individual, the *Defensoría* also investigates abuses by the police, prisons, and judiciary. When denouncing specific violations and advocating prosecution, it has at its disposal the range of legal processes: habeas corpus, *amparo* (the general recourse against illegal state actions), and, in some cases, challenges to laws' unconstitutionality or enforcement mechanisms.

Supported by both international institutions and national human rights movements, *Defensorías* grew out of popular demands to check the executive branch and strengthen the judiciary. Ecuador's *Defensoría*, created as one of 1996's constitutional reforms, was part of a larger program that included the 1999 National Plan for Human Rights, which strengthened protections for minorities and tightened restrictions on the police, and the constitution also adopted in 1999, which contains new human rights provisions such as a prohibition of amnesty for those guilty of egregious abuses. Venezuela established a *Defensoría* as part of the new "citizen" branch of government created in the constitution engineered by newly elected President Hugo Chávez in 1999. Restructuring the state and adding rights provisions such as the exclusion of rights cases from the military court system, the constitution was in part a response to previous governments' poor rights record. Several other countries, such as Chile, are in the process of legislating *Defensorías*.

Argentina also adopted a *Defensoría* as a constitutional reform, placing it in the legislative branch but giving it "full functional autonomy." The agency was actually first created by Congress in 1993 (Law 24.284), formulated and shepherded through by its Permanent Bicameral Commission of the Defensoría del Pueblo. This legislative impetus originally came from proposals in the 1970s and then by the Peronist senators of La Rioja province in 1985, following the lower house's earlier tabling of a senate proposal. As with the judicial council, this rare party agreement resulted partly from the fact that the opposition Radicals favored an institution that could check the executive itself, as did the then-opposition Peronists in the 1980s. Further political momentum came from positive media coverage (Tizón 1993: 31) and the success of *Defensorías* established after 1986 in San Juan, La Rioja, Salta, Córdoba, and Rio Negro provinces and the Federal Capital (the name used following the 1880 federalization of the capital city of Buenos Aires).

Most *Defensorías* have used the political support behind them to stake out defined areas of action. Amid privatization, decentralization, and spending cuts, for example, there has been a surge in citizen complaints about basic services. This has led many *Defensorías* to take on the public administration as well as private business.[14] Peru's *Defensoría* has worked against price-fixing by public utilities, charged companies with violating laws, and documented overcharging by energy companies. Colombia's *defensor* (the head of the agency) also has acted against utilities with violations, such as charging a major telecommunications business (the Empresa de Telecomunicaciones de Bogotá) of illegally altering users' terms of payments.

Merely the potential for such muckraking makes governments nervous. In some cases, it has even led the executive and other officials to delay enacting the laws necessary for a *Defensoría*'s functioning. Peru adopted a *Defensoría* in its 1993 constitution, for example, but largely because of executive obstinacy did not pass the necessary organic law until 1995 and did not appoint its first *defensor* until 1996. Bolivia created a *Defensoría* in its 1992 constitutional reforms, but created an organic law in 1997 and appointed its first *defensor* in 1998.

When a *Defensoría* does get off the ground, its actual functioning is still shaped primarily by executive politics and state bureaucracy. The agency's lack of political affiliations lends it popular legitimacy but also makes it less skilled at navigating officials' interests and bureaucratic demands. Dependence on state funds, overlap with other agencies, and lack of patronage networks also keep it in a precarious position. In some cases, such as Bolivia and Colombia, governments eager for a fresh approach to economic and political problems have given the *Defensoría* some leeway. But when most *Defensorías* test the limits of such benevolence, the usual response is negligence, stalling, or attack. Peru's *defensor* was sharply rebuked by the supreme military council when he asserted in December 1996 that the arrest of General Rodolfo Robles, following his criticisms of the government's human rights record, was illegal. In Argentina, despite Congress's authority to appoint and remove the *defensor*, the influence of the Peronists allowed President Carlos Menem to appoint a political crony to the job, negating the neutrality that gives the body its authority. In Venezuela, the political dominance of the Chávez government endangers the *Defensoría's* independence. Colombia's *defensor* has cast government action on displaced populations as vital to the "recuperation of the State's credibility,"[15] but the state's response has been one of low funding, poor coordination, outright denial, and harmful policies such as compelling displaced persons to return home without providing for their safety. As with other measures to increase accountability, the *Defensoría* is limited by the power and the bureaucracy of the very structures it is trying to open up.

Defensorías' work on behalf of journalists and human rights activists suffers from similar pressures. Throughout Latin America, journalists continue to be under attack by laws, threats, and other forms of intimidation and censorship. Peruvian journalists who expose rights violations or criticize the government have faced death threats, legal actions, and arrests on trumped-up charges of obstruction of justice or "apology" of terrorism, and *Defensoría* efforts on their behalf have not significantly slowed these practices. In April 1999, Bolivia's *Defensoría* was upbraided by the ministers of the government and of defense for its accusations of illegal harassment against a magazine. In Ecuador, the commission investigating the 1999 murder of three members of the opposition Democratic Popular Movement was repeatedly blocked. In Colombia, when the *defensor* blames military or paramilitary groups in killings of rights activists, political figures, and government investigators, the military often turns the blame on the rights organizations themselves. After the May 1998 murder of a top state official, for example, military officials passed along false information to the attorney general linking the crime to the Justice and Peace rights group and subsequently raided its office and threatened its employees. The government responded by installing bulletproof glass and security cameras in the offices of other rights organizations but has only slowly carried out its promise to cleanse government files of false accusations against those same groups.

Although a government can increase its popularity by supporting a *Defensoría*, it often gains more by targeting it. The most conspicuous of such attacks have been in Peru, prompted by the *defensor's* involvement in the 2000 presidential elections, from his questioning of the election's constitutionality to the logistics of the final runoff. When the *defensor* called for an inquiry into the president's registration drive after receiving hundreds of complaints of false voter signatures, for example, the president's congressional allies retorted that the *Defensoría* itself should be investigated for fomenting radicalism. The government can also use the more subtle tactic of simply cutting funds. Soon after appointing the country's first *defensor*, the Ecuadorian government instigated his resignation by denying him an adequate budget and reducing his term in office. A new *defensor* was then appointed following the adoption of a new constitution, but financial control continued: in 1999, the Finance Ministry delayed transferring funds to the *Defensoría*, whose budget request of 32,000 sucres was reduced to 19,000.[16]

Defensorías try to get around executive pressures by using actual or potential international reprimands and by focusing on specific cases. Citing cases before the Inter-American Human Rights Commission and a U.S. congressional report on Peru's lack of judicial independence, for example, the country's *defensor* pushed for action on these issues in order to avoid further reprobation. More effective is action on well-documented abuses by the state. In Colombia, subhuman conditions in several prisons were exposed only when *Defensoría* officials were barred from visiting members of the leftist Ejército de Liberación Nacional (ELN). Provincial-level ombudsmen can help generate further pressure to make the national *defensor* more independent and effective. The federal district *Defensoría* in Argentina has clashed repeatedly with the national government over police activities and social services—increasing publicity for the office and encouraging citizen action through it.[17] Colombia's provincial *defensores* document killings and kidnappings, relay communities' fears of attacks to the Defense Ministry, pinpoint areas of danger, and mediate talks between armed groups and local communities. In this work, the *Defensoría* has accused government soldiers of committing massacres while masquerading as paramilitary groups and of refusing to warn of imminent paramilitary attacks.

Such strategies, however, are less effective against the even bigger obstacles put in the way by judicial and law-enforcement agencies. Because no *Defensoría* can keep track of the daily activities in the street, prisons, police stations, and courts, its effectiveness depends on the cooperation of those in charge of these areas. Bolivia's *defensor* complains that she is constantly submitting legal recourses to stop unconstitutional governmental actions, from illegal roadblocks to intrusions on citizen privacy.[18] Police forces can be particularly unaccountable, especially when dealing with problems such as narcotics trafficking. Authoritarian regimes were more repressive, but blame was more easily affixed on its leaders; in many current democracies, responsibility and redress are more diffuse. Public opinion can also allow state practices to trump *Defensoría* efforts. In Colombia, for example, the regional *defensor* in Caldas Department publicly called on the police in 1996 to investigate up to eighty deaths in what it considered a deliberate act of "social cleansing." While bold, this statement is unlikely to lead to actual measures to resolve an endemic and deeply entrenched practice that society would rather ignore. As discussed in Chapter 7, a majority of citizens may not support some of the rights that a *Defensoría* does.

But the majority of complaints to most *Defensorías* regards the judiciary, upon which the *Defensoría* ultimately depends to make the rulings and impose the remedies needed to uphold basic rights. The *Defensoría* can muster up political and public pressure on officials but steers most of its cases, either directly or through the MP, into legal channels. But both the MP and public defenders—natural allies of the *Defensoría*—are overwhelmed, and most complaints end up in the disorderly files of untrained personnel. Bottlenecks of unresolved *amparo* petitions are common in many urban sectors of Ecuador, for instance, but the *Defensoría* has been able to do little more than urge area judges to quickly resolve these petitions.

Because of such barriers, *Defensorías* may find themselves limited to public advocacy, information collection, and individual cases. In most countries, specific incidents of torture by police officers have been resolved more easily than charges of general patterns of torture. Referring problems to congressional committees, or cooperating with executive agencies in nonthreatening projects like popular education, have more success than accusations against ministries. Responding to complaints of the use of electric shock against soldiers, Ecuador's *defensor* saw through a case of a soldier paralyzed after such treatment. Aware of abuse against street vendors, Colombia's *Defensoría* took up the case of a journalist beaten by the police in February 1999 while reporting on the eviction of some vendors.

Such successes show that state agencies best adapt to changes and demands incrementally. In trying to monitor the state under the triple pressure of government politics, societal needs, and interference by other state agencies, the *Defensoría* demonstrates the difficulty of bringing accountability to agencies protective of their authority.

Decentralization. In both administration and accountability, decentralization offers another route for state rule of law reform. Decentralization involves many different decisions, but the most important is whether the central government merely delegates policy execution to local governments or actually gives them real decisionmaking autonomy. Historically, centralization was encouraged because it was supposed to make state services more efficient, accountable, and powerful—for the benefit of both society and the executive. On the rule of law, however, centralization tended to reduce the state's presence in outlying areas, causing a de facto decentralization in which local powers oversaw the law, as during colonialism. Even constitutional federal states were centralized administratively and politically, allowing regional patronage and abuse to dig in.

Contemporary democracies, in an effort to be more efficient and accessible, are now decentralizing many state functions to provincial governments. But the process is highlighting the difficulties of juggling popular demands, administrative services, and individual rights. Decentralization of state rule of law functions can involve a range of authorities, including the creation and oversight of courts, the training of judges, and the operation of prisons. But such decentralization often imposes intolerable administrative burdens on unprepared provinces. Because of local bureaucracy, for example, a 1996 decree in Bolivia to decentralize the handling of court materials has not led to a speedier rate of justice. The balance of powers needed for a rule of law is often weaker at the provincial level as well. *Fiscales* and public defenders are even more beleaguered, police forces tend to have greater autonomy, and weaker local NGOs make public accountability less likely. Fiscal responsibility also tends to be scarcer at the provincial level. Representatives in Argentina's National Congress earned about $7,200 a year in 2001, for example, but assembly members in the country's poor Formosa province receive $1.9 million a year in salary and benefits. In Salta province each legislator gets $500,000 annually, and in Chaco province 90 percent of the legislative budget is earmarked for member salaries.[19]

Decentralization also depends on the manner in which it is carried out. Effective decentralization must increase both the "ability for officials familiar with local-level problems to tailor development plans" and the inclusion of local groups in formulating and monitoring these plans (Davis et al. 1987: 253). When constitutional protections are involved, this approach is most successful when the central government determines the rules and leaves their execution to regional or local governments, which are accountable to national standards but focused on their community's needs. In countries where the provinces have more administrative experience, effective decentralization is thus more likely to succeed. As discussed in Chapter 4, a model for criminal codes for all of Latin America came from the Argentine province of Córdoba, and reforms such as judicial councils and training programs were up and running in many Argentine provinces before the national government even legislated them.

But when functions are being transferred down for the first time, decentralization can weaken the rule of law. Even in Argentina, many efforts to establish local courts are being run aground by restrictions over the transference of national judicial powers to the local level.[20] Even more harmful is when the politics of decentralization overshadow its rationale. Decentralization is always political, of course, often initiated when the "center is unable to satisfy political expectations, and is compelled to seek local support and encourage the local generation of resources" (Mawhood 1987: 21). This does not necessarily mean decentralization will fail, but it is unlikely to work if carried out in a way that allows the central government to tie its support to political cooperation. In many countries, decentralization is even "instituted by executive decree and administered under severe central control" (Veliz 1978: 13). In Venezuela, the central government holds the purse strings and uses political patronage as part of its decentralization. Many plans only give state agencies the "freedom to do right": once a mistake is made, responsibility is rescinded and decentralization grinds to a halt.

Argentina

Emerging out of a particularly repressive regime in 1983, Argentina focused more on the immediate causes of rights violations with reforms such as those to introduce conscientious objection to military service, strengthen the right to privacy, adopt international rights treaties into national law, strengthen habeas corpus (Law 23.098 of 1984), and "consecrate the right to disobey [de facto] governments, rejecting the authority of their acts and punishing those who come to power through force or collaborating with them" (*Consejo para la Consolidación de la Democracia*: 48). Many changes in other state structures were not enacted until the 1990s, primarily through Radical-supported 1994 additions to the constitution, such as the *Defensor del Pueblo* and the *jefe de gabinete,* a presidentially appointed minister who coordinates the ministries' work and is their congressional liaison. Many of these ideas were developed in the 1980s by a Supreme Court advisory council and by President Raúl Alfonsín's Council for the Consolidation of Democracy (Consejo para la Consolidación de la Democracia). But these recommendations were too ambitious for what turned out to be the Radicals' tumultuous and short stint in power. Both bodies were terminated after 1989.

In Argentina, the two state agencies most responsible for the rule of law are the Interior and Justice Ministries. The Interior Ministry advises the president "on all matters of internal governance, the public order and the full exercise of constitutional principles and guarantees" (Law 22.520, title V, article 16). It oversees the rights of foreigners, political amnesty, national emergencies, immigration, interprovincial relations, federal intervention in the provinces, and parts of economic policy. The Justice Ministry formulates executive policy, helps in the MP's organization, develops legislation, and administers criminal records and related information. Its authoritative reach is limited because each province has its own Justice Ministry, and its political reach is limited because the justice minister is closely identified with the president. It does, however, have complete institutional authority over the "organization, functioning and supervision of [federal] penal establishments" (Law 22.520, article 20). (Provincial governments run provincial prisons, which comprise most of the country's facilities.) Insufficient attention was paid to the prisons after 1983, as they were associated with past authoritarian regimes and presumed not to be a human rights concern. But budget cuts, insufficient new construction, and increases in arrests— primarily because of overuse and "abuse of preventative detention" authority[21]—led to physical deterioration and growing rights violations in the twenty-eight federal prisons and in most provincial prisons.

Because the justice and interior ministers do not have much political independence, furthermore, their ability to alter criminal policies is limited. A lack of executive-level planning and policy long has been common in Argentina, with little public or institutional debate over crime and criminal policy. The Office of Criminal Policy, created in 1992 to formulate and direct criminal policy, has been hampered by poor access to information, a lack of criminology training, and inadequate infrastructural support.[22] The office's director complains that "we have improved slightly our focus on dissecting the same 'insects' that we have always dissected: those who commit minor crimes and are the only ones caught in the penal process' selectivity"; meanwhile, "the larger criminal policy and its normative and sociological approach have not changed" since the predemocratic era.[23] Indeed, a common response to such criticism from executive officials is that there are no funds for new crime initiatives and that the real problem in any case is that judges rule "habitually in favor of delinquents."[24]

As with the *Defensoría*, however, the harms of these national-level politics have been limited by decentralization. Despite the "near unanimity" in favor of political federalism in Argentina, many patterns of the past, such as military rule and state expansion, have "tended to reinforce the presence of the central government in areas" that constitutionally are under provincial jurisdiction (Quadri Castillo 1986: 116). With the return to democracy, the provinces have reasserted their constitutional prerogatives.[25] In particular, the constitution authorizes provinces to set up their own judicial systems and to legislate their own legal codes and procedures. Extensive use of that power after 1983 made provincial judiciaries a trove of state rule of law reforms and a source of advocacy for change at the national level. Long before similar reforms by the federal government, the constitutions of Salta and Córdoba included detailed provisions on the qualifications of judges, and Santiago del Estero set up a well-regarded training school for judicial personnel. In Córdoba, oral trials, defendants' rights, and a dependency by the judicial police on the Supreme Court were all established in the 1970s—later copied by Costa Rica and, in its 1992 penal code, by Argentina's federal government. Since the Luján Accord of 1990, furthermore, the federal and provincial governments have been clarifying relations between them, particularly regarding social services and political parties (Frías 1991).

The MP is another example of how provinces have bypassed executive power and judicial disarray. Most provinces have created MPs without the executive dominance long characterizing the national agency. Historically, the executive's power to appoint the national MP's chief, the *Procurador General de la Nación*, long undermined the agency's constitutional duty to "implement justice in defense of" society's interests.[26] Since 1862, the *procurador* had been selected by the president with the advice and consent of the senate and can be removed from office only through impeachment.

In its first days in power, the Menem government tried to remove the *procurador* through decree, leading to the *procurador*'s resignation. In addition, individual *fiscales* have had little sway in judicial processes and are "relatively isolated in investigation, only really appearing with any importance when a case comes to trial."[27] But Argentina's national MP was made officially autonomous by the 1994 constitutional reforms, inspired in part by provincial measures. The majority of provincial MPs are part of the judiciary, in Córdoba the MP is assigned much independent authority, and in Salta it is wholly independent. A 1994 law separated out the public defenders from the MP, giving both institutions more effectiveness. In 1998, in addition, Congress formulated a *Ley Orgánica del Ministerio Público* that further strengthened the agency.[28]

As in other countries, however, one problem still immune to decentralization's benefits has been the penitentiary system. Argentina was one of the first in the region to ban corporal punishment and hard labor, and its National Penitentiary prison was a model of security and humanity in the 1930s. But laws for probation and parole were not enacted, and the increasing repression by governments made the prisons overcrowded. After 1983, rising crime led to administrative and rights deficiencies, which were aggravated by being overlooked.

These festering problems in both federal and provincial prisons burst into the spotlight in 1996 with the worst prison crisis in the country's history. In March of that year, a botched escape attempt at Sierra Chica Prison of the Buenos Aires provincial penitentiary system led to a mutiny by some of its 1,000 prisoners and by 11,570 others in eighteen prisons throughout the country, killing at least seventeen and wounding more than fifty. The main cause of the upheaval was an overcrowding that was an average of 40 percent over capacity. Between 1985 and 1996, the federal prison population increased by 132 percent, the Buenos Aires provincial system's by 78.9 percent. About 75 percent of the actual prison population in Buenos Aires province has waited more than two years to be tried,[29] and more than 70 percent of all inmates at any given time are unsentenced, violating the criminal code's two-year pretrial detention limit.[30] Yet Buenos Aires province built only two new prisons between 1974 and 1995, with disease, malnutrition, substandard sanitation, unlocked jail cells, insufficient food, and illegal punishments increasing with overcrowding.[31] In Olmos Prison in Buenos Aires province, which was built for 1,800 inmates but holds 3,500, violence and neglect cause "one or two deaths each day" yet have led to few preventative measures.[32] Because of budgetary constraints, many complaints to the federal prison ombudsman go uninvestigated.

Rioting inmates demanded better conditions, faster legal processes, more relaxed visiting rules, more lenient penalties for car-theft convicts, and implementation in the provinces of the federal prison "two-for-one" law, which deducts two years for each year already served by unsentenced prisoners. The government blamed the riots on a small group of ringleaders but still agreed to implement the two-for-one reduction, create commissions with inmate representatives, reduce most car-theft sentences, move some inmates to prisons closer to their families, and set up a Justice Ministry AIDS commission.

Politics, judicial bureaucracy, and legal confusion, however, may well undermine new these and other reforms.[33] In 2000, the budget of the federal prisons amounted to $32,000 per prisoner. But 80 percent of that money went to personnel salaries, leaving little for actual prison improvements. The law regulating prison administration dates back from 1947, with modifications in 1973. A new national prison law went into effect in 1996 to establish a system of judicial monitoring of prison conditions, as did a set of regulations on pretrial detainees. But unless these two sets of laws are sufficiently regulated, the majority of inmates may be denied many of the prison law's benefits. Even less protected are the vast numbers of those held in police facilities. In 1996, the Justice Ministry estimated that between 28,000 and 31,000 of the country's 55,000–58,000 prisoners were confined in police lockups. As with all other reforms, equal rights must be incorporated into new administrative functions. But there is a danger that they will not be in Argentina's penitentiary reforms.

Since most inmates are detained for "crimes against property," in addition, the growing inequalities that fuel such crimes will only increase prison population.[34] Between 1990 and 2000, the rate of poverty among Argentines shot up from 22 to 43 percent. The top 10 percent earned 35 percent of national income and the bottom tenth 9.7 in 1990, but ten years later the figures were 36 percent and 8.2 percent, respectively.[35] Criminal rates changed in the same proportion. In 1999, reported crimes were double what they were in 1992 and were 28 percent more than in 1997. Even with faster judicial processes, new protections will have to be funded adequately to keep up with a prison population that is likely to grow.

In addition, the long-term penitentiary proposals formulated by the Justice Ministry have run up against executive pressures and judicial disarray even before their consideration. Citing the Penitentiary Law's stated goal to rehabilitate prisoners, ministry officials heading up penitentiary policy reported a serious state of deterioration at most facilities, lack of prison activities, and decreases in criminal sentencing rates. To resolve these problems, they put together an "integral reform" (Ministerio de Justicia 1994: 45) comprising proposals such as wider geographic dispersion of prisons, improved personnel education, and better medical services. But they also warned that these measures could not get off the ground without substantial increases in funding, a decrease in "excessive bureaucratization," and implementation of legislated treatment programs for offenders. But such requirements have been slow to materialize, largely because a lack of responsibility for them in the executive branch and because of the judiciary's administrative incapacity to help. The long recession that began in the mid-1990s has made new funding unlikely, and when the economy does recover these needs may be forgotten.

Sometimes, however, an institution functions so poorly that it draws unwanted attention and is connected with other failings of the government. And when it suddenly becomes beneficial for politicians to champion reform, actual change is likely because they can use studies and statistics to back themselves up. This is the case with criminal justice in many countries. As with penitentiary policy, formulators of criminal policy in Argentina have had more success in collecting statistics and outlining problems than in actually implementing plans. In 1991, the Justice Ministry's Criminal Policy Office began putting together a "national criminal policy plan" by studying criminal trends in the Buenos Aires area as a first step toward a "global strategy" incorporating the federal and provincial governments (Ministerio de Justicia 1996: 4). Although the study fell short of a national plan, it did bring together vital information on criminal trends that bolstered evolving reforms such as the new penal code and parole programs. Such unimplemented policies lay a foundation for change when political shifts open up opportunities for new legislation. Although the decentralized prisons have been no better than federal systems, they do provide laboratories for new reforms.

Venezuela

Reports of the Venezuelan state's demise have been exaggerated—but not by much. "The Venezuelan state is so disorganized," concluded the 1995 *Annual Report to the Congress of the Comptroller of the Republic*, "that it is at the point of disappearing—if it hasn't done so already." The same year, 92 percent of a national poll's respondents expressed their belief that neither the nation's leaders nor its institutions were capable of resolving the country's problems.[36] Despite oil wealth and political stability, the state's effectiveness in Venezuela had been trampled by executive power, party control, and bureaucracy. The ailing state of the state is displayed most prominently by its rule of law functions.

Two agreements defined Venezuela's 1958 transition to democracy. The first was the 1958 Pact of Punto Fijo, an informal, unwritten agreement among the leaders of the three main parties (AD, the Independent Electoral Political Organizing Committee [COPEI], and the Unión Repúblicana Democrática) to cooperate, abide by elections, split up cabinet posts, maintain a powerful executive, and dole out state resources. The other agreement, the 1961 constitution, institutionalized Punto Fijo's emphasis on stability and party control. It allowed party leadership to choose candidates for all elections, in which citizens voted for party lists, and gave the president wide-ranging powers, including that of appointing all state governors. Regarding judicial functions, the constitution granted the national government the "competency" of "the administration of justice and the creation, organization and competence of the courts" and the Public Ministry, as well as over legislation on constitutional, civil, penal, and penitentiary law (article 136). Through these agreements, AD organized civil society and the state along corporatist lines, with strong central government control over local administration. Although students were a key part of the 1958 regime change, for example, President Betancourt (1959–1964) "insisted that although student opposition was justified in a dictatorship, once there was a democratic regime, with free access to institutions through freely organized political parties, no justifiable basis for student political action remained. Here again, Betancourt is arguing for a compartmentalization of politics" (Levine 1973: 51).

To manage national growth, the government usually created more agencies. In 1958, it formed the Comisión de Administración Pública (CAP) to oversee the areas of education, housing, and public health. CAP helped legislate the 1969 regionalization law, which divided the country into economic regions and established new development corporations, and the 1972 administrative regionalization decree, which created regional offices of the eight national ministries and eighty-two autonomous institutions. These plans never went into effect, however, mainly because the executive stymied coordination among the ministries and corporations. Local services began expanding through the country's burgeoning cities but were sabotaged by party controls. Efforts by both COPEI and AD governments to improve *barrio* (shantytown) conditions were blocked by the opposition's protection of its own *barrio* networks. Municipalities' revenue-raising capacities were severely limited, and in 1968 Congress rejected a professionalization of local administration. It was not until AD and COPEI secured control of the Venezuelan Association of Municipalities that local government began to attain a voice in national politics.

The fight against corruption followed a similar pattern. Even when corruption was specifically targeted, its link with the party and public officials prevented effective reform. Betancourt revived the Comisión Investigadora contra el Enriquecimiento Ilícito (CIEI) to prosecute former officials accused of corruption, for example, but the CIEI received inadequate budget support and cooperation from the rest of the government, leading to only a few successful prosecutions. One of those successes was the 1963 trial against Pérez Jimenez, echoed by the 1995 corruption trial of President Carlos Andrés Pérez (1974–1979 and 1989–1993), both important symbols that nevertheless left corruption's root causes in place.

With the 1970s oil boom, state expansion continued to speed past state capacity. Ministry budgets were often rejected for being too low (Karl, 1995: 37), and the problems accompanying ever-increasing urbanization, such as crime, were smoothed over by expanding social services. Like many of his predecessors, President Pérez pushed through decrees in a poorly planned program of public works, worker benefits, the nationalization of oil, and the establishment of state corporations in refining, petrochemical, and other industries. As the number of agencies grew, coordination and efficiency predictably fell. The 1978 Law of the Cities did grant greater authority to the municipalities and established a city manager for those larger than 50,000. But as with the CAP earlier on, the law was not accompanied by necessary training and coordination provisions.

This combination of cash and party control came crashing down in the 1980s with a drop in world oil prices that devastated the economy (oil exports provided about 90 percent of the country's income). Just as significant as this high dependence on oil, which distinguished Venezuela's economy from those in the rest of Latin America, was the ambitious and expansive state-run model of development that the country had adopted. Based on distribution of its massive petroleum earnings, the state built a sprawling network of administrative agencies, social services, public works, and other programs. This approach led to unprecedented improvements in the living standards of most social sectors, who expected—far more than in any other Latin American country—that a proactive state can and should guarantee ongoing support and advancement. Facing economic problems, however, most other Latin American governments at the time began to adopt neoliberal reforms of spending cuts, privatization, currency devaluation, diversification, and an end to state subsidies and price controls. Not only was Venezuela's crisis more severe; so was its resistance to such policies. Both the parties and the popular sectors believed that oil would ultimately save them from a restructuring that would be more painful in Venezuela than in other countries because of the size and role of the Venezuelan state.

Yet poverty and other social ills continued to climb. The rate of acute poverty jumped from 22.5 percent to 54 percent of the population between 1981 and 1987 (Hillman 1994: 95), and the fourfold increase in hunger between 1979 and 1999 gave Venezuela a higher rate of hunger than China's.[37] In 1995, 62 percent of Venezuelans lived below the poverty line, and prices for basic foodstuffs rose beyond the reach of 75 percent of the population (Ministerio de la Familia: 23). Reported crimes jumped from 42,565 in 1961 to 64,365 in 1971 to 175,855 in 1986 (CTPJ: 1997). As societal needs from the state rose at the same rate as its ability to deliver them fell, the regime found itself squeezed by a vice of new pressures and old patterns. "Political clientelism, party factionalism," and the state's economic controls led to a severe "decrease in the capacity of rational action" by the country's leadership (Guevara 1989: 16). In 1983, the government was forced to enact the first currency devaluation in twenty years, and the following year it introduced a set of neoliberal policies. But those measures were derailed by opposition and the government's attempts to ameliorate them. And although the state had little capacity to raise tax revenue to make up for revenue losses, spending continued unabated and reached a level seventeen times greater in 1989 than that in 1972 while state debt ballooned to thirty-three times its 1970s levels, rising from 8.76 percent of gross national product (GNP) in 1970 to 50.46 percent of GNP in 1988 (Karl 1995: 37–41). By the 1990s, the state had 1.3 million employees for a population of just 21 million (a higher number of employees than in Japan, with a population of 120 million).

With patronage and corporatism quickening the state's deterioration and political pressures bearing down on the elites, the idea of state reform finally began to come under serious consideration. In December 1984, the government appointed the Presidential Commission for State Reform (COPRE, for Comisión Presidencial para la Reforma del Estado). Over the next ten years, COPRE made recommendations on political reforms, the rule of law, decentralization, "debureaucratization," and public policy. These efforts led to the establishment of mayors; direct election of governors; transference of many responsibilities to the states; and some streamlining of the penal process.[38] Proposals regarding state rule of law functions, however, got lost between the proposal and enactment stages. To improve oversight, COPRE recommended decentralizing the MP, creating municipal and state *fiscales*, and establishing the Council for the Prevention of Criminality, which would bring in civil society to design and disseminate criminal prevention programs (COPRE 1994: 102–111). These proposals were not considered. In addition, the central decentralization law, the 1989 Organic Law of Decentralization (LODDT), included no decentralization of rule of law functions.

The only clear state rule of law measure left standing was an LODDT provision to decentralize the prisons, followed up by a 1996 agreement between the Justice Ministry and fifteen state governors. Like other reforms, it was motivated primarily by crisis. As in Argentina, that crisis was an eruption in the country's prisons, which was also rooted partly in the assumption that prisons were not a major problem. Most of Gómez's prisons were torn down in 1937, and the new ones built as replacements were modernized and improved after the 1958 democratic transition. In Venezuela, the Ministry of Justice coordinates the executive's judicial policies, and its only institutional responsibilities are to run the federal prison system and most police forces.[39] Along with the post-1958 infrastructural improvements, this clear delineation of functions seemed to be a good foundation for effective penitentiary policy and administration.

But the ministry's limited political and financial capacity led to growing neglect of the country's thirty-two prisons and a lack of oversight of
inmate rights.[40] This neglect led by the mid-1990s to mass escapes and
uncontrolled violence that even became a real threat to national stability.[41]
Originally built to hold 15,426 inmates, the penitentiary system in the
1990s held anywhere between 24,000 and 27,000, with some facilities at
four times intended capacity.[42] Such overcrowding has fueled a spiral of
violence: whereas less than 100 prison deaths were reported each year during the late 1980s, more than 200 deaths were registered in 1990 and more
than 400 in 1999 (Inspector General de Cárceles 1999). In 1958, some 50
percent of all prisoners were awaiting trial, but by 1995 it was well over 70
percent.[43] Inmates are often transferred to prisons far away from the courts
that handle their cases, and even prisoners who remain in one spot wait up
to a year for transportation to the courthouse. Because of judicial bottlenecks, the average time from the detainee's initial declaration to sentencing
lasts four years, and some prisoners languish in jail for up to eight years
before being found innocent.[44] Despite legal prohibitions, all types of prisoners share cells: unsentenced with sentenced, minors with adults, petty
criminals with homicide convicts.

The most evident source of the crisis has been the insufficient amount
of spending, which led to collapsing physical facilities and subhuman living conditions.[45] Inmates must fight for floor space to sleep and depend on
family for food. Corruption, dangerous conditions, and an insufficient number of personnel leave whole areas of many prisons unpatrolled. Visiting
lawyers and family members bring in drugs and weapons to inmates, who
form heavily armed rival gangs that fight over territory and the lucrative
$3.5 million trade in cocaine and heroin, causing deadly riots.[46]

Also fueling violence is institutionalized abuse of inmates by prison
officials. Media criticism has focused on the Guardia Nacional's (National
Guard's) heavy-handed attempts to regain control over the most violent
prisons, yet abuse by regular prison officials is a daily occurrence. Inmates
denouncing abuses or demanding improvements often face harsh retribution. In 1990, the government packed off a group of 239 prisoners on a
hunger strike against prison conditions to the notorious Amazon penal
colony of El Dorado and, once there, limited contact with their families and
lawyers. Events following an inmate uprising at the General Penitentiary of
Venezuela in October 1991 reveals how the weakness of state oversight
agencies aggravates rule of law abuses. After the Guardia Nacional put
down the riots, prisoners claimed that rebellious inmates had been mur-
dered and their bodies dumped into "wells of death." The MP's investigation concluded that the inmates allegedly killed by the Guardia Nacional
had simply been transferred to other jails, and only continuing prisoner agitation led to follow-up that discovered the wells and several corpses within
them. But at that point the government halted this renewed investigation.

Despite the severity of the prison crisis, reform responses have been implemented and enforced haphazardly. The federal criminal code dictates that judicial officials inspect prisons every fifteen days and hear prisoner complaints, for example, but the few visits that do take place are rarely followed up with change. The Justice Ministry, responding to a ten-year-old request, only in 1994 completed an inmate census, which was immediately criticized as unreliable for depending on information provided by inmates themselves. Most of the agencies responsible for overseeing prisons and prisoners' rights work at cross-purposes or not at all; like the laws they enforce, they have been obstructed by executive power, incoherent policy, and judicial disarray.

Penitentiary policy is also shaped by politics. When inhumane conditions at El Dorado became an issue in the presidential campaigns of the 1970s, for example, it was alternately closed and reopened as political tides shifted. The many reasonable recommendations of the 1977 National Penitentiary Reform Commission, such as better personnel training and smaller prisons, went unimplemented (Bravo Oliveros 1977). The Western Penitentiary Center was earmarked in the late 1980s to be entirely for convicted inmates, but court delays quickly filled the prisons' cells with unsentenced detainees. In 1984, the Ministry of Justice showed that it was in charge by announcing plans to build a monstrous 3,000-inmate-capacity prison in the middle of Caracas, ignoring the fact that it had no money to do so and that international organizations had just recommended 300 inmates as the maximum size for any prison. As with many reforms, only crisis led to change. In Retén de Catia, one of the country's largest, most violent, and inhumane prisons, the government replaced hundreds of corrupt guards with newly trained personnel in 1994. When that didn't do the trick, four years later the prisoners were transferred and the prison was literally blown up. Disappearing along with the prison, however, were the chances of prosecuting many of the abuses that occurred there—such as a massacre of sixty-two prisoners in 1992.

The LODDT and later accords are attempting to address these problems by giving states control over prisons, as administration is more efficient at the provincial than national level. But the success of decentralization hinges on the balance between written policy and real decisionmaking power. The law allows extra discretionary state spending and encourages salary bonuses for personnel, but the Justice Ministry retains ultimate budget control. For needed physical improvements, the agreements only vaguely dictate that state governments "will collaborate" with the Justice Ministry. Yet constitutionally, the Justice Ministry is ultimately in charge of the penitentiary system. Given the country's financial constraints and political changes, the vague administrative and legal terms of this decentralization will mean that real reform will probably fall by the wayside. Three years after decentralization began, in fact, there were few apparent improvements. In response, the constitutional assembly declared a "prison emergency" and set up an interinstitutional commission to study it. This interinstitutional cooperation was a positive step, but so-called study may serve to merely block real change.

Penal process reforms, one of the three areas of enacted laws after 1984, has had limited impact because of a lack of support. The 1993 Law of Penal Process, the 1992 Bail Law, and the 1980 Law of Submission to Trial and Conditional Release (*Ley de Sometimiento a Juicio y Suspensión Condicional de la Pena*), along with legal aid and prisoner work laws in the early 1990s, began to reduce the prison population through parole programs, outreach to the poor, and alternative conflict-resolution mechanisms like mediation. Assistance Centers set up under the 1980 law, for example, supported nearly 130,000 persons and helped keep recidivism below 4 percent. But these programs soon became underfunded, unevaluated, and inconsistently applied (Elia de Molina 1992). The bail laws exclude the majority of detainees, such as those held for drug violations (Paolini de Palm 1993: 89–90), and a lack of personnel prevents the majority of prisoners eligible for release to actually be freed. More seriously, the executive blocked efforts to substitute incarceration with alternative approaches. It attempted to water down the alternative sentences provisions in the original bills and did not cooperate with them after the bills were enacted into law.

One of these reforms' biggest mistakes was to place many new programs under the authority of penal officials instead of into more efficient realms, such as the administrative courts. Poor-quality programs for resocialization inside prisons and for tracking former convicts on the outside make officials reluctant to release detainees, for example, and in some cases provisions to protect defendants actually keep them ensnared in the judicial bureaucracy. The automatic appeals of the 1984 Organic Law of Substances, Narcotics, and Psychotropic Drugs (*Ley Organica Sobre Sostancias, Estupefacientes y Psicotropicas*), coupled with bureaucratic incompetence, keeps many detainees incarcerated even after being acquitted twice. As with the other laws passed in the 1980s and 1990s, increases in overcrowding and violence also demonstrated these reforms' ineffectiveness.

Along with defects in the laws, poor penitentiary and decentralization policies also weaken criminal policy in Venezuela. As elsewhere in Latin America, Venezuela's crime rates have skyrocketed. Between 1990 and 1995, the murder rate increased by 73 percent, assaults by 16 percent, and robberies by 26 percent (OCEI: tables 631–634). Panic among the population threw the government off balance and created waves of vigilante justice in urban barrios as suspected criminals were lynched by angry mobs as well as organized groups. One of the sources of such deterioration is the executive's failure to adopt any coherent criminal policy to replace the *Doctrina Betancourt* (the name given to Betancourt's heavy use of security forces). Reflecting its policy drift, the government focused on misdemeanors such as loitering and lack of identification. As in Argentina, the "insects" were the first to get snared by law enforcement's web. In the early 1960s, almost 60 percent of prisoners were charged with crimes against persons. By the late 1970s, however, that percentage had dropped by half. Meanwhile, the percentage of those charged with property crimes jumped from 21 percent to nearly 50 percent and has remained steady since. Even in the face of the extremity of lynchings, the Venezuelan government has failed to devise coherent, viable policies. As in Argentina, the Justice and Interior Ministries' lack of political independence has also curtailed the formulation of effective criminal policy. Officials' insistence that the government does indeed have a criminal policy reflects their proximity to the executive's political interests, with ministers and other presidential appointees defending the executive and most others criticizing it. According to COPRE's executive secretary,

> We are very repressive but don't have programs for preventing crime. There are no resources. There are written programs, very good programs, but nothing is implemented. Part of the problem is a lack of coordination within the government. We have an institutional dispersion [without] common space for discussion among different policymakers. We have the Supreme Court, the Judicial Council, the Justice Ministry, the attorney general. All of them act separately on a specific area without taking into account the globality of the issues. There is no space for cooperative strategy. Each one only thinks in terms of its own piece.[47]

In Congress, strong party controls, lack of resources, and high rates of absenteeism have discouraged innovative or responsive legislation. Many congressional meetings lack quorums, and civil society groups are rarely asked to testify or otherwise participate in congressional proceedings (Peña 1978). In addition, attempts by several congressional bodies in the 1990s to scrap the entire system with a "judicial emergency" law clashed with efforts by other congressional bodies to piece together comprehensive reform. But the severity of the crime and prison problems, combined with goading by NGOs, the press, and academics, did eventually lead to some much-needed reform proposals. In 1999, Congress adopted a new penal process code (see Chapter 4).[48] In 1994, the government began to crack down on prison corruption, estimated to bring officials $10.6 million each year. In 1996, in addition, Congress's Legislative Commission urged a classification of inmates, improvement of prison facilities, and new administrative norms.

No matter how well intentioned, however, such proposals will not be effective without better judicial functioning. The experience of the MP reveals precisely how politics and practices can scuttle even carefully constructed reforms. The 1961 constitution made the MP autonomous and endowed it with a range of powers to oversee the state's rights obligations.

The 1970 Organic Law of the Public Ministry then gave it authority over "respect for constitutional rights and guarantees," the rights of detainees and inmates, court functioning, the actions of public administrators, and the "defense of the independence and autonomy of judges."[49] Individual *fiscales* can intervene in judicial processes, initiate penal actions, oversee police activity, require cooperation from state agencies, receive denunciations, assist judges in criminal investigation, and recommend whether an accusation should proceed to trial. Many of these powers include those given in other countries to a separate ombudsman.

Despite this authority, the MP has been hampered throughout the democratic period by a shortage of funds, poor cooperation from other agencies, and its image as the tool of the president. In particular, the MP's official role as directors of the *sumario*, the initial phase of criminal investigation, has grown weaker. In the inquisitive approaches characterizing systems dominating Latin American criminal procedures until recently, the *fiscal* had come to be overshadowed by the judge, who controlled most of the written material and made most of the decisions, and the police, which carried out most of the investigation. One exasperated MP official said that although *fiscales* are supposed to be present when a detainee gives his or her statement to the police, the *fiscales* are in one part of the station while detainees are held in basements where confessions are extracted through torture.[50] In 1995, the *fiscal general* insisted that the MP's role as head of investigation required establishment of a new criminal investigation unit within the MP, but this was not approved.

Similar obstruction limits the MP on other criminal procedures. The MP has the power to open a *nudo hecho,* the pretrial investigatory process against state officials, such as police officers, accused of "exceeding the exercises of their functions."[51] Although designed to be completed in under a month, the procedure was conducted in secret and was delayed for up to six years "by uncooperative police [or] indifferent or recalcitrant judges ... and neither the [MP] nor the victim has the legal means" (Human Rights Watch/Americas 1993: 16) to force the process forward. Such delays rob *nudo hecho* of its effectiveness because it is very difficult to produce witnesses and evidence for trial after such a long period of time. The immunity that the accused has during the process, in addition, "can become permanent in those not infrequent cases in which the statue of limitation runs out before the *nudo hecho* investigation concludes and criminal charges can be brought."[52] In 1995, the *fiscal general* tried to speed up the *nudo hecho* process with practices such as proceeding with the trial and waiting until the posttrial appeal to complete the process. His efforts, though, were resisted.

Above all, the MP is simply unable to carry out the tasks assigned to it. In other countries, this burden led to the creation of *Defensorías*. But proposals to create a *Defensoría* in Venezuela were rejected as merely creating "more bureaucracy" by top political officials, who considered the MP as the existing and only necessary ombudsman.[53] As seen by police detentions and accusations against state officials, however, vigilance over basic rights and accountability quickly get buried under the MP's mountain of responsibilities in overseeing both judicial processes and public administration. The creation of the *Defensoría* and the enactment of a new penal code in 1999 will help the MP recover its control over the criminal investigation. But whether this happens in practice will depend on both the executive and the judiciary. The executive may attempt to bolster the police's role, and the reorganization of the judiciary may defeat the purpose of a stronger MP. Even without such changes, the kinds of oversight and functional clarity that the MP needs to help improve prisons will require changes in day-to-day practices and attitudes.

Venezuela's prison decentralization plans, one of the few specific enacted state rule of law reforms, also shows how politics and practices overwhelm intentions. The LODDT's Regulation 8, the only long-term legal reform regarding prisons, puts state governors in charge of "administration of national prisons, [including] control of activities inside the prisons," and assisting in the improvement of conditions and in prison personnel selection. Prison decentralization is a cornerstone of the Justice Ministry policy. But unlike in countries such as Argentina, its implementation by central authorities in a context of crisis does not provide as strong a foundation as change from within the provinces themselves.

This lack of bottom-up planning characterizes Venezuela's overall decentralization plans. As discussed above, decentralization must be geared toward constitutional accountability and clear divisions as well as improved policy. Venezuela's policies fall short on these counts. According to the LODDT, authority can be transferred by state initiative, in which a governor requests the authority; by the president with senate backing; and by a procedure in which the state continues services run by the national government. But the law lacks needed clarity on the actual procedures of transferring authority from the federal to the state levels, as well as for hiring, training, and evaluating new personnel.

The result has been an uneven decentralization in which only some states have new authorities (de la Cruz 1992), and others, such as Miranda state, have been unable even to classify services under either state or national jurisdiction (Cupolo 1989). The LODDT includes a process to disperse money to both state and municipal governments, but the federal government has not been forthcoming with the money, and there are no local or state taxes or bases for regional revenue generation. State and local governments remain dependent on the federal state for their resources, with most states receiving more than 90 percent of them from the central government. Most decentralization has been of state-provided social services, not judicial functions. But a judicial decentralization would also be unlikely to improve administration or to improve rights protection.

Conclusion

Executive resistance and judicial obstacles to criminal policy and other state rule of law reforms were on clear display in Venezuela in February 1992, after a nearly successful and widely supported military coup attempt gave the democratic regime its first near-death experience. In its wake, President Pérez set up a council to recommend reforms that could help prevent a recurrence. Among those recommendations were five regarding the judiciary, including stronger disciplinary mechanisms and new appointments to the Supreme Court. Although these recommendations were feasible and uncontroversial, the government did not attempt to initiate them. Pérez probably felt that his shakeup of the military would prevent further coup attempts (it did not); and because he had only one term in office and was fighting with other factions of his party, he had little incentive or power to push for such changes.

Although attempted coups might not jar the state into enacting reform, the demands of administration and accountability eventually will. In particular, inhumane prisons and the *Defensorías* are now built-in reminders of the state's rule of law responsibilities. Corruption, poor training, insufficient funding, political meddling, private influences, and other symptoms of executive power and judicial disarray have caused state officials and agencies to become entrenched in undemocratic, unaccountable behavior within formally democratic structures. Such practices can be addressed only through measures and agencies strong enough to withstand such practices. Once in place, such reforms can begin to redirect harmful patterns and support further change. Because the MP watches over the state's protection of constitutional guarantees, for example, reforms strengthening that agency may lead to better respect for rights in the prisons. In Argentina, similarly, the executive's political dominance and the judiciary's disarray weaken the ability of state agencies to respect the rule of law, but the creation of a national *Defensoría*, the strengthening of the MP, and provincial reforms have all helped keep the state focused on the rule of law.

Reforms may help the state balance the demands of administrative effectiveness, the rule of law, political pressures, and citizen needs. But the ultimate test is the state agency with the single biggest impact on the rule of law: the police. Along with poor administration and accountability, coercive and unaccountable enforcement of the law has been a defining characteristic of the Latin American state. Like state rule of law functions, police power is rooted in historical trends, executive power, and judicial disarray. Chapter 3 examines how democracies are grappling with a legacy that alone could undo the rule of law.

Notes

1. "The state" is defined here as the network of agencies under executive authority and "all those individuals who occupy office that authorize them, and them alone, to make and apply" binding decisions (Nordlinger 1987: 362; Stepan 1978: xii).

2. Administration courts, which handle legal complaints against state administrators, in some countries represent a separate institution. In Venezuela, Bolivia, Brazil, Cuba, Haiti, Honduras, Mexico, Nicaragua, Peru, and El Salvador they are part of the regular judiciary. In Argentina the federal courts have only special procedures, whereas most provinces have separate administrative systems.

3. The MP is independent in Venezuela, Argentina, Guatemala, and Panama and is part of the executive branch in Costa Rica, Ecuador, El Salvador, Haiti, Mexico, Nicaragua, and the Dominican Republic.

4. As Guillermo O'Donnell (1993: 1360) asserts, "attributes such as 'democratic' or 'authoritarian'" correspond to the state as well as to the regime.

5. A constitution in 1824–1825 attempted to create a more balanced union by declaring Buenos Aires to be a federal rather than a provincial port (thus distributing its income throughout the country), as well as by creating a bicameral legislature where one body would have equal representation from each province.

6. The first coup against an elected government occurred not in 1930, for example, but in 1828 when revolutionary hero General Juan Galo Lavalle led the troops of Buenos Aires against the elected government of Manuel Dorrego.

7. Rosas originally attained power by overthrowing Lavalle. After resigning in 1832, he returned with increased powers in 1834. As Domingo Sarmiento (1929: 315) bitterly commented, "Before Rosas there was a federalist spirit in the provinces and the cities ... he obliterated it and organized [it] to serve his own ends."

8. Further constitutional touch-ups were necessary, however, and Gómez wrote new ones in 1922 (created two vice-presidents, filled by Gómez's brother Juancho and Gómez's son José Vicente), in 1925, in 1928, and in 1931. One consistency of his constitutions was congressional election of the president, which continued up until 1947.

9. Editorial, *La Gaceta Jurídica,* July 28, 2000.

10. "Overcrowding Main Cause of Riots in Latin American Prisons," Agence France Presse, December 30, 1997.

11. Author interviews, San Pedro prison, July 19, 2000; author interviews, La Paz FELCN prison, July 20, 2000.

12. Venezuela's new penal code, enacted in 1998, also ended the secrecy of the *sumario* investigative stage of the criminal investigation process, which hampered the accused's ability to form an adequate defense. Free from its traditional dominance by parties and the executive, Congress passed the bill easily. Luis Enrique Oberto, President of the Legislative Commission, Chamber of Deputies,

author interview, June 29, 1998; "El Código Orgánico Procesal Penal," Inter-American Development Bank, March 26, 1998.

13. Oscar Crespo Soliz, Fiscal General de la República de Bolivia, author interview, July 24, 2000.

14. Such complaints represent 75 percent of all complaints to Bolivia's Defensoría. *La Razón*, April 1, 1999.

15. Colombia Defensoría del Pueblo, Press Release No. 383, Santa Fe de Bogotá, March 12, 1999.

16. "El Defensor" (Newsletter of the *Defensoría de Pueblo*, Ecuador), February-April 1999, p. 5.

17. Antonio Cartañá, Ombudsman of the City of Buenos Aires, author interview, December 12, 1996.

18. Ana María Romero de Campero, Defensor Nacional of Bolivia, author interview, July 12, 2000.

19. "La Reforma Política," *La Nación OnLine*, February 28, 2001; "Advierten que Chaco no ajustará el Destino de los sueldos," *La Nación OnLine*, January 21, 2001; "Have Nots," *The Economist*, May 18, 2000.

20. "Habrá juzgado vecinales para conflicts porteños," *La Nación*, September 3, 1996. The *Ley Cafiero* restricts transference from the national to local judiciaries.

21. Ingeniero Freixas, Ombudsman of Argentina's Federal prisons, author interview, November 3, 1994.

22. Mariano Ciafardini, National Director of Criminal Policy, author interview, October 18, 1994.

23. Luis Niño, Oral Trial Judge, author interview, October 17, 1994.

24. Néstor J. Cruces, "Seguridad pública, tema de todos," *La Nación*, September 22, 1999.

25. Constant federal intervention in the provinces, allowed by constitutional article 99 with congressional approval, attests to its importance. Between 1853 and 1976, the federal government intervened in the provinces 148 times. More than seventy-two of these interventions were based on electoral fraud charges, with the real objective usually to give the government's party the victory that an election did not secure. Menem's August 1992 intervention in Corrientes province shows that the practice continued a decade into a democratic regime.

26. Article 120. There was no article for an MP in the 1853 constitution. In Venezuela and other countries, the *procuraduría* is in a separate office, in charge of defending the state in accusations brought against it.

27. Luis Niño, Oral Trial Judge, author interview, October 17, 1994.

28. María Fernanda López Puleio, Public Defender before the Supreme Court, author interview, December 17, 1996. Article 20 of Law 22.520 gives the Justice Ministry authority to organize the MP and name its officials.

29. Juan Scatolini, Director of the Human Rights Office of Buenos Aires Province, author interview, November 16, 1994. There are approximately 22,500 inmates throughout the country. The largest concentration is in the Buenos Aires provincial system, which has about 10,400 inmates in its 5,000-capacity system. Of the approximately 5,000 in federal prisons, less than 1,000 are dangerous or career criminals.

30. Law 24.390 of 1994 stated that preventative imprisonment should not exceed more than two years unless "complexity" in the case required it. Nine international treaties mention limits for waiting time to trial. One is the Pact of San Jose de Costa Rica, of which Venezuela and Argentina are both signatories, which states that detainees may be incarcerated for more than a "reasonable time" before trial,

although it does not specify an actual limit. But a denunciation by a detainee who waits more than two years, ironically, often extends the time in prison.

31. Internal rebellion is punishable with up to thirty days in an isolation cell. AIDS is a particularly bad scourge. According to the World Health Organization, 30 percent of inmates in Argentina's federal prisons are infected with HIV, the virus that causes AIDS, and some Argentina officials believe that it may be up to 40 percent in both federal and provincial penitentiaries. Many HIV-positive prisoners are not diagnosed until they have developed symptoms of AIDS, and only a few receive medical attention. One of the demands of rioting prisoners in 1994 was improved AIDS treatment and freedom for dying prisoners. Calvin Sims, "On Every Argentine Cellblock, Specter of AIDS," *New York Times*, March 22, 1996, p. 4.

32. Buenos Aires Province Police Officer Subalcalde Gustavo Romelio García, who works inside the prison, author interview, December 10, 1996.

33. Violent crimes rose by 65 percent between 1994 and 1999, with the resulting increase in police arrests and incarceration making the necessary reduction in the prison population unlikely. The numbers break down as follows: 1998 (608,602 criminal acts/15,571 sentences); 1989 (658,650/15,559); 1990 (560,240/16,262); 1991 (489,290/18,938); and 1992 (519,139/18,444) (INDEC; Registro Nacional de Reincidencia y Estadística Criminal: 38).

34. Some NGOs claim it is closer to 90 percent of trials. In 1988, of the 480,617 cases of criminal charges, 317,239 (66 percent) were for crimes against property; in 1992, 247,666 (59.6 percent) of the total 416,125 criminal charges were for property crimes (Ministerio de Justicia de la Nación 1993: 763–769).

35. In 1980, there were 7.1 million homes lacking some basic needs, and in 1991 there were 8.56 million such homes (INDEC 1994).

36. *El Globo* (Caracas), April 3, 1995, p. 7.

37. *World Press Review,* October 1999, p. 22.

38. Spearheading the change were three laws: the 1989 Election of Governors Law, which replaced the presidential appointment of governors with direct elections in the states; the 1989 Municipal Regime Law, which established direct votes for the newly created positions of mayor; and the 1989 Law of Decentralization, which specified in greater detail the division of powers in the federal arrangement, fiscal planning, and transference of services.

39. The Justice Ministry's work overlaps with that of the Interior Ministry, which, in countries such as Argentina, oversees the federal police. In Venezuela, in addition, the Justice Ministry has played only a minor role in state and judicial reforms, mainly because it has been overwhelmed by its own tasks.

40. There are no state prisons, but state and municipal police have jails to hold detainees temporarily.

41. In a January 1994 rebellion in the main prison of Zulia state, for example, more than 100 prisoners were stabbed, shot, drowned, burned to death, and/or decapitated.

42. Office of Penitentiary Security, Office of Information and the Press Department of the Office of Defense and Civil Protection, Ministry of Justice. This does not include the 2,826 in provisional liberty. About a third of all inmates are in prisons in Caracas. Venezuela's prison populations for the period 1979–1995 break down as follows: 1979, 17,000; 1984, 23,548; 1989, 28,623; 1990, 28,816; 1991, 30,543; 1992, 31,400; 1994, 26,656; 1995, 24,995.

The General Penitentiary of Venezuela prison in the state of Guárico was built for 750 but holds up to 2,100. Tocuyito, a prison in Valencia designed for 1,500, has held between 1,700 and 4,500 inmates. Space is at such a premium at Retén de

Catia prison that anyone lucky enough to find an empty stair or to string a hammock from the ceiling will not budge for days for fear of losing the coveted spot. About 70 percent of inmates are between eighteen and twenty-five years old, and 20 percent are between twenty-six and twenty-nine. Nearly 70 percent have not finished elementary school, and most are manual and agricultural laborers. (Source: Mirna Yépez, Ministry of Justice Director of Information, author interview, April 20, 1994; *Dirección de Seguridad Penitenciaría* officials speaking on condition of anonymity.)

43. Official speaking on condition of anonimity, Oficina de Seguridad Penitenciaría, Ministry of Justice, author interview, April 20, 1995.

44. Other prisoners end up serving more time than their sentences would have dictated. The release of a mentally ill prisoner from Ciudad Bolívar Prison, for example, was held up for eleven years because of official miscommunications.

45. Typhus, cholera, tuberculosis, scabies, and other viruses run rampant. The HIV infection rate may be as high as in Brazil, where about 25 percent of prisoners have HIV. The warden of Retén de la Planta, where inmates live three to a cell designed for one, blames inadequate budgets. The prisons "are collapsing," he says, because budgets are insufficient to train personnel and create a "professional culture." "Things fall apart and stay that way." Luis A. Lara Roche, author interview, May 19, 1995.

46. *El Nacional* (Caracas), September 2, 1988, p. D2.

47. Julio César Fernández Toro, COPRE Executive Secretary, author interview, April 24, 1995.

48. Oberto, Luis Enrique, author interview, June 17, 1998; "El Código Orgánico Procesal Penal," Inter-American Development Bank, 1998.

49. Article 6, *Ley Orgánica del Ministerio Público*, 1970. This article sets out the twenty powers of the MP.

50. Carolina Oliva, MP Liaison to the Congress, author interview, April 6, 1995.

51. The *antejuicio de mérito* (pretrial investigation) is a parallel process for top officials such as the president.

52. Human Rights Watch/Americas 1993: 16. *Nudo hechos* are sometimes never completed, resulting in a conviction rate of police officers in Venezuela of just 6–19 percent, a fraction of the rate for civilians.

53. Alicia Marquez, Director of Office of Citizen Defense, Fiscalía General, author interview, March 27, 1995. COPRE and others recommended a *Defensoría*. Carlos Blanco, COPRE Executive Secretary (1984–1989), adds that "the idea of a *Defensoría* is directly linked to the complaints and the claims of citizens in regard to the functioning of the public administration and of the state." Author interview, May 21, 1995.

3

THE POLICE:
NERVE CENTER OF THE STATE

We're extremely limited—in material, in cooperation, in funds. Our work
is seriously damaged.
    —Colonel Miguel Flores, Director, National Judicial Police of Bolivia[1]

LATIN AMERICANS HAVE ANOTHER GOOD REASON to be on edge about
the police: the police are on edge about themselves. With uncertain funding, poor coordination, and growing demands from both government and
citizens, police forces in the region are having trouble enforcing the law.
They may no longer be a tool of repression by authoritarian regimes, but
contemporary democracy has brought a whole new set of problems.
Attempts to resolve them, as with other issues, are held back by executive
interests and the judiciary's chaos. In the case of the police, reforms are
further complicated by police agencies' autonomy, the nature of their work,
and the schizophrenia of both government policy and public opinion.

Throughout history, the ways in which police officials carried out their
duties have had a stronger impact than most other activities on the rule of
law. Whereas the government makes and interprets the law, the police apply
it to the complexities of daily life. The police are so important, in fact, that
many consider "the character of government and police action" to be "virtually indistinguishable. A government is recognized as being authoritarian
if its police are repressive, democratic if its police are restrained. It is not
an accident that dictatorial regimes are referred to as 'police states.' Police
activity is crucial for defining the practical extent of human freedom"
(Bayley 1985: 129).

The police's importance is most pronounced when political and societal uncertainty are high and when the structures and rules that implement
policy are new—conditions common in new or unstable democracies. The
gap between the pace and the expectations of democratization, in fact, is

63

often widest on police issues. Police agencies in many Latin American and other countries lack coordination, have insufficient civilian oversight, are trained better for subduing rather than protecting citizens, and routinely act outside the law and public knowledge. New civilian governments contending with mounting crime and social unrest, furthermore, are usually compelled to enhance security forces' power even further.

Even amid these constraints, most democratic regimes do attempt to impose a rule of law on the police. They do so primarily through three kinds of reforms. First, there are reforms regarding the police's position in the state, which involves institutional dependency, training, discipline, budgets, and cooperation with other state agencies. Second are reforms on police-judicial relations, mainly to improve detention and investigatory procedures. Third are reforms regarding the police's action in society, including civilian review and individual rights. As with the rest of the state, such proposals are a reaction to executive power and judicial disarray. Specifically, many proposals stem from the executive's use of repressive and unaccountable policing and by the inability of the police and the courts to control crime. Both conditions bring pressure on elected officials, who don't want overly powerful and unpredictable police agencies or, worse, to be blamed for ineffective policing. Much of this pressure is channeled into demands for improved coordination or oversight. Just as judicial independence reforms focus on politicization, oversight and coordination are the most common rallying points for police reform.

Argentina and Venezuela have followed contrasting paths on the police, more than on most other areas of reform, because of differences in their executive and judicial branches. Both countries have changed personnel, reformed their penal codes, and eliminated certain police control. But because repressive policing was a much bigger issue in Argentina, that country experienced greater momentum to actually restructure its police agencies. Venezuela, in contrast, has been more concerned about ineffectiveness and therefore focused on "improving" police activity rather than curtailing it. The elimination of a major police faculty in each country, examined below, underscores this difference: Venezuela eliminated the regulation through the courts, but Argentina did so through citizen protest.

Reforms that do get implemented, however, then face the executive controls and judicial problems that made them necessary in the first place. Even with the increased transparency and accountability brought with democratization, enacted measures suffer from a lack of clarity over how to translate them into functioning, law-abiding operations that are effective under constantly changing circumstances. In particular, many proposals are fraught with tensions among competing values; for example, support for oversight clashes with support for law and order among both the police and society, preventing changes perceived to hinder police work.

This chapter's three sections explain the background and effectiveness of police reform in democratic Latin America. The first section creates the theoretical framework by showing how the uncertainty of the police's role is rooted in frictions between police power and the police's actions. The second section looks at policing in Latin American history, examining how the police's relationship with the state and society has affected the rule of law. The third section then examines how democracies attempt to embed the police more firmly within the state, to clarify the police's role in the judicial process, and to improve police relations with society. This analysis argues that reform is undermined by executives inclined to give police forces more power and by judiciaries unable to control that power. In this context, increasing crime rates, budgetary constraints, and long-standing practices by police forces all combine to limit the effectiveness of reform.

Latin America's Police:
"Police Power" Versus Police Actions

The role of the police in any democracy is inherently uncertain. Police forces are responsible for enforcing the law yet have no formal role in creating it. They participate in society's daily life yet are distrusted by most people. But such dislocation has less to do with specific policies or conditions than with the concept of the police itself. In particular, fitting the police within the three branches of government and the different sectors of society involves destabilizing frictions between "police power" and the police's actions.

Most authors take an expansive view of the police, asserting its rightful authority to regulate public order, to use physical force, and to support common "goods" such as public health and morality (Berthelemy 1923; Manzini 1926: 111). Missing in most conceptualizations of the police, however, is a delineation of the specific problems inherent in police relationships within the state, judiciary, and society. The police are, of course, institutionally dependent on the government and have structures similar to those of other state agencies. But because of their particular responsibilities the police are distinct from those other agencies, often causing them to be at loggerheads with the government, the courts, and other state bodies. Many specific clashes then arise because of the police's wide legal discretion in taking action when there is a violation of the law, even if such action intrudes on the laws or interests of other state institutions or officials.

The police's functions give it a unique relationship with society as well as with the rest of the state. Few other agencies carry out policy with such constant and direct interaction with the population, often in conditions of physical danger and resistance. In this position, the police shape the protection and interpretation of civil and political rights. They affect the freedoms of association and of speech, for example, by monitoring protests and other political gatherings. In much of Latin America, moreover, the police are put in the uncomfortable position of helping implement controversial policies such as land reform and price controls. The inability of officers to handle such policies, much less the conditions from which they spring, can lead to extrajudicial activity such as corruption and vigilantism. It also causes police officials to retreat into practices of secrecy, mutual protection, and disdain for civilian policymakers.

Most of this uncertainty boils down to the distinction between police power and the actual physical and legal actions of police agencies. In a democratic regime, elected officials have the sole authority to create all laws—the police power—and the police are simply the means to enforce them. Broadly defined, *police power* is the constitutional authority to legislate and regulate laws and "juridical norms that fix the powers and obligations of" police officials (Altamira 1963: 25) to prevent illegal acts, along with the authority to monitor the police themselves. Police forces have the separate authority to execute and enforce those regulations, which makes them the implementers of the decisions of those with police power. But in the process of enforcement, the police agencies themselves often redefine, reinterpret, and reformulate those same laws to the point where the police's actions become de facto police power.

Since the term *police power* was first used by Chief Justice John Marshall in the 1827 U.S. Supreme Court case *Brown v. State of Maryland* as the authority to limit citizen actions for the good of social order (Wheaton 1827: 44), it has been funneled into two general perspectives. The first, and narrower, conceptualization regards it as a limitation of rights in order to *protect public security*. Broader conceptualizations add the vague but significant *promotion of the general good*. This addition widens the range of possible police actions, such as controlling civil society organizations, which blurs police power and police acts. The second, broader, approach has been predominant in most of Latin American history. In 1922, the Argentine Supreme Court extended police jurisdiction to the "general good," especially to economic matters, and in 1950 it said that the power of the police is "justified by the necessity of the defense and strengthening of morality, health, collective fitness, and the community's economic interests."[2]

Police power in most democracies belongs to the legislative branch, which exercises it through legislation and budgets, and to the judiciary, which has authority over the interpretation and application of police action. Most constitutions make sure to clearly specify the separate police powers of each branch (e.g., by prohibiting the transference of authority among agencies or the substitution of a law with an ordinance). But the steady corrosion of this separation in the course of Latin American history has blurred the concept of police power and in the process has stretched the legal boundaries of police action, weakened the authority of elected officials, and reduced officers' accountability.

The only way for democratic regimes to now wrest police power out of the police's hands is through concrete reforms that define what the police need in order to prevent crime and maintain public order, and then translate those needs into laws and structures that are regulated by those with police power. But the police's use of and reaction to such proposals generate frictions between police power and the police's actions in all three areas of police reform. Within the state, tensions and uncertainties spring up over functional and geographic division, centralization, accountability, and the police's political influence. The police's judicial role, secondly, is rankled by continuous debate over policing issues, from the limits of police power to investigation procedures. Finally, regarding the police's societal role, frictions arise over the extent of the police's discretion through *proactive* and *reactive* approaches, which exemplifies the difficulty of balancing individual rights and crime prevention. Since police officers are usually the first persons to determine whether a law has possibly been broken, they are involved in most societal grievances against the law.

In a new or weak democratic regime, all these frictions are particularly acute because of the weak foundation for the decisions needed to resolve them. An authoritarian past means that regulations must be overhauled or built from the ground up. Proposals regarding the state's role, such as on interagency coordination, may spark a backlash by police agencies not used to sharing power, and measures to improve cooperation with the judiciary are often (legitimately) criticized as unfeasible. Oversight is a necessary part of democratization, particularly with agencies involved in past repression, but the police resist most outside monitoring as an infringement and a sign that they are not considered trustworthy. Internal mechanisms such as professional associations are more acceptable, but rarely do they succeed in ferreting out abuses, forcing governments to return to the choice between creating external checks and abandoning a key police power. Many measures on police-society relations, such as those to maintain public order, may even provoke the ire of a society victimized by past police repression. As a result of these frictions, police laws, organization, and practices in many Latin American democracies respond less to policing needs than to politics, displaying "remarkable permanence over time" despite "enormous changes in the political character of government" (Bayley 1985: 60). Such frictions, as Table 3.1 helps illustrate, are the real-life consequences of the gap between police power and the police's actions.

In a democracy, defining police power and police actions are first

Table 3.1   Frictions Between Police Power and the Police's Actions

Objectives of policing are carried out by police power through the police's actions:

1. Crime prevention	• Make laws	• Physical force to enforce laws
2. Public order maintenance	• Form structures	• Criminal investigation
3. National security	• Regulate/review	• Monitor society

The interaction between police power and the police's actions lead to frictions:

State:	Judiciary:	Society:
1. Functional/geographic proactive divisions and coordination approaches	1. Arrest and investigation	1. Discretion vs. reactive
2. Political influence	2. Legal confusion	

played out in the organization of the police as a state agency, which causes at least two sorts of frictions. The first sort occurs in the coordination of the different agencies with specialized functions, such as investigation and anti-terrorism, and of the many agencies divided by geographic jurisdiction, such as provincial and municipal forces. Functionally, most states divide their police forces into prevention/street forces, which work to prevent violations of the law, and judicial police agencies, which investigate violations. But even this basic division is often unclear. Venezuela's 1988 Judicial Police Law, for example, makes four bodies the "principal organs" of the judicial police, including the "competent organs" of the military, and nine "auxiliary organs," including the "authorities of State and Municipal police" (articles 6–8). What these assignations mean in practice is often undefined, leading to overlapping activities and spotty oversight. Other functional divisions—with military, border, customs, and special bodies like Argentina's onetime agency to enforce economic measures—only intensify such frictions. Aside from function, geography is the other principal organizational dimension. Provinces and municipalities in most countries have their own administrative and sometimes judicial police forces, often with wide enforcement powers. This multiplicity leads to frictions, especially amid the wide differences in accountability mechanisms and political dynamics among regions.

Steps to coordinate or centralize these bodies foment intrainstitutional conflict. Italy's three national police forces have clashed with one another over changes in coordination, and in France the unification of the civil and uniformed police caused conflicts between city police forces and the Ministry of Interior police. In countries such as the United States, in contrast, geographic and political separation resulted in a proliferation of police forces and less institutional conflict. In Latin America, the historical combination of authoritarianism, violence, and geographic disparities led to the worst of both patterns: institutionally rigid and politically powerful police at the federal level, and highly discretional, unaccountable agencies at the provincial and municipal levels. Trying to undo such a structure in any country, of course, is both politically and administratively difficult.

The second and related type of friction comes from the police's political influence. A basic part of state formation in Latin America, policing has been used since precolonial times to maintain control, expand the state's reach, and keep governments in power. And as independent republics, Latin America's states never made the formal distinction between external military and internal policing functions, further enhancing the police's role. Against this background, even after a transition to democracy, police agencies are likely to remain in politics and policymaking. With the increasing levels of violent crime in the contemporary democratic era—especially crimes that threaten political stability, like drug-trafficking—the police remain in a position to prevent or water down unwanted reform. As discussed above, they are often able to resist even basic oversight.

Related frictions plague the police's judicial roles. In all countries, the police make arrests and carry out steps in criminal investigation, such as collecting evidence and writing reports. These roles often lead to abuses and resulting calls for curbs on police action and a strengthening of court oversight. Increasing crime in turn generates demands for even greater investigative authority by the police and for curbs on judicial control instead. Frictions intensify when such contradictory demands occur simultaneously, decreasing the effectiveness, accountability, and clarity in the criminal process of judges, *fiscales*, and the police alike.

Confusion in the law itself leads to further frictions in police-judicial relations.[3] Latin America's policing is based on a complex legal foundation made up of penal codes, police codes, *ordenanzas, contravenciones* (both also called *faltas*; edicts are a category of *faltas*), *reglamentos* (regulations), prohibitions, police orders, *permisos* (exemptions to written regulations), special permits or authorizations, and customary laws made up of unlegislated but long-held practices. *Ordenanzas* are usually part of administrative penal law used primarily to regulate public order, and *reglamentos* are part of disciplinary penal law, usually for internal police matters like discipline. Both *ordenanzas* and *reglamentos* can be replaced, revoked, or annulled by those with police power—as well as by the executive agencies that oversee their execution, and they often do just that. And even though formal delegation of legislative powers to the executive branch is unconstitutional, a so-called general delegation of police power to the executive branch is often allowed in situations such as emergencies or an absence of needed norms. Even many legislatures and courts that guard their police power give police the benefit of the doubt or struggle to adequately "translate" the intentions of police power into law.[4] Resulting frictions are multiplied when the police are decentralized and thus vary widely in their practices. Like the national Congress, provincial legislatures and municipal councils have police powers, but many lack the political leverage or funding, even within their own jurisdictions, to effectively regulate police actions.

Regarding society, the police's general ineffectiveness leads to additional frictions over how much the police are to be reactive to violations of the law and how much they are to be proactive to head off potential violations. Much more than its investigative responsibilities, the police's preventative role to stop crimes from occurring infringes on individual freedoms. This proactive approach blurs the legal line between precriminal and actual criminal behavior. Police edicts in many countries were intended as proactive anticrime measures, for example, but their powers of unregulated, extended detention have made them a source of police abuse well into the democratic era. Pressures on the police in a democracy to maintain order and to respect basic rights—part of the dilemma faced by state agencies to be both restrained and effective (see Chapter 2)—are magnified in a transitional period by a high level of distrust, weak accountability mechanisms, professional insecurity, and judicial disarray. Curfews may be needed for public order, but when do they begin to foster arbitrary behavior by individual officers? Physical coercion is regulated through police power, but what about officers who hold a detainee beyond the legal limit because no judge is available to take the case? Such questions make it hard to know when the police have usurped police power or simply responded to a legitimate threat, weakening the separation between police power and police actions.

In varying combinations, these frictions diminish legislative and judicial police powers, increase society's distrust of the state, and lead to practices such as arbitrary arrest, mistreatment, torture, extrajudicial killings, and vigilantism.[5] As the police fight threats to public peace and national security, they may become an additional threat themselves.

Historical Patterns of Policing in Latin America

The predominance of violence in Latin America's past made security forces one of the main building blocks of state formation. From the beginning, presidents used them to stay in power, militaries used them to maintain order, legislative and judicial branches relinquished their police powers, and police agencies themselves solidified each newly acquired authority. In democratic Latin America, police reforms are intended to turn around these damaging historical patterns.

Although the term "police" derives from the Greek *polis*, meaning the totality of activity in a city-state, a distinction is made between the enactment and the enforcement of the law. In ancient Rome and Greece, the police were divided into internal and external forces, and police powers were differentiated from police actions. Legislative power was given to a people's assembly, a council, and magistrates who could enact decrees. Judicial functions were divided between special courts responsible for serious offenses and a so-called popular jury for minor ones. Functional and geographic specialization came later, during the imperial period of Rome, when the police were divided into four main parts, including secret and investigatory bodies. A set of police norms covered penal, civil, and commercial areas, and general legislative norms fell under the Law of the Twelve Tables, the foundation for Iberian law.

Police development stalled in the feudal era following the collapse of the Roman Empire. In most of Europe, police power, as well as police actions, were taken over by feudal landlords, who tailored the law to their own interests and carried out judicial functions as well. Landlord control over law enforcement continued well into the nineteenth century in many regions within Africa, Prussia, India, and China. Even in the twentieth century, many countries continue to have large private forces that help enforce (or evade) the law.[6] As state power gradually overtook feudal interests after the fifteenth century, governments began forming increasingly permanent cadres of police agents. To help consolidate outlying and colonial possessions, they also expanded the police, granting them *fueros* (separate charters of laws and legal functions given by the government to a colonizing institution such as the Catholic Church) and municipal charters, resulting in a wide range of police laws and practices. In countries such as France, different agencies policed rural and urban areas. Moral and religious policing, in addition, remained under separate ecclesiastical authority. Spain's monarchy developed its main police agencies after 1479, primarily through military training and religious-affiliated police associations. There was a modicum of control by judges at the time, but the possibility of using new laws against royal authority remained close to nil.

With the emergence of the modern bureaucracy and individual rights in the eighteenth century, police forces focused on the state's interests as well as the public good. In countries with less violent change, such as England and the United States, those forces developed in a decentralized but generally professional manner. In the Spanish Empire, police development occurred with far less uniformity and fewer standards. Police power resided within executive officials and a loose network of agencies, but most actual enforcement was carried out by private agencies through contracts with the Crown. After independence, the power of the executive, the role of the military, and the weakness of oversight led to a blurring between police power and the actions of the police. During the late nineteenth century, Latin

America's police consisted primarily of provincial militias and local forces. As central authority later grew, police forces were integrated into the armed forces and security apparatuses of authoritarian governments. This lasted from the late 1800s until the transition to democracy in the latter part of the twentieth century, when police forces came officially under civilian rule.

Argentina

A history of violence and instability shaped Argentina's police forces. Wars among provinces and political factions, armed territorial conquest, socioeconomic uncertainty, and class tensions all led to repressive policing by powerful executives. Even with a strong economy, state growth, and the durable 1853 constitution, professional and legal norms never caught up with police repression and autonomy.

Colonial Argentina had no professional forces, and in Buenos Aires the town council held all police powers. An irregular rural police force operated between 1755 and 1790, possessing summary power of judgment and a reputation for arbitrary violence. In 1799, the government established the Partida Celadora, an armed force under military direction responsible for general security in greater Buenos Aires. In 1810, after Napoleon's invasion of Spain, the provisional governing junta of Río de la Plata gave itself authority over laws "monitoring order, public tranquility and individual security" and created the Policía General (República de Argentina: 1879). After the war of independence, the government "began on a vigorous and rapid road to concentration of police power, a shedding of municipal and neighborhood structures, and the creation of a State Police" (Maier 1996: 133). In 1821, a government headed by Bernardino Rivadavia liquidated the Buenos Aires town council and named the first chief of police of Buenos Aires province. Soon thereafter Rivadavia replaced neighborhood law-enforcement officials with *comisarios* (station chiefs) and the so-called Police Monitoring Body. In 1826, the government created the Central Police Department in Buenos Aires city and replaced the monitoring body with new daytime and nighttime forces.

These two agencies were eliminated in 1872 and, after Urquiza's victory over Rosas, additional police forces were transferred from military to civilian control. The 1880 federalization of the capital city of Buenos Aires (now formally, the Federal Capital) then led to the establishment of the capital police and to the police of Buenos Aires province. Assertions of executive power were also taking place in the provinces, with "punitive social control of the disfavored classes" by caudillos' police laws and policies (Zaffaroni 1994: 254). The government introduced the first penal code in 1886 to help reign in growing crime rates, and later it introduced internal exile. Policing of the lower classes increased as the government turned its attention to the growing cities after the 1865–1870 War of the Triple Alliance against Paraguay. The government "needed a formalization of punitive social control that fit with a 'civilized' world." In the same decade and with the personal insistence of the Interior Minister, "the first penal process code was sanctioned in open violation of the constitution." Ignoring progressive proposals such as the 1873 measure to establish jury trials, the government based its code on the derogated code of the Bourbon Restoration—"the most inquisitive moment of Spanish penal process legislation" (Zaffaroni 1994: 254–255).

At the turn of the century, immigration and industrialization transformed the country even more. Police agencies adopted additional professional training and advanced technology as they repeatedly clashed with unions and socialist organizations while fighting climbing crime rates. The Buenos Aires police killed eight and wounded forty in a crackdown on a 1909 worker demonstration, and the notorious Tragic Week of 1919—in which the military violently crushed an outbreak of worker protest—began with the capital police's intervention in a labor strike. Such violence spawned antileftist vigilante squads that killed organizers, protested negotiation with labor by Radical governments, and became a precursor to right-wing hit squads such as the Argentine Anti-Communist Alliance (AAA) of the 1970s. In line with the government's stricter public-order approach, the Supreme Court became more restrictive of habeas corpus, denying it in many cases of preventive detention and the right of association.[7] Such divergence from the habeas corpus's basic intent was especially striking because at this time "it was obvious that judges could not ignore worsening police abuse" (Dromi 1985: 13).

After the Argentine military took power in 1930, the police became more institutionally integrated into the regime's repressive policies and more closely trained by an army restructured on a highly regimented Prussian model. Torture became routine in police stations. In 1934, for example, the *picana* (electric cattle prod) was invented and utilized regularly on detainees. Such practices did not stop with returns to democracy. During Perón's 1946–1955 rule, the authority of police agencies widened, and their use of torture increased as the government's popularity waned. Attempts were made after 1955 to eliminate such abuse, but it persisted under the elected Radical governments of 1958–1962 and 1962–1966, when the military continued to direct most of the police. After the armed forces returned to power in 1966, rising violence only deepened failing governments' reliance on repression. Left-wing guerrillas grew in strength during the 1973–1976 Perón governments, and the AAA conducted a campaign of attacks against leftists with "the active engagement of the Federal police."[8] When the military institutionalized and widened this repression after its 1976 coup, "all three armed services had the full support of the security branch of the federal police, forming espionage networks and clandestine operations with each" (CELS/Americas Watch 1991b: 7; Rock 1985: 363).

Before 1983, in sum, the police in Argentina steadily acquired power because of ongoing civil strife, repressive executives, a powerful military, the weakness of the legislature and the judiciary, the lack of established oversight bodies, and, finally, the police's acquisition of power itself. This was the legacy facing reformers after the transition to democracy.

Venezuela

As in Argentina, the police in Venezuela first developed under the auspices of the executive and the military, lacking professional and constitutional norms until the consolidation of central authority in the late 1800s. In the colonial era, "policing" was defined as covering all of a community's regulations and customs. It fell under the jurisdiction of each city's *cabildo* (the government of the local settlement), carried out mainly by *alcaldes de crimen,* who also had judicial power. In most cases, however, police functions such as arrests were shared by groups of residents and assorted officials like *alguaciles* (bailiffs/constables of the court). The main policing bodies, in fact, were sixteenth-century militia groups that captured runaway slaves and subdued indigenous populations. The first permanent police forces did not form until 1778, when four police districts were created in Caracas in response to high rates of violent crime. Since records were first kept, Venezuela and Caracas both registered among the highest rates of violent crime in Latin America, with the late-1700s murder rate of adults between five and seven per 100 inhabitants (Gómez Grillo 1995). With the advent of a pro-independence movement at the end of the 1700s, a third set of police agencies formed to promote rebellion and root out loyalists.

In April 1810, after independence, these three strains of police—the Caracas police districts, the pro-independence police, and irregular bodies operating in most regions—were brought together as the Tribunal de Policía. The junta created its own Tribunal de Seguridad Pública for common crimes as well as subversive activities. In enacting police laws, the government drew an increasing distinction between "minor" policing, in the colonial tradition of maintaining community standards and customs, and "major" policing of public order and political stability. This distinction was formalized by an 1819 decree by Bolívar, giving each province's military commanders the power of "major" policing and their civilian governors the responsibility for "minor" policing.

Police agencies, powers, and regulations expanded during the course of the century. In 1825, the Congress of Gran Colombia empowered local authorities to preventively apprehend delinquents and conduct summary investigations. Five years later, a series of laws granted municipalities the authority to organize police agencies. The 1854 National Police Code gave *comisarios* control over prisons and divided the police into administrative, judicial, and municipal forces. Later reforms restricted the police's judicial role. Police reports had "value" in trials, but the reformed penal process code (the *Código de Enjuiciamiento Criminal*, or CEC) of 1882 authorized police "to open the inquiry" only when necessary. A later version of the CEC allowed the police to carry out proceedings only "until the arrest of the prisoner; but [they] must pass the proceedings immediately to the respective judicial authority."

Despite such laws, police agencies' power in the street increased along with crime rates during the remainder of the nineteenth century. Under the centralizing Castro and Gómez dictatorships, this growing power occurred in tandem with that of the military. Although the 1888 Interior Regulation of the Police was the first serious attempt to bring coherence to the national network of police forces, those forces continued to be steeped heavily in military objectives and the maintenance of social control. Upon assuming power in 1908, Gómez created a mounted militia to maintain political order, recruiting officers primarily from his home state.

In the liberalization following Gómez's death, police specialization and centralization increased—but under strict executive control, largely within a military framework, and without adequate separation between the police's and the judiciary's investigative powers. A 1936 ordinance empowered the Urban and Rural Police of the Federal Capital "to discover plots ... against the public order and State security, persecuting and impeding subversive plans," and to arrest "vagrants and bad influences," defined as individuals ranging from common thieves to those who "walk in the streets promoting idleness with petty roguery."[9] In 1937, President López decreed the Law of National Security Service, which created the Interior Ministry's Body of Investigations, gave administrative and judicial forces wide investigative authority, and formed the powerful military-run National Security Police (Seguridad Nacional).[10] After assuming the presidency in 1941, Medina Angarita stepped up police training and equipping, but with little effect on crime or internal order.

Additional reforms took place during the 1945–1948 *Trienio*, such as the 1948 changes of the 1926 CEC "to avoid conflict of competency between police and judicial authorities" and to give the police "no more than 30 days" to hand over all material to the competent judge.[11] But in practice the judicial police continued to depend on the dictates of the military and executive's Interior Ministry at the national level and on governors at the state level. The 1948–1958 military regime headed by Marcos Pérez Jiménez used the National Security Police to quell opposition, and in 1949 it expanded the Body of Investigation. With a strong national organization and substantial governmental support, the Body of Investigation soon took charge of initiating and carrying out nearly all summary proceedings, aggravating problems such as overlapping investigations by the courts, unaccountable police operations, and detentions beyond the legal time limit. The 1950 National Codification Commission blamed these problems partly on the fact that the police were neither institutionally dependent on, or accountable to, either the MP or the judiciary. The main response, as it continues to be in the democratic era, was to create and strengthen police forces. Believing that police should have more expertise and opportunity to carry out criminal investigations, the government formed the professional Technical Police in 1954 and, for the first time, amended the CEC to include the judicial police as "the members of the Armed Forces [and] functionaries of National Security" (CEC, article 74-A).

The reinstallation of democracy in 1958 led to changes such as the establishment of women's brigades and the replacement of the National Security Police with the National Judicial Police (Cuerpo Técnico de Policía Judicial, or PTJ) in 1962. But the police's centrality continued. With an unprecedented rise in violent crime in the mid-1960s (which has yet to subside), the 1975 PTJ law granted judicial-agency status to most law-enforcement agencies, including many within the military, which gave them other powers such as initiating criminal proceedings.[12] The change was also intended to better incorporate all enforcement agencies into demo-cratic judicial norms, but with the existing broad jurisdiction of military law and courts, it served more to give the armed forces inroads into the civilian judiciary instead of the reverse.

Police Reforms and the Rule of Law in Democratic Regimes

New democratic governments rely heavily on civilian police agencies to help maintain order, as the military and security forces of the old govern-ment are usually discredited or nonfunctioning. But because policing is associated with authoritarian repression, those governments also need to bring it under the rule of law. They attempt to do so by readjusting police relations with the state, the judiciary, and society. Police reforms center on a single state function, but touch on many legal and political concerns. For the state, police reforms include budgetary and remuneration statutes, insti-tutional dependency and coordination, and training and discipline; for the judiciary, they include arrest and detention practices as well as criminal investigation and evidence; and for society, they include civilian review of police actions and respect for individual and due process rights.

Regarding the state, there are three general types of police reforms.

First are budgetary and remuneration statutes, which are important because salaries and material support shape police values and behaviors. The second kind regards institutional dependencies and coordination. As in continental Europe, Latin American ministries (Justice and Interior) have formal control over the main police bodies. But many other law enforcement agencies are placed in the military, the judiciary, the MP, or on their own, affecting both overall policy and coordination. Third is personnel training and discipline, which focus on officers' preparation, approaches, and accountability. The police relationship with the judiciary is also crucial, because police functions such as detention and investigation are parts of the judicial process and because the judiciary itself is needed to monitor police actions. There are two broad kinds of reform on police-judiciary relations. The first regards arrest and detention; the second involves criminal investigation. Because the police in most countries carry out most of these procedures, how they do so influences courts' judgments and interpretations.[13] There are also two types of police-society reform. First are those creating civilian review of police actions through special committees, ad hoc investigations, or regular civilian participation in police administration and policymaking. The other type of reform regards individual and due process rights in routine as well as special police operations.

Enactment of these reforms faces more obstacles than other kinds of rule of law reform. Many measures first garner support because an institution is unable to meet its own objectives. When it comes to the police and crime, however, political actors usually consider "society" as the problem and often perceive an inherent conflict between police efficacy and police accountability. Most of the changes they favor are geared toward strengthening existing police operations rather than reevaluating them. Legislators' enthusiasm for change is further dampened by police forces' military ties and political influence, along with the fact that little of the uncertainty felt by political actors is assuaged through police reforms. Sustained nationwide agitation for comprehensive reform is rare because of the concentration of police operations in poor areas and because the public usually focuses more on specific incidents than general trends.

But when the police behave badly enough, they increase the uncertainties that spur reform. Unchecked power and poor performance among the police usually lead to excesses such as corruption, for instance, making it clear even to political actors that police agencies are not functioning properly and so reflect poorly on the government. In addition, public pressure for reform can grow when persistent police abuses are associated directly with a specific law or when they feed into broader public demands. The public's impatience with a democracy's performance or anxiety over national security can also alter citizen views on policing, increasing political uncertainty and opening up opportunity for change.

When reforms are implemented, however, the two general obstacles to the rule of law reduce their effectiveness. The executive's control over policing, a lack of progressive policy, the judiciary's weakness, a lack of legal clarification of police powers, and demands from society all sidetrack many progressive measures. So even if reform does occur, it is squeezed by political interests during its formulation and by practical and legal constraints in its implementation.

Most of Latin America's democracies struggle to negotiate these constraints. In Bolivia, the police was reorganized into more clearly defined boundaries after the 1982 transition to democracy. But their historical role in suppressing civilian unrest reemerged with increasing antigovernment protests in the late 1990s. The restraints on police action have been loosened even more with the huge antinarcotics operations that began in the late 1980s. These operations have also revived the police's military training and militarized approach to internal order, which have been bolstered further since the late 1990s by new institutions such as antinarcotics police forces and courts funded by the United States.

At the same time, most Bolivian agencies have become more ineffective, corrupt, and distrusted. As reported crimes quadrupled between 1993 and 1999, top judicial police officials were accused of torturing detainees, senior officers were implicated in robberies, a police chief allegedly misused a pension fund, and an officer heading an internal corruption inquiry was beaten unconscious in a police cell. Government inquiries into these abuses lacked teeth, and in any case the police were beefed up with the $26 million Citizens' Security and Protection Plan in 1999. In the long term, however, the new penal code will help reduce the police's judicial power by handing over criminal investigations from judges to newly appointed prosecutors and, for the first time, by requiring police to give evidence in court.

The National Police of Colombia (PN, Policía Nacional), involved in serious rights abuses such as organizing paramilitary groups and killing suspected guerrilla sympathizers, also has a history of repression and weak accountability. During the 1948–1953 civil war, it fragmented into small units used by local powers for their own aims of revenge and control— practices reemerging under the current conditions of violence and corruption. Impunity has continued into democracy, as seen in the 1994 military-court acquittal of members of the navy's intelligence network charged with dozens of extrajudicial killings, despite strong evidence against them. Sometimes security and police forces have not carried out warrants for the arrest of paramilitary leaders, as when the Attorney General's Office had to use its own Technical Investigation Unit to capture an ally of the powerful paramilitary United Self-Defense Groups.

In Ecuador, most of the complaints to the *Defensoría* have been against the police and the armed forces, charging them with torture, beatings, arbitrary detention, and disrespect of the Constitutional Tribunal's rulings.[14] Despite the government's admission of responsibility in several detainee deaths, reports continue of torture, mistreatment, and disappearances, particularly by the National Police. The death toll from questionable police use of firearms also continues to rise, as do extrajudicial killings of crime suspects. Such practices often occur during the government's frequent crimefighting "states of emergency." During the one applied to Guayas province for most of 1999, hundreds of people were detained by police, and some who did not produce papers or pay a fine were held for more than forty-eight hours.

In Peru, increases in urban gang violence, organized crime, and attacks in wealthy areas have also prompted tough anticrime measures. In 1998, calling crime a national security problem, the government adopted ten decrees, many based on antiguerrilla measures that had resulted in rights abuses. From 155,000 in 1990 to 289,000 in 1994, reported crimes declined to 192,000 by 1998—suggesting that executive interests were as much a motivation for the change as crime itself.[15] In fact, these laws increased police and executive-branch authority by transferring many enforcement powers from civilian courts and the National Police to military courts and the notoriously abusive National Intelligence Service (SIN), forming a new SIN body to coordinate police intelligence, prohibiting courts from calling police officers who interrogate suspects, and allowing immunity or penalty reductions for those providing information. They also increased arbitrary and biased prosecutions, as Decree No. 895 has done (creating the crime of "aggravated terrorism" and giving police the power to detain suspects for up to fifteen days and military tribunals the power to try civilians charged with the crime). Decree No. 900, transferring many habeas corpus petitions from criminal judges to one specialized judge, stifles use of this important postconviction remedy. Because these policies were pushed through primarily by President Alberto Fujimori, however, the demise of his regime opens up both uncertainty and an opportunity for reform. In September 2000, the beleaguered president announced deactivation of the SIN, but his successors could very well reactivate it.

Constitutional rights are eroded not only by police practices but also by the enforcement of laws. Drug laws have proven particularly resilient to legal checks and administrative oversight, and often discriminate against marginalized populations. Bolivia's 1988 Anti-trafficking Law 1008, for example, violates basic rights, prohibiting pretrial release, and has fostered discrimination against indigenous people and *campesinos* (Laserna 1994), even after some of its more controversial provisions were eliminated. Rights officials in the drug-producing regions try to counter these trends, but in doing so they must carefully balance the interests of local communities and law-enforcement agencies, both of which are suspicious of them.

Drug laws and other special public-order measures pose a threat to human rights not only because of the judiciary's disarray but also because of the military's involvement. Bolivia's armed forces remain in control of many coca-producing zones and have been accused of beatings, illegal confiscation, violent raids, extrajudicial shootings, and collusion with cocaine traffickers. And although armed political violence has decreased in neighboring Peru, abuses continue in regions still under emergency law. Subordination of civilian authorities to military officials as well as limitations on personal liberty, inviolability of the home, and freedom of movement are all common. The Peruvian government has resisted international and national pressure to ameliorate the 1995 amnesty designed to deflect prosecution of military and police officials accused of rights violations. As in other countries, impunity and acquittals characterize many of the cases against officials that have been brought to trial.

Such conditions characterize policing in all Latin American countries and at all levels. Focusing on the three types of police reform during the democratic period, this section now turns to the main federal and municipal police agencies of Argentina and Venezuela. In Argentina, those agencies are the Policía Federal Argentina (PFA) and the police of Buenos Aires province, which long have been the country's two most important forces. The PFA enforces all laws in the Federal Capital as well as all federal laws, such as those regarding drug-trafficking; the Buenos Aires provincial police covers a large, mostly urban area that is home to more than a third of the country's population. In Venezuela, the agencies are the PTJ, the powerful national investigatory police, and the Federal District's Policía Metropolitana (PM), which carries out daily law enforcement in the nation's largest urban area.

In these and other countries, problems in police relations with the state, the judiciary, and society have been a catalyst for major reforms such as penal code revisions. In particular, concern over repressive tactics and a lack of accountability—that is, the gap between police power and police actions—has led to significant, if uneven, restructuring and restrictions. In Argentina, the Buenos Aires provincial police was entirely restructured, and the PFA had its edicts taken away. In Venezuela, where the priority for public order dampened the general desire for reform, the biggest change came out of the legal battle over the Law of Vagabonds and Crooks (LVM, *Ley de Vagos y Maleantes*).

Argentina

Along with a strengthening of individual rights and a new penal process code, since 1983 there have been three major areas of police reform: a law that reduces the amount of time officers can hold detainees; the elimination of police edicts in the Federal Capital; and a restructuring of the Buenos Aires provincial police. These changes stemmed from reaction to the overly repressive and discretional police power between 1976 and 1983, as well as growing awareness of institutional malfunctioning, corruption, and abuses after 1983. But as in other countries, these measures are threatened by executive power and judicial inefficiency, which are tipping the balance back toward tough discretionary policing.

Altogether, Argentina has six different sets of police forces. Because of the country's greater level of decentralization, the police in different geographic regions clash less than in other Latin American countries with both local and national agencies. Because of the collapse of the military regime, in addition, military-run forces do not have as much power as in countries where the military is more politically powerful. But as in the rest of the region, the Argentine police continue to be shaped by historical practices, political pressures, and problems in society. Post-1983, the police agencies of Argentina include:

1. Policía Federal Argentina: A federal agency, the PFA enforces all law in the Federal Capital and federal laws throughout the country.
2. Military Police: The mandate of this once-powerful national agency was drastically reduced to cover primarily discipline within the armed forces.
3. Penitentiary Police: Enforces regulations in the twenty-eight federal prisons.
4. Gendarmeria: Responsible for border control.
5. Provincial police forces: Enforce most laws in the territories of the twenty-two provinces.
6. Municipal agencies: Enforce transit and other areas of local law.

A spurt of reforms followed the transition to democracy in 1983. The Raúl Alfonsín administration replaced top police officials responsible for abuses during the previous regime and tightened discipline and accountability measures. But the government's real focus was police relations with the judiciary, particularly regarding *amparo* (general recourse against illegal state actions) and habeas corpus. Combined with Peronist obstruction in Congress and the economic crisis of the mid-1980s, however, this priority of rights over structures led to few substantial changes, even according to top Alfonsín officials.[16] It wasn't until the Menem era that police abuses and constitutional negotiations led to specific measures, most of them based on Alfonsín-era proposals. Similar patterns also occurred at the provincial level in the 1990s. Ironically, a more propolice government oversaw a larger number of police reforms.

In their relations with the state, Argentina's traditionally insular police have become more cooperative since 1983, but concern continues over low remuneration, poor training, weak discipline, and bias caused by the police's institutional dependency on the executive. The PFA, a key instrument of past repression, was a primary focus of concern. The PFA has always been institutionally affiliated with the Interior Ministry and, for all practical purposes, was directed by the armed forces until 1983. Although article 2 of the PFA organic law places the agency within the Interior Ministry, article 15 subordinates "the headquarters of the Federal Police to a superior official of the Armed Forces...with the Title of Chief of the Federal Police." The military and the police have been a steady part of the Argentine state since independence, moreover, and the Interior Ministry's power has been drained by continual changes in governments and ministers. Military regimes' long-standing use of police actions to carry out internal security policies, in addition, blurred the lines between internal and external threats and further enhanced the police's role. Although changes in the 1980s made it more professional than most provincial and municipal police forces, the PFA still required major reforms. Most everyone who enters the force possesses little education. Training, which lasts six months for subofficials and three years for officials, is very formalistic. It does include civil and human rights, but this material is not given much weight and is "just on the surface, without conviction, to show to society"; instead, as "a holdover from past eras," emphasis is on respect for authority and physical exercises like marching, "which doesn't serve for anything" in modern urban conditions.[17] Much of the human rights training, in fact, was instituted only in the early 1990s after the killing of one soldier by another. The PFA's paramilitary structure, meanwhile, reflects the legacy of long-running military rule.

Remuneration for PFA personnel is among the lowest in the executive branch, with the monthly average of $800 barely enough to maintain a middle-class existence in the Federal Capital. There are no associations or unions for grievances about salaries or other matters, and when they do arise the unspoken rule is to "obey or to leave."[18] Neither of two bodies that do investigate internal complaints—the Agency of Administrative Investigations and the Agency of Preventative Investigations—has "any independence. They can't do anything against the police chiefs. They can only take on small issues, individual problems."[19] Discipline is equally obtuse. Internal PFA disciplinary action takes one of four forms: warning, arrest, suspension, or dismissal. The PFA periodically announces the suspension or dismissal of officers, but the investigatory process is closed. It is assumed that most sanctions regard infractions of internal rules rather than violations of detainees' rights. The combination of low pay and low accountability has generated serious corruption within the PFA. Each city zone has one or two *comisarías*, many of which operate a system of bribery, intimidation, and threats. Some oblige neighborhood businesses to pay regular bribes of up to $2,000. This type of corruption may actually have increased under democracy, which loosened the military regimes' stricter mechanisms of internal functioning to prevent common corruption. And when other state agencies start to get a cut of the money taken by the police, "reform becomes virtually impossible, as civil officials stand only to lose if they cooperate in prosecuting corrupt police" (CELS and Americas Watch 1991b: 8).

Public concerns over crime and distrust of corrupt officials, however, have gradually increased pressure for PFA reform. This pressure increased with the 1994 change in the city's political status, which brought the opposition to power and allowed it to push for greater PFA accountability. The agency has stepped up its public-relations program, introduced human rights courses in the academy, and, upon receiving a complaint against an official, now removes that official from duty during the internal investigation.[20]

These patterns occurred in the rest of the country as well. Although most laws are established by Congress, the constitution gives nearly complete law-enforcement authority not to the national legislature but to provincial and municipal authorities. The largest and oldest of the provincial police agencies set up under this arrangement is the police of Buenos Aires province, with its approximately 48,000 officers making it about a quarter larger than the PFA. The two agencies' structures long were similar. Each was run by a chief reporting to a minister of the executive branch and based on a military-style hierarchy. *Oficiales* run basic agency operations, and *suboficiales* carry out investigations and patrols.

As in the PFA, pay for provincial police officers is extremely poor. Low-level agents receive less than $400 per month, station heads slightly more than $800. Most officers work other jobs. Training is poor, corruption is widespread, and officials protect each other when facing accusations. As in the PFA, external oversight is weak, and the unclear disciplinary measures "are used for political purposes ... not for systematic control of internal problems" (CELS and Americas Watch, 1991b: 9). The province's Office of Human Rights functions as an ombudsman, receiving complaints and publishing educational material. Its accomplishments include organizing an investigation of the 1990 disappearance of two youths, resulting in convictions of the police officers responsible. But this body's political authority is "limited"[21] because it does not have the facilities or independence to directly challenge executive policy.[22] The provincial legislature receives denunciations, meanwhile, but does not conduct investigations. The two functions of its Human Rights Commission—monitoring state officials and developing educational material and training—have had little impact on the police.[23] Institutional oversight over the police, key to defining police power, has been weak.

Like the state, the judiciary has unsettled relations with the police. Argentina's courts have the police power to determine the constitutionality of most police laws and to judge most police actions. However, the general lack of legal clarity over the extent of police power, added on top of judicial disarray and executive pressures, reduces such authority. Such confusion can be seen in regard to the "guaranteed limits" on police action, as defined by the judiciary: reasonableness, privacy, legality, necessity, and proportionality. There are gaps not only between these limits and actual police practices but also among judicial rulings on these limits themselves. Reasonableness means that police action "must fit ... public objective, ... justifying circumstances, ... adaptation of the elected method to the proposed end, and ... absence of manifest iniquity"; the judge is the final arbiter who decides when an action "has passed from the camp of reasonableness" to damage "the essence of individual rights" (Bidart Campos 1963: 570). Privacy extends to all areas, including the home, correspondence, and due process, during which no one is obliged to declare against himself or herself. Police conformity to legality means that they may impose no unlegislated rule or punishment (Constitution, articles 14 and 19). Finally, police measures "must be proportionally adequate" to their immediate and long-term objectives (Law 19.549).

Judicial rulings, however, are often at odds with these standards. The Supreme Court repeatedly has rejected claims of police violations of the inviolability of the home, arguing, among other things, that a private citizen opening the door constitutes an "implied invitation." Rules regarding detention as well as the exclusion of illegally obtained evidence during trial also have been given wide berth by the courts. In the 1984 *Adami* ruling, a Buenos Aires criminal court decided that the presence of "serious suspects," with or without material evidence, is a sufficient basis for detention. In the 1986 *Ferreira* case, another criminal court ruled that detention of a person in a public space does not require "strong indications of guilt" as stated in the Penal Process Code then in force. In addition, the Supreme Court ruled that the state's "rights" are equally important as individual rights, which should not be a pretext for "arbitrary" restrictions on public powers.[24] In 1934, the Supreme Court stated that "constitutional limitations must not be given an extension that destroys necessary state powers or impedes its efficient exercise."[25] This ability of the state to impose "limitations on the form, mode or extension of" rights (Dromi 1985: 793) is, in fact, the high court's definition of the state's police power. Although the judiciary recognized habeas corpus well before 1983, it often followed jurisprudence prohibiting it to challenge "the existence of 'probable cause'" (Carrió 1987: 114).

The gap between jurisprudence and police practices is also apparent in the penal system. The police's official role is primarily in the initial investigative stage of the criminal process, during which it can receive denuncia-tions, search homes, conduct seizures, detain suspects, and interview wit-nesses. Despite being the auxiliary of the courts and the MP during this stage, the police "far exceeds this function" (Maier et al. 1996: 168). First-instance courts and *fiscales* are overwhelmed with work, lack sufficient resources, have no investigators or specialists at their disposal aside from forensic experts and the police, and often "have no interest in investiga-tion."[26] As a result, they end up ceding a lot of their investigatory power to the police.[27] Reforms since 1983 have gradually improved the situation. Above all, the 1992 penal process code clarifies roles, bolsters the MP and public defenders, and clarifies due process rights. But it also maintains the fusion of investigating and trial judges, which contributes to judges' work burden and the police's "high level of autonomy" in investigations.[28] *Fiscales*, judges, and judicial officials were aware of corrupt networks in the police, for example, but could not muster enough strength to take action until the late 1990s.[29]

Most unsettled, however, are police-society relations. The police's actions throughout Argentine history have earned it deep distrust by most citizens, but since 1983 reforms in police-society relations, such as civilian review boards, have been rare. The first major measure to improve police-society relations did not come until 1991. In September of that year, Law 23.950/91 modified the Organic Law of the Federal Police to allow it to detain a person to establish his/her identity only if there was reasonable suspicion of criminal activity and when the person did not produce ade-quate identification; to require the police to specify the basis for each detention;[30] and to reduce from twenty-four to ten hours the maximum time allowed for such detentions. Although it was propelled by public outrage over the police station killing of a seventeen-year-old, Law 23.950/91 did not alter police structures or procedures. Nevertheless, the president vetoed the bill with the argument that ten hours was not enough time for adequate investigation, given the police's resources. In the end, though, he was over-ridden by Congress.

But mistrust and violence still characterize police-society relations. One manifestation of that relationship are alleged *enfrentamientos*—shootouts between police officers and criminal suspects in which the sus-pects are often killed but that often appear to be police killings of suspects who did not pose a threat to officers. Denunciations of such action are out of reach for most people because they require written statements in the police station, among other steps. Along with engaging in *enfrentamientos*, police use their powers of detention for *averiguación de antecedentes* (veri-fication of police record) and *razzias* (mass roundups or raids) as forms of preventative crime control and public-order maintenance. The enactment of measures to curb such practices, however, is hobbled by conflicting public opinion. Since 1983, most Argentines have been against giving more power to the police yet consistently list crime as a top concern and tend to overlook abuses if police are able to reduce criminal activity. Societal divisions also tip the balance toward societal "acceptance" of police excesses, with economic, geographic, and political divisions making coherent opposition less likely. Although the province of Buenos Aires is the country's richest, for example, it also has the poorest areas and relatively few strong civil-society organizations. Most other provinces are even less politically cohesive, making the possibility of police-society reform still more remote in most of the country.

Reform: restructuring of the Buenos Aires provincial police. Even more than the new penal process code or the elimination of the PFA's edicts, the restructuring of the Buenos Aires provincial police was the most dramatic police reform in democratic Argentina. Even before carrying out systemic human rights abuses during the 1976–1983 dictatorship, the provincial police were notoriously violent, powerful, and unaccountable. And since 1983, officers have been implicated in extensive drug-trafficking networks, bribery operations, extrajudicial killings, extortion, *gatillo fácil* (trigger happy) shootings, the brutal 1997 murder of a prominent photojournalist, and the 1994 bombing of the Jewish Community Center (AMIA: Asociación Mutual Israelita de Argentina) in the Federal Capital, which killed more than eighty people.[31] Edicts give the police wide leeway in making arrests, and torture continues to be common in police stations.[32]

The agency's assumption of police-power authority, which grew in many ways after 1983, was a primary cause of this abuse. Instead of controlling the police, the provincial government ignored abuses and let low salaries be supplemented by corruption. The training program for recruits, developed by the military regime between 1976 and 1978, shares the PFA's priority on physical formation. According to a top police official, "Six months [is] dedicated principally to formation, as if they were soldiers. They do not receive ... real training."[33] Little room is left for education on civil rights or even basic laws, with graduates lacking adequate study of laws on basic issues such as the use of firearms. Once on the force, "the surest route to advancement into elite squads" for officers eager to stand out seems to be *enfrentamientos* with suspected criminals (CELS and Americas Watch 1991b: 7). With their frequent use of *razzias* and *averiguación de antecedentes*, in addition, officers often hold youths for up to four days and, under the threat of additional detention, pressure them to sign confessional "statements," which they are often not allowed to read.[34] The agency's unclear disciplinary measures, finally, "are used for political purposes ... not for systematic control of internal problems" (CELS and Americas Watch 1991b: 9). Many of the disciplinary actions that are taken may be temporary. Of the 4,800 officials implicated in "irregularities" between 1983 and the mid-1990s, 3,600 were exonerated.[35]

For the province's citizens, crime-rate increases beginning in the early 1990s deepened support for such tough policing. Several prominent police officials with high-level positions during the dictatorship even gained popularity by advocating an "iron fist." One of them was Luis Patti. At the end of the military regime in 1983, Patti was a provincial police subchief accused of and subsequently cleared in the shootout deaths of two Peronist activists, despite evidence that the victims had been tortured and shot at close range. In 1990, Patti was made *comisario* in the provincial town of Pilar, where he became popular by reducing crime and solving some difficult cases. Advocating policing "outside the law" and asserting that the "police, to clear up a case, has to perform no less than four or five criminal acts,"[36] Patti admitted that he often "punished" arrested minors without bringing them to the courts. In 1990, however, an investigative judge wielding strong evidence ordered Patti's detention for the torture of two robbery suspects. Patti refused to surrender, saying that the judge "has a great animosity toward the police." Pro-Patti public demonstrations ensued, and the judge and his family received death threats. Both President Menem and the Buenos Aires governor at the time, Antonio Cafiero (and his successor, Eduardo Duhalde), spoke out for Patti,[37] and after a few weeks an appeals court removed the judge presiding over the case on rarely cited grounds of prejudice. The new judge then dismissed the case.

Societal doubts over the police grew, however, as the province's crime rate rose 10.8 percent in 1995, 15.2 percent in 1996, and 16.3 percent in 1997. Robbery alone shot up by 26 percent in 1997.[38] Public agitation was fueled by a succession of high-publicity corruption cases that were particularly galling because they occurred at a time of increasing economic hardship and, more important, because they revealed the extent to which police officials were distracted from the task of fighting crime. In July 1996, nearly a dozen officials in the Narco-trafficking Division in the town of Quilmes were implicated in selling drugs and covering up for and extracting bribes from area traffickers, and the division chief was put under investigation for illicit enrichment. These actions were the first real response to the long-suspected collaboration of police with traffickers and was one of at least four separate investigations into this unit. More than police corruption, police inability to reign in crime led to a proreform shift in public opinion. As citizens began to realize that the police were not effective in even the most basic responsibility, scrutiny extended from the agency's more disreputable elements to its basic structure. The police's image grew so poor—attracting even international criticism—that it began to impinge on the future of Governor Duhalde, a presidential aspirant.[39] Already burdened by rumors of organized crime connections and by his early misassessment of the police as the best in the world, Duhalde needed to move toward an accommodating position appealing to the political center.

In July 1996, Duhalde announced a plan to restructure the police. The

plan was formulated by León Arslanian, who presided over the trials against
military officers accused of rights violations during the 1976–1983 dictatorship. Arslanian was appointed to head the new Ministry of Justice and
Security and, along with the secretary of security, to oversee the revamped
police bodies and investigate police abuses. In mid-1998, the provincial
legislature approved the four bills presented by the judiciary to rewrite
police laws and restructure the agency. Subsequently, the province reformed
its penal code to expand oral trials and to strengthen the Public Ministry
and in 1999 enacted the Private Security Law (Law 12.297) to institutionalize cooperation between the police and private security agencies.[40]

The restructuring affected the entire force. Under the old structure, a
police chief headed a single hierarchy of nine departments, each in charge
of an area like training and narco-trafficking. The largest was the General
Security Office, responsible for basic policing throughout the province.
Under the new structure, however, the police chief is a civilian, with direct
oversight over five new, independent bodies. The two main forces are the
5,000-officer investigation agency and the approximately 35,000-officer
security police to take over the General Security Office's law-enforcement
role. The security police are decentralized, with eighteen departments corresponding to the provinces' judicial departments in order to improve coordination with police, judges, and *fiscales*. There is also a transportation
security agency, a specialized agency for the custody and transport of
police detainees and prison inmates, as well as a small force for economic
crimes. Finally, there are citizen forums at the community, municipal, and
departmental levels designed to advise police officials, develop community
policing programs, and provide channels for citizen participation.

Although the restructuring did more than any previous change to bring
constitutional rights and police practices together, it remains vulnerable to
the same kinds of political change that ushered it in. In fact, violent resistance by officers and poorly implemented civilian participation put the
reforms in doubt soon after they were implemented. The dismissal of
approximately 1,200 officers, along with corruption trials against officers
linked to a former police chief, Pedro Klodczyk, inflamed police sensibili-
ties. Dismissed and still-serving officers—including influential former
commissioners, the former head of the narcotics division, and Klodczyk
associates—began organizing to press judges and legislators to stop the
reform or at least the prosecutions of officers. The tensions often broke out
into violence. There were twenty-three killings of police officers in 1997 in
the line of duty; but in January 1998 alone there were fifteen officer
revenge killings among officers. Several members of the provincial legislature from the opposition Frepaso party received death threats from men
identifying themselves as police officials. In February 1998, the weapons
of the governor's bodyguards were stolen, almost surely by angry officials

with the cooperation of at least a few of the bodyguards. More ominously, the reform has had little impact on police activity: the number of civilians killed by the police in 1999 shot up to more than 200, up from approximately 120 in 1998 (CELS 1999).

But the real threat to reform came with the 1999 election. Patti, who had become a provincial mayor and gubernatorial candidate, said that delinquents "should be killed" and suggested forming armed civilian groups. More seriously, the national vice president and Peronist gubernatorial candidate, Carlos Ruckauf, associated police killing with justice, promising "bullets for murderers" and saying that "the bullet that kills the delinquent" is "society's response to the bullet that kills innocent people."[41] Such attacks prompted Arslanian's resignation, the first major blow to reform. The second and possibly fatal blow came with Ruckauf's victory. Because the reforms did not lessen the power of the governor over the police, doubts were immediately raised over whether the reform would be enforced at all. The new governor opposes most of the changes and favors restricting bail and widening the police's powers to question prisoners and to conduct random searches. Upon taking office, he even appointed Aldo Rico, a right-wing former military official who led a military uprising against the trials against the former junta leaders in the 1980s, as the province's chief of security.[42] But even if Ruckauf held back from such policies, rising crime—robbery and assault rose by 46 percent between 1997 and 1999—may alone lead to a popular clamor to scrap the reform in favor of more immediate action.[43]

Finally, the reforms might not institutionalize the oversight that roots out police abuses. With low salaries and budgets, the police have always depended on extracting bribes during the course of duty. The reform dismantled corrupt agencies, but without accompanying increases in the police budget—of at least sixfold, according to analysts—corruption will continue.[44] More officers will also be likely to join the swelling ranks of private security agencies, further confusing the relationship between police power and police actions. To slow down such trends, Congress needs to enact appropriate legislation, the judiciary needs to regain control over the investigative process, and oversight agencies such as the Human Rights Office need to have more power. Although such uses of police power would make the police more accountable, they are still unlikely to breathe life back into the 1998 reforms.

Reform: the PFA edicts.   Despite its historical lack of political autonomy, the Federal Capital has always been the country's political center. So when the city's new provincial status led to the writing of a constitution in 1995, its network of NGOs was ready to take advantage of the opportunity to push for reforms. Extensive neighborhood and other forums were set up, involving 400 organizations and 200 different proposals, which helped pass constitutional provisions such as strong new civil rights and environmental protections.[45] But the provincial assembly's most marked success was the elimination of the PFA's edicts.

In Argentina, police relations with the state, judiciary, and society—as well as the difficulty of distinguishing police power from the police's power, the historical legacy of the police, the difficulties of enacting reform, and the debate between reactive and proactive measures—all come together in the issue of police *edictos* (edicts). Internal police regulations allowing for the arrest and detention of individuals for up to thirty days based primarily on noncriminal behavior, edicts are usually the individual provisions of police codes referred to as codes of *faltas* or *contravenciones*. The PFA had twenty-three edicts, ranging from prohibitions of "scandal" and public drunkenness to unlicensed firearm possession, as well as an unknown number of secret edicts.[46]

These provisions have been a part of Argentine policing since at least 1772, when a viceroy dictated a *bando* (precursor of the edict) to detain vagrants.[47] New measures were added on in the course of the nineteenth century to regulate other populations regarded as dangerous, such as immigrants. Following this pattern, in 1889 a new penal code confirmed police authority over many kinds of detention and raised from eight to thirty days the time limit that police could hold a detainee. In 1899, the chief of the federal police refined the definition of "begging," allowing for a thirty-day detention of those who beg but are capable of working or who have sufficient resources (Ré 1937: 120).

Most modern edicts, however, were established between 1932 and 1956, primarily under military regimes. In 1944, edicts became official when Decree-Law 32.265/44 of the military government officially gave police the power to establish and apply edicts and to repress acts not specified in the law. In 1947, the Peronist Congress legitimized the edicts created between 1943 and 1946, including Decree-Law 32.265/44, thereby "automatically convert[ing] edicts into a law of the National Congress," an action that single-handedly neutralized the argument that "the police were violating the National Constitution by legislating in an area that is the exclusive competency of the Congress" (Gentili 1995: 8). In 1956, the military junta, in the wake of the moderating *Mouviel* decision by the Supreme Court (discussed below), enacted Decree-Law 17.189/56 to make legal all edicts up to the time. Two years later, the government passed the new Organic Law of the Federal Police. Remaining in force after 1983, this law gave the PFA authority to "apply" and "judge" edicts but not to "create" them. It thus partly reclaimed Congress's police powers but still left the police agency with the discretionary authority to apply edicts. In 1958, the Congress, under the Arturo Frondizi government, passed Omnibus Law

14.467, which ratified all of the previous military regime's laws, including 17.189/56.

No significant challenges to the edicts were made in the first years of the current democracy. In 1985, Congress gave the PFA new *contravenciones* that were based not on suspected predelictual character but on the suspected commitment of actual crimes. Although this was a major advance in the specification of police authorities, it neither delegitimized the police's ability to carry out existing edicts nor took away any of its specific authority. Under Menem, the edicts themselves had strong executive support, seen in particular by its pressure on the 1996 Buenos Aires Constitutional Assembly to retain the edicts.

Edicts have been further legitimized by the Supreme Court's inconsistent stand on them. In 1941, the Supreme Court ruled against an edict enacted by the Santa Fe provincial executive on the grounds that the executive had no such legal authority.[48] The high court struck down Decree-Law 32.265/44 in the 1956 *Mouviel* decision, arguing that the criminal code "grants [the police] the authority" to carry out edicts, "as they are written, and not to configure or define them, a power which is strictly of legislative character."[49] Although a major advance, like the 1985 legislation this ruling did not object fundamentally to police use of edicts. And in most cases, the courts explicitly upheld edicts. In the 1929 *Bonevo* ruling, the first to deal expressly with the issue, the Supreme Court sustained edicts' constitutionality on the grounds that even though Congress has the power to make laws, in the case of edicts Congress gives the police "the authority to dictate general *ordenanzas* and *reglamentos* necessary for security and the common good" and that granting such authority is simply "conferring administrative power" and not "legislative functions."[50] In 1942, the court declared, concerning an edict regulating public meeting of a university federation, that

> there is no constitutional obstacle preventing the Chief of Police, while Congress does not use its powers, in his character as a functionary dependent on the Executive in charge of the custody and defense of the public order ... to establish rules for the exercise of the right of association and sanctions for its non-fulfillment.[51]

During the Alfonsín administration, the high court rejected a measure to declare edicts unconstitutional, and the Menem Supreme Court argued that they are constitutional because appeals are allowed in the twenty-four-hour period after an edict detention and that striking down edicts would cause a "vacuum in legislation, incompatible with order and public security."[52]

Despite these many rulings, the judicial debate over edicts turns most fundamentally on defining the extent of the judiciary's and the legislature's police power. The 1984 Habeas Corpus Law (23.098), coupled with the difficulty of appealing an edict detention within twenty-four hours (Law 2.372, article 587), elicited many petitions questioning the constitutionality of the appeal process and of other edict regulations. These cases claim that edicts violate, among other provisions, article 109 of the constitution, which proscribes the president from "assuming judicial powers." Many first-instance courts have accepted such arguments and declared specific edicts unconstitutional.[53]

The course of this debate, however, may rest less on legal rulings than on broader notions of public order and the importance of precriminal character in maintaining it. For this reason, the return of democracy in 1983 (or in previous years) in itself did not have a decisive impact on edicts. Although the Habeas Corpus Law and other regulations widened citizens' legal recourses, the end of authoritarianism may in fact sway the judiciary toward allowing more rather than less police control. Courts often sympathize with police forces' claims to need mechanisms such as edicts in order to minimize democracy's legal restrictions and political uncertainties. As one PFA official believes, "During the military era the police had a lot of power, but now ... justice is too strong, and police officers are afraid to do anything, so they turn the other way when they see something happening."[54]

Legal analysis often boosts such an approach. Many proedict scholars distinguish *contravenciones* (*edictos*), akin to "infractions" from *delitos*, defined as "crimes." They assert that with *delitos* there is a specific individual whose rights have been violated, whereas with *contravenciones* the victim is society at large (see Rojas Pellerano, 1967: 77). This leads to the assertion that even though penal law and legislative authority over it deal with individual rights and thus *delitos*, public order and edicts are matters for administrative authorities such as the police. Edicts' maximum penalty of thirty days' detention, as opposed to the much more severe *delito* penalties, is also used to distinguish the two. Further supporting edicts is the fact that *contravenciones* traditionally reflect local customs and traditional uses, boosting the claim that each province should be able to establish them as its rightful police power.

Such reasoning is based on an exaggerated prominence of customary and provincial law, as well as on a specious distinction between the thirty-day edict limit and penal law's limits, some of which are also thirty days. More important, it reveals the historical gap between police law and police practice. Edicts allow police to punish people for who they are rather than what they have done, without being burdened by judicial processes and protections. Courts' acceptance of this approach indicates a prioritization of social order over penal law, which makes it difficult to bring the police into the rule of law. In particular, edicts violate the constitutional guarantees and legal procedures that are a basis of police-society relations. With a difference between penal and *convención* law, an individual detained for violating an edict has no guarantee of a lawyer at the time of making a statement, which, along with the detaining official's report, constitute sufficient evidence of guilt.[55] With no more than three days between detention and condemnation, the speed of the process undermines the rights to a legal defense.[56] Edicts also undermine these rights by opening loopholes for other laws. If the police detain somebody for *averiguación de antecedentes*, for example, checking on their record may take more than the ten hours allowed for this kind of detention under 23.950/91. But if they then charge the detainee with violation of an edict, they are still within their legal rights to hold that person for a longer period.

Such actions demonstrate how much edicts have been an instrument of social control. The police argue that edicts are a needed "tool for prevention. ... The only weapon we have in the street to confront on an equal basis those who rob."[57] Detention patterns, however, show that the vast majority of detentions are for undesired but not normally illegal behavior. In 1994, 49.7 percent of detentions were for the edict prohibiting "intoxication," 19.2 percent against the "scandal" edict that prohibits "publicly offending modesty," 16 percent against the "anti-vagrancy and begging" edict (similar to Venezuela's LVM, discussed below), 11.7 percent for "disorder," and 1.3 percent for "card-playing" in unacceptable locales (CELS 1996b: appendix). Most detentions occur in pubic gathering spaces like those outside cantinas and concert stadiums, and most detainees are from marginalized populations—youths, the poor, immigrants, transvestites, homosexuals, and the unemployed. In police stations, many are beaten, threatened, and denied rights, such as making a phone call, that are allowed even under the edicts.

Records also show how much more the police focused on controlling public order than on combating *delitos*. Of the approximately 240,000 annual detentions in the Federal Capital in 1995, more than 150,000 were based on edicts, about 50,000 on verification of identity, and 40,000 for suspicion of a *delito*. With such numbers, the alienation of and suspicion toward marginalized sectors became a self-fulfilling prophecy, as the social rifts upon which edicts fed grew wider. By giving officers wide authority over rights such as inviolability of the home, edicts blur the line between police power and police actions.

The difficulty of legal appeals against edict actions, in addition, weakens judges' ability to review the police's detentions under them. In fact, less than 1 percent of all PFA detentions were appealed—but the vast majority of those appeals were upheld (see Table 3.2).[58] The power of the police through edicts (officially, of the chief of police) to arrest, judge, and sentence also undermines other judicial functions because edicts give police chiefs the power "to commute or pardon" an edict sentence (article 65, *Reglamento de Procedimientos Contravencionales*), an authority that no

Table 3.2 Edicts and *Delito* Detentions in the Federal Capital

Year	Edict Detentions	Edict Appeals	Upheld Appeals
1992	35,350	313 (0.8%)	n/a
1994	106,451	115 (1.1%)	109 (95%)
1995	150,830	754 (0.5%)[a]	746 (99%)[a]

Notes: Figure for the number of upheld appeals in 1992 was not available.
a. Figures are approximate.

judge has ever had. They have further violated the division of powers by usurping judicial functions and contravening the constitutional prohibition (article 109) of the executive's "exercise of judicial functions."[59] Edicts also weaken constitutional article 19, which protects "private actions of men that in no way offend order or public morality, nor harm a third party" by allowing legitimizing detention based on perceived age, ethnicity, sexual orientation, or employment status.

During the 1990s, however, tension over policing grew as the crime rate spiked upward and as politics in the Federal Capital became increasingly polarized. The corruption, unemployment, and economic inequality associated with the Menem administration galvanized the traditionally Radical district when it formulated its provincial constitution in 1996. Harnessing a perceived societal consensus that the edicts did not work, NGOs mounted a lobbying campaign at the constitutional convention to prohibit edicts in the new province. The police and the executive tenaciously defended the edicts, arguing that it was democracy's restrictions and uncertainties that hurt crime control. In the end, however, each of the major district parties approved the abolition of the edicts.

Subsequently, in March 1998, the provincial government replaced the edicts with the new Urban Coexistence Code (*Código de Convivencia Urbana*). Although weakened at the last minute by pressure from the national government and the PFA, it is distinct from the edict system in important ways. First, it does not prosecute drunkenness, prostitution, or vagrancy per se, which were always legal under penal law but illegal under the edicts. It does, however, prosecute any activity that puts other people at risk; solicitation of prostitution is legal, for example, as long as it does not disturb or harm those nearby. Whereas the police chief under the edicts was the "judge" who applied the fine or sentencing, actual judges take over these roles in the new system. Finally, the code sets out explicit rules about detention. The police must now communicate to the detainee that a court appearance is required within five days, specify the *contravención* allegedly being violated, and take each case to a *fiscal* within three days. When the detainee is presented before the courts, there is either an abbreviated trial when the person pleads guilty, or an oral public trial.

Although a historic breakthrough, the uncertainty of the *Código* reform soon became apparent. One obstacle is the PFA's ability to substitute the edicts with similar mechanisms or powers, such as the *averiguación de antecedentes*. In fact, the PFA tested the limits of its power immediately after the initial derogation. In the first half of 1997—before the new code was enacted—the police detained an average of 413 persons per day, more than most days under the edicts. In contrast, there were only 900 registered actions during the code's first three months. The police now complain to the interior minister that the code leaves them without needed controls, citing these reduced detentions and a corresponding increase in crime. To make up for this limitation, and with sharp drops in the PFA budget making training programs on the code unlikely, the PFA is likely to step up its use of other detention procedures, demonstrating that there remains a fine line between detainable and nondetainable behavior. Although vague infractions such as "scandal" no longer exist, the police can still crack down on equally vague behavior that "disturbs" others. Combined with "lax control by *fiscales*" and a lack of personnel to implement the new code, this legal continuity means that officers' power over individuals on the street may not be fundamentally reduced.[60] Five months after the code took effect, there were only five *fiscales* when there were supposed to be eleven and two judges instead of the mandated three—and they all had to share phones and offices. This infrastructural inadequacy underscores the need for reforms to include effective oversight by the judiciary and other institutions.

Second, the relationship between the federal government and the new provincial government will be eased by their mutual rule by the Alianza (the coalition between the Radical and Frepaso parties), but a fall in their popularity or a rise in crime rates may reignite popular pressure for strong policing. Soon after its adoption, the code came under fire from the Peronists, the police, and the middle class. Then–Vice President Ruckauf criticized the code for allowing antisocial behavior such as prostitution and drunkenness, the justice minister said that it "does not foresee all the circumstances that we are going to have to confront, and that it is going to affect the security of the city," and the interior minister added that a "legislative vacuum" has "fomented pre-criminal and scandalous conduct that affect the security and public tranquility and that has given the citizens of the Federal Capital a sensation of insecurity and lack of protection."[61] Then–Mayor Fernando de la Rúa, later elected president, responded that the government's attack was purely political and that the most threatening and undesirable behaviors, in any case, remain punishable by law.

But de la Rúa's response missed the real point. Many of the Federal Capital's middle-class neighborhoods began organizing against the new code, with public marches and demonstrations. Residents of one neighborhood popular with transvestites complained of increases in noise and violence after the end of the edicts, and many high-profile neighborhood activists threatened to appeal for national government intervention. These protests reveal friction not only between the powers of the national and local governments but also between civil rights and the "right" to quiet neighborhoods. Civil rights and neighborhood security are not mutually exclusive, but the politics of public insecurity in Argentina had made them so. No government wants to be on the wrong side of a debate between transvestites and the middle-class. Responding to this political reality, barely a month after the code's enactment, de la Rúa said that the code "should be more severe" and that measures such as preventative detention and crackdowns on street prostitution should be used.[62] By taking such a position, the government not only conceded the terms of debate to the proedict forces but also appeared weak when rebuffed by the legislators and jurists in its own province. With President de la Rúa now facing a Peronist-dominated Congress, such a position is not promising for durable changes.

The most intensive pressure against the new code, however, came when Menem's government went on the offensive against it. In March 1999, after stating that "we are going to reinstate the edicts in the city of Buenos Aires," Menem signed a decree that gave the PFA power to arrest people engaging in any one of eight acts, including prostitution and the possession of hammers and other objects that indicate criminal intentions.[63] An even deeper intrusion into civil rights was the proscription of "tumultuous gatherings against a determined person," referring to the protests known as *escraches*, popularized by children of those "disappeared" between 1976 and 1983, in which charges are read aloud in front of the homes of officials believed to be responsible. Admitting that the decree was a replacement of the edicts, the interior minister said that "the President has ordered the police to respect the content of the edicts up until it covers the vacuum created by the code."[64] The decree was roundly condemned as unconstitutional for exercising legislative functions and intruding on the provincial powers of the Federal Capital. The District ombudsman set up a telephone line to receive complaints; de la Rúa called it an "act of propaganda," but the government did not back down, and the interior minister buffed up the police's powers by no longer requiring officers to clearly identify themselves and their actions before using their firearms.[65]

Police reform in Argentina, in sum, has made major advances during the democratic era. The executive's repression and the judiciary's disarray led to new laws, a new penal code, and major alterations for both the Buenos Aires provincial police and the PFA. These changes have already reshaped police relations with the state, judiciary, and society. But to function properly in the long run, functioning oversight of the new limitations on police actions will be needed. Without such oversight, public pressures over crime, continuing judicial disarray, police strength, and executive politics will allow old practices to continue even within reformed structures and laws.

Venezuela

In Venezuela, pressures for police reform came more from executive incompetence rather than executive repression, more from judicial ineffectiveness than judicial inaccessibility. Since repression is the biggest source of pressure for change, the movement for reform was not nearly as strong as it was in Argentina. In Venezuela, instead, the combination of high crime, societal wariness of the police, and party controls have channeled most reform efforts into improving coordination. Nearly all police forces continued to act with a high level of autonomy after the 1958 transition, even as the guerrilla insurgency gave way to economic and political stability. The breakdown in the economy and of public confidence in the regime in the 1980s, however, led to violence and uncertainty that increased the police's role as well as societal concerns over police practices. Most political actors, unwilling to support police reform that challenged a powerful clientelistic state, chose to interpret the police's ongoing ineffectiveness as a result of poor interagency coordination.

There are eight sets of police agencies in Venezuela:

1. Cuerpo Técnico de Policía Judicial: Created by decree in 1958 as part of the Justice Ministry, the PTJ is the largest national police agency, responsible for criminal investigations, forensic services, and new areas of investigation such as in narcotics trafficking.
2. Dirección Sectoral de los Servicios de Inteligencia y Prevención (DISIP; the Office of Intelligence and Prevention Services): Part of the Interior Ministry, DISIP is the other national investigative police and specializes in public security. It was created when it replaced DIGEPOL (General Office of Police, or Dirección General de Policía) with a 1969 presidential decree. With national jurisdiction and authority as a judicial police auxiliary, DISIP investigates threats to state security, individual liberties, and democratic institutions.
3. Policía del Estado (State Police): The police of the twenty-two states (some share one agency) are governed by state codes, and many are headed by Guardia Nacional officials. Reflecting the limits of Venezuelan federalism, the "organization of urban and rural police" is the only administrative responsibility given to the states by the constitution (article 16, ordinal 5).
4. Guardia Nacional (GN; the National Guard): Created by presidential decree in 1937, the GN is a military body responsible for securi-

ty around sensitive areas such as airports, highways, petroleum and industrial zones, and border areas. Long used in the penitentiary system, since 1990 it has taken control over many of the country's more violent prisons. The GN also fights contraband, supports state and municipal police, and as part of the judicial police can substitute for or work with the PTJ (CEC Article 74-A, Ordinal 2). Many of the GN's functions were originally granted it on June 22, 1946, by a military junta decree, which included a wide range of police powers. At that time, the GN was a special national administrative police overseeing areas under the Interior Ministry's jurisdiction.

5. Dirección de Inteligencia Militar (DIM; Office of Military Intelligence): DIM replaced the Armed Services' Information Service in 1971, is part of the Defense Ministry, and carries out intelligence operations relating to state security.

6. Dirección de Inteligencia del Ejército (DIE; Office of Army Intelligence): DIE heads the military's intelligence operations.

7. Policía Metropolitana (PM; the Metropolitan Police): Established in 1969, the PM is the country's largest local police force, and its central task is crime prevention and public order maintenance in the Federal District, which includes most of Caracas and the port zones north of the city. The PM can also carry out *expedientes*, and has been increasing involved in antidrug policing. (The *expediente* is the file of a criminal case created during the *sumario*, the first stage of the judicial process.) It is institutionally part of the Interior Ministry but in practice works primarily in the GN.

8. Municipal Forces: Taking advantage of decentralization laws, many municipalities within Caracas and other large cities have established their own law-enforcement agencies.

Because of both high crime rates and unsettled relations between the levels of government, problems of overlap and conflict have been greater in Venezuela than in Argentina and elsewhere. The agencies most central to law enforcement and most affected by reforms are the PTJ, which carries out most investigation, and the PM, which is responsible for policing the main urban area. Like the PFA and the Buenos Aires provincial police in Argentina, these two police agencies are the most important in their country.

The state.   After the fall of the military regime in 1958, presidential decrees brought police organization under the direction of newly appointed chiefs. President Betancourt (1959–1964) then initiated the so-called *Doctrina Betancourt* (Betancourt Doctrine), which was basically an ample application of executive authority toward the three most pressing needs of the time: crime, the leftist insurgency, and controlling a politicized society.

The police, long a part of the country's national security apparatus, was a key instrument in this strategy, often through stepped-up application of the LVM (discussed below), which, like Argentina's edicts, focused on undesirable rather than actual criminal activity. State institutions, public opinion, and political parties became so wedded to the *doctrina's* strategies, in fact, that their support for it continued beyond the Betancourt administration and the realization of its immediate goals.

Police structures underwent their most significant changes in the first few years of the new democracy and, later, were altered on an ad hoc basis when excesses and inefficiencies became apparent. The old Seguridad Nacional was replaced by new agencies, including, eventually, DIGEPOL, which had preventative and investigative powers "throughout the national territory...geared toward the conservation of order and of public tranquility."[66] Allegations of abuse plagued DIGEPOL, coming to a head in 1965 with the case of a communist professor who was probably tortured and killed, as judicial hearings revealed, by DIGEPOL agents. Although there were no prosecutions or reforms, in 1967 the *fiscal general* did suggest that DIGEPOL be ascribed to the Interior Ministry, arguing that such an ascription would give its actions a legal validity and, as would be discussed thirty years later, improve the efficiency of criminal investigation. But the executive countered that it needed maximum control to combat the leftist guerrillas. DIGEPOL's continuing rights violations and poor performance, however, finally led President Rafael Caldera to replace it with DISIP in 1969.

Despite the leftist insurgency's demise and the stability of the 1970s, changes were made more in police objectives than in actual activities, with reports of abuse dogging most police agencies through the decade. Several DIM officials were suspected of forming death squads in 1974 to target leftists after the assassination of a DIM inspector, and four years later reports uncovered a PTJ death squad. Such practices were only applied more widely with the shift in policy, during Caldera's 1969–1974 government, from suppressing armed opposition to fighting regular crime. The new laws and regulations of this new policy were epitomized by the massive police Operación Vanguardia of 1970 and its sweeps of urban barrios. By the time the operation had ended, it helped make abuses and arbitrary arrests, even as a response to behavior such as "disobedience or lack of respect for authority" (Santos Alvins 1992: 81), commonplace.

One of the few congressional actions on police matters during this period, aside from ad hoc hearings, was passage of the 1976 Organic Law of Security and Defense, which established the permanent National Council of Security and Defense that strengthened the police's arrest authority but had no provision for protecting constitutional guarantees. The legislative branch's reluctance to flex its police powers was caused less by the constitution than by the executive's continuing political hegemony. This was nothing new. Although constitutional articles 136 and 158 gave the legislature explicit police powers, including the authority to organize police agencies, it used these powers only rarely, such as when it established the National Guard of 1811. In the democratic era, party controls in civil society have dampened consistent and organized support for reform legislation. Even as police agencies grew after 1958, there was inadequate accompanying legislation on training, administrative organization, budgets and remuneration, acquisition and maintenance of materiel, and private security agencies. The senate and deputy human rights commissions receive reports of police violence, and the MP's annual report to Congress summarizes the charges against police officials, but there are no strong reporting or accounting procedures from the police to the Congress or the judiciary. With "empirical evaluation of police functioning ... virtually nonexistent" (Gabaldón et al. 1996: 188), the lack of external control effectively eliminates a large part of Congress's police power and its ability to promote police reform.

Despite the duration of Venezuelan democracy, in addition, its military has more control of the police than in many other countries. Police agencies' development under the armed forces has allowed them to become a reserve domain of power, particularly in the judiciary. The "competent organs" of the armed forces are "principal"—not "auxiliary"—parts of the judicial police, for example, and any "crimes against the independence and security of the nation, against liberty and against the public order"[67] are sent to military judges. The armed forces have also assumed most law enforcement connected to border areas, by military personnel, and of crimes listed in both military and civilian law. The courts often choose military law over civilian law in conflicts between them, in addition, and military courts have taken over trials of military personnel committing civilian offenses as well as civilians committing offenses in military-controlled areas. The alleged existence of a special police force called Manzopol, created to funnel arms and information to the police for antinarcotics and related efforts, reveals how the military also contributes to police excesses and lack of accountability. Such a force would violate Congress's constitutional police power to create new bodies in nonemergency situations (articles 136, 179, 190), but the justice minister claimed that Manzopol was part of the armed forces and therefore exempt from direct legislative oversight.[68]

The government's unwillingness to restrain or effectively oversee the police is expressed through its lack of criminal policies, which have allowed exceptional and emergency operations to become the basis of routine policing. Stemming in part from the *Doctrina Betancourt*, Venezuelan police forces have carried out "extraordinary" operations of raids, mass detentions, roundups, and related actions. In February 1981, the administration of Luis Herrera Campíns (1979–1984) implemented the Union Plan to institutionalize coordination of such operations, thus making them legal and "ordinary." This coordination was further institutionalized by Security Act 84 under the following Jaime Lusinchi government (1984–1989). The focus of the Union Plan and of extraordinary police operations in general is not to break up organized crime or address crime's causes but to arrest the greatest number of people. The Union Plan's 1981 report, for example, concluded that it "brought satisfactory results [by] making 31,714 arrests" (Policía Metropolitana 1981: 1).

In the economic downturn of the 1980s, however, stubbornly high crime and increasing complaints of rights violations convinced political officials that the police were not effective in their most basic responsibility. The regime was increasingly caught between the inability and the need to take action as violent crime rates accelerated even faster than those in the rest of Latin America. The murder rate over the span of the 1990s increased fivefold in Caracas and doubled in the rest of the country. Nearly every other indication of violent crime also grew. Between 1989 and 1993, the number of minors violating the law or in "situations of danger" jumped from 21,771 to 27,063 (OCEI 1993: 799–800). Between 1990 and 1995, assaults increased by 16 percent and robberies by 26 percent. Amid such violence, a sensation of lawlessness descended over society.

As in Argentina, poor standards, training, and job security aggravated the police's poor performance. The average workweek of seventy-two hours gives agents 40 percent more work than other state employees, without adequate vacation, health benefits, or retirement security.[69] Corruption has been rife, with individual officers as well as "mafias" conducting extortion, threats, and kidnappings. Many police agencies operate extensive networks in weapons distribution and sale (Controlaria General de la República 1989: 40).[70] Training is inadequate for lower-ranking officials. Heading each regional PTJ section is the chief of the delegation, under whom serve the chief of investigation, the chief of services, commissioners, subcommissioners, inspectors, subinspectors, detectives, and street officers. Detectives receive three years of education in advanced technology; subinspectors receive four years and receive the equivalent of a college degree.[71] But most personnel get only a short course in basic police functions, such as firearm use and investigative techniques. In the PM, training for officers consists of a three-month course, insufficient for the challenges they face in their job.

Disciplinary mechanisms in the PTJ are vague. The 1965 Regulation of the Disciplinary Regime prohibits the undue use of firearms and the physical or moral mistreatment of detainees (article 14), but it does not fully define either. The other disciplinary code is the Regulation of Ascensions and Punishments, an internal document whose only public exposure comes with sporadic "scandals and embarrassing cases known by the press"; individual citizens who denounce irregularities by officials rarely "know if there are sanctions and if sanctions taken had any effect" (Santos Alvins 1992: 99). In most cases, sanctions involve transfers or temporary suspensions without change or evaluation in the regulations or training. Egregious abuses have led to demands for a "reorganization" of police forces or the "dismissal of their directors" but rarely to follow-up legislation.[72] Such patterns only inoculate the police from effective reform, which in turn deepens its impunity and de facto usurpation of police power.

As in other countries, the police complain of inadequate budgets and support. But poor policy implementation is more damaging than poor financial expropriations. Although underfunded by objective standards, the PTJ is still among the state's best-equipped agencies, with a network of cars, communications equipment, archives of criminals and suspects, and funding through extraordinary allocations. It enjoys "a constant, intense, sustained, efficient, and vast investigative activity in thousands of processes in the initial stages of their respective proceedings" (Pérez 1985: 141). But judicial disarray and financial constraints still undermine the PTJ's work. The PTJ processes all serious crimes reported by other agencies, but its lack of personnel and organizational support are what a PTJ commissioner blames for constant bureaucratic delays.[73] In the Federal District, for example, the PM has approximately 15,000 officers, local municipalities 5,000, and the PTJ only 250. Combined with personnel insecurity, as well as a topography that makes law enforcement particularly difficult in Caracas, such delays alienate the police from the rest of the state.[74]

By the late 1980s, the government could justify neither abuse in the name of order nor inaction in the name of rights. The regime never formulated any real alternatives to the Betancourt Doctrine, which was not concerned with police abuse or judicial independence. Deteriorating conditions exacerbated and exposed the lack of policy cooperation between police forces and other state agencies, as well as among the Interior Ministry, the Justice Ministry, and other executive agencies with police or rule of law functions. Coordination of anticriminal duties is officially carried out by the Unified Police Commands (Comandos Policiales Unificados), which function in all jurisdictions under the control of the interior minister and the state governors. But officials still either do "not work together" or work under "contradictory instructions" (Gabaldón and Bettiol 1988), with the proliferation of agencies constantly straining coordination.

One of the few coherent policy responses was the attempt to improve poor coordination, which most officials chose to blame for police ineffectiveness. Between 1977 and 1990, bills were introduced in Congress to "give greater coherence to the ... organization, functioning and national coordination" of state police agencies.[75] The 1977 and 1990 bills would have unified the police under a military-type structure, the 1986 bill expanded some of Guardia Nacional's police functions, and others proposed moving the GN's police responsibilities to the Interior Ministry and to improve the police training academies. Most bills died at the committee level, due to police agencies' competing interests and the reluctance of municipalities to give up their new powers to organize their own police agencies. These failed legislative efforts, however, did lead to several partial regulatory reforms on coordination: the Regulation of Coordination of Police Services and Norms of Conduct of Police Bodies, the National Coordination System of Police Services, the Interior Ministry's National Police Commission, and regional police and coordination commissions.[76]

Reform efforts slowed during the political upheavals between 1989 and 1993 but picked up slightly after the 1993 election with new proposals to shift police agencies out of the Justice Ministry and to resurrect the Organic Law of the Police Career, as well as a PTJ-initiated restructuring of the criminal investigation process. But amid divided government, the rise of new parties, and economic crisis, these measures also failed to gain political traction. The most significant actual change of the time was initiated by municipal governments, which used the new decentralization law to form their own police agencies. There are now more than 450 state and municipal forces. Although they are legally only auxiliary organs, these agencies have become a central expenditure of wealthy municipalities and have further widened the differences in police services and lack of coordination that were a cause of the 1977–1990 legislation.

Like these efforts by state and government officials, the judiciary has also tried to better define the police's role. But in both cases, interpretations of written laws have not meant a rule of law. In Venezuela, the law actually gives the police more authority than it does in most countries. Combined with infrastructural strength, such legal authority often forces the judiciary to take a backseat in criminal investigation. "In the activities of the police pre-trial, judicially-speaking, there are no controls. Except for the presence of the fiscal in the declarations to the police investigators"; and at the other end of that process, the police exhibit "blunt resistance ... to obey judicial decisions."[77] Because these power dynamics infuse each stage of the judicial process, judicial-police reform has been particularly difficult.

Gómez's security forces and Pérez Jimenez's Seguridad Nacional first gave the police a central role in judicial investigation, which passed to the PTJ in 1958. The PTJ was ascribed to the Justice Ministry, causing the hybrid of organizational dependence on the executive but functional dependence on the judiciary. This position has led to many political frictions. A justice minister asking a PTJ commissioner to manipulate an open investigation, for example, might force the commissioner to choose between violating legal procedures or risk being replaced. In many countries, the judicial police is placed in MP because it is responsible for proceedings, preparation of trial, and preparatory proceedings. But one reason why the PTJ was not part of Venezuela's MP was because the MP was not the large, autonomous functioning institution that it subsequently became.

From the democratic regime's outset, police forces were part of the administration of justice. During the Betancourt and Raúl Leoni (1964–1969) administrations, pressure was put on police and judges to jail guerrilla suspects and to curtail due process, creating almost complete reliance on confession in criminal investigations. The CEC itself "gives great weight to testimony for proof of the action and guilt of the accused" (Gabaldón 1996: 212), and police officials admit that many cases without witnesses hinge on no more than the word of the accused against the accuser. Although the MP is supposed to monitor detainee rights in police stations, as discussed in Chapter 2, *fiscales* at police stations are usually in the main rooms while abuses happen in secret basements. Affirming the provision that the police can only take an "informative statement" from a detainee, the MP pointed out in its 1966 congressional report (MP 1966: 200–201) that the CEC "incurs a grave error in considering the judicial police as investigative functionaries." At the same time, however, CEC article 248 states that the "extra-judicial confession rendered before judicial police authorities will be taken into account as evidence ... according to the character of the person who makes it and the motives and the circumstances in which he is found." Coupled with the police's dominance over investigation, this legal focus on the detainee's character makes it difficult to prove abuses such as coerced confessions.

The police have increased their authority by extending it into most judicial processes. As in other countries, the police have the powers to inspect crime scenes, retain evidence, and question suspects and witnesses. But unlike in other countries, the penal process itself in Venezuela often begins with the police, who can initiate the *sumario* (CEC, article 75). With these rules, the CEC (especially articles 71 and 72) "conferred a great power to police officials to shape the legal proceedings that should be decided by the judge" (Gabaldón 1996: 186). Unlike in many other countries, in particular, CEC article 75-B obliges police officials to "maintain absolute" secrecy in these proceedings, which not only violates due process rights but also enables the police to withhold information from judges and *fiscales*. The police continue as an auxiliary after the information is turned over to the judge, and all police action has force of proof unless proven false. In practice, most detainee declarations are taken by the police with or without the presence of a defense attorney or *fiscal*, despite the fact that only the court is authorized to take detainees' formal statements. But due to the courts' weakness and the police's ascription to an executive that places primacy on crime control, the police have gradually assumed many of the functions of both the MP and investigating judges.

This power has allowed abuses to spread throughout the judicial process. Police officers regularly "use false witnesses, invent facts, ... bring false charges against innocent persons,"[78] destroy evidence, defy court orders, protect accused officials, harass political activists, and sometimes charge suspects "money to not bring charges."[79] Such behavior is often justified by the belief that judges let delinquents free and frustrate the use of preventative detention. Many officers even argue that detainee access to legal counsel puts the police at a disadvantage, accusing public defenders of telling their clients to withhold incriminating information. Detainees' rights to legal defense, indeed, have required a "long and painful sermon" (Colegio de Abogados del Distrito Federal 1983) in the Judicial Police School. Combined with such beliefs, the vagueness of many laws fuels the police's tendency to punish allegedly precriminal behavior.

A set of judicial and CEC reforms in 1962 included one granting judicial police "delegated" judicial powers and another allowing judges to return judicial proceedings back to the judicial police.[80] Such wide involvement in the judicial process, and the lack of clear boundaries between judges and these auxiliaries, reduce judges' independence by explicitly and implicitly giving judicial duties to nonjudicial officials. Strengthening the police's judicial role by placing it on equal judicial footing with the first-instance courts, these changes violate the separation of powers by granting judicial powers to an executive agency. Altogether, the police's infrastructural advantages, the judiciary's bureaucracy, and courts' chronically overloaded dockets lead many Venezuelan judges "to base [their] decisions on police actions without an investigation of them and without a deep conviction regarding the veracity or falsehood of the facts" (Santos Alvins 1992: 86).

Like the PTJ, the PM also derives judicial powers from the vagueness of the law and the judiciary's failure to clarify much of it. Although the Organic Law of the Federal District says that police officials "are able to act as investigatory officials" and therefore "have the attributions and obligations expressed in the CEC to such functionaries," the Judicial Police Law and the CEC limit the police to initial investigations. But the hierarchy of laws is unclear, allowing the police to control most criminal investigations in practice. Suspension of constitutional guarantees boosts such power—even when, as with the 1994–1995 suspension, regular policing has little connection with the suspension's rationale. "The lack of [constitutional] guarantees certainly does make our work a lot easier," says one PM inspector at the time regarding the sharp increase in raids and detentions in Caracas barrios; whereas normally a warrant for searches must be served three days in advance, with a suspension "we can enter homes without order ... and hold people without all the regular paperwork. It cuts down on the bureaucracy. The courts can process cases more directly."[81]

Drug laws—most of which have been enacted during the democratic era—further entrench such patterns and make the possibility of reform more remote. Although house searches remain illegal without a judge's order, drug laws have allowed wide discretion in conducting them (CEC, article 75-F). The 1984 Organic Law of Substances, Narcotics, and Psychotropic Drugs does not allow bail under any circumstances (articles 62 and 168) and keeps the procedure secret except from the defense and participating authorities (article 98). The law does specify treatment and rehabilitation for drug abusers (articles 50 and 106), but a lack of such programs makes these provisions moot. Meanwhile, the law has generated an increase in raids of private homes without a judge's order, even though such action does not effectively address the causes of drug-related crimes.

High levels of police impunity also demonstrate the Venezuelan police's power. Between 300 and 1,000 people were killed in unresolved circumstances during the *Caracazo* (the mass riots of 1989 protesting austerity measures), for example, but only three sentences were passed down against the many security and police officials accused of killings and other rights abuses. Two of those sentences were later absolved, and the third ended with the officer's release for good behavior. There were long delays in exhuming the mass graves of people killed in the riots, partly due to the PTJ's unauthorized channeling of reports to military courts. Such impunity can be seen even more clearly with *nudo hecho*, about two-thirds of which were against police officers. After the denunciation is made, a first-instance judge must decide within ten days if there is sufficient evidence for trial. But, as discussed in Chapter 2, this deadline is rarely met unless the judge has a *fiscal* breathing down his neck, causing *nudo hechos* to take up to six years or to never be completed. The resulting conviction rate of police officers is between 6 and 19 percent; in similar murder charges, police officials receive an average sentence five-and-a-half years shorter than convicted civilians.[82] The *fiscal general* and other officials have criticized the PTJ, DISIP, and the GN for holding up *nudo hechos* and blamed the PTJ's ascription to the executive branch for biasing them.

These judicial distortions, combined with the police's inability to stem crime, led to opportunity for reform after the 1993 election loosened the AD-COPEI hold on the executive and legislative branches. Previously, the government blocked proposals to transfer responsibility over *nudo hechos* from first-instance judges to a *Defensoría* and to curb the PTJ's roles in the penal process. But growing pressure from NGOs, international agencies, and new parties eventually pushed Congress to include police reform in the new penal process code. Instead of focusing on police coordination, as in the 1977–1990 bills, the new code clarifies the roles of the judiciary and the police in criminal investigations. As with Argentina's 1994 constitutional reform, a new balance of political forces and the excesses of judicial disarray opened up efforts to reseparate police power from the police's actions.

But such late reforms may not be able to make up for damages in police-society relations. In the absence of restructuring and oversight after 1958, practices from the authoritarian era combined with new police authority. Political protests and violence did not dissipate after the fall of Pérez Jiménez, for example, and neither did police repression to crush them. Up until the 1970s, "primitive" tactics were used against protests, and incidents of both torture and disappearances were common. The first Caldera government, in fact, registered more cases of student deaths at the hands of the military police than during any other administration since Gómez (Rico 1985: 115). Ten years into the democratic regime, "political violence, persecution, repression, and torture are daily occurrences. ... The primitiveness of Gómez's violence is being updated technologically, [and] torture modernized" (Araujo 1968: 250).

Violent crime, however, continued its steady increase. The police were ineffective in reducing it because they were not held responsible by policymakers and because they became a criminal element itself. Many of the drugs and arms flooding to urban barrios stream in through police-run operations or through organized crime syndicates that buy off police officials. Especially antagonizing to *barrio* residents are constant police roundups, daily detentions "for investigation," and exorbitant bribes demanded by officers to release a suspect detained for drug possession. The concentration of such tactics in the poor barrios (home to nearly three-quarters of Caracas's residents) only increased along with violent crime and the political instability after the 1989 riots.

As in Argentina, public opinion on policing in Venezuela follows two contradictory currents: suspicion of the police and support of individual rights, on the one hand, and fear of crime and support for police crackdowns on the other. In one poll in Maracaibo, the country's second largest city, 91 percent of respondents did not "feel secure" with any of the police agencies, and 86 percent felt that police operations affect innocent people. In another survey, only 22.1 percent of respondents expressed confidence in the police while 89.2 percent were confident in private security (Hillman and Cardozo 1998). Still, 89 percent of the Maracaibo respondents feared being victims of crime, 60 percent favored more violence to combat crime, and an astonishing 47 percent favored police killing of delinquents (Gabaldón and Bettiol 1988). Such contradictions—simultaneously demonstrating a lack of respect for constitutional rights and a perception of runaway violence—are both a cause and effect of drifting government policy. Citizens may distrust police agencies yet support the harsh means they adopt.

Such patterns are fueled by police views, with many studies estimating that about 70 percent of police officers believe the public to be hostile to the police. Most officers come from the areas they patrol, and 56 percent live in the barrios (Gómez Grillo 1988); thus, they often share their neighbors' contradictory opinions about individual rights and public order. These attitudes are likely to be expressed through violence. In one study of the use of violence by police in Mérida state, police agents justified the use of violence by a person's behavior or attitude—such as "aggression"—in 83 percent of the cases, the need to have "control" in 45 percent, and punishment or maintenance of police image in 7 percent (Gabaldón 1996).

As in the judicial process, the "lack of a clearly defined conception regarding the duties and attributions of the police in the area of security" has further damaged police-society relations.[83] Vague legal definitions of "public order" not only make officials less sure of their role and enhance the discretion of individual officials but also add to public insecurity. Article 282 of the old penal code allowed agents to use arms in cases of legitimate defense and of defense of the public order but did not define these conditions, except through article 66, which drew the line of police action at "not trespassing the limits imposed by the law." The 1990 Organic Police Law bill attempted to specify the bases of police action—such as stopping an occurring crime—but still did not define their limits. As in Argentina, the police and police lawyers filled this vacuum with assertions that torture and coercion are integral parts of police work.

The distance between the police and society also comes from the extreme economic and geographic fragmentation of urban Latin America. As with the waves of immigration to Argentina at the turn of the century, the 1920s oil boom in Venezuela sparked massive urbanization, immigration, unionization, and growing adherence to leftist ideologies. Urban growth outstripped planning, resulting in chaotic and insecure urban environments in which most of the poor are concentrated in large zones surrounding, but economically marginalized from, the central downtown area. This physical division then created facile demarcation of "problem" areas, with the endless ring of barrios becoming a mix of heavily policed areas or "free territory for organized crime."[84]

The government has been trying to mend police-society relations through presentations at Junta de Vecino meetings and "cooperative" programs such as UNIPROVE (Unidad de Protección Vecinal) of 1992, which established a network of police kiosks in the poor areas of Caracas.[85] But many residents see such measures as only helping the police tighten their control. Even with good intentions, such measures will fail without neighborhood-controlled organizations, permanent participation in police matters through review boards, regular and secure opportunities to provide testimony, and trust in the judicial system. In other words, there needs to be a comprehensive change able to reverse existing patterns and take in the totality of police-society relations.

Reforms: the Law of Vagabonds and Crooks.   The two major police reforms in Venezuela's democratic era were only partly about the police. The decentralization law allows municipalities to create their own forces, among other things, and the penal process code refines the police's role in criminal investigation, among other provisions. A third major reform, however, more directly addressed the frictions between police power and the police's actions. In 1997, after decades of legal and political wrangling, the Venezuela Supreme Court ruled unconstitutional the Law of Vagabonds and Crooks, a key criminal law that underscored the police's power in daily law enforcement as well as the country's traditional approach to public order. A knockoff of a fascist law from Spain, the LVM was first enacted as a military-era statute on August 14, 1939, and was strengthened in 1943 and again in 1956.[86] The LVM allowed the "preventative" detention of persons who have not committed a crime but are deemed a "threat to society" or to themselves. The law's definition of these "vagabonds" was wide, ranging from individuals "who habitually and without just cause do not have a profession or licit business and thus constitute a threat to society" to individuals "who habitually walk the street ... fomenting idleness and other vices" (article 2).

As with Argentina's edicts, the impact of the LVM on the rule of law came from its focus on precriminal behavior. Although the penal law deals with the gravity of specific acts defined objectively and in a postcriminal state, the LVM focused on criminal potential decided in a highly subjective manner. By attempting to "correct" individuals in a "state of danger," the LVM turned an observation into a de facto crime. Given the wide police discretion and vague terms such as "habituality" and "morality," understandable resistance to arrest only added to the suspicion of a detainee being an actual "vagabond" or "crook."

As with many drug laws, furthermore, the LVM intended to be rehabilitative yet provided for little or no actual rehabilitation; as with the edicts in Argentina, its punishments were far less specific than under the penal law. There were eight possible punishments to be taken against those arrested under the LVM, including internment in a "work" or "agricultural colony" or in a "Work and Reeducation House" (article 4). These "corrective measures" often led to further abuse. An entire wing of the notoriously inhu-

mane El Dorado Prison in the country's remote south, for example, held
LVM detainees, many sent there without knowledge of the judges presiding
in their cases. After a person was charged under the LVM three or more
times, more severe punishments are allowed, such as three years of incarceration. Approximately 500 people were arrested each year under the law,
about 100 of them being held without trial at any given time. As with the
edicts, most of those detainees were from society's marginalized sectors:
prostitutes, the unemployed, immigrants, youths, and transvestites.[87]

Because the LVM was a "special" law, many argued that it should in
fact be exempted from regular penal law. After an LVM arrest, indeed, all
of the different "partial" decisions and officials involved in regular criminal
processes were compacted. Article 4 allowed "competent authorities" to
decide the punishment; the Justice Ministry decides the place of confinement and can prolong confinement if the "correction" of the prisoner has
not "been obtained" (article 12). Article 17 stipulated that the investigation
and first-instance decision is made by first-instance courts or by the regional PTJ. Although public defenders write a report on the detainees (article
22), it is the governor that officially sentences them, and after six months
the case moves to the Justice Ministry. Such control by executive officials
transgresses the CEC and judicial authorities, but it was this very control
that made the law so indispensable to its supporters. The role of the governor "of course violat[es] sacred constitutional rights, but allows for the
immediate way to deal with those who are considered scourges."[88]

Most legal scholars—from the Inter-American Court of Human Rights
to local lawyers—considered the LVM unconstitutional, but neither of the
first two petitions for nullity before the Supreme Court, in 1985 and 1988,
were heard by the court. The reason for the court's inaction was its position
that the law is to be interpreted and utilized at the discretion of state governors[89] and, as with constitutional suspensions, that the LVM is simply
regarded as "a problem of the Executive Branch."[90] Many even argue that
the LVM is in fact constitutional, citing constitutional article 70, which
allows for preventative laws, as well as the existence of preventative laws
on minors and on narcotics. "I asked for the nullity of the [LVM] because it
does not allow for the proper correction of anti-social behavior," asserts
José Fernando Nuñez, a lawyer who spearheaded the 1985 Supreme Court
petition for nullity and the 1990 Social Defense bill. "But, I repeat, such a
law is absolutely necessary" because it is "more advantageous and more
fruitful for a modern state ... than a penal law."[91]

In the political arena, a change or abrogation of the LVM was never
seriously considered. On the contrary, proposals to change the law focused
on correcting its weaknesses rather than questioning its basic premise.
There were three congressional bills to replace the law, in 1989, 1990, and

1994. Nuñez says that because the law contains no "mechanism to permit the correction" of potential delinquents, it does "not even fulfill its own basic purpose."[92] The intention of his reforms was to strengthen the LVM. Like the Supreme Court, however, Congress did not act on the proposals before it. One of these bills, the Bill of Citizen Security, was drafted originally by the MP but got mired in some of the same legal problems as the LVM. Although the bill called for elimination of "conceptual categories and discriminatory, degrading and anti-juridical adjectives," it referred continually to the need for "public order" but did propose concrete alternatives to the LVM acceptable to national and state executives (Ministerio Público 1990). The MP circulated the draft of the bill to several civil-society organizations but then submitted a revised bill that those groups did not see. As with Argentina's edicts, at stake for those involved was the executive's power over the rule of law and the continuation of a long-standing approach to public order.[93]

But controversy over the LVM never dissipated, particularly as citizens saw that police actions were not making a dent in violent crime. Then, in October 1997, a third petition of unconstitutionality against the LVM was introduced to the Supreme Court by the court's recently elected president, Cecilia Sosa Gómez, a long-standing LVM opponent. Ruling that the law violated prohibition of punishment for acts not defined as crimes and that its implementation by executive officials violated the right to a "natural judge," the tribunal declared it unconstitutional (Corte Suprema de Justicia 1997). The about-face was due not only to Sosa but also to apprehension over judicial disarray and to changing political dynamics that gave the high court a rare opportunity to take on a political question. The decrease in power of the two main parties and of the popularity of President Caldera gave some breathing room to the normally cautious, party-bound judges. The decision was met with great criticism, however, and has prompted attempts to resurrect the law in a different form—similar to the executive's reaction to the edict derogation in Argentina.

The 1998 election and the 1999 constitution, however, may erase these progressive steps. The constitution fortifies civil rights, but the power of law enforcement agencies may negate them. The new government champions society's underprivileged, for whom police abuse is a major grievance, but all societal sectors have repeatedly prioritized order over rights and supported strong policing—a position probably shared by President Chávez, a product of the military. The new government has not linked state corruption and inefficiency to the police's abuse of power, moreover, and seems to regard many legal mechanisms as less a victim than a prop of elite democracy. Even though crime has jumped 30 percent since Chávez took office, his government and allies have developed police reforms yet held back from criticizing police or reducing their power. Even if the president is willing to reign in police forces and abolish practices like those under the LVM, it will take many years of concerted effort to alter entrenched practices. The police's authority weathered the change from uncertainty in the 1950s, to stability in the 1970s, and back to instability in the 1990s. They are likely to survive the changes to a new constitutional order, even with radically different paths under it. A drift toward authoritarianism would certainly involve stepping up tough policing, and a decay of the state might also increase police agencies' strength; they would likely be among the few functioning institutions.

New restrictions on the courts, secondly, may destroy the judiciary's police power. Chávez has substituted an unresponsive executive with a dominant one and, from that position, has dealt with judicial disarray by remaking the judiciary altogether. After his election, the president attacked the corruption and patronage saturating the public administration and assumed basic powers of both the Congress and judiciary, such as to dismiss judges, which prompted the resignation of top jurists, including Sosa. He then saw through a new constitution that increases executive power by abolishing the senate, giving the executive authority to dissolve Congress under certain circumstances, lengthening the presidential term from five to six years, and allowing the president's immediate reelection. It also replaced the Supreme Court and liquidated the judicial council. A weakened judiciary and limited Congress dominated by Chávez supporters will now be less able or likely to challenge new laws or resist the derogation of old ones. The new penal process code and the LVM ruling, in particular, may be threatened by the fact that the rewriting of the constitution has opened up scrutiny of all laws from previous governments.

Conclusion

Frictions between police power and the police's actions have made their way through history into contemporary democracies. For Latin America, bringing police forces in line with the rule of law requires sorting out those frictions in ways that establish institutionalization against executive power, improve cooperation with the judiciary, and address the real needs of society. Once enacted, every type of police reform can support others. Improved disciplinary measures help sift out officers who do not cooperate with the judiciary, for example, and clearer public-order laws and better remuneration reduce corruption. As with other measures, however, these reforms will also need to be part of a larger process of democratization encompassing all institutions responsible for the rule of law. For the success of state reforms, particularly crucial is an independent and effective judiciary, which is the subject of Chapter 4.

Notes

1. Author interview, July 13, 2000.
2. *Ercolano c/Lanteri de Renshaw*, April 28, 1922 (Buenos Aires: *Jurisprudencia Argentina* 1922, vol. 136, p. 170). The broad approach was dominant in the United States until 1877. *Aron Rabionovich* (Buenos Aires: *Jurisprudencia Argentina* 1950, vol. 217, p. 469). Most Argentine scholars support the narrow interpretation, citing the dissenting opinion in *Renshaw*.
3. Many areas of law deal with the police. Disciplinary law delineates police responsibility; administrative law defines sanction authorities and processes; penal law regulates constitutional order and internal state security.
4. *Anglo c/Gobierno Nacional* (Buenos Aires: *Jurisprudencia Argentina* 1934, vol. 171, p. 366).
5. Argentine law distinguishes "torture" from "*apremios ilegales*" (illegal pressures), which is mistreatment less "severe" by law than torture. This distinction has confused prosecution of continuing practices such as *submarino seco* (dry submarine), in which a detainee's head is held in a plastic bag up to the point of asphyxiation.
6. Private security agencies are becoming increasingly prominent in Latin America. In Argentina, for example, private security officials outnumber state police officials, often have police or military backgrounds, and get paid up to 50 percent more than state police. Roberto Sausa, President, Seguridad Magnum, author interview, October 24, 1994. According to the Cámara Argentina de Empresas de Seguridad e Investigación and the Unión del Personal de Seguridad (*La Nación*, November 6, 1994, p. 3), as of 1994 there were approximately 90,000 private security officers, more than the combined total of the federal police and the police of Buenos Aires province.
7. Although not constitutionally guaranteed until 1994, habeas corpus already had been a part of Argentine jurisprudence and legal recourse.
8. PFA official who spoke on condition of anonymity, author interview, December 13, 1996.
9. *Edición Oficial* (Caracas: Editorial Bolívar, 1936), chapter I, section III, ordinal 3; chapter II, section II, article 66.
10. Article 1, *Ley el Servicio Nacional de Seguridad, Gaceta Oficial* No. 19.637, August 4, 1938.
11. Article 87 (75-H of the current CEC). *Ley de Reforma Parcial del Código de Enjuiciamiento Criminal, Código de Enjuiciamiento Criminal* (Caracas: Edición Oficial de la Imprenta Nacional, 1959). In July 1941, the executive created the Central Office of National Investigation.
12. Crimes reported to the PTJ (*Estadística Delictiva, Cuerpo Técnico de Policía Judicial*) rose from 42,565 in 1961 to 261,630 in 1996.
13. Police-judicial reforms intersect with state reforms in many areas. Regarding police discipline, for example, either regular (judicial) or special administrative courts (executive) try police officials charged with wrongdoing.
14. *El Defensor*, January 1999, p. 12. Of the 900 complaints received between October 1998 and March 1999, more than 50 percent were about excessive use of illegal preventative and arbitrary detentions. *El Defensor*, February-April 1999, p. 7.
15. Instituto Nacional de Estadística e Informática, Gobierno de Perú, available on the Internet at www.inei.gob.pe.
16. Jorge Bacqué, Supreme Court Magistrate (1985–1990), author interview, December 6, 1996.
17. A top PFA official who spoke on condition of anonymity, author interview,

December 13, 1996. Completion of elementary education is required for subofficials and at least three years of secondary education for officials.

18. PFA official speaking on condition of anonymity, author interview,
December 13, 1996.

19. Articles 114–121 detail the PFA's disciplinary structure but do not specify
the specific structures of discipline or of the possibilities of appeal.

20. Carlos Alberto Solá, Comisario, PFA, author interview, August 14,
1998.

21. Laura Taffetani, Bar Association of La Plata, author interview, November
16, 1994. She points to article 13 of the Organic Law of the Police, as well as the
Código de Faltas of the *Ley de Procedimiento* as a source of edicts.

22. Juan Scatolini, Director of the Human Rights Office, author interview,
December 10, 1996.

23. "More of a problem than the law is the attitudes of the police. They are for
repression, not prevention. This is part of the history of the police, of decades of the
same pattern," asserts the commission's president. Deputy Juan Carlos Lema,
author interview, December 1, 1994.

24. In *Jaime Andrés Font*, the court said that "the principle that there are no
absolute rights justifies reasonable limitations imposed by the authorities, such as
administrative resolutions dictated during the course of a strike with the objective
of controlling it" (Buenos Aires: *Jurisprudencia Argentina* 1962, vol. 254, p. 56).
See also *Héctor Luis Cuello* (Buenos Aires: *Jurisprudencia Argentina* 1963, vol.
255, p. 293); *Antonio Dri v. Nación Argentina* (Buenos Aires: *Jurisprudencia
Argentina* 1966, vol. 264, p. 94).

25. *Carlos Sarde e. Provincia de Mendoza* (Buenos Aires: *Jurisprudencia
Argentina* 1934, vol. 171, p. 79).

26. Sofía Tiscornia, Centro de Estudios Legales y Sociales, author interview,
September 27, 1994.

27. Those who do run thorough investigations often are subject to physical
threats and attacks. In the widely publicized case of a young man allegedly killed by
the police, which led to the first trial over a "disappearance" in the post-1983 era,
those running the investigation were subject to attack.

28. This according to the assessment of Mariano Ciafardini, Director of the
Office of Criminal Policy, author interview, October 18, 1994. The 1992 CPP in
some ways built upon the reform proposed under the Alfonsín administration.

29. Writer on judicial issues for a major national daily newspaper, author
interview, December 1, 1996.

30. The distinction remains between arrest, which requires a written order in
most circumstances, and detention to establish identity, which before Law
23.950/91 was subject to few regulations. But citing antidrug policy in 1994, the
Justice Ministry tired to negate Law 23.950, which was originally opposed by the
executive.

31. In this case, in which fourteen provincial police officers were arrested, the
police chief at the time, Pedro Klodczyk, said that he did not take more initiative to
investigate the case because the courts did not request it, although by law the police
are supposed to automatically exhaust the investigation.

32. Law 8031 (*Código de Faltas Policial*) contains many of the provincial
police's edicts. Law 8031 was established by a military regime and made the chief
of police a judge in the edict process.

33. Roberto Vicente Vasquez, Sebsecretario de Seguridad, Police of Buenos
Aires Province, author interview, August 19, 1998.

34. Ciro Annichiarico, provincial lawyer who defends detained youth, author interview, November 23, 1994.

35. "Examen a fondo en la Policía Bonaerense," *Clarin,* November 23, 1996, p. 16; "Retiros y falsas renuncias," *Página/12,* November 26, 1996, p. 15.

36. "Me voy a presentar a la Justicia, pero no ante ese juez," *Clarín,* October 4, 1990.

37. "Movilización en favor de un comisario," *Clarin,* July 19, 1991; "Duhalde propone como modelo a comisario Patti," *Clarin,* August 6, 1991.

38. "Crecen las cifras del delito en la provincia," *Clarín,* August 28, 1998, p. 43.

39. In 1998, charges against the provincial police went to the Inter-American Human Rights Commission. It involved a young man, Sergio Schiavini, killed during a police shootout with robbers who took Shiavini and others hostage in a cafeteria when the police arrived. The young man was killed by police during the ensuing battle, but the police were absolved of wrongdoing during an investigation and oral trial plagued with irregularities, including the accusation that the police and forensic experts made it look as if Shiavini had been killed by one of the robbers.

40. This new code transfers many police investigation functions to *fiscales* and judges, who, if they were unable to take on the investigation, would return it to the police. This makes the reform, in some opinions, a joke because neither judges nor *fiscales* have time for the extra work. Duhalde originally opposed the reform but was pushed into it by the police scandals. Leopoldo Schiffrin, Federal Criminal Appellate Court Judge, author interview, December 11, 1996.

41. Eduardo Oteiza, "Consecharás tempestades," *Clarín,* August 8, 1999.

42. Rico was on record saying that "it is necessary to kill [delinquents] in the street without any doubt and without having pity." "El carapintada por la boca muere," *Página/12,* March 10, 1998, p. 12.

43. "Quieren usar custodios privados para prevenir y reprimir delitos," *Clarín,* July 28, 1999, p. 38.

44. In addition, in February 1999, the provincial government formulated a plan to allow an increase from twenty-four to forty-eight hours the time that the police can hold someone detained for identification and to ease the ability of the police to carry out inspections without previous court authorization.

45. The provincial constitution's environmental protections include education and impact reports, whereas the national constitution simply provides citizens' rights to a clean environment, which may be enforced through *amparo*. New political rights included the approval of recall elections and plebiscites. Regarding civil rights, the constitution became the first one in Spanish-speaking America to prohibit discrimination based on sexual orientation.

46. In Buenos Aires province, Law 8031 (*Código de Faltas Policial*) contains many of the provincial police's edicts. Law 8031 was established by a military regime and made the chief of police a judge in the edict process. Among its edicts include one that says "all who do not show work or dependency may be subject to a checking of records." Ordinarily, edict detainees are kept in police-station jails.

47. This *bando* dictated that "all vagabonds and persons that do not live from work or office or position, must leave this city within three days and if this time span passes they will be...punished with four years of exile in the Malvinas Islands" (Policía Federal Argentina 1935: 7).

48. *Esio Bruno Cimadamore* (Buenos Aires: *Jurisprudencia Argentina* 1941, vol. 200, p. 161).

49. *Raúl Oscar Mouviel y Otros* (Buenos Aires: *Jurisprudencia Argentina* 1956, vol. 237, p. 636).

50. *Sumario instruido a Ricardo Bonevo, por violación de la ordenanza policial de Corredeores de Hoteles* (Buenos Aires: *Jurisprudencia Argentina* 1929, vol. 155, p. 178).

51. *Cuomo, Eduardo y otro, Fallos de la Corte Suprema de Justicia Jurisprudencia Argentina* (Buenos Aires: *Jurisprudencia Argentina* 1942, vol. 201, p. 73).

52. *La Ley,* 1987-A, p. 22; *La Ley* 1992-A, p. 412.

53. Because the police do not appeal the antiedict rulings of first-instance courts, however, there are very few rulings by appellate courts on the issue. But in February 1985, a federal court upheld a ruling of unconstitutionality by a first-instance court, and in August 1996, a criminal judge upheld an appeal against a "scandal" edict, declaring the police actions null for not guaranteeing the detainee rights such as choosing a lawyer and for interviewing him prior to the investigative declaration. *La Ley,* 1986-C, p. 240; *La Ley,* 1987-A, p. 501; *La Ley,* 1991-C, p. 74.

54. Officer Schwartz, author interview, November 22, 1994.

55. Article 155b, *Reglamento de Procedimientos Contravencionales.*

56. Edicts violate the Pact of San José de Costa Rica, an inter-American rights treaty to which Argentina is a signatory, and nearly every clause of constitutional article 18, which states that no citizen may be punished "without previous trial based on a law previously established, nor judged by special commissions, nor taken from judges designated by the law in the crimes involved. Nobody may be forced to make statements against themselves; nor arrested without a written order of a competent authority. A defense by trial of persons and their rights is inviolable." (One legitimate exception to these guarantees is with crimes caught *en flagrante delicto.*)

57. "Presiones que dan frutos," *La Nación,* September 8, 1996, p. 15.

58. Registro Nacional de Reincidencia y Estadísitica Criminal; "Se cuadruplicaron las detenciones por edictos," *La Nación,* September 8, 1996, p. 15.

59. Many argue that this prohibition is meant only for the president and not necessarily executive agencies such as the police (Bidart Campos 1963: 789).

60. Gaston Chillier, "Una fuente de corupción," *Página/12,* July 3, 1998.

61. Raúl Granillo Ocampo, "El Código incompleto," *Página/12,* March 17, 1998, p. 19.

62. The city government subsecretary stated that prostitution and other activity may not be crimes but "may be the precursor to crime." Gabriel Reches, "De la Rúa quiere que el Código de Convivencia sea más severo," *Clarín,* August 22, 1998. The new decree does prohibit the police from holding people for more than ten hours, the limit set by Law 23.950. One proposal, to establish officials to sanction persons found in a suspicious behavior, was supported by the national government but then rejected by Congress.

63. *Clarín,* March 4, 1999, p. 3.

64. Natanson, José, "Si no hay ley, que sea por decreto," *Página/12,* March 4, 1999, p. 3.

65. "Los policías ahora pueden disparar sin aviso previo," *Clarín,* August 6, 1999.

66. Decree No. 51 of April 29, 1959; *Gaceta Oficial,* No. 25.948, April 29, 1959.

67. *Reglamento Orgánico del Ministerio de Relaciones Interiores,* article 8, June 5, 1979.

68. See "Sistema de Drogas y Reciclaje de Químicos Eran las Funciones del Cuerpo Parapolicial," *El Nacional,* February 13, 1988, p. D-22. The minister said that *Manzopol* was dissolved in 1986.

69. Rafael Rivero M., "Cuánto y qué Gana un Policía," *El Diario de Caracas,* June 14, 1990, p. 20. In 1991, salaries were raised to an adequate wage (15,000 bolívars), and officials were given health coverage for hospitalization, surgery, and maternity. More than half of all police officials want better professional treatment and better discipline. C. T. Valdez, "Ser Policía: Una Vocación que Tiene Cara de Hambre," *El Diario de Caracas,* June 15, 1989, p. 20.

70. Excessive use of arms is also a problem among officers. The fifty-year-old Law of Arms and Explosives limits the use of arms to the "legitimate defense or in defense of the public order." The Law of Political Parties, Public Meetings, and Demonstrations encourages other methods, such as tear gas. Matías Camuñas, a director of the neighborhood association Justicia y Paz, has seen police distribution of arms to neighborhood gangs over the past twenty years; Camuñas, author interview, March 20, 1995.

71. Detectives and subinspectors receive training at the University Institute of Police Science. All PTJ personnel must be high school graduates; PM agents must have finished the ninth year of elementary education, an official at least five years of secondary education (Dirección de Coordinación Policial of the Ministry of Interior Relations).

72. José Vicente Rangel, "CAP y los Policías," *El Diario de Caracas,* June 12, 1989, p. 2.

73. Victor Amram Lazes, PTJ Commissioner, author interview, July 2, 1998.

74. Author interviews with PM and PTJ officers, July-August 1992, January-July 1995. Frictions in police-judiciary relations can be seen by judge's comments. Directors of the Federation of Associations of Judges of Venezuela agree that relations "are very bad" (author interviews, March 29, 1995), and another top judge adds that "if the police is run by a person ... who understands that the police is our instrument, fine. But if it is a person who believes that since they have guns ... that they are better than judges, that they are above us, then it's very serious." Mercedes Medina de Villarroel, President, Association of Judges of Caracas, author interview, March 29, 1995.

75. *Anteproyecto de Ley Orgánica de Policía,* 1986, p. 2. The Law of the Federal Police, which would coordinate activities of the GN, DISIP, and PTJ, was approved by Congress but left unsigned by President Caldera.

76. *Gaceta Oficial,* No. 35.317 of October 14, 1993; Decree No. 3,179; COPRE 1994: 112.

77. Saúl Ron Brasch, Superior Court Criminal Judge, author interview, March 22, 1995.

78. "La Ley Antidroga es una Patente de Corso de Jueces y Policías," *El Nacional,* September 9, 1988, p. 12.

79. "PTJ: Un Cuerpo que Vive Entre la Enfermedad y la Depuración," *El Diario de Caracas,* June 21, 1989, p. 18.

80. *Gaceta Oficial,* No. 148 Extraordínario, February 3, 1962, paragraph 1, article 72. CEC article 72 designates the "organs of the judicial police" as one of the penal process's five investigating authorities; article 74 designates five broad areas of officials as "organs of the judicial police."

81. Marco Hurtado, Inspector, Policía Metropolitana del Distrito Federal, author interview, March 15, 1995.

82. La Red de Apoyo por La Justicia y La Paz and PROVEA, *Informe Anual, 1995.* But Raquel Pointevien, an official in the MP's Human Rights Office, denies such charges of impunity, saying that officials and civilians are "subject to the exact same criminal justice system" after being formally accused of a crime; Pointevien, author interview, May 2, 1995. There were 3,310 *nudo hechos* in 1994. The highest

number was against state police: 1,310, followed by the PM (720), the GN (485); the PTJ (369); and DISIP (228) (Fiscalía General 1971: 13). Most *nudo hechos* are for an allegedly illegitimate use of arms.

83. Former police commissioner Rafael Briceño Muñoz, in *El Diario de Caracas,* June 4, 1989, p. 20.

84. "1,400 Barrios Constituyen Territorio Liberado para el Hampa," *El Nacional,* September 9, 1990, p. D-10.

85. Antonio Ledesma, Governor of the Federal Capital; Gonzalo Sánchez Delgado, Chief Inspector of Information and Inter-institutional Relations of the Metropolitan Police of Caracas; UNIPROVE staff; author interviews, August 1992.

86. These changes aimed "to eliminate certain procedures, facilitate punishment, eliminate appeal to judicial authorities, and give more latitude to executive officials. In a word, to eliminate 'all the procedural shackles' in its application." *La Esfera,* June 9, 1943, pp. 1, 8. A motion to eliminate the mobile colonies housing LVM detainees was rejected.

87. Raids by the PM on prostitutes on the street and homosexuals in bars are two examples of the LVM's societal dimension. The Movimiento Ambiente de Venezuela, the country's gay rights organization, sends letters regarding this practice to both the MP and the senate human rights commission but receives no response.

88. José Fernando Nuñez, author interview, April 25, 1995.

89. Hildegard Rondón de Sansó, Supreme Court Magistrate, author interview, June 9, 1995.

90. María Antioneta Acuñade V., President of the Association of Public Defenders, author interview, 1995.

91. José Fernando Nuñez, author interview, April 25, 1995.

92. Ibid.

93. Article 22 of the *Ley Orgánica de Policía Judicial*, by giving the PTJ part authority in the "vigilance and control of vagabonds (*vagos*) and crooks (*maleantes*)," adds to the executive's authority.

4

INDEPENDENT
JUDICIAL FUNCTIONING

"Mr. President, the opposition says that the judiciary is not independent."
"Well, the opposition doesn't understand. Before, the judiciary was like
 an old car—it ran poorly, was slow, and broke down in the middle of
 the road. Now, in contrast, the judiciary is like a sleek red Ferrari."
"It's faster?"
"No—it's mine, mine, and mine."
                              —Rudy and Bik, *Página/12*, September 19, 1999

A LACK OF JUDICIAL INDEPENDENCE is a long-standing criticism of
Latin American democracy. It is so long-standing, in fact, that its meaning
is easily taken for granted. Behind the stereotype of judges as political
chess pieces are the numerous daily practices in which the legal and political authority of courts is compromised. Focusing in on such practices, this
chapter argues that the low independence and efficiency of Latin American
judiciaries come from internal disarray and politicization by outside
actors—particularly the executive.

A necessary starting point for such an examination is the idea of judicial independence itself. The chapter's first section reformulates the meaning of "judicial independence," defined as an impartial and functioning
judiciary's ability to make binding rulings on how the law applies to the
state and the citizenry in cases presented to it. The second section then
looks at the history of Latin America's judiciaries, bringing out the long-
term interactions among actors, processes, and functions that have weakened and continue to weaken the courts. Bringing these two dimensions
together, the third section examines democracies' measures to strengthen
judicial independence and functioning and how executive power and internal chaos undermine them.

Judicial independence is part of most democratization as well as legal
studies, because a judiciary carries out functions necessary for a democratic

regime. An independent judiciary mediates grievances of citizens against citizens and citizens against the state, enforces the contracts that maintain an economy, resolves conflicts among state actors, decides the constitutionality of new laws, and formulates remedies to legal injustices. An independent judiciary is especially critical to a new democracy, as it can ameliorate new laws' uncertainties, biases, and inefficiencies (Hart 1961). And it carries out these functions not in "isolation from the democratic political process" (Nino 1992: 705) but through meaningful participation in it. An independent judiciary, in short, defines the actions and accountability of the state itself. Of course, the principle of checks and balances requires that the elected executive and legislative branches exercise some control over the unelected judges—such as through appointments and budgets—as judicial "independence" based on insularity could destabilize democracy. But in most countries that is not the problem. Instead, many laws are decreed or forced through a legislature by a powerful executive or ruling party, many state officials act outside the law, and courts do not receive adequate support.

Because of the judiciary's role, measures to increase its independence have been at the forefront of contemporary Latin American reform. Such measures fall into four main categories, each of which focuses on checking the executive's power over the courts or on bolstering the courts themselves. First, there are changes in procedures for nominating judges to loosen the executive and ruling party's grip over them, such as raising the congressional majority needed to nominate Supreme Court *magistrados* (justices). Second are improvements in training, education, and discipline—through measures such as new schools for training and judicial councils for discipline—to make judges and judicial personnel more effective. Third are measures to increase the transparency and speed of court processes, primarily through revisions of the penal codes. Lastly, there are new rules and agencies, like the judicial council, for managing judicial budgets and resources.

Like most other reforms, such measures are prompted by problems in the executive and judicial branches. Authoritarian pasts, societal and business demands for judicial services, damage to basic rights from judicial bureaucracy, and general disillusion with the government all generate demand for change. Although resulting measures are similar across the region, in countries like Argentina they stem more out of a push to check the executive's power and in countries like Venezuela mainly from efforts to make it more responsive.

Even when enacted, however, many such measures are ineffective because they do not get to the real sources of the judiciary's vulnerabilities, such as politics and money. New rights for defendants are negated by a lack of funding for public defenders, and new oral procedures will bring limited change without the training to wean courts from dependence on written material. Even entirely new norms and institutions might not bring the real administrative and political support that a judiciary needs day after day.[1] Reforms may also fail to confront many of the executive's influences on the judiciary. Augusto Pinochet's court appointments in Chile and Fujimori's dismissal of judges in Peru are clear influences, but more common is the ability to prevent issues from arising or to make the courts quietly acquiescent. In Honduras, for example, basic judicial reforms were blocked after the transition to democracy in the 1980s by members of the ruling Liberal Party as well as "business leaders and political king-makers who have profited from the system."[2] Latin American democracies are better at creating constitutions and laws than at deflecting threats to them, and without change in the routine actions of the executive and the judiciary—beyond the written law—even well-trained and disciplined judges can have a difficult time actually being independent and efficient.

Underlying the weakness of reform are oversimplifications and distortions of the concept of judicial independence. Because most studies and proposals focus on a single issue and use inadequate measurements, they tend to overlook the wide range of actors, structures, and functions involved. Only inclusion of all these components yields a full understanding of judicial independence by bringing in its political context, its daily obstacles, and the effectiveness of reform. After the first section of this chapter lays out this reconceptualization, the second section looks at its historical development; the final section analyzes how contemporary democracies try to redirect it.

The Judiciary and the Concept of Judicial Independence

Most studies of judicial independence focus on the two endpoints of the judicial process: the selection of judges, and judges' rulings. On the first point, executives in Latin America long have selected permanent, temporary, and auxiliary judges (and manipulated the selection procedures as well), based almost entirely on political interests. On the other end of the process is judges' "freedom to judge" unencumbered in their final rulings. As the culmination of the judicial process, in fact, a judge's ruling provides the clearest "proof" of independence because that is when effects of any influence would most clearly emerge.

Many studies thus use selection or rulings to "measure" judicial independence. One study of the Mexico Supreme Court concludes that it "operates with a certain degree of independence with respect to the executive power, sometimes exercising a controlling action over the President" but nevertheless "generally follow[ing] executive policy" (González-Casanova 1965: 23–24). But this approach largely overlooks actors' interests and specific judicial procedures. It does not, for example, account for "the importance of the challenged acts or laws to the Executive," which may lose interest in them after "typical litigation delays."[3] Because of that wider political and procedural context, it is less productive to try to measure independence than to explore how it is affected by actors, institutions, and functions. Rulings may be a judiciary's main product, but they are a product of many influences and decisions, ranging from executive policy to investigatory biases, which change along with a country's society, economy, and politics. Independent judicial functioning is a moving target. It is about knowing who can influence the judiciary and how and when they do so.

Although structure differs from country to country, most Latin American judiciaries have a basic set of courts. As Table 4.1 shows, that structure is almost always comprised of the Supreme Court at the top, superior appellate courts (usually called Cámaras Federal de Apelaciones and Cortes de Casación) directly underneath, and a range of first-instance, municipal, and district courts at the bottom. They are supported by administrative agencies and, in some cases, complemented by institutionally separate constitutional courts at the Supreme Court level that rule on issues of constitutionality.[4] Together, these institutions have many functions: settling conflicts involving citizens and/or state agencies; deciding on the constitutionality or meaning of a law; investigating crimes; and administering internal matters like budgets and discipline. Usually, courts share these functions but specialize in some of them. The Supreme Court's role is primarily to rule on laws' constitutionality and, in most countries, to act as a court of third instance. The superior courts also have these two functions,

Table 4.1 Institutions, Functions, and Actors Affecting Independent Judicial Functioning

Institutions	Functions	Actors
• Supreme Court	• Constitutionality	• Executives
• Constitutional court	• Settling conflicts/grievances	• Political parties
• Superior courts	• Managing resources	• Public administrators
• First-Instance courts	• Investigation	• Legislators
• Specialized courts	• Discipline	• Economic interests
• Special courts (e.g., military)		• Citizens
• Administrative courts[a]		• Other (e.g., judges)
• Labor courts		
• Family/juvenile courts		
• Provincial courts		
• Municipal courts		
• Community justice forums		

Notes: a. In much of Latin America, separate administrative courts are used in charges against public administrators. In Uruguay, Colombia, Bolivia, Brazil, Cuba, Haiti, Honduras, Mexico, Nicaragua, Peru, Venezuela, and El Salvador, these courts are officially part of the judiciary. In Argentina, most provinces have separate administrative courts.

although their rulings can be appealed to the Supreme Court. First-instance courts concentrate almost exclusively on conflict settlement but in some countries share superior courts' authority to declare laws unconstitutional. When not in the hands of a judicial council, administrative matters are usually run by the Supreme Court.

In carrying out these functions, judicial structures involve a range of actors. They include presidents and executive officials such as cabinet ministers; public administrators; legislators and legislative staff; political parties; business interests; citizens with cases in the courts; judges; and judicial personnel, such as secretaries and bailiffs, who administer most first-instance courts. Certain individuals, of course, can represent two or more institutions, such as the legislature and a political party. But judicial independence signifies something different for each actor. For private enterprises it can mean sensitivity toward business needs, and for citizens it usually means fair and speedy hearings.

With this range of institutions and actors, most cases offer some opportunity to influence the judiciary's actions. In a Supreme Court case regarding privatization, this opportunity to influence the outcome will likely involve executive manipulation of *magistrados*, and in a first-instance case involving a local business it is more likely to come in the form of bribery from individuals. Sometimes independence is bombarded from all sides. In an early 1990s case in a provincial capital of Argentina on whether to grant a legal exemption to a private electric company, promises and threats were unloaded on the judge by local party officials, area residents, and the electric company itself.[5]

Such cases show that judicial independence involves not only the selection and the rulings of judges but also all the functions in between. Reforms like judicial councils, "career" judiciary laws, entry examinations, and public forums help break the executive's hold over selection and improve independence in the long run if supported by nonjudicial actors necessary for the courts' functioning. A legislature that does not provide an adequate judicial budget or clear laws, a police force that does not report all information to judges, and a government agency that disrespects rulings can thus be as much a threat to judicial independence as direct manipulation. Even with full institutional autonomy, a judicial system without such support will be vulnerable to corruption and inefficiency. All these components' interactions form the basis for identifying—and thus knowing how reform can alter—the ways in which independent judicial functioning is compromised in a modern state.

But when is judicial independence most often compromised? The points of vulnerability cluster around uses of the executive's power and the weaknesses of the judiciary's power. Whether they are repressive or unresponsive, first of all, executives get involved in most judicial functions by strong-arming nominations, dominating the legislature's lawmaking powers, meddling in court cases, ignoring unfavorable rulings, and implementing the law on their own. The first vulnerability is rooted in the personal and political background of judges, which executives have learned to exploit. Perhaps judges themselves do not know how independent they are "until circumstances arise that test their independence," but when handpicked by the executive or a certain political party, judges are aware of at least some issues on which they are unlikely to be independent.[6] In every democracy, the selection of judges is political because politicians choose candidates who best match their own views, sometimes to the degree that they must pass a "litmus test" on issues such as capital punishment. Nominees' general legal predisposition and positions are thus legitimate considerations and are usually balanced by professional requirements and public opinion. But in Latin America, that balance is thrown off by candidates' political and personal affiliations—which are dominant and sometimes exclusive criteria—and by the lack of citizen engagement in the process. Even when criteria are more neutral, political considerations may still be central, as with the importance of regional representation in Bolivia. Although usually honoring the letter of constitutional regulations, most executives are less interested in creating an effective judiciary than in making it loyal to the governing party. Emboldened by control over regular nominations, many executives go farther by altering the size of the Supreme Court, pressuring judges up for reappointment, or dissolving courts altogether.[7]

Even much of the influence of political parties and legislatures comes from their connection with the president. Most executives dominate the usually divided legislatures, complementing its pressures on their nomination and lawmaking authorities with political-party patronage and its administration of legislatively funded programs. In many countries, for example, election lists make legislators dependent on their parties for their seats and oblige them to follow the parties' legislative agenda. For those in the president's party, this means following the executive's agenda. In addition, many of the laws, regulations, and decrees governing Latin American countries are created wholly or partially through the use of presidential decree, decree-law, state-of-siege, and other "discretionary" powers that undercut legislative and judicial authority.[8] Below the constitution in Latin America's legal hierarchy are the organic laws (*leyes orgánicas*), which set out the outlines of a general area, such as the Supreme Court or the role of the police. After the organic laws, are, in order, regular laws, regulations, and decrees. Unlike the permanence of organic and regular laws, regulations and decrees are usually temporary, and common use of them by Latin American presidents has blurred the legal hierarchy, undermined permanent laws, and allowed the executive to circumvent lawmakers.

Such powers encourage executives to engage in subtle and not-so-subtle but perfectly legal interference in the judiciary. In Argentina, President

Menem told the Peronist mayor of Buenos Aires in 1996 to ignore a court's indictment against him for corruption. In Venezuela, a series of terminations by the president of high-level drug and racketeering cases in 1992 and 1993 included pardons that were unconstitutional because they were granted prior to any conviction.

But judicial independence ultimately depends as much on the strength of external influence as on the ability of the judiciary to withstand it. In much of the region, judicial independence is constantly being undermined by poor infrastructure, faulty internal coordination and planning, uneven institutional modernization, inadequate personnel policies, and contradictory or inconsistently applied codes. Judicial weaknesses also derive from four particular aspects of the law and legal history: implementation and application of criminal law, the lack of stare decisis, restraints on judicial review, and the use of special tribunals. In a new democracy, where the law is less settled and citizens' judicial needs are stronger than the judiciary's capabilities, the effects of these conditions are amplified.

First, problematic implementation and application of criminal law has weakened judicial defense of due process rights even alongside democracy's revived guarantees. In the civil law systems of continental Europe, criminal procedure is composed of two stages. The first is the investigation into a crime (*sumario*), based on written material; the second is a trial (*plenario*), which decides guilt and is largely based on the material of the first stage. In Spain during the colonial period, both stages were characterized by secrecy, lack of counsel, and torture of defendants. French reformers moderated these abuses by establishing rights for the accused, juries of citizens, and a separate MP to prosecute crimes. Because judges were seen as unaccountable to popular will, in addition, civil law countries began to limit judges' role to one in which they only apply the law rather than interpret or shape it. Such reforms were instituted in the 1808 *Code d'Instruction Criminelle,* known as the Napoleonic Code.

Latin American republics further reformed this two-part penal procedure by adding the individual rights detailed in the U.S. Constitution. This system was strong on paper, but there were long delays in actually codifying it. Argentina adopted commercial and civil codes in the 1860s, for example, but not its criminal code and code of criminal procedure until the late 1880s. Many of the codes' provisions reflected trends in European reform brought back by legal scholars (with the notable exception of oral trials), but without the modification needed for their application to Latin American conditions. And when new codes were put in place, necessary administrative support was rarely forthcoming. But most damaging was the advent of civil war and authoritarianism, during which governments tacked on many abusive laws that obviated due process guarantees.

Judges in contemporary Latin American democracies must therefore deal with legal codes weakened by a history of poor codification, inapplicable provisions, a lack of institutional support, and repressive laws. Like judges everywhere, those in Latin America make decisions based on the law's text and, where the text is unclear, need to interpret it. Because of vague or ambiguous language, for example, only judges can decide in each case the meaning of pivotal words such as cruel, reasonable, excessive, proper or equal. Because authoritarianism tends to freeze laws in place, a democracy's judges need to help the law catch up with social, economic, and other changes. But doing so makes them appear to be practicing a judicial activism antithetical to civil law's formalism.

Along with gaps in the law, this uncertainty over judges' roles allows influence from outside at different points in the judicial process. A judge's final decision is the product of a set of "partial decisions," such as interpreting laws, analyzing evidence, and, when the accused is found guilty, deciding on a penalty within the law's parameters. Each partial decision is a point of possible interference. A history of politically biased legislation and of jurisprudence can narrow a judge's realm of interpretation from the start, and material evidence may be withheld or manipulated by state actors like the police. When a case triggers political pressure by interested officials, such effects on partial decisions can result in a biased ruling. Since judges need to be consistent in all these partial decisions so that they follow logically from one to the next, for example, a politician's pretrial public statement of her "interest" in seeing "justice" done with an innocent verdict in a corruption trial might color judges' view of evidence, reports, and testimony. In Venezuela's 1988 *El Amparo* case, in which members of the security forces were accused of killing fourteen fishermen on the Colombian border, political pressure led the courts to indefinitely delay the case and return it to the military courts, based on earlier biased decisions, despite the MP's assertion of serious irregularities in the judicial process.

A second, related influence on judicial independence is stare decisis, often one of the biggest distinctions between common law and civil law. In civil law systems, most rulings apply only to the case at hand. Gradual changes in a law through a series of rulings may be considered "judge-made law" and an unconstitutional usurpation of legislative authority. The wider interpretive leeway of common law courts, combined with the binding nature of previous decisions, allows for jurisprudence to keep up with changing circumstances. The best way to establish such a pattern is through specific rules to allow jurisprudence to change the law, but such rules are rare in Latin America. Article 148 of the Mexico Constitution, for example, dictates that if the Mexico Supreme Court rules in a series of five consistent and consecutive decisions on a particular constitutional question—or if one of its four chambers does so by a certain majority vote—then that decision becomes binding on all federal and state courts. Other countries have had such provisions, but with much less effect. Article 95 of the 1949 Argentina Constitution stated that Supreme Court decisions on cases arriving through extraordinary appellate channels or for review would create binding precedent on all courts. Because of the frequent changes in government after 1949, however, article 95 was given little chance to be put into effect, and the current constitution contains no such provision.

Restraints on judicial review—the power to review laws' constitutionality—may also undermine judicial independence. Most countries' courts have authority "to declare the total or partial nullity of national laws and the rest of the acts of legislative bodies" as well as of "regulations and other acts of the National Executive, when they are violating the Constitution."[9] In the Argentina Constitution, any court may find all or part of a law or decree unconstitutional and inapplicable to the case at hand. But whether from a regular or constitutional court, declarations of unconstitutionality often have been resisted by the executive and legislature as an intrusion on their powers. And even when the government agrees to derogate or replace an old law, new norms need to gain legal footing through application by the state. Courts may thus have to rule repeatedly on the same issue, which can cause inconsistency. Even when democratic constitutions restore judicial review, therefore, it usually remains stronger in name than in practice.

A particularly tricky challenge to judicial review power comes from "political questions" in court cases deemed not to "present a justiciable controversy" (Bickel 1986: 184) and therefore more appropriate for political authorities such as the executive. Politics is vigilantly separated from principle, with elected officials the guardian of the former and the judiciary of the latter. This approach is applied whenever the court feels a "lack of capacity" created by "the strangeness of the issue and its intractability to principled resolutions; ... the sheer momentousness of it, which tends to unbalance judicial judgement; ... the anxiety, not so much that the judicial judgement will be ignored, as that perhaps it should but will not be; [and] the inner vulnerability, the self-doubt of an institution which is electorally irresponsible" (Dworkin 1985: 184). Amid unsettled laws and politics, judiciaries in new democracies have a greater share of such "intractable" and "momentous" cases, especially because "executive pressure tends to increase in direct proportion to the political importance of" a case (Moreno 1943: 377). Many questions certainly are political, but executives often go out of their way to define them as such, citing civil law's long-standing concern that an unrestrained judiciary will tread on legislative and executive turf. In its 1960 *Sofia* decision, for example, the Argentina Supreme Court used a broad interpretation of the political-questions doctrine to uphold a ban of a public meeting without questioning either the government's state of siege or its sole justification for the ban that the meeting's organizers were radical leftists.[10] Although possessing the power of judicial review, the Argentina Supreme Court "has defined as political any issue that might lead to a major conflict with the executive branch—a conflict that all Justices realize they would certainly lose" (Snow 1979: 123). Although interpretation as a political question in itself does not prove a lack of independence, it may do so when involving issues clearly within the judiciary's realm.

Threats to judicial independence are also posed by the executive's power to create new or special courts and to appoint judicial "auxiliaries."[11] Special tribunals have been a part of Latin American judiciaries ever since colonial administrations began using them for matters such as mining and taxation. Although Latin American republics usually prohibited "exceptional" tribunals after gaining independence, they have nevertheless been unable to resist establishing them.[12] Colombia, Peru, and Bolivia, for example, have "faceless" or other special courts for narco-trafficking and terrorism.[13] In creating its drug courts under Law 1008 (see Chapter 3), Bolivia got around the constitutional prohibition of "special" courts by calling them "specialized." Some specialized permanent courts, such as juvenile courts, can speed up the judicial process and better handle technical questions. But especially if they established ad hoc, they weaken the independence of the judiciary by creating a parallel structure without many of the regular channels of internal accountability and management, as well as by assuming that it cannot handle such problems. The ensuing complications can be seen in many kinds of special courts.[14] Venezuela established its Tribunales Superiores de Salvaguarda del Patrimonio Público (TSS, Public Patrimony Courts) in 1982 to handle high-level embezzlement and corruption, with wide-ranging powers to investigate and punish corruption. The TSS courts have second-instance jurisdiction over most corruption charges and serve as trial courts on charges of corruption by high-level officials. But these courts were not given enough resources and as a result have passed down very few sentences.[15] The regular courts, meanwhile, found themselves restricted from acting on most corruption cases.

Among special courts, the military courts enjoy the most power and the least controversy. Existing in every country and rooted in colonial *fueros*— separate charters of laws and legal functions granted by the government to settler institutions such as the Church—these courts reduce judicial independence by blurring the line between military and civilian justice. In many countries, the law exempts military personnel from civilian courts, and the government allows expansion of military courts over civilians.[16] In Argentina, the use of military courts and the military's control of civilian courts by the 1976–1983 dictatorship led to the drastic curtailment of military justice after 1983. In Venezuela, however, military courts had been moving in on the civilian judiciary since the early 1980s. The 1967 Code of

Military Justice (CJM) traditionally covered only those matters involving personnel or occurring in areas of military control, but that jurisdiction subsequently expanded over civilians in many cases. The Security and Defense Law gives the military jurisdiction over crimes around any zone considered "necessary" for national security and defense, such as basic industries and bodies of water (CJM, article 15), while the 1984 Drug Law placed several large regions, such as the Colombian border area, under military authority.[17] The use of the armed forces to quell violent protests has expanded military justice in urban areas as well, with numerous civilians imprisoned for "altering the domestic peace" cited in the vague "military rebellion" clauses.[18] Leaders of political movements have been detained under "extraordinary" military measures, presidential motions have exonerated soldiers accused or convicted of offenses such as murder, and the armed forces retain the power to try civilians involved in crimes of a "military" nature.

Even though the civilian and military legal systems are separate in Venezuela, their competence over cases is not. The Venezuela Supreme Court can choose between a federal military and a federal ordinary judge when there is a dispute over jurisdiction and can place it under military law by citing the relevant CJM provision. It has been granting cases to the military on a stepped-up basis, particularly since the Supreme Court's 1978 ruling that the military courts could hear cases involving civilians accused of fraud on military bases.[19] Civilian judges handling cases affecting Venezuela's military, meanwhile, often have to contend with more than just the cases themselves. The Venezuelan military interfered with one penal judge on eighteen different occasions and has "requested" investigations into judges who dissented from the release of military officials charged with corruption. Such incursions weaken the authority and independence of civilian courts and add to executive power over the judiciary because the military is under the president's command.[20]

Most of the influences on judicial independence, in sum, come through executive power and judicial disarray. Pressure from the military, political parties, business, and other powers often originate in or are linked to the executive and its agencies. And that pressure usually works because the judiciary is tangled up in its own corruption, careerism, and legal confusion.

The Judiciary's History in Latin America

In the past, the level of independent judicial functioning has been determined primarily by the type of regime in power. A judiciary acting independently but closely affiliated with the political elite is common in a stable authoritarian regime, as in late-nineteenth-century Germany and

Francisco Franco's Spain, because it lends legal legitimacy and carries out needed functions. Political instability and regime change, in contrast, diminish judicial independence by opening up opportunities to replace judges, alter court structure, and derogate laws.[21] Because authoritarianism and instability have been the historical rule in Latin America, judicial independence has been the exception.

Courts' vulnerability goes as far back as courts themselves. In the Roman Empire—a foundation for continental European and Latin American law—judicial rulings were not mandates or orders with the force of law, only opinions. In the Middle Ages, nonjudicial specialists memorized the law and decided legal norms, with most disputes settled between the parties themselves. When urbanization and economic development began to require the unification and centralization of authority, the "source" of law continued to be the monarchs. Castile's 1347 Ordinance of Alcalá, for example, said that while courts carry out the law, "to the King belongs, and has the power to makes *fueros* and laws, and to interpret, declare, and amend them."[22] Most Iberian state courts, in addition, were based on Catholic Church tenets. In 1612, Iberia's High Commission, which was an administrative court established for the government by the Church, began to incorporate temporal matters and secular trials.

But in some common law countries during this period, the role of judges as the king's servants started to clash with the law's evolving role in limiting royal authority. In 1612, judges challenged the king of England's control over judicial decisions with the argument that legal matters require a background and knowledge that the king lacked. Although the challenge failed, it eventually led to the Act of Settlement of 1701, which allowed judges to continue in their positions as long as they maintain good conduct. Although such developments allowed common law judges to become increasingly separate from the executive, as discussed in the beginning of this chapter, their counterparts in countries such as Castile remained little more than functionaries.

This pattern continued in the Spanish colonies, where the judicial system operated on a largely ad hoc basis, with three general spheres of authority. The first sphere, formed directly by the monarch when needed, was composed of *audiencias* (with the highest courts), *intendencias* (administrative agencies), *corregimientos* (committees), and ecclesiastical agencies in charge of resolving certain issues. Appeals could usually be made against an *audiencia*'s ruling to the Consejo de Indias, the central authority of the colonies, or sometimes even to the monarch himself. The second sphere was made up of *alcaldes de crimen* (criminal judges), *jueces capitulares* (who oversaw regular criminal and civil judicial affairs), and special magistrates responsible for Indians, water rights, and other issues. The third sphere consisted of *audiencia*-appointed magistrates to oversee particular areas of legislation, such as inheritance or property. Because each sphere was made up of officials who also had executive, administrative, and legislative responsibilities, the judiciary did not become a distinct, non-political institution.

Spain's efforts to control colonial life from afar also confused the region's legal framework, with the Consejo de Indias attempting to run everything "from high-up policies to detailed geographic information" (Malagón Barceló 1966: 86). Although colonial law was officially given preference over Castilian law, "in practice it only applied to very specific material" and "covered a small zone of judicial life" (Bravo Lira 1989: 9). Because of this limited applicability, informal and unwritten modifications of law became necessary and common. Disregard for formal law was also caused by colonial demographics. With only 3–5 percent of inhabitants living in the cities, the huge distances between settlements made uniform application of law impossible and rendered state authority "inversely proportional to the distance from" regional capitals (Editorial Nacional 1956: 418). In rural areas, landowners, miners, and businessmen utilized their de facto judicial authority to make rules, block access to the courts, and manipulate judges. Many judges were relatives of landowners, whose haciendas were the sites of many jails. Many judicial decisions went unenforced, and even colonial officials used laws "selectively and astutely, to further their purposes. This allowed for disregard of the law without implying disloyalty to the crown" (Crahan 1982: 28).

Meanwhile, many judicial functions were given to other institutions, particularly the Church, which "served as a political and strategic instrument [of Iberian colonialism] to secure and advance positions in zones away from the big power centers" (Editorial Nacional 1956: 397). Church officials had great influence not only because of the extensive land holdings the Church acquired through these and other settlements but also because of the large number of religious authorities with administrative and political powers. Many viceroys came from religious orders, and Church missions got the lion's share of *fueros*, allowing them to develop their own political and legal bases. Although many Church officials promoted Indians' well-being, the colonies' economic and social structures played down individual rights. Fervor to Christianize the New World and dependence on cheap Indian labor encouraged the view that "inequalities in terms of property, status, and accomplishments were considered the result of imperfect human nature" (Crahan 1982: 27)—and institutionalized such views into law.

As in most areas of government, nepotism and clientelism pervaded the *audiencias* and other judicial structures. A 1607 meeting of the Consejo de Indias even identified the Consejo itself as a source of the problem, saying that its members appoint relatives whose "authority is powerful enough to tie the hands of judges of inferior courts."[23] *Alcaldes* and chief magistrates, for example, were put in charge of extracting economic resources from their respective jurisdictions. Although legally prohibited, such activity became so frequent that it practically constituted a form of customary law, which is made up of unlegislated practices that are so common that they merge into a legal system over time. As the fortunes of the Crown declined in the seventeenth century, public offices were put up for sale, including, in 1687, most of those in the judicial system. The first sale of an *alcaldía de crimen* garnered 17,000 pesos, and by 1749 it got 47,500. By the time they dwindled out in 1750, these fire sales had filled the judiciary with corrupt and incompetent officials. Professionalism did advance in subsequent years, but not enough to make up for past practices.

The judiciaries of the empire's successor states, as a result, were born with malfunctioning institutions, nonfunctioning laws, bad reputations, and uncertain futures. It wasn't until the 1850s that stable constitutional rule gave judges a veneer of independence and influence amid a lack of challenge to the dominant conservative parties. Judges helped codify laws, uphold government policy, and interpret constitutions at a time of state growth and economic expansion.

This limited but comfortable role came to an end at the turn of the twentieth century, when violently competing political forces exposed judiciaries' inherent weakness and whipsawed them between radically different uses of the law. As new social and political movements upturned settled notions of power, judges were left "without a model of the country, without political identity, without ideology," and in the process they became "disposable, technocratic, limited to formal solutions, evasive of real problems, as a tactic of survival amid a growing and threatening instability" (Zaffaroni 1994: 271). Courts responded to escalating conflict with an accommodation that undermined their independence but maintained a semblance of continuity. They did this by writing in vague language, diluting the ideas of "rights," growing closer to political parties, and making occasional antigovernment rulings that served less to question unconstitutional policies than to legitimize them. But when the turmoil culminated in military takeovers in most countries, the courts were forced to take a stand.

Venezuela

After Gran Colombia's 1830 breakup, Venezuela inherited a Supreme Court with five members, appointed through a process in which Congress would select one of the three candidates presented by the president. But the subsequent years of civil strife and weak central government did not allow the Supreme Court to play any significant role. The destructive Federal Wars from 1859 to 1863 finally overcame caudillo conflict with a weak federal structure, and the 1864 constitution replaced the Supreme Court with the High Federal Court (Alta Corte Federal), composed of five judges elected by Congress from a list of names submitted by the state legislatures. Although this constitution gave each state the same civil and criminal laws, it made the courts of each state fully independent with exclusive jurisdiction over all cases submitted to them. The Alta Corte had little impact, as a result, despite Congress's 1876 *Ley de Casación* that established appeals principles to the tribunal. The Guzmán constitution of 1881 finally created a Corte de Casación, which, though limited by the federal structure, could hear appeals (*casación*) from the states.

As the central government solidified its control at the turn of the century, the 1904 constitution combined these two courts into the single Corte Federal y de Casación, and the many constitutions of the Gómez regime (1908–1935) left the judiciary decentralized.[24] Anti-Gómez protest, increased labor organizing in the late 1920s, and AD's mass organizing in the 1930s all helped push the post-Gómez governments to liberalize. The 1945–1948 *Trienio* held to the country's first democratic presidential election, but its policy of filling the courts with its allies reflected both a lack of organized civilian opposition and a desire to build the foundation for a controlled democracy. The 1945 constitution "nationalized" the judiciary, ending Venezuelan states' judicial power by reserving for the federal government the authority over the administration of justice throughout the country. The 1947 constitution reestablished the Supreme Court, and the 1948 National Organic Law of the Judiciary replaced all of the states' organic laws on their respective judicial branches.

The 1948–1958 military regime that succeeded the *Trienio* continued the process of centralization by creating the Ministry of Justice and expanding the state in general.[25] Nearly all judges and judicial officials at the time were loyal to the military and its political program. With its power to hire and fire anyone in the judicial branch, the Justice Ministry made sure it did so.

Argentina

From independence until 1853, Argentina was convulsed in a struggle between Buenos Aires province and the rest of the country, relieved by occasional cease-fires and periods of enforced calm during the Rosas regime. Recognizing the need for a functioning judiciary, the governor of Buenos Aires called for a grand "General Plan of Judicial Organization" in 1829. Citing the judiciary's slowness, inapplicability, and subservience to the executive, the French jurist contracted to draw up the plan recommended a complete overhaul as "the only way to prevent a complete disaster" (Binder 1993: 17). But when the plans were finalized, the government was unable to muster up the financial and political resources needed to implement them.

Although the 1853 Argentine constitution finally established a unified state, it addressed judicial issues only tangentially. Most of the country's legal codes were established in the following decades as part of the federal government's expansion, with the era's scant jurisprudence centered on supporting federal power and preventing internal rebellion. In Buenos Aires province, though, court support for de facto executives began to take shape. In 1865, the high court ruled, regarding a questionable seizure of power, that "the Governor of Buenos Aires and Commander of its army was the competent authority" who "exercises provisionally all the national powers … with the right of the victorious revolution and granted by all the peoples and in virtue of the serious obligations that the victory imposed upon him."[26]

But the high court's greatest uncertainty and inconsistency regarded its own authority. In 1865, it declared unconstitutional an executive decree giving judicial powers to a military official and declared that each government branch is "sovereign and exclusive in its own sphere."[27] But in the *Montana* case of 1870, it said that the judiciary had no jurisdiction over a man detained for assassinating Justo José de Urquiza. At the turn of the century, more damagingly, the Supreme Court did not challenge many of the constitutionally questionable laws being enacted at the time as a response to the rising tide of labor unrest and leftist agitation. The 1902 "residence law" (Law 4144) gave the executive the authority to expel or permit the entry of any foreigner without judicial recourse, for example, but despite open criticism from some constitutionalists, the court took no action. In 1903, when the government established internal exile that could only be reversed by executive commutation, again the high court did nothing. In addition to implicitly supporting the 1910 Social Defense Law and justifying anti-immigrant restrictions,[28] the high court also became more restrictive of habeas corpus, denying it in favor of police powers.[29]

Reflecting the executive's dominance, however, the judiciary did become more supportive of civil rights when power shifted toward the Radical Party, which held the presidency between 1916 and 1930. The Radicals helped push through landmark reforms such as the 1912 Sáenz Peña Law establishing the secret ballot and universal suffrage for adult men. The Supreme Court—which hears all cases brought before it, either in original or appellate jurisdiction—generally supported these changes. A 1928 decision, for example, held up a government-supported interpretation of constitutional article 19 that constructed a broad realm of personal sovereignty out of government reach.

In the 1930s, however, the judiciary was on its own as the parallel tracks of liberalism and repression running through Latin American history crossed over on the constitution. As the primary source of law and the ultimate check on power, a constitution is the last stand of conflict among those claiming to be the legitimate defenders of the national interest. Although Latin America's constitutions began to take root during the nineteenth century, the turmoil of the twentieth century turned them into battlefields. De facto governments dismissed them as a luxury or a "suicide pact" to be set aside by firm leadership in times of crisis, and elected governments often reassembled them to fit their own interests. A constitution is most useful during crises and instability, of course, as it provides continuity and written guidance. But in many countries the leaders emptied the constitution of these benefits, reducing it to just another blunt political instrument. So when Latin America's modern democracies turned to constitutions as a basis of stable rule, they inherited the manipulation and suspicion surrounding them. The most dangerous extreme of that legacy is suspension of or questionable changes to the constitution itself. Because the primary task of any democratic judiciary is to defend the constitution, its response to such action most clearly demonstrates its level of independence.

When constitutional reform is about fortifying institutions and processes to defend basic guarantees, then it builds a rule of law. In most countries, such as Argentina, such changes have been a way to affirm democracy after a history without it. But when suspension is borne out of frustration and when reform tries to redefine instead of refine democracy, then constitutional alterations may imperil the rule of law. In a growing number of countries, Venezuela most conspicuously, such changes are more a criticism than an affirmation of the existing democratic regime. By attacking the institutions of such a regime instead of the processes eroding it, this approach usually misses the real sources of weakness.

In Argentina, chronic suspensions of the constitution came through seizures of power by the military—legitimized, with very few exceptions, by the country's Supreme Court. Despite removal of sitting judges by each incoming government, which robbed the high court of having a single composition for more than four years, this legitimization continued from the first coup in 1930 to the latest, in 1976. The 1930 ouster of elected President Yrigoyen was headed by General José F. Uriburu and supported by a loose but wide coalition of Conservatives, right-wing nationalists, and a few left-wing parties. Mindful of its obligations but rejecting a renunciation in protest, the high court's reaction appeared measured and reasonable. It recognized the new regime's de facto power but stated that is would reestablish such guarantees that were violated. Specifically, on September 10, 1930, the Supreme Court declared:

That this government is in possession of the military and police forces necessary to ensure peace and order in the nation, and consequently, to protect the life, liberty, and property of all persons and has, moreover, declared in public that it will uphold the supremacy of the constitution and of the basic laws of the country while it exercises power.

That the foregoing facts undoubtedly represent a de facto government as regards its nature and that the officials who now constitute it, or who may be appointed in the future, partake of said nature, with all the consequences derived from the doctrine of de facto governments with regard to the possibility of carrying out validly the necessary acts for accomplishing the objectives it seeks.

That this court has declared, with reference to de facto officials, that constitutional and international doctrine is uniform in the sense of considering their acts valid, whatever the deficiency of defect in their appointment or election, on the basis of public order and need and for the purpose of protecting the public....

That this notwithstanding, if, once the situation is normalized in the course of the activities of the de facto government, the officials constituting it should ignore personal or property guaranties or others safeguarded by the constitution, the court charged with enforcing compliance with such guaranties would restore them in the same manner and with the same effect as it would have done under a de jure executive branch.

This conclusion, mandatory under the organization of the judicial branch itself, is confirmed in this case by the declarations of the provisional government which on taking office has hastened to take an oath to comply with, and make others comply with, the constitution and the basic laws of the nation, a decision that entails the consequence that it is ready to lend the support of the force at its command to obtain compliance with judicial decisions.

That the provisional government that has just been formed...is, therefore, a de facto government, whose title cannot be successfully challenged judicially by individuals since it exercises administrative and political functions derived from its possession of power as the key to social order and safety. (Ciria 1974: 10–11)

This careful language did not respond to the court's limitations as much as it did to create them.[30] In placing the "forces" necessary for social peace and individual rights in the hands of the new government, first of all, the court minimized the possibility that the government itself could be a threat to both peace and rights. Consideration of the new regime's acts as "valid, whatever the deficiency or defect in their appointment or election," also downplayed connections between a "deficiency" in the regime's use of power and its respect for the constitution. Passively worded descriptions of the government as having "been formed" lent further legitimacy to the unconstitutional seizure of power, and the high court limited its own role by restricting judicial challenges to the junta.

The so-called Infamous Decade from 1930 to 1943 rolled right over the court's balancing act. The judiciary grew increasingly helpless in the face of government abuses, including widespread arrests, summary dismissal of judges who could not legally be removed without trial, repeal of laws such as the Sáenz Peña Law, an executive decree that gave itself final decision-making power to carry out capital punishment, and the annulment and control of elections. The court did not act against these actions and upheld existing restrictions, such as provisions of the 1902 Residence Law.[31] But after the June 1943 coup by the Group of United Officers (GOU), the Supreme Court began to regain its voice. Like many elite groups, it opposed the GOU's non-Conservative stances, such as expanding social rights, and began to hold the line against executive powers. Although the court recognized the de facto government, the rotating rulers' tentative hold on power allowed the court to reject the military rulers' power to legislate, create new courts, and arbitrarily transfer most judges.[32]

The junta's disunity led to the rise of General Juan Domingo Perón, who came to thoroughly dominate national politics. As under Yrigoyen and Uriburu, the high court adjusted accordingly. But only a year after Perón's election, the court's recent history came back to haunt it, as all but one of the court's members were impeached and tried by the Peronist-dominated Congress on charges, among others, of legitimizing the de facto regimes of 1930 and 1943, assuming legislative powers by denying application of labor legislation, denying benefits to fired workers, and applying inconsistent legal criteria to political prisoners. Replacing three charged *magistrados* with three who publicly declared allegiance with Peronism, the trial was technically legal, but its real purpose was to create a progovernment Supreme Court. Executive power over the judiciary increased in 1949, when a new constitution purged lower court judges and eliminated the guarantee of judicial immobility. This constitution also gave the president enhanced powers, such as to declare a "state of internal war."

The 1955 coup that overthrew Perón ushered in the so-called Liberation Revolution that included decrees for suspending and removing judges. The new Supreme Court proclaimed the new government legal and expressly accepted its promises to "carry out the revolutionary program for the re-establishment of the rule of law and the return of the country to an authentic democracy," all "in conformity with" the constitution.[33] As in 1930, the court ignored the fact that an unconstitutional seizure of power is unlikely to lead to constitutional rule and that the biggest danger to rights may now come from those entrusted to protect them. The court did sometimes defend its authority, as in its 1957 *Siri* decision to uphold the right of citizens to require judicial intervention when a state authority violates a constitutional guarantee.[34] But this latter ruling, like those in the early 1940s, was made when internal divisions and Peronist pressures had weakened the executive. Otherwise the court usually supported the government, as in its affirmation of Decree 4161, which prohibited the mention of the name "Perón" and any promotion of Peronism.

Radical Arturo Frondizi was elected president in February 1958 but rescinded his campaign promise to the Peronists to fire all the Supreme Court *magistrados*. Three left anyway, and with the new Court's backing the president and senate raised the court size to seven *magistrados* (although Frondizi wanted nine). The court legitimated actions taken by previous de facto regimes as long as they didn't conflict with those of de jure regimes, and it rejected the habeas corpus petitions of labor leaders arrested and placed in military courts under the executive's plan to handle internal disturbances. In the *Rodríguez* case, the court justified the use of force against those employing violence to attack state institutions, supporting its ruling with an obscure English court case regarding an Irish uprising.[35] But when a military faction arrested Frondizi and occupied the Congress on March 28, 1962, the court used its constitutional power to name the president of the senate, José María Guido, as head of state. The court stepped in simply to resolve the "unsettled situation of the Republic," insisting the political-questions doctrine proscribed it from addressing the actual causes of an "absence" of the president or vice-president, even when resulting from unconstitutional actions.

Arturo Illia, head of another Radical Party faction, won the 1963 elections and while in office generally respected the court, although the lower house of Congress blocked his attempt to raise the number of high court justices to ten. In June 1966, Illia was ousted in the so-called Argentine Revolution, a military takeover that dissolved Congress and the Supreme Court, prohibited political activity, and made no pretense of being "provisional." Although the government was validated by the high court *magistrados*, the junta still replaced them with handpicked choices on the grounds that it was "essential to have a Supreme Court whose members have sworn to respect" the government's norms.[36] The junta even demoted the constitution itself, bumping it to third place below the "Revolutionary Objectives" and the "Statute of the Argentine Revolution." It also issued a proliferation of executive decrees, most of which came to be considered full-fledged laws. Growing internal violence led to even harsher measures, such as the 1971 creation of federal penal courts for those accused of revolutionary activity.[37] The Supreme Court upheld these special courts, as well as most of the government's other measures, such as its self-appointed authority to seize publications without any legal accusations against them.

After Perón's return from exile and assumption of the presidency in 1973, the court declared the invalidity of laws made under de facto rule, but the government still pressured judges into retirement (Law 20.550). After Perón's death in 1974 and the military's overthrow of his widow and successor, Isabel Perón, in 1976, the country spent seven years under the military government of the *Proceso de Reorganización Nacional*

(*Proceso* hereafter). As in 1930, the Supreme Court recognized the new regime by citing the need to end the violent institutional crisis racking the country while also affirming constitutional rights. The result was a repetition of the 1930s: the regime removed the high court *magistrados* and began violating all basic constitutional rights through systemic use of torture, "disappearances," and other practices.[38]

As before, Supreme Court legitimization of the new government, its laws, and its actions left little maneuvering room, and the few decisions defending constitutional rights were more of a legitimization than a challenge. In *Pérez de Smith*, a habeas corpus petition on behalf of the disappeared, the court declared itself incompetent and asked the executive to carry out investigations to locate the disappeared individuals, but it later reversed itself.[39] The court accepted Law 21641, which subjected civilians to military tribunals, and also stated that "the measures adopted to assure the realization of the 'basic purposes and objectives of the Proceso'... cannot be considered either arbitrary or unreasonable" (Broisman 1990: 19). In a reversal of its 1928 decision on constitutional article 19, the court (along with provincial courts) upheld a series of laws severely restricting personal rights, including the prohibition and seizure of certain books. Only twice during the *Proceso* did the Supreme Court unequivocally defend constitutional rights. One case was the detention of newspaper editor Jacobo Timerman under Institutional Act 18, which allowed the executive to determine all arrest procedures. After winning two habeas corpus recourses, Timerman was released but forced out of the country. In the other case, the court overturned the arrest of lawyer Carlos Zamorano, who had defended political prisoners on the grounds of the arrests' lack of specificity. But instead of annulling the sentence, the court sent it back to the executive, which then justified it by Zamorano's alleged links with subversives, arguing that now "the connection between state policy and the detention" was concrete.[40] Although such decisions were contrary to the government's position, they did not question government policies per se.

Throughout history, the judiciaries of Argentina and other Latin American countries have found themselves cornered into various but always politicized positions: cooperation and irrelevance during oligarchic regimes, tenuous relations with de facto governments, and uncertainty during democracy. In nearly every context, the interactions of actors, institutions, and functions whittle away at independent judicial functioning. Up until recently, for example, the Argentina Supreme Court never recognized any claims of judges removed by the military. The judicial independence required of a consolidated democracy therefore means not only a prohibition of external influence in a judge's selection or rulings but also reforms that get to the heart of court processes. Even when judges act independently, they can remain subject to undue pressures and insufficient support. Because the judiciary derives its legitimacy from impartiality, when it becomes an extension of politics it cannot sort out the fundamentals of democracy. How are the executive's "extraordinary powers" to be defined? Who is ultimately responsible for a false arrest? Only a fully independent judiciary can provide binding answers to such questions. It "does not give the final word because it is infallible," in sum, "but it is infallible only because it gives the final word" (Bielsa 1993: 11, paraphrasing U.S. Supreme Court ruling *Brown v. Allen*, 1953).

In democracies such as Argentina, past suspensions of the constitution strengthened the resolve to let the judiciary grow into its rightful role. But even as threats to judicial independence from authoritarianism have receded, others have multiplied along with the growing number of daily interactions within the judiciary. Such threats have become so serious in such democracies as Venezuela, Peru, and Colombia that they have led to a questioning of constitutional democracy itself.

Judicial Independence Reforms in Democratic Regimes

Beginning in the 1980s, Latin America's new regimes began to adopt four main types of judicial independence reforms. Each area includes several kinds of specific measures. The first and most prominent area of reform is the selection of judges. To reign in the executive's power to appoint judges based on personal or political interests, one of the first things many Latin American democracies did was to change rules for the selection and reappointment of judges. Many established *concursos públicos* (open forums), where candidates' records are publicly reviewed and debated, and also required a two-thirds majority of Congress, rather than a simple plurality, for approval of Supreme Court *magistrados*. Other measures clarify reappointment. In most of the region, Supreme Court *magistrados* now serve terms that vary between four and twelve years, usually renewable by Congress.[41] Lastly, many countries established judicial councils to nominate candidates to the bench and, in most countries, to discipline judges and manage judicial budgets.

The second category of reform is the training, professional stability, and discipline of judges and judicial personnel. Judges receive an education heavily steeped in highly formalistic and theoretical approaches, with inadequate emphasis on practical matters such as speeding up trials. Few law students want to join the ranks of overworked and underappreciated judges. To improve such conditions, many countries limit the number of cases in each court, adopt more rigorous career guidelines, and establish *escuelas de la judicatura* (training schools) or special training programs for students as well as presiding judges. Regarding discipline, the power to remove judges and judicial officials is usually given to the Supreme Court, a high-level appellate court, or the judicial council.[42] To increase the clarity and enforceability of the actual processes of discipline, many countries adopt stricter standards, adopt more detailed infractions and sanctions, and rotate judges through area circuits (which itself can endanger judicial independence).

The third reform category is geared toward increasing the transparency, fairness, and speed of criminal trials by quickening pretrial investigations, clarifying officials' roles, and replacing the traditional written and inquisitorial procedures with oral and accusatorial trials. This task is so broad that it is usually tackled by altering the entire penal code and the laws governing each state agency involved. In particular, reforms attempt to respect due process guarantees in practice by redefining and monitoring the interactions of judges, police officers, *fiscales*, and public defenders. Countries such as Costa Rica, Panama, and Peru also require judges to write logical, law-based opinions explaining their decisions, which makes it harder to hide undue influences and helps ensure that decisions conform to the law.

The fourth category of reform relates to the need for adequate finances and control over them. Most Latin American judiciaries traditionally received less than 1 percent of their country's annual budget, on the low end of the world range, and have had to fight for even this allocation.[43] And the judicial secretaries, bailiffs, and administrators who work in the courts are among the lowest-paid government employees. Although money alone does not guarantee sound administration and political independence, a judiciary in financial straits will certainly have neither. The main response is to earmark a higher, fixed percentage of the national budget for the judiciary. To manage those resources effectively, most countries give a judicial council control over proposing and managing the judiciary's budget, as well as the responsibility to modernize judicial facilities through computerization and improved accounting.

In sum, there are four main areas of reform for independent judicial functioning. These include:

For selection and reappointment of judges:

- public forums
- higher legislative vote for Supreme Court judges
- judicial councils

For education, training, and discipline:

- less formalistic education
- training schools, educational programs
- "career" judiciary laws
- clear and enforced disciplinary rules

For transparency in judicial processes and trials:

- oral procedures
- clarifying each agency's functions
- new rules for writing opinions

For budget and financial management:

- judicial councils
- resource management

Although the interactions in the judicial process allow the meddling that reduces judicial independence, in a democratic regime they also create opportunity for reform by exposing institutional malfunctioning and harmful influence. In particular, the executive's overbearing authority triggers reform when an authoritarian past leads to greater checks on the executive, as in Argentina, or when the executive's ineffectiveness incites efforts to give nonexecutive actors more power, as in Venezuela. In both instances, change usually occurs when a shift in the political balance between the executive and legislature or between the ruling and opposition parties allows popularly supported proposals to be enacted against the executive's wishes. Judicial structures, for their part, often malfunction to the point where political officials alter them because they do not want to be burdened with or be blamed for their deficiencies. Such pressures on officials can come from societal demands for judicial access, or from executive demands for judicial support of economic liberalization. In either case, the judiciary's problems and their consequences are so widespread that judicial reform must be comprehensive to succeed. So in addition to enacting new penal codes, as mentioned above, many Latin American countries are refurbishing a wide range of other code and institutional laws. Since 1997, for example, Bolivia has formed a constitutional court, a judicial council, a *Defensoría*, and a conciliation center and developed legislation on the public ministry, the judiciary, intellectual property, and the commercial code.

When such reforms are enacted, however, they often are not as effective as planned because of the very conditions that promoted them. The severity of judicial bureaucracy can limit the impact of better training, and delays in raising salaries and making infrastructural improvements—often due to limited budgets and executive foot-dragging—generate even more conflict and bureaucracy. In Honduras, a majority of judges supported the 1987 career law but did not expect it to be applied because of budgetary limits, political obstacles, and a lack of administrative regulations. In Bolivia, judicial personnel regularly strike to protest low salaries, broken promises of raises, and huge salary differentials between higher-ranking and lower-ranking judicial officials.

Meanwhile, political shifts among the three branches of government can allow the executive to regain leverage and minimize the reforms intended to check its authority or to increase that of the judiciary. Such patterns have impacted each area of judicial reform in Latin America. Despite new nomination procedures, most judges continue to be chosen for their political affiliations; many training programs are stalled by ruling parties in the planning stages; discipline is undercut by politically motivated accusations and by special tribunals; and either new management or more money makes little difference without the other.[44]

Executive power and judicial weakness, then, limit reforms' effectiveness. The executive rarely loses its determination to stock the judiciary with friendly judges, sidelining new merit-based procedures in the process, and practices such as patronage, favoritism, and discriminatory prosecution are engrained into internal judicial functioning. Much of that bias comes from political parties, seen in the fact that countries with more entrenched parties tend to be have more politicized nominations.[45] Decentralization and privatization increase the number of new actors involved in the judiciary, and their influence is often hard to detect and therefore monitor or reduce. Amid a high number of unresolved legal questions under civil law's traditional limitation of judicial powers, judicial independence reforms are effective only if they can prevent such limitations from closing in on them. When reforms are able to stem these ongoing pressures, however, they are effective. A judicial council that establishes its own political base is likely to have an impact, for example, and training schools can provide knowledge and skills that enable judges to be effective. When political changes open up opportunity for change, as when executive interests shifted with Governor Duhalde and the police in Buenos Aires province, the judiciary can fully utilize these newly acquired supports.

Penal code reform demonstrates both the pitfalls and the potential of judicial reform. Throughout the region, democracies have reformed their penal codes to speed up criminal process and protect constitutional rights. As Table 4.2 shows, most of these changes were enacted during the 1990s. Many of the new codes were inspired by other countries' models and, demonstrating the benefits of a decentralized judiciary, on the code of the Argentine province of Córdoba. The two principal changes adopted in the region's new codes are changing inquisitorial and written procedures to oral and accusatorial ones, and transferring control over criminal prosecution from judges and the police to the MP. Such reforms were responses to biases in criminal procedure that the Napoleonic Code addressed but that Latin America failed to carry forward. Reliance on written material slowed

Table 4.2   Penal and Penal Process Code Reforms, Post-1990

Country	Year Formed	Major Provisions/Changes
Argentina	1992	Oral trials, stronger Public Ministry
Bolivia	1999	Oral trials, stronger Public Ministry
Colombia	2000	New crimes (e.g., torture, disappearance, genocide)
Ecuador	1999	Inquisitorial to accusatorial trials, stronger Public Ministry
El Salvador	Formed 1996; reformed 1999	Clearer delineation of crimes, new protections for victims
Guatemala	1994	Role clarification, stronger Public Ministry control, oral, accusatorial trials
Honduras	1999	Stronger control by Public Ministry and judges, inquisitorial to accusatorial trials, restrictions on incarceration
Nicaragua	2000	Stronger Public Ministry
Paraguay	Implemented 1998 and 1999	Oral, accusatorial trials, stronger Public Ministry
Uruguay	1997	More oral procedures, less investigative responsibility for judges
Venezuela	1999	Abolish secrecy of the *sumario,* oral trials, introduction of *escabinos* (citizen judges), abolition of *nudo hecho*

down the process and built in bias against defendants, whose poor representation and access to documents during the *sumario* affected the outcome of the *plenario*. The limits on Latin America's multitasking MPs, as discussed in Chapter 2, allowed investigations to be taken over by judges and police officials, who were less vigilant regarding due process. Along with complementary reforms of the judiciary and other agencies, these long overdue code alterations promised to be a boost for judicial efficiency, fairness, and citizen confidence.

Legal and infrastructural disarray in the judiciary, however, can derail even these reforms. Most codes consider an adequate defense an absolute right, but (with the exception of Costa Rica) do not provide enough public defenders to make it a reality (see Chapter 6). In El Salvador, increased salaries have led to a larger corps of public defenders, but working conditions remain poor. In Guatemala, budgetary constraints have prevented language interpretation, which is required in the new code, and numerous pretrial motions cause *sumarios* to violate the provision that they be completed "as soon as possible." Continuing concentration of investigative specialists in the police and the dual position of some MPs as both prosecutor and investigator can also negate the codes' delineation of roles. Due process can be further imperiled by what other provisions do and do not cover. In many countries, for example, there is a lack of guarantees for offenses that are minor but may nevertheless involve extended periods of incarceration without access to counsel. In the Dominican Republic, the *sumario* is limited to sixty days but can be and often is extended as many times as deemed necessary. In Bolivia, the *defensor* has criticized the approval of clandestine agents in that country's new code as a threat to constitutional rights.

Argentina

Even though important judicial independence reforms were added to Argentina's constitution in 1994, most judicial, government, and party officials still consider judicial independence to be low and judicial functioning to be inefficient. In particular, they blame historical patterns, executive dominance, economic interests, political parties, and a "culture" of interference.[46] Even as the effects of such problems vary, they cannot be fully overcome without reforms targeting the judiciary's routine functioning.

Judicial independence was very weak when democracy returned to Argentina in 1983. Newly elected Radical President Alfonsín replaced about one-fifth of the judges, with the resignation of additional 6 percent allowing for more appointments. Many of the new appointments were made through negotiations between the two main parties. The president also placed new *magistrados* on the Supreme Court, most of whom were not linked with him politically (his attempt to increase the court's size in 1987 was thwarted by the Peronist Congress). The result was a court that acted independently. It ruled against a 1985 executive decree suspending habeas corpus during a spate of urban violence, for example, and later struck down provisions of the government's economic plan that used workers' pensions. But the judiciary generally backed the government's promotion of democratization and individual sovereignty. In the 1987 *Sejean* decision, the Supreme Court ruled that the prohibition of divorce was unconstitutional because the constitution "ensures all of the country's inhabitants the right to choose their personal plan of life, insofar as it does not harm third parties or offend public morality." The court used its new freedoms to strengthen itself as well, such as by reviewing the method of impeachment of provincial judges in 1987 and by arguing against establishment of special courts.[47]

But the new government's main rule of law reform focus was to modernize penal and criminal laws. Recognizing "that the current system of criminal trials and of judicial organization in Argentina belonged to the colonial era, and were old in Spain when they arrived in America," proposals were put together that eventually served as a basis for the 1992 penal process code.[48] Alfonsín gave much of the responsibility for developing these reforms to the Council for the Consolidation of Democracy.

The Consejo recommended trials by special juries for judges accused of breaches of duty and the application of stare decisis to Supreme Court rulings. It also favored a Constitutional Council to "resolve conflicts of powers that results from the new organization of government" and thereby free regular judges from political conflicts; unlike European versions, however, it would leave decisions of laws' unconstitutionality in the courts.[49]

But demands on the judiciary quickly overwhelmed such plans. With expectations running high and a big backlog of pent-up demands, the number of cases in the federal courts doubled between 1983 and 1989. Judges responded to the influx in different ways, such as one who hid 220 files in an office cabinet. But the inability to keep up eventually caught up with the courts, diminishing both their efficiency and citizen confidence in them. Up to 55 percent of Argentines expressed confidence in the judiciary in 1983 (Carballo de Cilley 1987: 68–73), but in 1989 more than four-fifths deemed it inefficient and inaccessible (Buscaglia and Dakolis 1996), and in 2001 less than one-fifth had confidence in it. More significant, Alfonsín's human rights trials led to military backlashes and uprisings, forcing him to either risk a coup or abandon one of his administration's most important pursuits. His ultimate decision to bring the trials to an end precipitated a drop in popular confidence in both the government and the courts. Within the courts, in addition, there was a spate of resignations of high-ranking judges, such as in the federal criminal courts, in protest of the president's decision. So what looked like a "judicialization of politics" at the beginning of the transition turned into a "politicization of the judiciary" (Malamud-Goti 1996: 4).

Along with the military unrest, economic downturns and hyperinflation after 1987 led to a decisive victory for Peronist*s* in the 1989 presidential and congressional elections. One of President Menem's first actions was to increase the Supreme Court from five to nine *magistrados*. Although Menem asserted that his so-called Project of 1989 was necessary because a paucity of judges was forcing functionaries to take on judges' responsibilities, the Peronist-controlled Congress gave just forty-one seconds of debate to this unannounced change, and Menem filled the open positions with candidates close to him or the party.[50] From the outset, then, it was clear that independent judgment would not be forthcoming from these judges in cases involving political questions important to the government. Politicization also sunk deeper into the nominations to superior and lower courts, aided by nomination processes that "happen in secret," with "very little discussion when they do become public," according to one Alfonsín adviser.[51] Such practices were intensified by Menem's own accusation of judicial politicization under his predecessor. He asserted that during the "entire decade of the 1980s, 'mafias' of judges and experts [were] dedicated to draining the treasury" and that "discussion has been politicized to that extent that there is no way in which judges" could "reclaim their independence"; in particular, he criticized the trials of military leaders as helping "to transform [the judiciary's] crisis of legitimacy into an incurable disease" because they were a political "connivance between the government and certain judges and *fiscales*."[52]

The judiciary as a whole supported Menem's early policies, including his most controversial: the 1989 amnesty decree of officials convicted of *Proceso* crimes, justified by the need to prevent a repeat of the 1987 uprisings. This support for a wide use of the executive's decree powers helped justify an unprecedented number of decrees in the course of the Menem administration. Whereas only thirty executive decrees were made between 1853 and 1989, Menem issued 398 between 1989 and 1996.[53] These decrees were constitutionally questionable on the grounds, among others, that they gave legislative power to the president, but the high court did not strike them down or modify them. In the 1990 *Peralta* decision, for example, the court upheld Menem's decrees to convert bank deposits into state bonds, to deregulate the economy through laws' abrogation, and to regulate the constitutional right to strike. In some cases, such as on the privatization of Aerolineas Argentinas, the economic minister lent a hand by calling up the *magistrados* personally. With conservative backgrounds, judges in the high court as well as federal courts returned to pre-1983 interpretations of personal sovereignty. In one case, the gay rights group Comunidad Homosexual Argentina appealed after a civil court rejected its petition for legal recognition, and President Menem, startled by protests on a world tour, pressed the Supreme Court to allow recognition to be granted.

The Menem administration's use of administrative and special courts also reduced judicial independence. As discussed above, courts outside the main judiciary opened new inroads for external influence. In Argentina, they grew in number throughout the country's history, numbering more than 300 by the 1970s, despite consistent judicial rulings attempting to limit their power.[54] After a reduction in the courts in the 1980s, Menem began establishing them mainly for regulatory purposes. Many of these courts now have jurisdiction over several kinds of complaints formerly directed to the regular courts, and their judges can be removed by the executive for "good cause"—which has happened on numerous occasions.

Along with the military amnesty and the economic decrees, the biggest controversy of the Menem government was the widespread accusations of corruption, some proven in court, within the government and the president's family. By the end of Menem's second term, well over 100 government officials and their relatives had been charged—and acquitted. To help minimize such embarrassments, Menem established a superior criminal court, second only to the Supreme Court, "endowed with the judicial faculty to review and reverse any criminal court in the country" and staffed "almost entirely" with the president's allies (Linz and Stepan 1996: 201). Like other special courts, this one seriously diluted judges' authority.

Such politicization has been countered by the many judges who assumed the bench during the Radical government and by the profound impact of the *Proceso* on nearly all judges. Although state inefficiency tends to bolster views of the law as a constraining impediment, state aggression tends to bolster views of the law as a necessary control. In most countries, judges are often split between those who abide by judicial restraint—in which they apply the law irrespective of policy implications and personal values—and those who follow a judicial activism to go beyond narrow legal thinking. Despite civil law's emphasis on restraint, a history of constitutional manipulation and layers of contradictory laws cause more judges to adopt activism in order to shore up the gaps and weaknesses in the law with progressive jurisprudence. This is most true in countries such as Argentina, where authoritarianism is associated not with policy efficiency but with legal abuse.

Restraint and activism will always coexist, but reforms can use the tension between them to make the judiciary more open and relevant. Judicial schools in particular will help. The first serious attempt to begin a judicial school was a proposal by a 1991 commission of the Supreme Court and bar association, which received support from USAID and the World Bank.[55] But a lack of funding put off the school's development until 1999, when the judicial council began planning and requesting appropriations for one. Given large bodies of judges from the Radical as well as Peronist governments, different perspectives can become part of the judiciary's functioning and provide a check on political bias.

During Menem's first term, increasing awareness of court inefficiencies and a growing reliance on private international capital opened up other opportunities for reform. The administration expanded public defense agencies, increased the number of clerks to handle the administrative tasks that took up so much of judges' time, and established a judicial studies center. Menem also initiated a large ADR program. These reforms were geared toward creating a more efficient and balanced judiciary, necessary to attract the foreign investment that was a cornerstone of the government's program of privatization, export growth, and currency parity with the dollar. Businesses and economic interests long had decried Argentina's administration of justice. Unlike in Venezuela, where dependence on oil allowed such necessary but politically difficult improvements to be put off indefinitely, the Argentine government's embrace of neoliberalism obliged it to do everything possible to be competitive and to attract investment.

In 1992, in addition, Congress passed a new penal process code and restructured part of the judiciary in order to improve judicial efficiency. As in Venezuela, impetus came from international organizations, legal scholars, and NGOs. Based to a large extent on proposals put forth during the Alfonsín administration, the new code included the establishment of oral trials in federal courts and many criminal courts, the creation and reduction of courts in other issue areas, and greater rationality in sentencing. More than 200 oral courts were established, boosting court transparency and efficiency. In its first years of operation, in fact, about 80 percent of oral trials ended in a sentence. But the quicker pace of trials also led to even greater demand, increasing case backlogs as well as prison overcrowding. Many courts also continued to be bogged down in written procedures, which are so ingrained that even many judges aware of the drawbacks of the written format still believe it to be more secure and just.[56] In addition, the new code kept the investigatory judge as head of investigation as well as administrator of evidence collection, leading to a confusion of roles and responsibilities that allows "the police to continue having autonomous action in the investigation."[57]

Also creating momentum for national judicial reform was provincial judicial reform. As discussed in Chapter 2, provincial governments with real authority provide both good and bad examples for the rule of law. On measures to improve judicial functioning, Argentina's provinces led the way. Córdoba enacted a rigorous selection process for judges and, along with Santa Fe and Mendoza, initiated an integral reform of the judiciary. Mendoza put resources into creating courts specializing in mediation and in family law. To deal with the persistently poor distribution of basic information, Río Negro began putting laws and rulings on the Internet. Chaco, despite its freewheeling financial reputation, pioneered judicial reform with its establishment of a judicial council and judicial school in 1934. As with the national government, much of the reform was motivated by the costs of judicial disarray. In a 2000 survey, 72 percent of businesses said they shunned investments in provinces with inefficient and biased courts.[58]

More significant, however, was the constitutional reform of 1994. Because the Peronists wanted an amendment allowing for presidential reelection, the opposition Radicals were in a position to push through their own proposals. The most important of those reforms were: changing the senate majority required for appointment of Supreme Court *magistrados* from a plurality to two-thirds, and creating a judicial council to select candidates for lower courts (see Chapter 5).[59] Executive-branch politics opened up opportunities for reform, and the opposition responded with measures checking executive power.

Reflecting this impact of politics on the judiciary, the next major test of judicial independence came with the 1999 elections. Menem sought to run for a third term, arguing that the reformed constitution did not apply to his 1989–1995 term, therefore making the 1999 elections his first reelection.

When the final decision over the constitutionality of a Menem campaign was placed before the Supreme Court—in the form of a request by the president to have a transitory article of the constitution declared null, permitting him to run—the progovernment majority broke down. In March 1999, contrary to expectations, the court ruled unanimously against Menem's request. The ruling was in part a response to presidential politics: the opposition campaigned vigorously against the reelection effort, threatening a "political trial" against the five *magistrados* that worked "on line" with the president and publicly took the position that it would regard a ruling for reelection as a constitutional violation itself.[60] More important, a split within the ruling party, its losses in provincial elections, and anti-Menem votes in Congress created an atmosphere in which a ruling against reelection was both uncontroversial and politically astute. A decrease in the executive's power, that is, led directly to an increase in judicial independence.

Although executive politics can increase judicial independence at the top, poor administration keeps judicial efficiency low at the bottom. While crime rose inexorably during the 1990s, judicial functioning did not keep up. The probability that an arrested person would be sentenced by a court fell from 7.3 percent in 1990 to 5.6 percent by 1997. And of the record 1,043,757 crimes reported in 1999, the courts tried and convicted the guilty in only 1.26 percent of the cases.[61] Unlike in other countries, one change not adopted in the 1994 reform was to give the judiciary a fixed percentage of the national budget. This divergence from other countries was probably due to realization that judicial disarray was due as much to mismanagement as to executive manipulation. In fact, the judiciary's budget is about proportionally double that of the United States, with about 40 percent more support staff and nearly 70 percent more funds per case (Fundación de Investigaciones Económicas Latinoamericanas 1996). In 2000, a whopping 32 percent of the judicial budget went to administration, depriving the courts of new technology and training and practically starving functions such as forensics, which received only 3.1 percent.[62] Such figures underscore the importance of administration and are a warning to countries that fix the judicial budget.

But budget politics and processes only make it worse. Allocations have varied widely, from a high of 3.8 percent in 1900 to a low of 0.79 percent in 1984 (Serra 1985c). Budgets have always been prepared by the executive, but Law 23.853 of 1990 (the so-called Autarky law), gave the Supreme Court the authority to formulate the first draft. But this reform made little difference. Although the high court now makes the first requested allocations, the executive revises them before sending them to Congress for final approval. Invariably, the executive lowers the high court's request, and Congress does not alter the executive number.[63] Since 1992, the judiciary's budget has steadily declined. In 1994, there was a 15 percent difference in the amount requested by the Supreme Court and that recommended by the executive; in 1996 the Supreme Court requested $900 million but got $600 million; and between 2000 and 2001 the judiciary's final budget dropped from $800 million to $600 million. Such decreases have fueled a cycle of inefficiency in which poor administration leads to lower allocations, which only worsens administration further. Once the budget goes through, in addition, spending on unforeseen expenses is nearly impossible. Modernizing and other projects, as a result, are perpetually delayed.

Since the return to democracy, in sum, Argentina has enacted very significant judicial independence reforms: a judicial council, a higher senate majority for Supreme Court nominees, and a new penal code. Each of these reforms, rooted in desires to improve the judiciary's efficiency and to check the executive's power, were channeled through congressional legislation, reform councils, and constitutional amendments. But in order to succeed in the long term, these new measures must hold up against continuing practices of judicial politicization.

Venezuela

More than forty years after it became South America's first contemporary democracy, Venezuela lacks judicial independence. It is a result of manipulation not only by the executive and political parties but also by nonstate actors as well. Of a sample of eighteen opinions of Venezuelan officials on judicial independence and functioning, five stressed the parties' complete control over court nominations, eight highlighted the influence of economic interests in the daily actions of the judiciary, and only four said it was not a serious problem.[64] Reflecting the infighting of judicial reform politics, many officials point to a lack of independence in areas of which they are not a part: a Supreme Court magistrate said that the Judicial Council was far more politicized than the Supreme Court, but an MP official claimed that there was far more interference in the judiciary than in the *fiscalía*.

More than other rule of law issues, Venezuela's poorly functioning judiciary has attracted serious reforms, including a new penal process code, alteration of the judicial council, and new budget guarantees. But these reforms still have to contend with both old and new patterns. Despite the thorough battering and reconstruction of Venezuelan democracy in the 1990s, neither executive-party control nor judicial weakness has dissipated. Although executive power had been declining since the 1980s, Chávez has reasserted it with a vengeance. New laws have clarified the judiciary's role, but politicization and bureaucratic disarray continue to threaten it.

Federal control over the judiciary as well as a commitment to judicial independence were affirmed with the 1961 constitution. AD's unprecedented levels of citizen mobilization, along with its pact with the right-of-center religious party COPEI, also led AD leaders to assume the mandate to structure the new regime. The new constitution, accordingly, granted the executive the "competency" of "the administration of justice and the creation, organization and competence of the courts; [and of] the Public Ministry," as well as over all legislation dealing with constitutional rights and with civil, penal, and penitentiary law (article 136, No. 9, Ordinals 23–24). Inheriting the attributes of the Alta Corte Federal and Corte de Casación, the Supreme Court was given the power to declare the total or partial nullity of laws conflicting with the constitution.[65] Constitutional article 208 proscribed removal or suspension of judges except in extraordinary situations, and the Organic Law of the Judiciary prohibited reductions in judges' salaries (article 13), spells out sixteen different infractions, and gives the judicial council and superior courts the power to carry out disciplinary action through warnings, fines, suspensions, and removals.

Despite such powers in writing, from the beginning judicial officials chafed at executive controls and judicial weaknesses in practice. In 1959, the Convention of Criminal Judges complained of lack of cooperation by police and prosecutors, as well as the need to reform many criminal laws and introduce measures such as provisional liberty. Reflecting a growing consensus that continued into the 1990s, Ramón Escovar Salom, a key architect of the 1961 constitution, pointed out the need for modernization, administrative change, and the judiciary's infrastructural inability "to put the juridical order into practice."[66] As time went on, however, politicization only magnified these weaknesses. Since anyone in a top judicial position has or is perceived to have gotten there with party support, the courts became fair political game. Opposition parties attacked AD's dominance of the high court in the 1980s, pointing to the court's refusal to try former President Jaime Lusinchi and other AD politicians accused of corruption, as well as its decision to allow justices personally close to former President Carlos Andrés Pérez to preside in the corruption trial against him.[67] A 1991 petition of 5,000 national luminaries that called for the court's mass resignation further politicized the court.

Politicization increased as powerful economic sectors, as well as well-connected law firm–business alliances called *tribus* (tribes), came to not only enjoy favorable treatment by judges but also to utilize the courts for their own purposes. One of their more innovative uses has been "judicial terrorism," in which they have judges order arrests or bring charges as a means of intimidation or revenge against personal enemies. Under such pressures, each of a judge's partial decisions becomes an opportunity for external interference. A journalist who named names in a 1995 book on corruption, for example, was attacked, threatened, and, in an unusually speedy process, jailed for libel.

As in the rest of Latin America, judicial disarray brought international financial institutions to Venezuela. As the government braved adoption of neoliberal economic policies in the 1990s, it began working with IFIs on judicial reform. But several obstacles blocked the government's ability to see these changes through. Violent opposition caused neoliberal reforms to be introduced on a piecemeal and inconsistent basis, and nearly every year judicial employees either threatened to strike or did strike for stretches of up to three months.[68] Politicization also brought hesitation to even basic reforms such as judges' training. A school operated by the judicial council was opened in 1982, but a lack of funding and party backing forced the school to shut down in the mid-1980s. It opened again in 1990 for short preparatory courses on the new competitive exams required for selection, then expanded in the late 1990s as part of Congress's judicial reform package.

Inadequate funding has also increased the judiciary's disarray. Up until recently, the courts received a small fraction of the country's budget, their deficits were among the highest of all state agencies[69] and, as everywhere else, nearly every judicial official complained of chronic inadequacies and of the humiliation of having to plead for funding.[70] Although the Supreme Court and the judicial council were able to pump up these anemic budgets with World Bank funds, the budget process itself remained highly politicized through control by the executive and the lower house of Congress, the Cámara de Diputados. After the executive presented the budget to the Cámara, its commissions made recommendations and changes. Congress, however, could not allocate funds beyond the estimated national income. Alterations could be made by the executive but required congressional approval if involving additional credits or large sums. The Supreme Court did make an initial budget request, but it was not open for negotiation, and about two-thirds of the requested total was usually granted. Only after a petition to Congress could more money be released.[71]

The results of all these shortfalls are predictable: Computers are rare, basic office supplies are always low, and until the mid-1990s the central palace of justice in Caracas had just nine telephone lines for more than 1,000 employees. More serious is the chronic lack of judges. When democracy was established in 1958, there were approximately 700 judges for a national population of about 7 million people; in 1994, with more than 22 million inhabitants, the country had just 1,400 judges.[72]

These limitations affect all judicial processes. The average time for a criminal trial is 4.5 years, and the average detention from initial declaration to sentencing lasts nearly four years. *Amparo* has also fallen victim to the lack of efficiency. The provision that judges must decide *amparo* petitions within forty-eight hours has caused an *"amparicitis"* by lawyers eager to avoid the usual delays. This has overloaded the courts and spurred the outright dismissal of nearly 90 percent of *amparos*, sometimes years after filing. Judicial independence is also reduced through "auxiliary" and "temporary" judges, despite constitutional article 210's assertion that such posts must not lessen judges, "autonomy and independence." But with a lack of full-time judges, there is a burgeoning number of temporary judges, who stay long past their sixty-day limit and usually account for more than half of all sitting judges.

As the consequences of the judiciary's poor financial state became increasingly obvious, efforts to give it a fixed percentage gained ground. Unlike in Argentina and other countries, in Venezuela executive power and judicial disarray led to support for a clear, simple solution that avoided the more difficult and unpopular task of making judicial operations accountable to basic administrative standards. In the 1999 constitution, the judiciary was, in fact, guaranteed 2 percent of the annual national budget. If the budget shrinks, this may actually mean less money. But even if it means more, the additional funds will not create better functioning unless accompanied by change that addresses the causes of corruption and waste.

This judicial politicization was a low-priority problem until it got channeled into growing citizen disillusionment with the overall political system. More of a motive than attracting international capital was responding to growing popular demand for justice and criticism of the judiciary's functioning. Many of the ideas under consideration in the 1990s originated in the Justice Ministry Draft Commission from twenty years before. One of the biggest causes for slow and abusive due process was dependence on written materials, which creates bias against the defendants. A 1976 bill attempted to introduce orality into criminal procedures, but it was quickly torn apart by amendments and controversies. Judicial disarray only continued, and greater societal awareness of it in the 1980s and 1990s forced officials to respond with actual reform.[73] After the end of the AD-COPEI control over Congress in 1995, legislative reformers tapped into the technical training and political support around the region to step up their efforts. After three more years of debating, compromising, and beating back challenges, they then succeeded in enacting a comprehensive package of reforms.

Although this package was centered on the penal process code (COPP, *Código Orgánico Procesal Penal*), it encompassed all of the agencies involved in the rule of law: the police, the MP, public defenders, and judges. Because much abuse resulted from a confusion of roles in criminal investigations, a simultaneous clarification of each agency's authority was considered critical to the new code's effectiveness. The Legislative Commission, in charge of the reform, stressed the importance of an "integral solution" (Oberto 1998: 28) because of agencies' interlocking roles and because of the need to change the mentality of their personnel. Accompanying a new penal code, therefore, were reforms in the organic laws of judiciary, the judicial council, the MP, the PTJ, and judicial careers.

The new Judicial Career Law added new qualifications for potential judges, for example, and the new MP law enhanced that agency's authority.

Above all, the long-standing criminal process had built-in bias against basic due process rights. In the *sumario*, the police would carry out nearly all of the investigation and then hand over the results to the judge. The judge, without independent support to evaluate the material, would then order the arrest of the suspect. This same investigative material would then be the basis of the *plenario*, by which time it was exceedingly difficult for the defendant to counteract it. This process led to a confusion of roles as well as unofficial control by the police over the *sumario*. Under the new code, the investigative phase is directed by the MP, affirming the spirit of the Napoleonic Code. The MP would be ensured adequate support by the police, whose role would be strictly limited to presenting evidence to the MP. A judge would then use the presented material and decide whether to proceed to the *plenario* and to which court the case would go. The accused would be informed of the investigation and have an opportunity to appear before the judge, who could then order further investigation. In this manner, the secrecy of the *sumario* was ended. Before, suspects were informed of the charges and the evidence at the time of detention, stacking the deck against them and fueling abuses such as judicial terrorism. As the reform began in 1995, in fact, in a move that underscored the judiciary's lack of action on key issues, the house of deputies unanimously regarded the secrecy of the *sumario* as a violation of the constitution and directed the Legislative Commission to eliminate it.

After the *sumario*, a case goes to a separate trial court not biased by previous involvement. A confusion of roles and a weakening of due process occurred before because the judge involved in the investigation usually decided the verdict. Instead of being run by one judge, in addition, under the new code most trial courts are headed by panels of judges and *escabinos* (citizens), who, like the judge, would be able to question witnesses, the accused, and experts. The criminal trial process itself was changed from a written to an accusatory oral process between the plaintiff (represented by the MP) and the defense. The trial is then followed by a sentencing phase, headed by a separate judge also responsible for corresponding security and rights measures. With these additions, the original two-phase process was replaced by a four-phase process to more fully ensure the principles of transparency, speed, and balance. The new code also eliminates *nudo hechos*, which is also a big step toward applying the same standards of justice to citizens and state officials.

Congress—acting in part to save itself from the rising antigovernment tide—unanimously approved the new penal code. In fact, the head of the Legislative Commission said that along the way there were almost "no differences" among the parties.[74] But the executive's role was a mix of stalling, indifference, and counterproposal. To help finance the new reform package, Congress proposed amending the budget process so that the executive would be obliged to accept the judicial council's budgetary request. The executive blocked this change, however, and proceeded to reduce expenditures, crippling the reform by depriving needed funds for training *fiscales*, hiring judges, and educating the public. The president's 1997 budget proposals signaled a clear lack of support for the changes, and as the reform progressed, there were further reductions in the following two years. During the actual formulation of the new laws, the executive did intervene with eleven specific proposals, but they all primarily involved replacing judges rather than reforming structures and processes. Above all, it pushed for creation of a High Commission of Justice to hire and fire judges, which would disempower the judicial council. It also delayed providing information on the administration of state agencies such as the MP and public defenders.

Opposition also came from the police. As part of its "integral solution," both Congress and the MP stressed that the MP could not carry out its new obligations without sufficient and trustworthy police support. The PTJ, however, blocked any move to alter it or to pass its powers to a new investigative unit within the MP. It also attempted to reclaim its power to direct criminal investigations by backing bills in Congress and by trying to convince the public that the new code would reduce its crime-fighting ability. The MP also publicly opposed the COPP, and the bar association brought a petition of unconstitutionality against use of *escabinos* to the Supreme Court, which rejected it.

Although political change opened up the opportunity for these reforms, it also endangered them. One big obstacle was high turnover in Congress, with about 70 percent of legislators removed in the course of the 1990s. In a foreshadow of the future, even bigger obstacles were parallel legislative measures introduced to reform the entire constitution. In particular, the Judiciary Subcommittee of the Senate Constitutional Reform Commission declared the judiciary in a "state of emergency," which legally requires a drastic overhaul above and beyond the reform measures being developed.

The reformers, in fact, were trying to stop rising political tides from sweeping away what they considered the only practical response to poor judicial functioning. As described above, the political shifts that open up opportunity for reform can be caused by a questioning of the entire system, which ultimately leads to the end of both reformed and unreformed institutions. Chávez's election took Venezuela to that final step. After the president took office, the National Constitutional Assembly writing the new constitution declared the judiciary to be in a state of emergency and proceeded to restructure it. Only months after enactment of the most serious and successful measure to address the judiciary's institutional malfunctioning, the government began to unravel it. Since then, the public has also grown increasingly hostile to the new code, even to the point of staging mass street demonstrations against it.

The uncertainty surrounding these reforms is so high because the agencies responsible for the rule of law depend on the constitution. And as in other countries, Venezuela's constitution is the principal zone of conflict among those responsible for a rule of law. The 1961 constitution provided stability, but growing inequalities and injustices transformed it into a lightning rod for attacks by citizens and, because it lost the ability to maintain order, by politicians as well. Such attacks made the 1990s a decade of constitutional erosion and suspension. The constitution gave the president the power to "declare a state of emergency and to decree the restriction or suspension of guarantees in cases" (articles 190 and 240) "of emergency, of disturbance" affecting "the peace of the Republic, or of serious circumstances that affect economic or social life" (article 241). The declaration of emergency or constitutional restriction is to be submitted to Congress within ten days following its publication (article 242), and the suspension order is to be revoked by the "National Executive or by the Congress in joint session, at the cessation of the causes which led to it" (article 243). Only the executive can respond swiftly enough to respond to emergencies, of course, but emergencies requiring constitutional suspension were declared so frequently that the judiciary was frozen out of what had become the most important exercise of constitutional power.

Since the advent of democracy in Venezuela in 1958, constitutional guarantees have been suspended twelve times. Although the initial suspensions were broadly supported, by the 1990s they were declared without popular consent and amid deteriorating conditions. The fact that these suspensions took place under democracy made them more damaging to judicial independence and to democracy than if they had occurred under authoritarianism. Although the unconstitutionality of any law or decree can be challenged directly in the Supreme Court or lower courts through a "popular action," in addition, no suspension was ever questioned by any court or challenged from outside the judiciary until 1995. Between 1958 and 1996, in fact, there were only two references to the pertinent constitutional articles. In the first reference, which foreshadowed a later decision, the Supreme Court turned down a habeas corpus petition in 1967 on behalf of a man whose detention was justified by the suspension of guarantees, asserting that it was "not of competence" in such an appeal (*Gaceta Forense, 2 Etapa*, 1967, No. 57: 407–411). In the other reference, the court rejected a petition against a court-martial during a constitutional suspension, arguing that there was "no relation between" the appeal and the defendant's "constitutional" rights (*Gaceta Forense, 3 Etapa*, 1973, No. 79: 382–395).

The first constitutional suspension was declared in concurrence with the promulgation of the constitution itself on January 23, 1961. President Betancourt justified the move by alleging plots by groups such as the Left Revolutionary Party and the Communist Party to overthrow the government. Carlos Andrés Pérez, then the Interior Ministry's political director, said that constitutional guarantees would not be reinstated until the country had a "climate of political peace and citizen harmony," even though he added that current conditions were "completely normal."[75] Shortly thereafter, the interior minister said that the "fundamental obligation" of the new constitution was to support the democratic regime that it created but that under certain circumstances the regime itself reserves the right to use "temporary and extraordinary instruments of defense to impede its liquidation." Like Pérez, he contradicts the need for the suspension by stating that those arrested for causing disturbances "are in the process of investigation in" the courts and that the activity by those associated with the military dictatorship that ended in 1958 "is in large part controlled by the authorities."[76] These statements promoted the perception of the constitution as a handicap in the face of national security threats. In May 1962, after a rebellion by the Marine Infantry Battalion, the president again suspended constitutional guarantees, shut down newspapers, banned parties, and jailed political opponents. Betancourt's incorporation of "extraordinary" into "ordinary" constitutional practice continued through the administration of his successor, Raúl Leoni, until the leftist rebels were defeated.

Along with the insurgency's end, a strong economy and continuing AD-COPEI domination led to a respite from suspensions after 1969. But political instability beginning in the late 1980s brought a revival. Several constitutional guarantees were suspended in March 1989 following violent national riots against austerity programs, twice again in 1992 following attempted military coups in April and November of that year, and once in 1993 due to protests against alleged electoral fraud.[77] Just as during the 1960s, the action was justified by an assumed inability to overcome emergencies under constitutional protections.[78]

With a collapse of the country's top nine banks a few years later, President Rafael Caldera suspended five basic guarantees with Decree 241 on June 27, 1994.[79] In the spring of 1995, Supreme Court Magistrado Hildegard Rondón de Sansó sponsored a popular action contesting the decree and requesting the restitution of three of the five suspended provisions.[80] The popular action accused Decree 241 of lacking sufficient motive, absence of regulation, disproportionality to the problems it was intended to tackle, and procedural errors. One of those errors concerned an executive-legislative tussle over the suspension itself: when Congress derogated Decree 241, the president promptly replaced it with Executive Decree 285, which continued the suspension. Rondón de Sansó argued that because Executive Decree 285 was created for the same reasons and objectives as the struck-down Decree 241, the judiciary should rule on the first act.

The court's unusual spate of assertiveness came about partly from the president's growing unpopularity, as well as the split between the parties controlling the executive and legislature. That split, however, did not prevent pressures from being exerted both inside and outside the courtroom. The day after the Supreme Court began its hearings on Decree 241, the president issued the veiled threat that "there are people who want to end" the "equilibrium" that his government is "guaranteeing to achieve the transformation of the country."[81] The press and the *magistrados* questioned the motives and legitimacy of the two university lawyers who brought the suit, despite the legality of such a popular action. On the case itself, the *magistrados* disagreed most pointedly with the suit's contention that suspension of many of the guarantees was disproportionate with the decree's goals of bringing the country's financial crisis under control. The final vote, on May 18, was 10-2 against the petition, with three *magistrados* absent. Some *magistrados* seemed to contradict prior support for constitutional rights. Cecilia Sosa Gómez, for example, had been a vocal opponent of written criminal investigative processes for violating defendant rights yet voted against the petition. Rondón de Sansó would not comment on the petition but complained of the judiciary's "insecurity and of the press's 'irresponsibility.'"[82] As with Argentina's 1999 reelection case, the high court took on a critical case at a time of executive weakness and increasing scrutiny of its own actions. But unlike in Argentina, uncertain politics and a volatile populace stopped it from taking the next step and issue a bold ruling.

Such practices eroded the ability of the Venezuelan courts to maintain a rule of law and pulled the constitution down with the judges into the arena of partisan politics. Repeatedly declared and unchallenged, suspensions almost turned into regular government policy, and the enhanced power each one brought to already powerful agencies such as the police increased momentum to declare further suspensions. Blind support for a constitution is not a prerequisite for judicial independence, but continuing attacks seriously complicated the judiciary's most fundamental task: to determine if legislative or executive acts violate basic rights and, if so, to nullify those acts. The loss of power by the two main parties over the legislative and executive branches opened up opportunities for change in the mid-1990s that was used to introduce a new penal process code and to make some controversial rulings. But these changes may now be reversed by the powerful Chávez government's unapologetic revamping of the judiciary and the constitution.

Conclusion

In the current democratic era, the judiciary has a chance to reach back to its original constitutional role. But with all the irrelevance, co-optation, and repression in between, such a task requires a commitment to durable reform. Almost all of Latin America has adopted important judicial independence measures, in all four areas, since their transitions to democracy.

But different historical and political experiences will determine the success of these changes. Because many detrimental interactions among actors and institutions were established under democracy in Venezuela, rule of law reforms in that country face more obstacles than do those in Argentina. Although a history of suspensions weakened judicial independence in Argentina, those suspensions took place under previous, nondemocratic regimes and were ameliorated by a more active Supreme Court. And although political officials still control court nominations in both countries, in Venezuela interference by nongovernment actors is more serious and widespread. Furthermore, the networks of party patronage and nepotism in the judiciary are more extensive in Venezuela than in Argentina. Most important, citizens' experiences with dictatorship in Argentina have created a stronger push for accountability on constitutional rights than in Latin American democracies dominated by entrenched parties.

But with economic recession, disillusion with government, and problems like crime and inequality, countries such as Argentina are not in the clear. Aware of their limited ability to enact effective reform amid such conditions, many democracies are attempting to permanently remove the task of judicial reform and oversight from the whim of politicians into the hands of separate judicial councils. Whether such councils are the true path toward independent judicial functioning—or a dumping ground for unsolvable problems—is the focus of Chapter 5.

Notes

1. Even the Supreme Courts in Latin America suffer from growing bottlenecks. The percent change in median delay for Argentina's high court jumped from 17 percent between 1973 and 1982 to 48 percent between 1983 and 1993. During the same two ten-year time spans, delays in Brazil increased from 2 percent to 39 percent, in Colombia from 3 percent to 28 percent, and in Venezuela from 3 percent to 48 percent; 12 percent to 29 percent in Chile, and 7 percent to 34 percent in Mexico. Edgardo Buscaglia Jr., "Judicial Reform in Latin America: The Obstacles Ahead," *Latin American Affairs* 4 (Fall/Winter 1995): 9.

2. *New York Times*, November 30, 1993, p. 3.

3. Keith Rosenn, "The Protection of Judicial Independence in Latin America," *Inter-American Law Review* 19, no. 1 (1987): 11. See Argentina Supreme Court case *Pérez de Smith Ana F. y otros* (Buenos Aires: *Jurisprudencia Argentina*

1978, vol. 237, pp. 87–88). Another way to measure judicial independence is to categorize Supreme Court independence, such as with the typology developed by Joel Verner (1984).

4. There are many variations of this basic structure. At the first-instance level, courts vary in their territorial and functional jurisdictions, whereas most countries have additional administrative and military courts.

5. A federal court judge with direct knowledge of the case, author interview, December 1996.

6. Rosenn, "The Protection of Judicial Independence in Latin America," p. 9. Judges' values are also blamed for a lack of judicial independence. Those values are a product of many factors, including a judge's knowledge of the law, social and economic backgrounds, and "cultural conditioning during judicial education, training and practice" (Wróblewski 1987: 25).

7. In Venezuela, the Supreme Court was dissolved totally in 1945, 1947, 1948, 1953, and 1955. In Argentina, Supreme Court judges were replaced in 1945, 1947, 1955, 1976, and 1983.

8. Decree-laws are usually decrees with the force of law taken in unusual circumstances, as when the legislature is not in session. But decrees and decree-laws have been such an integral part of governing in Latin America that legislation used to be "practically unenforceable because of the absence of a presidential decree to implement it" (Clagett 1952: 15).

9. Article 215 of Venezuela's 1961 constitution. In some countries, the courts have the power to pass judgment or write advisory opinions on the constitutionality of a bill still in Congress, particularly when questions of constitutionality generate opposition or threats of an executive veto. In Venezuela, when a presidential veto is overridden by two-thirds of Congress, the president must sign the bill into law. If the veto is overridden by a majority of less than two-thirds, however, the president can return it to Congress, which, if it overrides the veto again, obliges the president to sign. But if the president's opposition is based on alleged unconstitutionality, he can refer the bill to the Supreme Court, which must make a ruling within ten days. If the high court does not do so, the president must sign the bill. In the country's democratic era, there have been few cases in which the courts have struck down laws as unconstitutional. In 1969, President Caldera vetoed a congressional act limiting his judicial appointments. When the veto was appealed, the court ruled in favor of Congress, which was the first time it and the Congress united against the president—largely because the party in the executive controlled neither of the other two branches. Latin American countries have adopted divergent regulations on unconstitutionality. In some, any person or group can bring a direct "popular action" against the constitutionality of a law or legislation without allegations that someone has been directly harmed by it, but in other countries such actions can be taken only through extraordinary appeals and if someone was harmed. Some countries require the opinion of the Supreme Court on a bill's constitutionality before it becomes law, but usually declarations on constitutionality can be taken only against a promulgated law. Argentina's constitution grants the judiciary "jurisdiction over decisions in all cases that deal with matters governed by the Constitution, and by the laws of the Nation." *Control difuso*, in which all courts can declare a law's unconstitutionality, was established in the 1853 constitution.

10. *Sofía, Fallos de la Corte Suprema de Justicia* (Buenos Aires: *Jurisprudencia Argentina* 1959, vol. 243, p. 504).

11. In Venezuela, for example, the Organic Law of the Judiciary empowers the executive "to create and endow new ordinary courts of finance, work, and minors,

[and] to abolish existing ones." "Special" courts (ad hoc or temporary courts) usually deal with a specific problem, and "specialized" courts focus on a legal issue such as corruption.

12. In Argentina, special courts were usually a response to economic instability; Law 12.833 of 1946, for example, created administrative police tribunals in each provincial capital to enforce price controls.

13. Bolivia's 1988 *Ley de Régimen de la Coca y Sustancias Controladas* (Regulatory Law of Coca and Controlled Substances) created sixteen narco-trafficking courts with national jurisdiction. Throughout Latin American history, in fact, cases that are "the most germane to political issues" go not "before the regular court system, but before special judicial bodies or tribunals" (Needler 1965: 155).

14. Most Latin American countries also have electoral courts, which function under the executive, leading to conflicts of interest; as part of the judiciary, leading to criticism of the judiciary for handling "political questions"; or, most commonly, as specialized bodies. Under any arrangement, however, manipulation of electoral procedures and results weakens these courts. Argentina established the Federal Electoral Court and inferior courts in 1946, but these courts have often been ignored. During his first term, for example, Menem intervened in many provincial votes, such as in Estero and Corrientes during his first term. In Venezuela, the rulings of the Supreme Electoral Council are routinely challenged by parties and the executive.

15. One reason for the lack of cases were questions over these courts' approach, such as prohibiting bail and placing the burden of proof on the accused. In the 1995 banking crisis, many bankers accused under the law fled into exile. A proposal to set up new courts to handle the crisis set off a firestorm of debate and lawsuits.

16. The coherence and efficiency of military law are rooted in the Spanish Crown's disproportionate granting of settling *fueros* to military explorers, giving the military from the outset "special legal privileges," their "own special systems of laws and courts," and exemption from state legal jurisdiction (Karst and Rosenn 1975: 32).

17. The National Commission Against the Unlawful Use of Drugs stated that "drug-related offenses...concern the security and defense of the Venezuelan nation" and so "are subject to military justice."

18. CJM articles 476 and 486, under which some people have remained incarcerated and untried for up to ten years.

19. The case was decided on September 28, 1978 (cited in Elichiguerra 1978: 18–20). In military courts, the accused are not afforded basic guarantees. Military trials are consistently subject to longer delays than civilian ones, their prohibition of bail violates the presumption of innocence, and the fact that the prosecutor, judge, and defendant's attorney all belong to the armed forces impairs impartiality. Despite constitutional article 69's declaration that "no one may be judged except by his regular judges nor sentenced to a punishment not established by a pre-existing law," and article 154's statement that "the Law be one and the same for all citizens in punishment and in protection," the trial of civilians in processes with which they are unfamiliar violates rights to equality and to the natural judge.

20. Although the 1999 constitution clearly limits military courts to military crimes, the armed forces have become more involved in formulating and implementing national policy than at any previous time in the democratic era.

21. The Chile Supreme Court in the early 1970s, for example, "was widely regarded as very independent because it had openly clashed with the executive,

publicly accusing the Allende regime of violating the Constitution." But after the military's ouster of Allende, the court "was widely regarded as subservient because it failed to stand up to the military and defend individual constitutional rights." Indeed, "public perceptions of judicial independence may change even though a court may regard itself as possessing the same degree of independence" (Rosenn 1987: 8).

22. The main document of Iberian Law, the *Siete Partidas*, specified the roles of judges and lawyers and outlined the judicial process, but these regulations primarily addressed inheritance and property law.

23. *Consultas del Consejo de Indias*, Documents Room, Archivo de Indias, Sevilla, Spain.

24. There were new constitutions in 1909, 1914, 1922, 1925, 1928, 1929, 1931, and 1936.

25. The 1947 constitution was initiated by the *Trienio* government. The 1953 constitution of the following military regime returned the Supreme Court to its previous division of the Alta Corte Federal and the Corte de Casación. In the 1949 constitution, article 220 stated that any court, after a review of the case can refuse to apply a law, a decree, or specific provisions of either, on the basis of unconstitutionality, and that a general declaration of unconstitutionality can lead to a law or decree's nullification even when no case is involved.

26. *Fallos de la Corte Suprema de Justicia* (Buenos Aires: *Jurisprudencia Argentina* 1865, vol. 2, p. 141).

27. *Ramón Rios y otros (causa criminal)* (Buenos Aires: *Jurisprudencia Argentina* 1865, vol. 154, p. 500).

28. *Ameder Spagnol, María E. Alvarez de Schuster y otros*; *Fallos de la Corte Suprema de Justicia* (Buenos Aires: *Jurisprudencia Argentina* vol. 191, p. 388).

29. Although not guaranteed by the 1949 constitution, habeas corpus already had been a part of Argentine jurisprudence and practice.

30. The court's position was confirmed with its 1935 upholding of the dismissal of a suit brought by a first-instance judge against his 1931 dismissal. Avellaneda Huergo, *Fallos de la Corte Suprema de Justicia* (Buenos Aires: *Jurisprudencia Argentina* vol. 172, p. 344).

31. *Don Francisco Macia y don L'cutura Gassol, Recurso de habeas corpus* (Buenos Aires: *Jurisprudencia Argentina* 1928, vol. 151, p. 211); *Recurso de habeas corpus deducido en favor en el transporte "Chaco" de la Armada Nacional, Fallos de la Corte Suprema de Justicia* (Buenos Aires: *Jurisprudencia Argentina* 1932, vol. 164, p. 344); Bernardo Groisman, Recurso de Habeas Corpus, *Fallos de la Corte Suprema de Justicia* (Buenos Aires: *Jurisprudencia Argentina* 1935, vol. 173, p. 135).

32. The main ruling on these issues was the *Municipality of the City of Buenos Aires c/Mayer, Fallos de la Corte Suprema de Justicia* (Buenos Aires: *Jurisprudencia Argentina* 1945, vol. 201, p. 249).

33. *Fallos de la Corte Suprema de Justicia* (Buenos Aires: *Jurisprudencia Argentina* 1955, vol. 233, pp. 15–16). A decree of April 27, 1956, declared the 1853 constitution as the one in force.

34. *Siri* (Buenos Aires: *Jurisprudencia Argentina* 1957, vol. 235, p. 459). After the government jailed the leaders of a 1956 military uprising, some were never legally charged, but there was no response from any court.

35. *Rodríguez* (Buenos Aires: *Jurisprudencia Argentina* 1962, vol. 254, p. 116).

36. Preamble, *Estatuto de la Revolución Argentina, Anales de Legislación Argentina* (Buenos Aires: 1966), p. 756.

37. The high court supported the military's June 1970 installation of President Roberto M. Levingston and did the same when Levingston was replaced by General Alejandro A. Lanusse in March of the following year.

38. The military probably planned its strategy of disappearances during Isabel Perón's administration, according to Emelio Mignone, a principal human rights opponent of the 1976–1983 junta; Mignone, author interview, October 18, 1994. Many of the abuses during the *Proceso* were carried out by newly established clandestine intelligence services. The estimated number of disappearances ranges from 10,000 to 30,000 people.

39. *Pérez de Smith, Ana M. s/pedido* (Buenos Aires: *Jurisprudencia Argentina* 1977) of April 18, 1977, was the original case; *Pérez de Smith* (Buenos Aires: *Jurisprudencia Argentina* 1977) of December 21, 1978, was the reversal. *Fallos de la Corte Suprema de Justicia* (Buenos Aires: *Jurisprudencia Argentina* 1978-III, vol. 1978-IIII, p. 87). Freedom of press remained officially in place, but more than 150 journalists disappeared.

40. Carlos Zamorano, author interview, October 25, 1994.

41. In Costa Rica, high court magistrates are reelected to eight-year terms unless two-thirds of the legislature votes to dismiss them. In El Salvador, members of the Supreme Court stay in office for renewable five-year terms unless Congress votes against them. Members of Uruguay's Supreme Court may not be reelected after a ten-year term until a five-year waiting period has elapsed. Venezuela's Supreme Court judges serve one period of twelve years. Several Latin American constitutions ensure tenure pending good behavior until a specified retirement age; in order to prevent conflicts of interest, most proscribe judges from nonjudicial economic or political activity besides writing or teaching. To protect judges from financial retribution for rulings displeasing to the legislative or executive, several Latin American countries such as Argentina prohibit reduction in judges' salaries while they remain in their positions. Other countries, such as Venezuela, make no such guarantee. In Panama and Uruguay, the salaries of Supreme Court judges (which determine the salaries of the rest of the judiciary), cannot be less than those of ministers. Mexico's constitution also prohibits raising Supreme Court salaries during service, but inflation forced a modification to call for adequate compensation to be determined each year (Rosenn 1987: 15–16).

42. "Chile has a review system in which all judges below the level of the Supreme Court are graded annually by the Supreme Court. Judges whose performance is deemed substandard for two consecutive years and those graded unacceptable for a single time are automatically dismissed, regardless of their tenure.... Brazil, Haiti and Paraguay provide for impeachment by the Senate for members of the highest court, while other members of the judiciary are tried before the Supreme Court in Brazil and Paraguay" (Rosenn 1987).

43. Most of Latin America guarantees their judiciaries a fixed percentage of the budget. Costa Rica gives its judiciary no less than 6 percent of the nations' annual receipts; Honduras provides an annual appropriation of at least 3 percent of annual receipts; Peru allots 2 percent of the central government budget; and the constitutions of Guatemala and Panama give the judiciary at least 2 percent of ordinary annual receipts. Those without guarantees do not fare as well. In the Dominican Republic, the highest rate for the judiciary in recent years was 0.6 percent in 1984. In Colombia, the percentage never rises above 3 percent and is usually under 2 percent. The percentages in Bolivia and Ecuador are usually under 1 per-

cent. In Argentina, the judiciary gets about 1 percent of the budget, and the Venezuelan judiciary receives between .44 percent and 1 percent (Sagüés 1986; Rosenn 1987: 16–17; Cavagna Martínez et al. 1994: 45–50). Large chunks of governmental spending are often not in the budget, effectively reducing the judiciary's share.

44. Most involuntary transfers are punishments or an invitation to resign. Some Latin American constitutions prohibit such a practice, and others limit it to the Supreme Court. Judicial independence can also be undermined by lawsuits claiming injury by judges' malicious or negligent use of the law. Most countries protect their judiciaries from such suits though different forms of immunity. But many Latin American countries have yet to adopt strongly protective approaches and often allow judges to be sued for wrongful application of the law.

45. In Mexico, for example, no judge "is likely to be elevated to the bench who is not a member in good standing of the" PRI (the long-ruling Partido Revolucionario Institutional), and "judicial decisions conspicuously incompatible with the policy positions supported by the PRI and its allied major interest groups would have no independent power base to sustain them and could not maintain themselves" (Baker 1971: 272).

46. Of the eighteen officials who wished to discuss the issue, five stressed the problem's historical roots, three said that the biggest issue was executive control of the nomination of judges, three pointed to endemic corruption, primarily by economic interests, one blamed a lack of internal independence, two said that all judges were too closely linked to the parties, two complained of interference in the judiciary's daily procedures, and two cited a "culture" of political interference. This cross-section of officials is made up of five presiding judges, four current Justice Ministry officials, one former justice minister, one former Supreme Court magistrate, one assistant to a presiding Alfonsín-appointed Supreme Court magistrate, one lawyer linked to the 1976–1883 military regime, one executive official, one official of the bar association, one adviser in the Alfonsín government, and two deputies in the Congress of Buenos Aires province. Author interviews, August 1994–January 1995, November-December 1996, and August 1998.

47. *Sueldo de Posleman, Mónica R. y otra.* In this case, the court declared that the "system of designation and removal of judges and the laws that regulate" the courts are based above all on the idea of judicial independence, a "necessary requisite for the exercise of control that judges should exercise on the other powers of the State, and this independence is reflected in the elimination of special ad hoc courts, so that *magistrados* are free of all pressure of interests involved in their designation" (Buenos Aires: *Jurisprudencia Argentina* 1987-II, pp. 137–138).

48. "La reforma judicial que propiciaba Alfonsín," *Todo es Historia* 13:8 (Buenos Aires), February 1996.

49. It would also maintain a "disperse" rather than "concentrated" control, in which judges at all levels instead of just at the top could declare laws unconstitutional (*Consejo para la Consolidación de la Democracia* 1986: 56–57).

50. Rodolfo Barra, who stated that "my only two bosses are Perón and Menem"; Mariano Augusto Cavagna Martínez, a longtime Peronist activist who said upon his appointment that he was a "Peronist always" (Verbitsky 1993: 54); Eduardo José Moliné O'Connor, brother-in-law of the secretary of intelligence; Julio Salvador Nazareno, former minister in Menem's home province of La Rioja and a chief of police, who had no professional or intellectual background to recommend him to the court who shared a study with Menem and was close friends with Eduardo Menem, the president's brother and president of the senate; Antonio

Boggiano, recommended by the Vatican's ambassador; and Ricardo Eugenio Gabriel Levene, a drafter of the new Buenos Aires penal code who earlier in his career promoted forced sterilization of "delinquents" (Verbitsky 1993: 53).

51. Carlos Rosenkrantz, author interview, September 13, 1994.

52. All quotes from Mario Baizan, "La Justicia en la Picota: Conversaciones con Carlos Saúl Menem," *Administración Pública* (Buenos Aires), September 1993, pp. 4–10.

53. *La Nación*, November 24, 1996.

54. The Supreme Court's 1942 ruling in *Parry* (Fallos 193–408) demanded that administrative courts should assure the due process of law, for example, and in *Fernández Arias vs. Poggio* of 1960 (Fallos 247–266) the high court required all administrative court decisions have control by regular judicial courts.

55. See Fundación La Ley, "Una Escuela Judicial para la Argentina: Proyecto de creación de la Escuela Judicial Convenio AID" (Buenos Aires: Fundación La Ley, August 1992); World Bank, "Encuentro Sobre Reforma de la Administración de la Justicia," vol. 2, chapter 19, pp. 24–39 (Buenos Aires: World Bank, December 1994). Many officials assert that dependence on foreign aid prevents the internal planning and societal participation needed for effective reforms. Luis Moreno Ocampo, former *fiscales*, author interview, December 13, 1996.

56. Rafael Bielsa, Judiciary Ministry official, author interview, November 9, 1994; and 1993, p. 94; and Rafael Bielsa, *Transformación del Derecho en Justicia* (Buenos Aires: La Let, 1993), p. 94.

57. Criminal Judge Luis Niño, author interview, October 17, 1994.

58. National Survey conducted by the Foro de Estudios para la Administración de Justicia, 2000.

59. Law 24.050 of 1992 clarified that the nominations for the national appeal courts, oral courts, and other courts need only review the candidates' professional background as a lawyer.

60. "Cinco jueces en peligro," *Página/12*, February 21, 1998, p. 7.

61. "En 1999 hubo casi 3000 delitos por día," *La Nación*, April 3, 2000.

62. "La burocracía judicial consume el 32 por ciento del presupuesto," *La Nación*, November 18, 2000.

63. According to former Supreme Court Magistrate Jorge Bacqué, author interview, December 6, 1996.

64. In a survey of eighteen officials regarding judicial independence in democratic Venezuela, the question was asked, Who has most influence in first and superior courts and the Supreme Court? The responses break down as follows, with each number representing how many repondents considered the corresponding group or agency to be the most influential: Executives: 0; Economic Interests: 8; Legislatures: 0; (Other) Judges: 1; Political Parties: 13; Citizens: 0; Public Administrators: 0; Sufficient Independence: 4. This cross-section of interviews was composed of one Supreme Court magistrate, one presiding cabinet minister, one judicial council member, two executive-branch officials, two Fiscal General officials, one senate aide, two members of a presidential reform commission, three officials of lawyers' association and government advisers, two congressmen from minority parties, and three judges. Author interviews, 1990, 1992, 1995, 1998.

65. *Ley Orgánica del Poder Judicial, Gaceta Oficial,* No. 3.995 (Extraordinario), August 13, 1987. The 1961 constitution describes nullity of laws by the Supreme Court but does not mention such power for the lower courts. But article 8 of the Organic Law of the Judicial Branch says that "in addition to the attributions that this law confers upon ordinary courts ... they will also exercise

those that are assigned to them by the rest of the National and State Laws and Municipal Ordinances so long as [they] do not conflict with" the constitution and federal laws.

66. Salom, Ramón Escovar, "¿Cual Constitución?" *El Nacional*, May 26, 1959. Salom went on to serve as Fiscal General and as interior minister in the 1980s and 1990s.

67. Impeached in May 1993, Pérez was tried and found guilty of embezzling $17 million of state money that he alleges went for security of Nicaraguan President Violeta Barrios de Chamorro.

68. Alfonso Ochoa, President of ONTRAT (National Organization of Judiciary Workers), author interview, June 2, 1995. Specifically, Ochoa complained of a lack of resources, inadequate salaries, a lack of meritocratic evaluations, and poor Labor Ministry policies.

69. In 1995, the Venezuela Supreme Court's deficit was among the highest of state agencies, at $5,372,781. The judicial council's was $19,656,805; the TSS's was $289,941; and the contentious-administrative courts' was $207,101.

70. "We have to beg Congress like poor blind souls, desperately trying to convince them not to cut our funds." Cecilia Medina de Villarroel, author interview, April 1995.

71. Alvaro Leal, Director of Studies and Projects, Project of Modernization, Supreme Court of Venezuela, author interview, July 3, 1998.

72. *El Universal*, March 19, 1995. These 1,400 judges amount to about one judge for every 15,000 citizens, below the United Nations recommendation of one for every 4,000 (Ministerio de la Familia 1995).

73. "Nuevo Código de Procedimiento Penal cambia juicio a acusatorio y oral," *El Nacional*, December 26, 1995, p. 2.

74. Luis Enrique Oberto, President, Chamber of Deputies Legislative Commission,, author interview, June 29, 1998.

75. "No Seran Restituidas Las Garantias Mientras no Exista un Clima de Paz," *El Nacional*, January 7, 1961, p. 19. Carlos Andrés Pérez suspended guarantees several times as president between 1989 and 1993.

76. Statement by the executive sent to the Congress, January 30, 1961. *El Nacional*, February 1, 1961, p. 25.

77. Riots throughout the country in February and March, protesting the rise in prices and other government actions, led to the deaths of approximately 1,000 civilians. The president suspended guarantees to "personal liberty and safety" (article 60), the inviolability of the home (article 62), the freedom of association (article 71), and the right to peaceful demonstration (article 115).

78. As a deputy minister of justice in the Lusinchi and Pérez (1989–1993) governments asserted, suspension brings "greater ability to establish tranquility and progress." The "important thing is not to criticize the government ... but to let it do its job." Confidential author interview, April 26, 1995. Although the suspension was declared in order to help investigate those responsible for the collapse of the country's top banks, it actually had very little effect on this investigation.

79. Suspended were the constitutional guarantees of the freedoms from arbitrary arrest and search without a warrant, as well as for travel, to pursue profitable activities, to own private property, and to receive compensation for assets confiscated by the state. The executive restored the guarantees in July 1995 under pressure from Congress and society. *El Nacional*, June 2, 1996, p. D2; *El Nacional*, June 9, 1995, p. D2.

80. It petitioned restitution of article 60's prohibition of detention without a

written order; article 62's guarantee of inviolability of the home; and article 64's protection of free transit. The action would maintain suspension of article 99, the "right of property," and article 101, which allows for state expropriation of goods.

81. "Caldera persionó a la Corte Suprema para que no restituyera las garantías," *El Nacional*, June 1, 1995, p. D2.

82. Hildegard Rondón de Sansó, Supreme Court Magistrate, author interview, June 9, 1995.

5

JUDICIAL COUNCILS

Caught *in flagrante* with a bribe in the sting operation, Judge Melida Aleksic Molina tossed nearly one million *bolívars*—about a third of her $18,000 payment for a favorable ruling—out of her 20th floor office window.... The lucky pedestrians below will not soon forget "the night it rained money."

—*El Nacional*, Caracas, Venezuela, May 2, 1995

IN THIS ONE ABSURD MOMENT, Judge Molina exhibited every stereotype of Latin American judiciaries: corruption, incompetence, and tragicomedy. In reality, of course, many judges are honest, intelligent, and hard-working. The problem is that no one is quite sure how many of each kind there are. Finding out is the task being handed to the region's newly established judicial councils (Consejo de la Judicatura, or Consejo de la Magistratura). Empowered to choose, monitor, and discipline judges, such councils now have major responsibilities over nearly every area of judicial independence and functioning. The high hopes pinned on judicial councils have made them a primary judicial reform in Latin America. Although only a few countries had judicial councils at the beginning of the 1980s, twelve had them at the end of the 1990s (see Table 5.1).

But these councils' ultimate effectiveness—and existence—will be determined by executive power and judicial disarray. Even a council with wide-ranging authority stands little chance against an executive determined to outmaneuver it or against a judiciary whose problems are beyond any single agency. In particular, Latin America's judicial councils have already been caught up in party politics, institutional rivalries, and counteraccusations from the officials being investigated. Executive interference and judicial disarray can also be mutually reinforcing: a council's inability to make headway into judicial matters can encourage the executive to target it, and executive attacks often encourage judicial officials to ignore council direc-

Table 5.1 Judicial Councils in Latin America

Country	Formation			Members
	Legislated	Formed	Reformed	
Argentina	1994	1998		20
Bolivia	1994	1998		5
Brazil	1977	1979	1988	5
Colombia	1981	1991		13
Costa Rica	1989	1993		5
Dominican Republic	1994			11
Ecuador	1992	1998		8
El Salvador	1983			11
Mexico	1995		1999	7
Panama	1987			5
Paraguay	1992			8
Peru	1969	1981	1979,1994	7
Uruguay	1981	1981		8
Venezuela	1961	1969	1988	eliminated

tives. Any lack of clear guidelines on council activities, from formulating budgets to naming personnel, makes them even more politicized and ineffective.

Such obstacles nearly killed off the councils of Argentina and other countries before they were even formed, and they threaten to do so today in countries such as Bolivia. And in Venezuela, one of Latin America's first democracies to establish a council, it was killed off altogether. Only when a council gains the upper hand can it truly address the judiciary's corruption, politicization, and inefficiency. When a judicial council's establishment emerges from a broad democratic consensus, as in Bolivia and Argentina, it is likely to survive. But when it is the product of a nondemocratic regime or temporary political calculations, as in Venezuela and Peru, a council will be weak. As with other reforms, in short, councils are susceptible to the problems they are mandated to solve. Executive power and judicial disarray motivate judicial councils but return to undermine them.

With very few exceptions, councils endure years of haggling and politicking between the time they are legislated and the time they actually start to operate. The political parties, the three branches of government, and interested societal organizations all get involved in determining the council's authority. Particularly controversial are composition and appointment, as no one seems to trust any kind of selection mechanism to adequately sift out political bias. As with other reforms, those entrusted to create an officially neutral agency do not trust each other to make it neutral in practice. The only way out has been to divide appointments based on each sector's official status and unofficial influence. Most countries' councils thus end up with appointments by the executive, legislative, and judicial branches, along with representatives of bar associations and university federations. But less dominant executives tend to have fewer or no appointments. Thus, the military government that created Peru's original council gave itself appointment power over two of ten members (as well as influence over the others), but the council created in the wake of El Salvador's civil war had no executive-designated members.

Although watered down by the same institutional suspicion of new agencies, council authority is more uniform. At the end of formation negotiations, all of Latin America's councils have been granted controls in four areas of judicial functioning: nomination, discipline, finance, and policy. Most councils nominate slates of candidates for openings on the bench, investigate and sometimes prosecute judges guilty of illegal acts, manage the judiciary's budget, and develop policies and plans for the judiciary. Variations and specific restrictions in these four areas, however, can be significant. Councils whose decisions can be overruled, for example, will be weaker than those with final decisionmaking powers. Countries that raise the senate majority needed for Supreme Court *magistrados* help councils battle against politicization more than do those that allow the Supreme Court to retain most nomination authority.[1]

Like the 1974 Italian and 1978 Spanish councils after which they are modeled, most of Latin America's councils arrived during unstable or undemocratic conditions. Some countries, for example, first created a council during military rule. The Brazilian Consejo Nacional de la Magistratura was formed in 1977, with very limited powers, and was replaced in the 1988 constitution by the Consejo de la Justicia Federal, as a complement to the high court, to oversee most of the federal judiciary's budgets and administration. Uruguay also created its council during the authoritarian era but, unlike Brazil, gave it wide powers over court administration and the discipline of its judges.

Most councils, however, were part of democratizing constitutions. Paraguay established a judicial council in its 1992 constitution and regulated it with a March 1994 law. This council is very limited, and its biggest authority is to propose sets of candidates to the Paraguay Supreme Court. Venezuela's council was part of its 1961 democratic constitution, and Ecuador mandated a council in December 1992 as a constitutional reform. The Mexican Consejo de la Judicatura Federal came into being in 1995 as part of President Ernesto Zedillo's constitutional reform packages, which also included elimination of the life tenures of Mexico Supreme Court judges. The Mexican council is in charge of carrying out judicial career laws, overseeing judicial functioning, and selecting judges at all levels under the Supreme Court. Modifications in 1999 further clarified its specific powers.

Most of Central America's judicial councils were formed as civil wars were dying down in the 1980s. El Salvador's council was founded in the 1983 constitution and modified in October 1991 with a constitutional amendment that affirmed its independent status and expanded its appointment authority from first- and second-instance courts to the Supreme Court. In 1980, Honduras created the Council of the Judicial Career, institutionally affiliated with the Supreme Court. The council's members (*magistrados*) are selected by the Supreme Court from a list of ten candidates presented by the court's president. An implementing regulation for the council was passed in 1987. Panama's Law 29 of 1984 established a judicial career law and mandated a judicial council to enforce it. The council has wide powers, with authority to oversee the functioning and planning of the courts and agencies such as the MP.

The structures of most Central American councils are modeled after Costa Rica's. A prototype of that country's council was formed in 1937, and the modern version, called the Consejo Superior del Poder Judicial, came with a 1973 law. A second body, the Consejo de la Judicatura, was established in 1993. The council has a role in administrative policy, career laws, and discipline. It examines candidates to lower-court vacancies; the Supreme Court continues to name superior court judges. The Administrative Council manages much of the judiciary's administration, including appointment of support personnel, and the Judicial Inspection Court (Tribunal de la Inspección Judicial) investigates personnel conduct and determines punishments. But the full Supreme Court reviews appeals of the Inspection Court concerning high court–appointed judges and many of the Judicial Council's disciplinary actions.

Although several additional countries are in the process of creating judicial councils, others, such as Peru and Venezuela, have hounded them out of existence. Peru established the National Council of Justice in 1969 to select and discipline judges. Partly because it was created by the military regime and composed of military officials, the council generally intimidated instead of supported judges. The council was reformed following the 1979 transition to a democratic regime, then underwent further changes after the 1992 suspension of democracy, in the new constitution of 1993, and in the December 1994 organic law reestablishing the body. Subsequently, however, the government stripped the council of its powers. In 1996, executive commissions headed by government appointees were given the council's control over the reorganization of the judiciary and over the public prosecutor's offices. A March 1998 law rescinding the council's constitutional powers to appoint prosecutors was reportedly prompted by its impending investigation of six judges alleged to have signed a forged ruling ordering the Central Reserve Bank to pay U.S.$40 million in a compensation claim to a private corporation. Tensions rose in April 1998, when the dean of the Lima Bar Association—who was one of the judges impeached and dismissed in 1997 from the Constitutional Court for ruling against President Fujimori's plan to run for a third term—fled the country after receiving death threats. The bar association's request to investigate the conduct of several judges linked to the dean was one reason why Congress limited the council's powers. Hostilities finally came to an end in 1998, when the entire council resigned in protest of a law restricting its authority to investigate and dismiss judges. Executive power thus succeeded in crippling the council while sparing the president the trouble of actually eliminating it formally.

Although they have so far avoided such trauma, most other judicial councils still find themselves criticized and embattled. Ironically, they are accused of weakening the independence of judges, for allowing greater executive power in judicial affairs, for creating imbalances among the branches of government, and for bringing party politics into the courts. Far from causing such problems, however, judicial councils are victims of them. One of a council's most important authorities is over the selection process, for example, but in most countries that process remains politicized. Councils are designed not simply to break the president's hold on nominations but to open up and broaden the nomination process beyond the vague and minimum requisites for judges. But even with new rules, councils are blindsided during the nominating process by ongoing disputes over nominations, a lack of qualified judges, executive maneuvers like "horizontal" nominations, and other practices. And once these practices allow unqualified and biased judges onto the bench, both independence and efficiency are that much harder to create.

The experiences of Venezuela, Argentina, and Bolivia illustrate how executive power and judicial disarray determine the effectiveness and the fates of judicial councils. Venezuela's council was reformed and restructured but ultimately undone by the executive's manipulation and the judiciary's disarray. In Argentina, politics delayed and almost ruined the council, but its formation at a time of popular demands for change has given it substantial support. In Bolivia, finally, the council was established successfully but is being hammered by outside interference and judicial problems. Its precarious condition is being closely watched by the many countries whose own councils also face uncertain futures.

Venezuela

Venezuela's post-1958 democracy was made up of strong institutions run confidently by a dominant party elite. The main exceptions were agencies requiring a certain level of independence and power-sharing. The 1961 constitution mandated a judicial council, but the AD government, despite its pact with COPEI, did not want a neutral body choosing judges.[2] Thus, it put off legislating the organic law needed to actually establish the judicial council, conveniently allowing the executive's Ministry of Justice to continue appointing judges. But the organic law was quickly patched together in September 1969, following the unexpected election victory of COPEI. AD, no longer controlling the executive but still having a congressional majority, pushed through the law to limit the new executive's power over the judiciary. The hurried pace of enactment was criticized for not involving a wider sector of officials and for lacking background studies. Almost immediately, President Caldera filed a petition of unconstitutionality before the Supreme Court, which upheld the enacting law by one vote.

Luckily for AD, however, the council never really gained its footing before the party returned to power. From the start, the council got bogged down in bureaucracy and politics. The lack of an implemented judicial career law, above all, impeded the council from its primary function of selecting and processing judges. Disciplinary functions did not work much better. Accusations filed at the council were reviewed by an inspector, who, if finding wrongdoing, began a disciplinary process. But most of this initial processing had to be dedicated just to separating substantive from spurious accusations. When investigations were actually initiated, bureaucracy slowed them down and politics made them nearly irrelevant. Of the 148 cases reviewed by the council between 1971 and 1980, 42 percent ended with absolution. Only thirty judges were suspended and only twelve were dismissed (Calcaño de Temeltas 1982: 76–86).

Not surprisingly, citizens and officials alike became more and more reluctant to present cases to the council. Between 1983 and 1985, the number of cases dropped by a third. Aware of the frustration that led to this drop, the council picked up the pace and dismissed seventeen judges in those two years alone. But even though processes speeded up, politicization continued. Certain rules, such as the requirement for unanimity in most decisions, allowed the government's appointees to continue protecting judges affiliated with it. The council's ineffectiveness led to a reformulation in 1988, when judicial inefficiency and corruption could no longer be ignored. Its condition was part of the state's larger deterioration in the 1980s, which generated growing societal protests, leftist and populist political movements, and, eventually, officials' belated support of reform. The 1988 law reduced the judicial council from eleven to five members—three named by the Supreme Court, one by the president, and one by the Congress—and required both the Supreme Court and the Congress to approve their selections by a two-thirds vote. The council was also given wide-ranging powers over administration, court inspection, and discipline.

As political realignments shook up the executive and legislative branches in the 1990s, the council unexpectedly emerged as one of the more stable and independent state bodies. It took the offensive with promotion of reforms throughout the judiciary, boosted by its administration of a $30 million World Bank grant for such changes. The council even ventured out of the capital, braving the thickets of favoritism and nepotism around the country.[3] In some states, such as Nueva Esparta and Carabobo, personal or political networks dominate court processes and appointments. In 1991, the judicial council began to address these conditions by creating oversight officials called the *juez rector* (rector judge) and the Consejo General de Jueces (General Council of Judges) in each of the country's juridical jurisdictions.[4] The council also became more legitimate and effective in this period because of its more balanced appointment from all three branches of government and because of the growing weakness of each of these branches and the parties dominating them.

Politicization and bureaucracy, however, were far from vanquished. The council still did not directly name judges, allowing executive officials to continue interfering in the nomination process and, in turn, the courts. As in most other countries, Venezuela selected most judges through *concursos públicos* (public forums and competitions). For all levels below the high court in Venezuela, such *concursos* were run by members of the judicial council and at least one judge, which reviewed candidates' credentials, practical experience, and legal views.[5] But Congress was not obliged to accept nominees, and judges at all levels needed only a majority to be elected (and in votes were not required to be open to the public; article 4, *Ley Orgánica de la Corte Suprema* 1977). With the AD and COPEI continuing as the majority parties in Congress, as a result, nominations continued to be a party affair, sent to a vote only after closed interparty agreements.

Meanwhile, many judges, angry at their own weakness, resented the judicial council's authority. As in other countries, they complained that the existence of a judicial council entails giving too much power to nonjudicial officials and that the council had just become another channel for executive and party domination.[6] In August 1992, one of the country's biggest associations of judges lent support to a congressional proposal to eliminate the council and give its appointment power to the Supreme Court. Two months later, the MP publicly opposed the new president of the council for her political alliances. High-publicity cases of court corruption at the time continued to keep the spotlight on the council for not sifting out poor candidates.

Regarding investigation and discipline, the 1988 law did not prepare the council for the increases in accusations and diminishing funds during the 1990s. In 1995 alone, the council processed more than 1,400 denunciations of corruption and other irregularities against the country's 1,400 judges. But hundreds of other charges went uninvestigated, and many dismissed judges were reinstated by the government with back pay. "Of all the denunciations, the majority have no relevance," asserted one council *magistrado* that year; "corruption penetrates the judiciary, but not in the dimensions...whipped up by the media. But of course it doesn't help that we have neither the budget nor the personnel to solve the problem."[7] A year later, the same *magistrado* publicly complained about the lack of administrative and policy support. The judicial council "is 26 years old and all of its procedures are done manually," she said; "it manages 10,000 officials, 1,109 courts, and everything is manual. There are no plans or policies, since no one bothers to make them. The only thing officials worry about is controlling the judiciary."[8]

Rampant favoritism also remained. According to one of its former presidents, the judicial council helps "its friends, who are many, and 90 percent of the denunciations" are absolved because the council buys the flimsy defense that a controversial ruling is simply "an independent interpretation of the judge" (Ojeda 1995: 87). Immediately prior to the inauguration of the Caldera administration in 1994, the council reportedly absolved hundreds of pending denunciations to minimize the possibility that the new government would dismiss the judges against whom the denunciations were made.[9] The council's authority was whittled away further by legal setbacks such as the Supreme Court's ruling in favor of an *amparo* lodged against it by the TSS. Angered by the council's opposition to Congress's budget for the TSS, that court's judges brought the first use of *amparo* in an interinstitutional clash.

In this period after its 1988 reform, the council was subjected to attacks from all three branches of government. The country's largest association of judges criticized the *concursos de oposición,* in which the council conducted public reviews of potential judges, as "showy" and argued that such spectacles would not even be needed if the council did its job of properly vetting candidates.[10] Congress also expressed antagonism toward the judicial council. In 1992, for example, it rejected a list of council recommendations for the Supreme Court because it was submitted "out of place" with congressional deadlines and procedures.[11] The council underwent further criticism by the Caldera government, which attempted to appoint temporary "roving" judges without going through the council. It also continued its efforts to replace the council with a High Commission of Justice, an idea promoted by Caldera as a senator in the early 1990s. The justice minister even proposed handing over the council's authority to open investigation of corrupt judges to the PTJ. The council itself wanted reform—but mainly to strengthen its disciplinary authority.

Yet it was Congress that took the initiative on the council as the executive became increasingly caught up in the country's economic crisis. As part of Congress's Integral Reform of the Judiciary package, the council underwent a further reformation through the new Organic Law of the Judicial Council of 1998. In order to make the agency more professional and transparent, the new law divided it into separate administrative and disciplinary *salas* (chambers or divisions of the court that specialize in a particular area such as labor), the former with three members and the latter with five. The Supreme Court appointed one administrative member and three disciplinary members with a two-thirds vote, Congress appointed one member in each *sala* with a two-thirds vote, and the president also got one appointment in each *sala*. The law fortified the council by affiliating the Autonomous Service of Public Penal Defense with it, by tightening up disciplinary measures, and by strengthening the judicial school. Under the new Judicial Career Law, also approved in 1998, the council was given control over new and stricter entry requirements and was made responsible for reviewing candidates records, the "quality" of their rulings, their hours of work, the speed of their processes, and other details. As in other countries, these measures showed how much the council continued to be the best hope for real change. But growing criticisms of the overall judicial reform, along with an upcoming election, prevented real change from happening. In particular, disagreements arose over many of the new law's provisions, and Congress took more than five months after the law was signed to appoint its members. The executive kept up its steady criticism of the council as well.

The judicial council's rocky journey came to an end in 1999, when the new constitution replaced it with the far more limited Executive Judicial Office (Dirección Ejecutiva de la Magistratura) within the new high court (Tribunal Supremo de Justicia). Dominated by the president's allies, the assembly that drafted the constitution took over many legislative and judicial functions, using its newfound power to dismiss more than 120 judges—and review more than 3,500 further accusations—on charges of inefficiency and politicization. In a bad omen for Venezuelan democracy, the measures liquidating the judicial council and the Supreme Court were taken *after* the popular election endorsing the constitution.

Argentina

One of the most surprising recommendations of the Alfonsín administration's Council for the Consolidation of Democracy was that nominations of judges be public without use of a judicial council. Citing the negative experiences of countries such as Spain, the administration argued that a council would create an establishment of judges impermeable to societal needs. This stance, of course, was also rooted in a desire to minimize the Peronist opposition's leverage over the judiciary. During the constitutional negotiations in 1994, however, the Radical Party was in the opposition and favored the creation of a judicial council. This about-face was similar to that in Venezuela during the 1960s, when AD pushed for a council after it lost the presidency.

Support for a judicial council also came from the judiciary's poor financial planning and the government's poor handling of charges against judges.[12] As in most countries, judges in Argentina can be removed only for ineptitude or misconduct, whereas employees and auxiliaries can be punished with warnings, a fine of up to a third of remuneration, temporary suspension, or dismissal.[13] Throughout history, of course, even life terms did not prevent judges from "being resigned" or impeached for alleged failure to perform duties. But the end of such illegitimate dismissals after 1983 did not mean that they were replaced by legitimate investigation of actual wrongdoing. Of the 176 requests for impeachment made between August 1990 and March 1993, about half went to the Supreme Court and promptly became backlogged. The senate wound up trying a mere thirteen cases and removed seven judges, fueling charges of inefficiency and favoritism.

During the formation of the constitutional reforms, the opposition Radical Party proposed creating a judicial council to nominate judges at all levels, including the Supreme Court.[14] But the Peronists, according to one of their representatives, "defended the participation of the political powers" in the nomination process because that process "interests not only [those] connected professionally with judicial activity" but "all social sectors" (García Lema 1994: 218). Others argued, more speciously, that a council would be foreign to the country's legal tradition. But the idea of a national judicial council gradually gained support because, as with other state reforms, many provinces had been establishing their own well-functioning councils.[15] This decentralized approach created structural models as well as political momentum for a national council.

But the council was approved in the end primarily because the ruling Peronists wanted the new constitution amended to allow for presidential reelection and was willing to compromise on other matters. In the constitutional negotiations, as a result, the parties agreed to create a judicial council whose members would be appointed by a range of agencies, which would have authority to administer the judiciary, nominate all judges below the high court, and help carry through punishments against wayward judges. The 1994 constitutional reform also created a special panel, the Jurado de Enjuiciamiento (jury trial), composed of "legislators, judges and lawyers" (article 114), to try judges. Although this body was also subject to controversy over its representation, the negotiated compromise between the two main parties was to have no executive representatives on it.

Subsequently, however, the council got stalled over its composition. Because the constitutional reform did not include detailed agreement on precisely how council members would be appointed, politicization quickly took over.[16] In the parties' fight over appointments, most contentious was the division between judicial professionals—judges and lawyers—and those from other areas. The Peronists were particularly opposed to giving the bar association too many slots because of its leanings toward the Radical Party and the city of Buenos Aires. The two sides became entrenched into two camps—"whites," who wanted a weak council; and "blues," who favored a strong one. More than three years and many careers later, a compromise was reached on an unwieldy composition of twenty members: one executive appointee; four judges elected by colleagues and representing different court levels; four senators (two from the majority, one from each of the two largest minority parties); four lower house representatives (two from the majority, and one from each of the two largest minority parties); five lawyers elected by bar association members; and two academics elected by colleagues.

But while the Peronists calculated that they could count on deciding seven of the government appointees and the Radicals six, based on controls over the government, the council's lawyers and academics were up for grabs. Continuing to suspect that these members would likely be Radicals, the government in June 1998 proposed changing the judicial council law to transfer administration of the academics' election from the Radical-associated National Inter-university Council to the more government-friendly Council of Universities. Denying any political motivation, the government argued that the change would allow for "representation of the entire academic community."[17] But with the approaching 1999 elections widening internal Peronist rifts, the proposal collapsed under the weight of party politics, as did the legislative appointment of council members.

Along with such wrangling, executive pressures and institutional conflict undermined the council before it even began operating. Nearly 150 petitions for trials against judges were held up by Peronist senators, who argued that until the judicial council was formed the petitions could not go forward. This generated accusations of political cover-up by the opposition as well as backlogs for the council when it finally started up. During this ongoing debate, five provinces managed to establish their own judicial councils, and many others passed laws clarifying regulations on transference, dismissal, remuneration, and professional stability in the judiciary.[18]

The judicial council finally came into existence in November 1998. Although political divisions were blurred by the council's defense of its authority, it still faced serious bureaucratic and political obstacles. Almost immediately, it came under criticism for slowness in selecting and sanctioning judges. This lack of action was due primarily to a complex selection process that involved selecting panels to review nominees and a lengthy study of nominees' records. Within that process, further delays were caused by disagreement over how much weight to give different areas of experience. In particular, most members' tendency to emphasize past legal practice elicited criticism that the council would simply maintain the judiciary's status quo. One possible resolution—to create expert bodies to review nominees without the involvement of the council—was not considered. The council did not do much better with discipline. Its Disciplinary Commission had not actually sanctioned any judge in its first year, and not for a lack of cases. But mostly to blame was the house of deputies, which during the previous years held back many cases and, after the council's formation, dragged its feet on at least forty more, many of which were against judges affiliated with the Peronist opposition.

When the judicial council did move forward, political conflicts reemerged. Internal political factions led to delays when one faction, sensing that it would lose a vote, would derail discussion on the matter at hand. Both inside and outside the council, other clashes arose over the composition of council committees. Weak disciplinary action against sitting judges, for example, was blamed on the judges who formed the majority of the disciplinary committee. More serious was the fact that the government-appointed president of the Supreme Court was also head of the judicial council, which led to charges of behind-the-scenes executive control. Such charges appeared to be confirmed with Menem's many unilateral horizontal appointments of judges from one court to another, in order to fill key openings with Peronist allies. Members of the judicial council reacted harshly to this practice, declaring that it violated the constitution's clear mandate that judicial appointments be made through the council.

The judicial council clashed with the Supreme Court, primarily over disciplinary power and salary determination. Despite what the judicial council law said, the high court claimed that it alone, as the top judicial body, retained disciplinary powers in the judiciary. Overcoming internal political divisions, eighteen of the judicial council's members—the president conspicuously not among them—signed a resolution affirming its exclusive authority for discipline of judicial personnel. In what the council took as an act of "hostility," the high court rejected the resolution and went ahead to take on specific cases.[19] Budgets also sparked disputes with the high court. When the judicial union petitioned for higher salaries, the president of the Supreme Court directed its claims to the council. The judicial council approved of the increase, but only on the condition that the Economy Ministry increase the overall judicial budget. But the high court claimed that such an increase was impossible and that the 1990 Autarky Law granted the high courts complete determination over the judicial budget. The council retorted that its creation in 1994 superceded the 1990 law. The low budget given to the council did not help: the Economy Ministry denied the Supreme Court the $1 million for the initial functioning of the council, leaving the new agency without even a permanent office. Overwhelmed with its most basic tasks, it had to indefinitely put off long-term authority, such as developing a comprehensive judicial reform plan and a judicial school.

But its performance was still slow, and in all of 2000 it accused only one judge of inadequate performance. The council defended itself by complaining of the huge workload it was given upon its formation and that its founding law was excessively regulatory because the requirements to ensure transparency had become unwieldy. In particular, it pointed out that the process of selecting judges—involving a review of the record, an exam, and a round of interviews—takes time. President Fernando de la Rúa formulated legislation to allow the judicial council to quickly fill the many vacancies in the courts while the formal nominations were proceeding, and the agency's members also earned some breathing space with their suspensions of a few notoriously corrupt judges. But these developments have not stemmed criticism to date. The council's budget jumped from $10 million to $15.8 million and its personnel from 100 to nearly 200, prompting criticisms of waste. On several occasions, candidates to the court with exemplary records have been denied support from the council at the last minute because of technicalities or protests from council members that they did not have "the best democratic values."[20]

This has led the Supreme Court, whose members have anonymously characterized the council a "monster" that "should be dissolved," to try to reclaim some of the council's powers.[21] The council's authorities are to preselect judges, administer the judiciary, and dictate regulations. But the high court, arguing that the council should focus on hiring judges, has tried to wrest the others powers away from it. In March 2000, the Supreme Court decided to deny the council the power to dictate regulations. In response, a council member moved to request a political trial against the entire court. The Jurado de Enjuiciamiento, the body created to try accused judges, has also been pulled into this melee. The body is dominated by Peronists, who see it as a check against the judicial council's power. In several cases, in fact, the Jurado has been accused of limiting the types of evidence used in council charges of Peronist judges.

The council will probably weather these attacks, primarily because of a lack of alternatives as well as the strong public desire to cleanse the judiciary. Although the Radicals' return to the executive might have diminished their interest in a strong judicial council, such reluctance is largely overcome by the political and economic gains it would reap from presiding over judicial improvements. But the president still resists perceived intrusions on his authority, such as his outright rejection of council requests that he relinquish his power to accept the resignations of judges under investigation. Each of its disputes may serve to strengthen the agency by ironing out

poor regulations and unsettled political relations. But even with acknowledgment of the harms of both politics and bureaucracy, the council will still
have to manage to show concrete results if it is to gain the institutionalized
power needed to bring real change. Attacks over its slowness, administration, and internal disputes will keep it permanently on the defensive. Until
it has been allowed to figure out a way around both judicial bureaucracy
and national politics, the council could be undermined by both.

Bolivia

A similar pattern—an ambitious judicial council caught up in bureaucracy
and conflict—has played out in Bolivia. Modeled after the Spanish judicial
council and established by law in August 1994, the council began functioning in mid-1998. Its five members, headed by the president of the Supreme
Court, have the authority to propose candidates for most courts, formulate
the judicial budget and administer resources, and investigate and discipline
all judicial personnel. The council hit the ground running on all of these
tasks. Trying to fill the many openings in the judiciary, it set up a new system for evaluating candidates, reviewed more than 10,000, and formulated
reforms to further streamline nominations.

The second priority was financial. Estimating that about 70 percent of
judges' time goes toward financial management and that the judiciary pays
overinflated prices for property and material, the council has begun to
rationalize management and accounting. Smarting at such criticism, the
agencies that were previously in charge of budgets attacked the council's
campaign. The senate accused the council of corruption for spending excessive amounts for property and equipment. One Supreme Court judge
claimed that the council ate up 28.3 percent of the judiciary's budget, causing the notoriously low salaries of judges and judicial personnel.[22] Because
of the importance of salaries to judicial personnel, the court knew that such
criticism would be a particularly potent attack on the council. The minister
of justice as well as Congress's Constitutional Commission also blamed the
council for the World Bank's decision to freeze a $25 million credit for
judicial reform, 80 percent of which was earmarked for modernization and
salary increases. They claim that the council failed to formulate career
laws, appoint key officials, and undertake other tasks that the council says
it completed. The World Bank itself, however, said it froze the program
because of bickering between agencies, the council's failure to appoint a
director, and the government's failure to approve an MP law, appoint *fiscales* and modify certain aspects of the organic law of the judiciary. But by
that time the government's attacks on the council had stuck. As in other

countries, domestic politics was used to turn the judicial council's efforts against it.

The council's investigation of corruption brought even greater political wrath. Council investigators had caught judges in their offices accepting money, cavorting naked with assistants, and conducting other unjudicial activities. In its first fifteen months, the council sanctioned nearly 100 judicial personnel—the first time in history any sanction had been imposed. But before long the backlashes began. One started with the trial of a court officer on fifteen charges of collaboration with drug traffickers. The officer appealed to the Constitutional Court on the grounds that the dismissal violated his due process rights. Although it upheld the council's disciplinary authority, the court ruled in the officer's favor and returned him to his post. Immediately thereafter, the lower house of Congress eliminated the judicial council's power to dismiss judges and limited punishment to suspension of up to five years. The senate then reduced it to a range of three months to three years. Derogation of the power to dismiss judges in particular has left a great "legislative hole" that effectively eliminates the council's main power and allows serious criminal corruption to continue.[23]

As in Argentina, the council has also clashed with the Supreme Court. Although the Supreme Court agrees that the council has disciplinary powers, it says that the lack of clear regulations has caused abuse of those powers. These largely unfounded accusations were intended to tilt power toward the high court. Specifically, as in Argentina, the Supreme Court's president is the judicial council's president, causing an inherent conflict of interest that was intensified by the senate's decision to allow the council to call a quorum with only the president and two council members—practically turning the council into an "appendage" of the high court.[24]

Such tensions between the council and other state agencies led to the council's February 2000 letter to the president of the Congress (Consejo de la Judicatura 2000), in which it asserted that the judiciary—including the Constitutional Tribunal—was undermining the council's work and even threatening its members' lives. It accused courts of conspiring with political parties as well as officials, and of protecting accused judges, many of whom were using *amparo* petitions as a legal escape from disciplinary action.

These tensions blew up when council members began blaming legislators for the judiciary's corruption. When two council members accused several senators of being corrupt, an outraged senate ordered them to appear to explain their statements in person. When the council responded that the senate had no subpoena authority over it, the senate reiterated its demand, and the minister of government ordered the police to retrieve the council members forthwith. One of the two, Luis Paravicini, came to the senate voluntarily. But the meeting disintegrated as soon as it started when Paravicini opened with a declaration that that he would not cooperate with a "pack of *corruptos*"; he then followed up with two writs of habeas corpus against the commission and the government minister, accusing the commission of usurping the council's disciplinary powers and the minister of justice of being "inept."[25] The commission—led by a legislator associated with a notorious bribery case—counterattacked with charges of sedition and contempt against Paravicini, and the justice minister asked all the council members to resign.

Although Bolivia succeeded in forming a judicial council that has not shied away from taking on the most difficult challenges, the ensuing resistance to its efforts makes it a case study of how underlying processes limit a new institution's effectiveness.

Conclusion

Although structural, financial, and moral disarray in the judiciary slow down the judicial councils in Latin America, political interests remain the biggest threat. When a council is not scared off by chaotic administration and widespread corruption, it often rebuffed by executive and legislative officials whose interests are threatened by actual change. Put simply, judicial councils are subject to the vagaries of politics and corruption—the very things they are designed to root out.

Notes

1. In Paraguay, the president appoints Supreme Court judges with senate consent, but only for five-year terms. The president also appoints the other judges, with the consent of the high court. Chile now has a model in which the president fills vacancies on the Supreme Court and the courts of appeals from a list of names proposed by the Supreme Court. The Mexican president, with the approval of the senate, appoints the members of the Supreme Court, which in turn selects the circuit court and district court judges. In Panama, the cabinet council (the president and his cabinet ministers) appoints members of the Supreme Court for ten-year terms. The Supreme Court appoints judges to the appellate court, which in turn appoints the judges immediately lower in the hierarchy.

2. Constitutional article 217 created the judicial council and gave it the authority "to assure the independence, efficacy, discipline and respect of the courts and to guarantee judges the benefits of the judicial career. In this it must give adequate representation to the Public Power's other branches." A judicial council was also included in the 1947 constitution.

3. The growth of the drug trade and drug cartels in Venezuela has also exacerbated judicial corruption. Bombings, death threats, assassinations, and gun attacks

have been carried out against judges and judicial personnel involved in drug cases, and there have been many pardons of those accused of drug offenses. In the state of Miranda, for example, First Instance Penal Judge Ana Teresa Morazzani released several narco-trafficking suspects who had been captured by the PTJ. When the suspects were rearrested, she then ordered the arrest of the chief of the PTJ's antidrug division. It is said that this judge is a member of the tribe known as Las Chicas, headed by a former magistrate of the Consejo de la Judicatura.

4. Resolution No. 1184 of the *Consejo de la Judicatura*, November 6, 1991. One example was Penal Court Judge Clotilde Condado Rodríguez, a relative of President Caldera, who was awash in allegations of corruption yet was given an important case against a top bank official. Although prohibited from fleeing the country, the banker did.

5. Articles 25–28 of the *Ley Orgánica de la Carrera Judicial*, December 1980. For superior-court nominees, the reviewing judge is from the Supreme Court; for lower-court nominations, the reviewing judge is from a superior court. Laws establishing "career" judiciaries with entry based on competitive examination also promote judicial independence by assuring more competent judges.

6. Mercedes Melina de Villarroel, President of the Association of Judges of Caracas and Superior Juvenile Court Judge, author interview, March 29, 1995.

7. Gisela Parra Mejías, judicial council Magistrado, author interview, April 11, 1995.

8. "Elementos políticos interfieren con el proceso de reforma judicial," EUD.com, October 7, 1996.

9. In January 1995, the judicial council president said that the number of expedients or denunciations against judges in the Consejo was 3,000, 2,500 of which were left over from the previous administration and 500 accumulated during 1994. He added that his predecessors sanctioned, with notices or suspension, many judges who deserved dismissal.

10. "El Congreso desechó lista de candidatos de la Judicatura," *El Universal,* May 2, 1992, p. 1–17.

11. Ibid.

12. "There is no base-zero budget, no results-based budget, no planning budget, or budgeting for 'management' or administration of the [judicial] apparatus." Rafael Bielsa, author interview, November 9, 1994.

13. Decreto-ley 1285/58, articles 3, 13, 14, 15, 16, modified by Ley 24.289.

14. Article 99 of the constitution allows the president to "name the *magistrados* of the Supreme court with consent of the Senate by two-thirds of its members in session," and to name "the rest of the judges of inferior federal courts based on a proposal of three names by the *Consejo de la Magistratura*, with consent of the Senate."

15. At the time, the provinces of San Juan, San Luís, Río Negro, Chaco, Santiago del Estero, Tierra del Fuego, and Formosa all had or were in the process of creating judicial councils.

16. Despite agreements that professional lawyers would not form a quorum, for instance, then–Justice Minister Barra argued that the judicial council "should be integrated, in its majority, by members outside of the judiciary." Adrián Ventura, "Entrevista al Dr. Rodolfo Barra," *La Nación,* December 5, 1994.

17. The minister of education, quoted in "El Turno de los Profesores," *Trespuntos,* July 8, 1998.

18. Twelve provinces give their supreme courts the power to prepare the judi-

ciary's budget and, in some cases, to administer it: Catamarca, Córdoba, Corrientes, Chubut, Formosa, La Pampa, La Rioja, Mendoza, Neuquén, Río Negro, San Luis, and Chaco (Cámara de Diputados de la Provincia de Buenos Aires 1987).

19. "Nueva pelea de la Corte y el Consejo de la Magistratura," *La Nación,* March 15, 2000.

20. "Una nueva cultura judicial," *La Nación*, July 12, 2000.

21. "Demasiados empleados," *La Nación,* June 7, 2000.

22. "Una piedra en al zapato de la Corte Suprema," *La Gaceta Jurídica,* July 28, 2000.

23. Luis Carlos Paravicini, Judicial Council Member, author interview, July 14, 2000.

24. Ibid.

25. "Paravicini llama 'mediocre e inepto' al ministro de Justicia," *Presencia,* July 22, 2000.

6

JUDICIAL ACCESS

ULTIMATELY, INSTITUTIONS ARE NOT TRULY REFORMED unless they are accessible to citizens. Civil, commercial, and criminal courts must be able to resolve justiciable conflicts, enforce agreements, and allow citizens to take legal action against the state, private enterprise, and other citizens. But a constant backlog of cases, contradictory and outdated laws, and a range of physical, education, and linguistic obstacles effectively thwart justice for more than 80 percent of all Latin Americans. The exhaustion of those trying to break down these barriers have led them to develop alternative structures as well as to apply political pressure.

Limited access to the judiciary is a sensitive and sometimes explosive problem in new or unstable democracies. Unprecedented freedoms ushered in by the transition can create overwhelming demands for justice not only regarding past human rights violations but also current conditions. In the modern era, legal responses to problems like corruption and economic inequality often become part of national politics, with many citizens employing actions such as lawsuits and denunciations "as a form of political activity" (Zemans 1983; Giles and Lancaster 1989). When suddenly expecting justice after a long authoritarian era, however, society can short-circuit a judicial system unprepared for such demand. This pressure is heightened by the novelty of the very notion of judicial access. Even in industrial democracies, where the movement for judicial access began, advances have been slow and patchy—even with the support of civil rights protections and institutional stability. In democracies without such benefits, creating judicial access is that much harder and riskier.

On one level, structural limitations prevent or discourage the majority of citizens from resorting to the courts. Bureaucratic requirements, poor infrastructure, and lack of judges test the patience of even the most determined litigants, and investigations and trials in nearly every country in Latin America are seemingly interminable.[1] The average time for criminal trials in Venezuela and Argentina is 4.5 years. In the 1990s Venezuela's 22 million people were served by just 1,400 courts.[2] This average of one judge for every 15,000 people is far below a United Nations recommendation: at least one judge for every 4,000 people.

On a deeper level, judicial access is limited by less transparent conditions such as social discrimination and byzantine procedures. Legal formalism also restricts access in indiscernible ways. Basing court decisions on the letter of the law is, of course, necessary for the defense of constitutional rights. But an exclusive attention to the semantic form of a law can frustrate its larger purpose and spirit, leading to unjust application or unfair interpretation in real-life cases. This danger is high amid contradictory statutes, overloaded dockets, political pressures, and a lack of stare decisis. In Brazil, the courts took a formalistic interpretation of a housing law by rejecting petitions to decrease payments that hurt the law's intended working-class beneficiaries (Trubek 1978: 256). In Venezuela, the Supreme Court rejected a 1990 *amparo* action by the Kari'ña indigenous people against a local government that declared them extinct and confiscated their land, arguing that the Kari'ñas's delay in taking action implied their consent with the measure. Many believe that the courts, in fact, use "premeditatively impenetrable language" (Bielsa 1993: 19) to paper over its inability to deal with real-world problems.[3] "The use of very archaic expressions [and] excessively technical [and] inconsistent use of terminology," along with obtuse logic, makes satisfaction or even comprehension impossible for the majority of people (Bielsa 1993: 82).

This range of obstacles, from a lack of judges to judges' attitudes, can be overcome only with specific reforms. Although such reforms respond most directly to judicial disarray and would apply almost entirely to the judiciary, the executive is seen as critical to getting them formulated and making them effective. Because of the judiciary's long-standing weakness and subservience, it is largely regarded as a headless system whose improvement depends on an authoritative president. More and more, however, the executive's own actions are a motivation for access reforms. The public's frustration with court limitations and discrimination tend to simmer, but its intolerance of illegal executive activities that escape court scrutiny are more likely to spur concrete measures. When society believes that executive and ruling-party manipulation is preventing resolution of individual and societal injustices, as in Argentina during the 1980s and Venezuela during the 1990s, new popular legal channels are opened. Otherwise, reform tends to be more moderate. When court inefficiency scares off foreign investors or when special tribunals generate international criticism, for example, access reforms will be limited to those specific problems.

In varying combinations, such pressures have given way in Latin

America to four areas of judicial access reform. First, there are measures to provide free legal aid to criminal defendants lacking means. Second are related reforms to set up and operate centers that provide legal aid and information on criminal as well as civil cases. The third area of access measures is government-sponsored mechanisms for alternative dispute resolution (ADR), such as mediation, to replace regular court procedures. The fourth major kind of reform goes beyond ADR, allowing individual communities to set up parallel judicial structures.

The long-term effectiveness of such changes depends on how the changes affect and accommodate the judicial and the executive branches. Most reforms, including legal aid and government-sponsored ADR, focus on widening access to existing agencies. Because they improve efficiency and can be monitored by officials, such measures usually enjoy broad political support. Yet because they often do not take on the most intractable inefficiencies and external controls, their long-term impact is mitigated. A smaller number of reforms, community forums especially, avoid executive controls and judicial disarray by circumventing the executive and judiciary themselves. But because such changes scramble the traditional power dynamics of judicial procedures, and because they are harder to control, they usually have less political support. Innovation, then, is the source of their promise and their vulnerability.

Because access reforms by definition involve citizens far more compared to other reforms, societal divisions and weaknesses also reduce their effectiveness. Indigenous groups demanding land rights share little in common with urban sectors concerned with garbage disposal, for example, and conflicts over property are likely to pit societal sectors against each other. Access measures that get enacted, therefore, tend to lack new ideas opposed by large sectors of the population—that is, they are often vague and unthreatening by design. Still, the judicial and executive branches will undermine even watered-down proposals. Administratively challenged judicial structures are slow to adapt, and state officials discourage class actions or use of civil and commercial courts, which are daunting prospects for citizens under any circumstances.

More generally, officials look down on the majority of less-educated and less-skilled citizens. With governments' inability to resolve economic problems or stem violent crime, such attitudes have led to a gradual blaming of the poorer and marginalized sectors of society. Political pressures can combine with ongoing state practices to turn whole sectors of society into suspects, burdens, and threats. Media analysis and political discourse associate unemployment with illegal immigrants, moral decay with homosexuals, underdevelopment with indigenous peoples, and drug-trafficking with young men from the barrios. Change that increases access for these sectors—with all the rights that entails—therefore often lacks the political support to be enacted or to be effective. Efforts to stop extrajudicial killings and other forms of social cleansing, for example, have stirred up popular support for such practices in Brazil, Colombia, and Peru. In Mexico, Ecuador, and other countries, efforts to defend constitutional protections of homosexuals have led to fierce backlashes by municipal officials and citizen groups.

Finally, even new proreform governments may continue or step up interference that weakens access. They often do so under the guise of getting rid of judges affiliated with discredited parties, putting in more capable administrators, or making the judiciary responsible for ending problems such as civil violence. If these new judges do prove to be "able", then the executive is emboldened to continue this approach, particularly if the executive enjoys political popularity and a legislative majority.

To understand the enactment and effectiveness of judicial access reforms, however, it is first necessary to understand the conceptual and historical context of judicial access itself. The first section reconceives the idea by unpacking the actors, structures, and functions involved in judicial access, and the second section looks at its historical development. The third section then examines the process of enacting access proposals, and their effectiveness after enactment, in new democracies.

The Concept of Judicial Access

The limitations of many reforms stem first from unclear or limited conceptions. In general, *judicial access* can be defined as the equal opportunity by all citizens to use, and receive remedies from, mechanisms of conflict and grievance resolution. As with other areas of the rule of law, this involves a wide set of actors, institutions, and functions that interact in many ways. The most important interactions can be sifted out with three questions: Access by whom? Access to what? and Access for what? These three questions capture the main determinants of access by individuals in Latin America. They also show how and when those individuals fall into the gap between constitutional standards and daily practices.

Access by Whom?

What individuals and social sectors do and do not receive adequate access? Most generally, access is determined by the citizen's relation to the mechanisms being used, that is, whether he or she is bringing an individual complaint in a minor conflict, is a criminal defendant, is part of a group lodging a lawsuit, or has some other role in a judicial procedure. Within a country, for example, there may be greater access for those with minor complaints than for those facing criminal charges or with collective claims.[4] Access is also determined by individuals' makeup, regardless of the type of judicial procedure in which they are involved. Throughout Latin America and other regions, officials provide different levels of service based on citizens' socioeconomic status, language, race, ethnicity, gender, and other personal traits. Such discrimination is sharpened when certain crimes are associated with certain social sectors, such as drug-trafficking with young males. Levels of access also vary with the strength of social networks and customs. Demands for use of judicial structures are low when different groups have functioning mechanisms of conflict resolution, but demands can be high when interaction among communities requires state intervention.

Access to What?

Are there differing levels of access to the many judicial and nonjudicial agencies that dispense justice? Access by defense attorneys to documents, access by a defendant's family to legal support, and access by a community to knowledge of environmental laws are examples of different needs by different people in the judiciary. Access to nonjudicial agencies such as police forces, public administrators, and oversight commissions can also help resolve conflicts and grievances—especially when money is part of the process. Connections with political parties and nongovernmental organizations, which are likely to have influence in the judiciary and state agencies, are likely to be useful for the same reasons.[5]

Access for What?

This last question centers on upholding the results of access, which requires actions ranging from supportive legal interpretations to unbiased rulings. Above all, it is about the ultimate objective of judicial access: remedies. Remedies are measures, dictated by courts and some nonjudicial state agencies, to redress specific injustices. There are three basic kinds: injunction, damages, and restitution. An injunction "directs the defendant to act, or to refrain from acting in a specified way;" damages are "a judicial award in money, payable as compensation to one who has suffered a legally recognized injury or harm"; and restitution is "a return or restoration of what the defendant has gained in a transaction" (Dobbs 1993: secs. 2.9[1], 3.1, 4.1[1]). Access to justice means little if it does not result in implemented remedies, whose effectiveness depends in part on the type of conflict involved.[6] There are many kinds of conflicts: between citizens, between citizens and private enterprises, between citizens and state agencies, between groups of citizens and private enterprises, and over laws' constitutionality or meaning. Enforcement of court rulings on these different conflicts can differ markedly. The state may have a good track record of enforcing small-claims decisions from lower-level courts, for example, but may not be able to carry out the remedies ordered by superior courts in big corruption cases.

Basic constitutional rights mean little without remedies. But many countries are too "occupied in defining rights" to give sufficient attention to "the absolute necessity for the provision of adequate remedies by which the right they proclaimed might be enforced" (Parker 1975: 4). On one hand, courts are responsible for deciding how laws apply to important national issues but often lack the independence or support to hand down the remedies needed for such application. On the other, much of society is too unorganized—and most political parties too concerned with patronage and power—to mobilize "antiremedies" able to bring about working remedies. Like remedies, antiremedies are an overlooked component of the rule of law and of democratization. Whereas remedies are court directives to enforce a ruling, antiremedies are actions to force a remedy or correct an inadequate one. The union and civil rights movements in the United States, for example, were antiremedies that led to remedies like labor laws, voting rights, and school desegregation. Remedies and antiremedies together advance a country's democratic development by helping it settle and apply the law. In Latin America, however, low educational and literacy levels, economic and political marginalization, and control by local powers make grassroots action difficult. Tasks as basic as publicizing information on judicial nominations and police violence, for example, are often carried out by underfunded NGOs that in turn depend on irregular media reports.[7]

The cycle of remedies and antiremedies speeds up when society starts to express broad and often unformed political and economic grievances as matters of justice. Such expression has been explored in studies of violence and change, as in Ted Gurr's study (1970) of the "relative deprivation" between what people feel entitled to and what they actually receive, and Charles Tilly's examination (1978) of violence sparked by political conflict between groups vying over resources. In contemporary democracies, such grievances are more diffuse but do not dissipate. They are stoked over time by a lack of closure on prior abuses, the distribution of power and wealth, and the impunity and arrogance of state officials. Because these grievances are vaguely articulated, and because they usually materialize in the form of general discontent and a withdrawal from political participation, governments often choose to not respond directly. But grievances are also part of a more positive side of democratization: widespread demand for a basic level of rights, dignity, and fairness. Most citizens do not know how to achieve or measure such respect, but they know when it does not exist. Abusive state actions or policies, unobscured by an immediate crisis or political manipulation, can be seen as an affront to this basic minimum. In cases such as favoritism in a privatization program, an unexplained cut in social services, or police complicity in disappearances, citizens are likely to react. Whether they do so with violence, calls for reform, or other political mobilization depends in part on how the state itself treats their demands.

Judicial access, in sum, involves actors (Access by whom?), structures (Access to what?), and functions (Access for what?). These elements interact in many ways, from a language minority suing a state agency to a group of lawyers questioning a law's constitutionality. If they are denied institutional outlets, such grievances will find political outlets. In most democracies, the frustration of limited judicial access feeds potentially destabilizing nonjudicial actions.

The Uneven Development of Judicial Access

Although the idea of universal judicial access took off in the twentieth century, rules structuring the relationship between the law and citizens go back much farther. In the initial years of state formation, a person's socioeconomic status determined access to judicial processes. The first rights to be promoted in the West were on civil and political issues, from redress against the king to basic religious freedoms. Those who promoted these rights were not economically deprived and therefore did not make economic needs a priority. With each of the major landmarks in human rights—from the Magna Carta in 1215 to the Treaty of Westphalia in 1648—economic guarantees fell farther behind civil and political guarantees. It then became normal for those who lacked economic independence, such as women, to relinquish their civil and political rights to those who had them, such as men. Within this conceptual hierarchy, individual rights were confined to "negative" liberties of freedom, requiring only an absence of state interference, as opposed to "positive" liberties involving economic needs, requiring active state policy and expenditure.

Another reason for differentiated rights and access to justice was that big chunks of the law itself were often delegated to institutions such as the Catholic Church and the military. Many of these divisions proved quite durable. In England, merchant laws and courts did not merge with common law until the eighteenth century, and in Russia special courts for peasants existed until 1912. Such divisions were marked in Iberia, which carried them to its colonies via laws and *fueros*. Access was not considered a formal right in the Spanish Empire, and "differences among potential litigants in practical access to the system or in the availability of litigating resources were not even perceived as problems" (Chayes 1976).

After the revolutions in France and America, however, countries began to adopt constitutions recognizing positive as well as negative rights. Modern European legal codes were formed during this era, based on "interrelated notions of neutrality, uniformity, and predictability" (Unger 1976: 176–177) and with a state commitment to accessible conflict and grievance resolution. Such access was seen "as the most basic requirement ... of a modern, egalitarian legal system [that] purports to guarantee, and not merely proclaim, the legal rights of all" (Cappelletti and Garth 1978: 9). But even though this development increased judicial access for the growing middle classes, it actually decreased it for the poor, beginning a pattern that has continued in many countries. Most court use, in fact, was against the lower classes in civil and criminal cases for nonpayments of debt; eighteenth- and nineteenth-century court records in Spain (Toharia 1974) and other countries show that the majority of defendants were servants and workers. Costs of legal action grew when governments, realizing that litigation tied up resources and slowed down economic activity, raised court fees. Such increases did not end up reducing actions against poor debtors, for urbanization and industrialization multiplied the use of credit and contracts, causing the levels of debt to grow faster than the costs of legal measures to recoup them. The biggest price was paid by debtors themselves, whose use of effective defense, payment alternatives, and appeals were effectively blocked by increasing court expenses and fees.

Rapidly growing social movements and slowly growing democratization did lead to better legal support for the poor. During the nineteenth century, countries such as France, Spain, and Portugal incorporated the idea of assigned counsel into their judicial systems, in which the courts required private lawyers to provide free assistance to the poor. By the end of the century, most of Latin America had followed suit. Some courts began to pay these private lawyers.

In the twentieth century, ideas of universal access finally began to take hold—but not always progressively. Mauro Cappelletti (1978) identifies three main kinds of judicial access demands, which in most countries tend to follow each other chronologically: basic counsel for criminal defendants, resolution of diffuse and class actions, and, most recently, mass access to judicial institutions for civil action. Even when extended over time, such demands are difficult for any country to accommodate. In new democracies, all three kinds can build up and rush in simultaneously during a relatively condensed period of time. Strapped with organizational limitations, economic instability, and societal unrest, most governments cannot even absorb even some of those demands—which can heighten pressure for them even more.

Argentina

Most of Argentina's judicial access measures predate democracy. In 1722, the *cabildo* of Buenos Aires took responsibility for legal services for the poor, and in 1814 it established a permanent center for such services. In 1878 the Supreme Court began to provide limited professional help for some criminal defendants, and eighteen years later the Federal Capital created the position of Defender of the Poor and Missing Persons as part of its new court system. In November 1898, in addition, the conservative newspaper *La Prensa* began to provide free legal consultation, employing about five lawyers and publishing periodical reports on its services.[8]

In the modern era, most legal aid has been conducted through provincial and local government programs, like the legal assistance office of the city of Buenos Aires, and state *defensores públicos* (public defenders) for indigent criminal defendants. Most such services began in the 1940s. Some of them were manipulated by the executive, such as the Ministry of Social Welfare's free legal clinic, which dealt with economic issues such as rent disputes but came under the increasing control of the regime's Eva Perón Foundation. The National Minor Service was established in 1956, and the Labor Ministry set up a small legal clinic in 1959. Most of the state's legal aid, however, has been carried out in conjunction with bar associations. In 1947, Buenos Aires province required all lawyers to belong to the bar association, one of its objectives being "the defense and juridical assistance to the poor."[9] In 1972, the military regime decreed that the Lawyers Forum of Buenos Aires would also be obliged to provide legal defense to poor defendants. Bar associations became increasingly active after 1983, and by 2001 there were more than 100 of them throughout the country.

Most of the university legal clinics were developed between the 1930s and 1970s. In the early 1930s, the law school of the University of Buenos Aires required students to participate in the city bar association's legal advice services. Couching these services within the schools' education mission was to come in handy during the purges of faculty by governments from the 1950s to the 1970s, especially under Juan Perón. Some smaller law schools established services in the 1972–1973 academic year, the same time the University of Buenos Aires law school set up clinics in some of the area's largest shantytowns.

Venezuela

In the colonial period, judicial functions were managed by the municipalities, primarily by officials called *alcaldes ordinarios*. This decentralized approach continued after independence with the Justicia de Paz (Justice of the Peace), an agency created by the 1812 Gran Colombia constitution to try to resolve "citizen controversies." The 1819 Gran Colombia constitution then dictated that in "each parish there will be a *Juez de Paz* before whom will come all civil and criminal cases that do not proceed in the official processes. He will listen to the issue without a trial format, attempting to bring the sides to a compromise and agreement, as a referee or arbitrator" (article 8). Only if "these means do not work" is the case then sent to higher-court authorities. In 1825, Bolívar decreed that all legal disputes would be required to go before these judges. Venezuela's 1830 constitution reestablished the *jueces* (article 178), and laws over the next thirty years established specific regulations on them.

The 1864 constitution phased out the Justicia de Paz by creating a national judiciary to preside over all cases at all levels "without being subject to any other authority." But nineteenth-century civil-procedure codes did provide court support for individuals settling noncontentious issues who lacked the means to pay for legal help. Legislation in 1928 and 1936 created some channels of access on labor disputes, which were carried forward by AD and enacted into law during the *Trienio*. When the Ministry of Justice was established in 1950, in addition, it created a legal support office in order to help persons "who do not exercise or defend their rights due to a lack of resources, of knowledge and of adequate information."[10] Subsequent decrees severely limited the power of attorneys working for the office, however, gradually reducing it to serve primarily as a reference to other services.

The first actual guarantees of judicial access were made in the 1961 constitution, which stated that all citizens can "use the organs of the administration of justice for the defense of their rights and interests, in the terms and conditions established by law, which will fix norms that assure the exercise of this right to those who do not have sufficient means" (article 68). The Municipal Federation of the Federal Capital established a free legal clinic in 1963 that focused on mediation, and other municipalities and states followed suit. The Central University of Venezuela founded a clinic in 1964; other major universities later followed suit. Most other professional services were established in the 1970s. The Center of the Venezuelan Lawyers Federation, one the country's largest clinics, was founded in 1981.

Judicial Access Reforms Under Democratic Regimes

Measures geared toward increasing judicial access fall into four main categories, each with different approaches and objectives. First is improvement of legal defense in criminal cases. With the majority of people in Latin America unable to afford private legal aid, democracies strive to improve the availability and quality of free counsel for indigent criminal defendants. All countries in the region guarantee free legal representation for the poor in criminal cases and in many civil cases as well. Most rely on one of two kinds of assigned counsel programs: The first uses a list of lawyers in each jurisdiction, often without pay; the second is an agency of full-time government *defensores* who work full- or half-time. In either case, public defense has fallen far below basic standards and expectations throughout Latin America.

A second and related area is to establish government and private legal aid centers to provide representation and information. Many of these programs are designed to reach out to low-income citizens, laborers, youths, the elderly, and other groups with traditionally low use of judicial mechanisms.[11] Although many such services are provided by the state, there are clinics run by unions, universities, law schools, bar associations, professional organizations, law firms, and NGOs. In Bolivia, legal claims against the state have been brought into the legal system with programs such as the Popular Judicial Consultancies, started in 1978 by the Center of Juridical Studies and Social Investigation. In Venezuela, human rights groups such as La Red de Apoyo por La Justicia y La Paz (Support Network for Justice and Peace) have organized popular legal actions.

Public-interest law firms, often modeled after those in the United States, are becoming more common. Such firms have expanded in Mexico, Peru, Chile, and Colombia, and others are affiliated with universities, such as the so-called Popular Law Firms of Guatemala's San Carlos University and of Nicaragua's Central American University. Universities also house more general legal clinics and institutes, such as the Legal Consultancy of the University of Costa Rica and the Free Legal Consultancy of the Catholic University of Ecuador. Law schools also provide a great many legal services. Chile, Brazil, and Costa Rica were the first to use law school clinics to teach students by having them support the poor. Currently, law students in nearly every country are required or encouraged to work in legal aid.

The most avowedly political of these clinics are those of workers' unions, which have been at the forefront of revolutionary and democratizing movements throughout the region. Labor rights, such as those guaranteed in Mexico's 1917 constitution, are among the earliest popular victories in Latin America. Aware of unions' power, states have responded by controlling them through regulatory laws and prescribing the membership, service, financial, and even ideological requirements needed for legal recognition. In countries such as Argentina and Venezuela, the ruling party succeeded in co-opting the main trade union entirely. Along with their historical role, these attempts have made unions more insistent on representing both workers in general and individuals in particular. In a few countries, such as Brazil, labor unions are legally required to provide free legal representation. Most countries channel such grievances into the regular judiciary, and some have created separate labor courts. Brazil and Colombia, for example, have entirely separate structures made up of local, appellate, and high labor tribunals. Most countries have labor courts within the judiciary and a constellation of other mechanisms, however, such as the networks of conciliation and arbitration boards in Mexico and Chile. These forums allow for extra attention to labor problems and provide a more level playing field for workers.

No matter what their backgrounds or priorities, legal aid centers have many advantages. They are, of course, essential to those unable to afford legal defense, much less to file civil or commercial suits. They are also key to the legal advancement of social sectors, such as women, because they bundle individual grievances and articulate general demands.[12] Violence against women in the home and in the street, for example, would be treated on a case-by-case basis without organizations that link specific cases with the sources of the problem. Such holistic approaches help break down educational, linguistic, and psychological barriers to legal action. By distributing leaflets, drawing comic books, and organizing rallies, these groups empower citizens through knowledge. Governments often choose to ignore marginalized people or regard them as "rich without resources" (Pérez Perdomo 1987a: 71) who lack only financial means. But the pursuit of a legal grievance also requires a persistence to face bureaucracy, intimidation, economic penalties, and possible social disapproval.

Many countries' *Defensorías* also work to straddle this gap between specific cases and broader patterns and, in the process, have become central channels of judicial access. The agency resolves specific cases, gathers information, gauges public opinion, mediates conflicts, and helps groups like youth and the elderly to organize and express their concerns. Ecuador's *Defensoría* helped form consumer defense organizations in twenty provinces, Colombia's *Defensoría* has brought attention to the overlooked problem of child abuse, and a 1999 agreement between the *Defensorías* of Bolivia and Argentina dealt with the plight of Bolivian immigrants in Argentina.[13] In Bolivia, the *Defensoría*'s multilingual radio broadcasts and regional information-gathering provide a basis for policymaking and help expose regional imbalances of resources and patterns of discrimination. Peru's *Defensoría* is one of the country's most credible and politically independent institutions; the 500 people who lined up outside on the first day of operation revealed the extent of demand for its help.

As with legal aid centers, special offices and adjunct *defensores* on women's rights illustrate the agency's effectiveness. Colombia's *Defensoría* has pressured the president to respond to the feminization of poverty, and Peru's *Defensoría* successfully worked with NGOs against a government sterilization program targeting poor women and has taken up charges by women against police agencies for illegal and inadequate responses to domestic violence reports.[14] *Defensorías* also improve access to nonjudicial institutions. In Peru, elderly pensioners have filed thousands of complaints through the *Defensoría* against the public administration—mostly regarding the agency that issues pension payments (*Defensoría del Pueblo* 1998). *Defensoría* officials have also opened up access on less traditional issues, such as the environment. Backed by the *Defensoría*, a Bolivian environmental rights group cited the adverse impact of a local government development project as constituting a violation of the national Environment Law.

The third kind of access reforms is ADR, composed of four different mechanisms: negotiation, conciliation, arbitration, and mediation. These mechanisms differ primarily in emphasis and structure. *Negotiation* is a voluntary approach taken on by and limited to the parties in a case; *conciliation* and *arbitration* are each run by a neutral third party that makes a resolution binding on the two sides; and *mediation* involves a framework tailored to each specific case. Such procedures usually get their start in special tribunals, such as labor courts, but increasingly are brought into regular courts. They reduce legal costs and save time and are more accessible to the parties involved, who usually decide the basic terms of interaction.[15] More important, ADR promotes mutually satisfactory solutions instead of imposed, zero-sum rulings based on distinguishing right from wrong in which one party wins and the other loses. Even in cases involving poor *favelas* (shantytowns) and drug gangs in Brazil, for example, mediation proved to be an effective form of conflict resolution (Santos 1977).

Although ADR is speciously attacked by lawyers and judges who fear a loss of control, many of the criticisms of ADR are valid. For example, companies requiring consumers or suppliers to submit to arbitrators instead of the courts may be railroading them into processes that the companies can better manipulate. Unequal powers and resources may simply transfer over to ADR forums, and the informality of the procedures can help the wrongdoer avoid the public scrutiny that courts bring. In other cases, poorly drafted and implemented ADR mechanisms only marginalize the poor even more, as their real interest is not to expand grievance resolution but to slim down court dockets.

Even though ADR is not always balanced, it is generally less intimidating and more flexible than regular court procedures.[16] Regular court procedures treat individual matters outside of their societal context, but ADR creates more harmonious relations by allowing disputants to bring in any and all relevant legal and nonlegal issues (Friedman and Bierbrauer 1978). It also helps publicize the idea of citizen participation in general. ADR is thus considered particularly useful to Latin America's polarized societies and, since the 1980s, has been promoted throughout the region by government ministries, social agencies, private firms, and bar associations.[17] Beginning in 1998, for example, Guatemala established a network of rural community mediation centers as well as urban court-annexed mediation and conciliation centers. The rural centers take on issues such as women's rights, indigenous rights, and labor disputes and have resolved about three-quarters of all disputes mediated (MINUGUA: 2000).

The most sweeping and controversial types of access reform, however, are those creating entirely separate procedures of conflict resolution. Adopting ADR's conciliatory approach while rejecting state involvement, the most common of such reforms are community justice forums. Unlike the defined set of policies that comprise related reforms, these forums are designed to be as open-ended, flexible, and accessible as possible. With this approach, discussed in Chapter 7, community justice goes the farthest in putting justice into citizens' hands.

In sum, there are four main areas of judicial access reform. These include:

For legal defense:

• better public defense system

For legal aid and information support programs:

• government programs
• Defensoría del Pueblo
• NGO and university clinics

For alternative dispute resolution mechanisms:

• negotiation
• conciliation
• mediation
• arbitration

For parallel judicial structures:

• community justice forums

Officials support access measures, as with other rule of law reforms, primarily because of a public push to improve the dismal record of existing mechanisms and to give people a legal instrument independent from executive control. Argentina experienced a broad consensus on the importance of judicial access in the aftermath of the *Proceso*, opening up debate over which reforms would be effective without undercutting other tasks such as combating crime. In Venezuela, the exclusion of most of the population from judicial mechanisms, combined with widespread disillusionment with the state, led in the 1980s and 1990s to the enactment of new access mechanisms and the revival of some that had died out.

Like other reforms, however, judicial access measures are effective in the long term only if they establish institutionalization against political pressures and judicial disarray. They must not only be well run and financed but also careful to avoid reproducing or abetting the judiciary's discrimination and inefficiency. Legal aid clinics must be capable of guiding people through bureaucratic mazes, public defenders must have adequate time and support, and ADR mechanisms must be able to create a level playing field for unequal opponents. But to do more than hold the line against such weaknesses and infringements, access reforms must also challenge the judiciary. The most generous legal advice means little without speedier trials, and the best public defenders can do little against implacably biased judges. Even comprehensive reforms, such as new penal codes, often fall short of the larger goal. No matter how many officials they hire or shuffle around, new codes will not succeed without changing officials' attitudes as well as helping turn citizens from passive recipients to active participants in legal processes. For this reason, the lack of appropriations for public education and personnel training on the new codes will seriously compromise their effectiveness.

More than other reforms, the success of access measures is also dependent on the public. Just as growing confidence stimulates demand for access, the low levels of confidence persistent throughout Latin America have depressed demand for judicial solutions, which only deepens the judiciary's exclusionary tendencies.[18] In a March 1994 Gallup Institute survey in Argentina, a full 80 percent could not find anything positive to say about the judiciary; 65 percent considered it unjust, partial, slow, corrupt, politicized, biased in favor of the right; and 45 percent were unaware of any noncourt alternatives for resolving conflicts. A 1996 nationwide poll revealed that the judiciary continued to be the second-least least trusted institution in Argentina.[19] In Venezuela, there is an almost complete lack of confidence in every public institution, with all major institutions besides the Catholic Church having the confidence of well under 40 percent of the population.[20] Even a judiciary that throws its doors open will not be used by a population that distrusts it. With confidence around the region remaining persistently low, access reforms require even more proactive support from officials to get them past the expected political and bureaucratic obstacles.

It will be a long road to achieve successful access reform, particularly on public defense, as the public not only lacks confidence in the criminal justice system but also is unsupportive of its guarantees for criminal elements. As mentioned in Chapter 4, only Costa Rica actually supports the right of public defense with a sufficient number of public defenders. Nearly every other country suffers from a chronic shortage of *defensores*; in 1994,

for example, Ecuador had just twenty-one. New as well as established public defense agencies are poorly run and provide inadequate representation.
In many countries, defendants might not be assigned counsel until the
major steps of the criminal process have been taken, and there is rarely
enough money to compensate witnesses or carry through investigations.
But most countries today are trying to hire *defensores*, improve their working conditions, and make public defense in general more effective. Many
reforms, such as the 1995 Public Defense Program in Bolivia, focus on
improving or creating public defense offices in underserviced regions.
State-financed counsel is also provided in civil cases, but the requirement
to attain a certificate of poverty, as well as the usual rule of allowing the
winning party to recover legal costs from the losing party, keep out many
deserving plaintiffs.

Even as these issues get ironed out, rising crime and changing criminal
laws also threaten to inundate criminal public defense, because increasing
arrests bring in more people than even an improved agency can process.
Defendants' rights are perhaps most precarious in Peru, where antiterrorism
laws have increased illegal arrests and unfair trials. The *Defensoría del
Pueblo* has drawn up lists of those convicted of terrorism or treason without sufficient proof, headed a commission to recommend pardons or short-
ened sentences for these and other cases, and pushed legislation to allow
those who repent terrorism to file appeals. Combined with international
pressure, the work has led to the pardoning of about 500 prisoners from
prison since 1996.[21] But, as discussed in Chapter 2, executive power alone
can halt or reverse such progress.

Because they are more independent, legal aid centers face fewer obstacles. Along with the human rights and related NGOs that have flourished
under democracy, these clinics have been among the biggest proponents of
judicial access in Latin America. Because of their legal expertise, their
biggest successes have come with representation of individual cases. With
the hope that such rulings may become important legal precedents, many
popular law firms and women's rights groups have scored their biggest victories on behalf of individuals and demands for accurate documentation. In
both Venezuela and Argentina, for example, the major achievement of
human rights groups has come from their push for an accounting of the
number of victims of the *Caracazo* and the *Proceso*, respectively.

But these organizations tend to be organizationally and financially limited. Law school clinics, for example, have high turnovers, sketchy organizational guidelines, inadequate outreach efforts, and irregular communications with each other. Students required to work in them in order to
graduate often become inured to the legal problems of the poor. In addition,
law clinics and human rights organizations taking on broader political
issues risk backlashes that they may not be able to withstand. Members of
Bolivia's Permanent Assembly of Human Rights have been arrested and

tortured by police officials, and members of established Peruvian organizations like the Lima Bar Association are regularly harassed. After Venezuela's devastating coastal floods in December 1998, the government harshly attacked a report by a reputable rights group documenting abuses by the military during its recovery efforts. These organizations may also run up against public as well as government opposition, as *Defensorías* have learned, especially when they advocate on behalf of unpopular social sectors.

For these reasons, many of those shut out of the judiciary turn to organizations, such as trade unions, that prioritize political over legal action. Legal aid clinics focus on providing access *to* the law, but often they do not help provide access to justice *through* the law. In Bolivia, for example, many laborers found that they were not benefiting from agricultural reform laws. Even when they won legal battles, they rarely attained meaningful remedies or legal guarantees of control over their lands. As a result, peasants organized unions willing to take their legal claims into the political realm. Beginning in the 1930s and especially after the 1952 revolution and the 1953 Agricultural Reform Law, poor rural populations have put more confidence in unions, such as the United Confederation of Rural Workers of Bolivia, than in the existing legal system. With more than 90 percent of cultivatable land still in the hands of capitalist enterprises, Bolivia's indigenous and peasant majority continues to see the limits of judicial access. Unpopular mass eradication of coca plants, clumsily applied crop substitution policies, and fatigue with a neoliberalism that began in the 1980s only reinforce this state-society division. Use of the legal system is a political compromise, on the state's terms, which most citizens are not yet willing to make.

Argentina

The most significant reforms to improve legal defense in Argentina have been provincial efforts to help courts resolve local conflicts and national efforts to improve the state public defense agency (Defensoría General de la Nación). Good private criminal lawyers are hard to come by, because most experienced lawyers are in civil and business law and few have criminal expertise. Because of the length and complexity of the criminal process, in addition, private defense is prohibitively expensive for the majority of the population. Of all those sentenced for property crimes, for instance, about 95 percent were represented by *defensores*. Despite this great need, *defensores* are outnumbered three to one by *fiscales* in most of Argentina. *Defensores* have far too many cases to be effective and are constantly obstructed by a lack of infrastructure, resources, and coordination. Most of them say only about 20 percent of their time is dedicated to actual counsel, with the rest spent on paperwork and other administrative tasks.

As with judges, the appointment of public defenders in Argentina has been politicized. As part of the MP, defenders faced political pressures from the *procurador general* (head of both *fiscales* and *defensores* until the 1994 constitutional reform created the Defensor General), who often dismissed them at will and thus further politicized the judicial process. *Defensores* usually have far less experience compared to *fiscales*, and they often harm due process through actions like pressuring detainees to confess in the first hearing. In addition, there long has been poor coordination among *defensores* working in first-instance, appellate, and oral courts. As these weaknesses slowed down and confused court processes, they led to efforts for reform. Most of those efforts came together in Act 24.946 of 1998, which gave *defensores* more organizational autonomy, created a professional career law, required a two-thirds senate majority to appoint the *defensor general,* and established *defensores volantes* to coordinate the work of defenders at various levels.[22] But the law, and subsequent developments, have several deficiencies. Article 31 requires a "duty of obedience," for example, which could bring back the practice of obliging individual *defensores* to follow questionable orders. In order to save money, in addition, the government created the position of adjunct *defensores* who are paid less than full-time *defensores*. In many cases, due process is endangered when these adjuncts are up against more experienced *fiscales* in criminal trials.

Less directly affected by judicial bureaucracy and politics are legal aid and support clinics. These clinics have been expanding rapidly in Argentina since 1983 because they provide an outlet for the underserved on issues unlikely to be resolved quickly or satisfactorily by the courts. Two of those issues are family violence and housing disputes. Family conflicts account for about 60 percent of university clinic cases and more than 70 percent of the cases handled by *La Prensa*. Rent disputes represent approximately 20 percent of university clinic caseloads, and most of the cases in the Buenos Aires municipal clinic address housing, financial, and family conflicts.[23] Such disputes are a low priority for the courts, but of course not for the people caught up in them.

Most of the country's legal clinics, moreover, are hampered by programmatic problems that started well before 1983. Although political intervention in university clinics has stopped, for example, rapid turnover and inconsistent supervision of participating students continue to limit their effectiveness. As with the public defense, the poor quality of free legal services in Argentina "derives from the inexistence of a unified planning that allows the coordination of efforts, avoids the overlapping of tasks, and above all, permits the adequate coverage of the legal needs of particularly needy sectors" (Berizonce 1987: 67) such as immigrants and the urban poor. Many clinics have been at a loss to help residents in Buenos Aires neighborhoods like La Matanza, for example, where Paraguayan and Bolivian immigrants misunderstand and reject offers of legal help. Clinics have been generally ineffective on health care and property rights issues, which are of critical importance for populations throughout Latin America living on land of uncertain ownership. Argentina's clinics are also sometimes limited by the law itself, as with democratic-era court restrictions on certain actions against the state as well as the suspension of trials under certain "emergencies." Decree 2196 of 1986, for instance, temporarily suspended all trials concerning debts with state pension funds.

As with the courts, the most effective clinics are those with independent institutional and political foundations. Argentina's umbrella union, the General Confederation of Labor (CGT, for Confederación General del Trabajo), has provided legal services for members since its founding in 1930, with a high rate of successful litigation. Through its clinics, the CGT takes on specific cases and often uses private lawyers who receive up to 15 percent of a settlement. Bringing together workers from all areas, the CGT also takes political and legal action on issues such as safety, unemployment, sick leave, and family support. The CGT has also enjoyed a high level of popular backing because of its concern for workers' lives outside of the workplace. Its extensive educational, cultural, and recreational programs have been a source of support through many periods of political and economic change. With the withdrawal of Peronist backing and the economic difficulties in the 1990s, however, the CGT's political and legal influence has declined.

Argentina's ADR, with a level of government support higher than in most of Latin America, has enjoyed steadier progress. The number of conflicts taken on by ADR grew three times over during the mid-1990s, with mediation centers successfully concluding 65 percent of cases in 1993 and 75 percent four years later (Buscaglia et al. 1995: 4). More important, ADR mechanisms increase access of marginalized sectors: about 90 percent of users of the country's mediation centers were poor and about 60 percent were female (Blair 1994: 42–43). Municipalities and provinces throughout the country have also used mediation as a basis for community justice forums (see Chapter 7). Despite this "popular participation in justice" and support for it by institutions such as the World Bank (World Bank 1994b: 80), however, the government has promoted ADR primarily in courts where most citizens do not participate. It established arbitration tribunals for economic, industrial, and other associations, for example, and in 1994 the Supreme Court created a pilot mediation center for the civil courts. So even though ADR increases judicial access, popular usage has been a secondary priority for the national government.

Venezuela

Access reforms in Venezuela have been propelled by both societal and individual demands. As Venezuelans increasingly felt the consequences of financial and political misrule, popular ideas of justice became a part of national politics. After a boom in the 1970s, the economy had a rough landing the following decade. As mentioned in Chapter 2, poverty and violence soared. By the mid-1980s, more than two-fifths of laborers were working in the informal sector and three-quarters of families could not afford minimum food needs. The unexpected implementation of austerity measures in 1989 by a newly elected president tapped into an intensifying frustration that first exploded in the *Caracazo*. Three years later, growing resentment among the lower ranks of the military led to two popular and nearly successful coup attempts. Pervasive corruption—from police bribes on the street to the trial of President Pérez over a $17 million discretionary fund— also became a populist rallying point. Society's perceptions of such "injustices" led to Caldera's 1993 and Chávez's 1998 presidential victories.[24] The state had betrayed society's expectation of respect for its basic rights and dignities.

Limits on individual access to judicial structures also began to receive greater attention as the national crisis put civil and commercial courts even farther out of citizens' reach. While the average monthly salary stayed at about 1,000 *bolívars*,[25] under the *reformed* Judicial Tariff Law of 1994 the costs of all court services rose—the price for sending a document between offices, for example, jumped from 70 *bolívars* to 250 *bolívars*.[26] As in most countries, a hefty chunk of these fees makes its way into the pockets of administrators, who add on their own "personal" charges. The least expensive private legal consultancy fee was equivalent to one day's earnings for an average-income family, with the appointment itself often requiring the personal contacts that most people do not have.[27]

In the criminal courts, judicial disarray severely weakened Venezuela's public defense system. Public defenders' work long has been blocked by a lack of clarity over their "obligations and duties"; a code to establish professional norms was proposed in the 1980 Judicial Career Law but was not formulated.[28] Before such changes were incorporated into the new COPP, they did not receive adequate support allegedly because of budgetary reasons, but mainly because *defensores* do not have strong alliances in either the judiciary or in the legislature. *Defensores* are paid much less than most other lawyers, have little job security, do not receive regular bonuses or promotions, and are subject to little accountability and oversight. At the same time, *defensores* are saddled with far too many cases to provide adequate defense on nearly any of them. In 1979, each *defensor* took on an average of just under sixty-nine cases per year; by 1993, that average shot up to 291 cases. In some jurisdictions, it was up to 381, by 1995 to 348 (in some areas to 625).[29] In 1999 there were 159 public defenders for the entire country—just one more than in 1994. The COPP attempted to resolve these problems by bolstering the Public Penal Defense Service with new training and better benefits. It also helped guarantee job security by allowing suspensions and dismissals only through formal mechanisms. But even with such change, long-term improvement requires more actual defenders.

These problems severely limit access for *defensores'* clients, who represent about 85 percent of all detainees. Despite legal requirements for regular visits, two-thirds of prisoners awaiting trial report never even meeting with their defenders, and 16 percent report meeting only one time (Torres 1985: 90). The first meeting is often at the detainee's investigative declaration, which states their version of events—but when options such as challenging the charges or appealing the detention orders are no longer available. The CEC establishes a maximum of forty-six days between arrest and the declaration, yet the average has been about 285 days (Consejo de la Judicatura 1994). When there is contact beforehand, sometimes it is so quick that many detainees cannot identify their own lawyer at the time of the declaration.

At the same time, however, Venezuela has developed an impressive range of legal aid clinics since the 1960s. Many of them are run by the government, with the Ministry of Justice, the Federal Capital, and each state operating its own free clinic. There are also centers operated by bar associations, universities, professional organizations, and most unions. Some of these clinics specialize in particular areas of the law. The Municipal Federation of the Federal Capital provides mediation in housing disputes, for example, and labor unions represent members in legal cases and ADR forums on most labor issues.

Despite their extensive growth, these clinics have not been particularly effective or even accessible. The Ministry of Justice's clinic feels "abandoned" by the ministry because of its skeletal budget, for example, and the guards at the door frequently use their ample discretion to turn people away. Many university clinics have solid records, but they are always low on resources and do not provide students who work there with adequate pay or coverage of work-related costs. The resulting high turnover had led to poor institutional continuity. More significant, entire areas of the country still lack any clinics whatsoever. About half of all services and two-thirds of all lawyers are concentrated in Caracas, home to about a fifth of the population (Pérez Perdomo 1994: 33), and even there most people lack knowledge of such help. Unlike in Argentina and other countries, neither the government nor international funders have strongly promoted ADR mechanisms in Venezuela. Without detailed plans and support from agencies such as the World Bank and COPRE, a critical mass of political support for new legal aid is unlikely to form. Higher-ranking judges are too embittered by their experience with the judicial council to give authority to another nonjudicial institution, and legislators do not wish to risk any of their own influence.

Conclusion

Although judicial access has a history in Latin America, it did not lay a strong foundation for democratic-era reforms. State defense and private aid are widely available, but too often they are unable to challenge practices that make such aid necessary. ADR mechanisms attempt to get around most of the practices but are not immune to political pressures or judicial disarray. Solutions that do not involve existing institutions, as a result, are becoming more and more attractive. Leap-frogging traditional access reforms—both conceptually and in practice—have been measures to create community justice, the focus of Chapter 7.

Notes

1. In Paraguay, the average duration of a civil trial in 1995 was more than five years and a labor trial 3.5 years; in Bolivia in 1994, the average first instance of a civil procedure lasted 3.5 times longer than required under law. In Brazil, only 58 percent of the 4 million first-instance cases filed in 1990 were resolved in the same year. In 1993, about 500,000 cases were pending in Ecuador and 4 million in Colombia, with some trials lasting up to twelve years. In Argentina, there were about 1 million pending cases in 1996.

2. Juan Martín Echeverría, "Preguntas a la Justicia," *El Universal,* March 19, 1995.

3. In addition, judicial authority is ceded to nonjudicial state agencies in the many cases interpreted as administrative rather than constitutional and therefore belonging to the state officials' and not judges' discretion. In 1989, a labor court rejected a petition brought by street merchants against a forcible eviction on the grounds that the workers were unprotected by labor laws because they were not engaged in "real" work, despite being among the 40.8 percent of Venezuelans in the informal economy.

4. There are generally two types of such claims: a *collective interest* on behalf of a group of people injured by a certain action, such as an indigenous community whose land was confiscated; or a *diffuse interest,* such as to protect the population as a whole from a harmful consumer product. Collective action laws are not as well developed in Latin America as they are in common law countries but have advanced during the 1990s. In general, there exists two forms of collective actions in the region: giving the government, usually in the form of the MP, the responsibility of protecting collective interests; or allowing private attorneys to bring collective interest suits.

5. Further complicating the picture is access on other kinds of rights, such as

social and economic rights, on needs such as health and education, and communal rights such as on the environment.

6. In *Seste y Seguich vs. Gobierno Nacional, Fallos de la Corte Suprema de Justicia* (*Jurisprudencia Argentina* 1864, vol. 1, p. 319), the Argentina Supreme Court argued that the judges' power includes employment of means to require obedience to their rulings.

7. In Argentina, such efforts are led by two NGOs: the Centro de Estudios Legales y Sociales, begun during the *Proceso*; and Poder Ciudadano, which focuses on judges' records and public participation in judicial nominations.

8. This service was shut down by Perón in the 1940s but reappeared again in 1957 before fading out in the 1970s.

9. Article 1, Ley 5177, Buenos Aires Province, 1947.

10. Decree No.462, *Gaceta Oficial*, No. 24.000, November 29, 1952.

11. For example, Argentina's National Institute of Social Services for the Retired and Pensioners set up free legal services in 1984.

12. The Women's Study Institute of El Salvador, the Women's Legal Services Center in the Dominican Republic, and Bolivia's Judicial Office of Women in Marginal Urban and Rural areas are some examples.

13. Estimating that nearly 8 million children suffer from some form of abuse and that the number of children sexually exploited alone has risen 600 percent between 1996 and 1998, a 1999 *Defensoría* report blamed a lack of state funds and increases in poverty. With limited budgets, every *Defensoría* depends on the growing numbers of NGOs to provide cases and support. With evidence gathered by the Comisión por la Vida y por la Paz Social, for instance, Ecuador's *Defensoría* complained to the Defense Ministry about the operations of military bands in certain regions, linked to abuses such as the 1998 murder of a union activist.

14. The *Defensoría* estimates more than 6,000 cases of rape annually in Lima alone (although some rights groups assert this to be the monthly figure). In the agency's investigation of the sterilization program, medical officials reported that they were given bonuses for reaching sterilization quotas. The *Defensoría's* efforts led to enforcement of a seventy-two-hour waiting period for sterilization operations and a drop in their number from 109,000 in 1997 to 26,000 in 1998. Matt Moffett, "The Go-Between: Peru's Ombudsman Takes on Fujimori," *Wall Street Journal,* March 9, 2000.

15. In El Salvador, mediation is conducted without a lawyer and within a time frame of two months (Dakolias 1996: 37). In some countries, mediation is used to cover issues excluded from the courts, as in Ecuador, where immediate family members may not pursue legal actions against each other.

16. For example, 69.1 percent of Brazilian judges interviewed in a study said that the administration of justice would improve with a broadening of extrajudicial conciliation procedures (Terez Sadek and Bastos Arantes 1994).

17. Colombia began employing ADR techniques in 1983 and in 1991 set up a pilot program under presidential decree that allows judges to delegate stages in the judicial process to conciliation (decree articles 2–10) or to arbitration (articles 11–20). In El Salvador, the mediation mechanisms in the office of the *procuraduria* on child support and alimony cases settles 90 percent of these cases within two months—without lawyers. ADR approaches are also effective in addressing sexism in the judiciary and the greater lack of access by women to the courts. In Ecuador, for example, ADR has proven to be the most accessible form of conflict resolution for poor women, and family-related cases constitute Ecuadorian ADR mechanisms' second-largest area of work.

18. In poll questions about the judiciary—in Chile, Argentina, Mexico, Brazil, and Peru—public confidence above 60 percent has never been recorded. In Chile, poor people with no experience with judicial mechanisms have about a 20 percent rate of confidence, but those with experience have higher rates of confidence (Dakolias 1996: 361). In a 1993 Venezuela poll (conducted by Javier Otaegui y Asociados), 22.8 percent of respondents thought judges were independent, and 77.2 percent thought they were not. In a 1994 Gallup Poll in Argentina, 84 percent of respondents said that the judiciary favors the rich and powerful, 72 percent said that judges were influenced by the current government, 69 percent said that Supreme Court decisions were "very or quite politicized," 78 percent felt that the high court was influenced by the government, and 79 percent worried that the high court "would be able to be" influenced by the government.

19. Respondents were asked about their trust in nine institutions and social sectors; public schools enjoyed confidence from 56 percent of respondents, the press 53 percent, the church 42 percent, the military 25 percent, Congress 20 percent, the business sector 14 percent, the police and the judiciary 13 percent, and the unions 7 percent. Estudio Graciela Römer y Asociados, reported in *La Nación,* November 17, 1996, p. 24. In *Estudio de Opinión Acerca de la Justicia en Argentina,* the Gallup Institute of Argentina reports that 49 percent of the population consider judicial structures "bad" or "very bad" on all matters due to corruption and influence by the executive. In most countries, 3–10 percent of poll respondents place "constitutionalism" and "human rights" as a top concern, below unemployment, inflation, crime, and corruption.

20. In 1997 national surveys by RAC and Mori International, only 37 percent expressed confidence in the judiciary. In a poll by Conciencia 21 and the Konrad Adenuaer Foundation, reported in *El Globo* (April 3, 1995, p. 7), 92 percent of respondents said that they did not believe that the nation's leaders or institutions could solve the country's crisis.

21. Conscious of provoking a counterattack, however, the *defensor* has been careful not to overplay his hand. To help the military save face, for example, he recommended that it pardon rather than exonerate many prisoners.

22. María López Puleio, Secretaria Letrada, Defensoría General de la Nación, author interview, December 17, 1996.

23. In June 1972, for example, of the 2,773 cases handled by this service, 721 were rent and housing issues, 417 were financial, and 854 were family matters (*Dirección de Asistencia Jurídica* 1972).

24. The issue was further fueled in 1994 after the country's top banks collapsed and their directors fled the country with more than $7 billion, an amount equal to about 45 percent of annual national income. In just "the first half of 1994, half of Venezuela's banks ended" up being seized by the government in a $6.1 bailout, equaling 11 percent of the country's gross domestic product and 75 percent of the government's budget. Some 80–90 percent of the banking industry was involved in one way or another; Banco Latino alone had 1.2 million depositors— about 10 percent of the country's adult population. *New York Times,* May 16, 1994. Among the causes of the failure were weak government supervision.

25. In Mexico, high examination standards prevent widespread use of the courts; in Ecuador and Peru the number of notaries is limited by law, with a monopoly of high fees.

26. Article 17, *Ley de Arancel Judicial,* enacted June 23, 1994. Although adjusted for a devaluation of the *bolívar*, the price changes still represent an actual increase in costs.

27. Rogelio Pérez Perdomo (1987b: 67). "Many bailiffs charge you according to how far they have to take a document, as if they were taxis," complains one civil lawyer waiting in line to the Palace of Justice in Caracas, April 20, 1995. In Bogotá, Colombia, for example, to pay for four hours of the least expensive private attorney's time, a service-sector worker would have to work 4.4 days, an agricultural worker 4.3 days, and a laborer 4.0 days (Lynch 1948: 99).

28. María Antioneta Acuñade, President, Public Defenders Association of Venezuela, author interview, May 22, 1995.

29. *Memoria y Cuenta del Consejo de la Judicatura,* Dirección de Planificación, Consejo de la Judicatura. As of 1994, the judicial council estimated a need for an additional 100 defenders in addition to the 158 then serving.

7

COMMUNITY JUSTICE

Our efforts to resolve neighborhood tensions are starting to work. But it's still hard when those at the bottom of the hill distrust the rest of us, and when going to the top of the hill can get you killed.
—Amanda Castro, Community Activist, *barrio* of Los Erasos, Caracas[1]

COMMUNITY JUSTICE HAS POSITIVE as well as negative aspects. On the positive side, it means that Latin American communities are returning to more efficient and harmonious methods for resolving disputes. On the negative side, it can mean those same communities are resorting to vigilantism, lynchings, and other forms of violence outside the rule of law. Community justice reforms try to get the positive side to prevail over the negative. In particular, neighborhood forums, social centers, and related programs have been established in order to prevent or peacefully resolve disputes by bringing people together in cooperative and noncombative ways. Like more traditional access reforms, community justice measures are a practical alternative to the judicial system's inability to deal with anything more than a small fraction of legal disputes. But they are also a form of political expression and a challenge to the judiciary's legalistic, impersonal, and centralized approach.

The needs addressed by community forums are as diverse as communities themselves. One of the most developed areas of community justice, for example, is among indigenous populations. During the 1990s, countries such as Colombia, Ecuador, Peru, and Bolivia enacted constitutional provisions recognizing the legal traditions of indigenous peoples and allowing them to administer justice in their regions. Many of these communities long have regarded state justice with a "mix of distrust and rejection," as well as an instrument of domination; as state law was regarded as the polar opposite of indigenous values, resorting to it was tantamount to "eroding com-

213

munal autonomy and perverting the criteria of equality and justice" (Gálvez 1987: 243–244). Now most of these populations are able to designate and empower community leaders and groups to judge disputes and dispense sanctions. Their legal traditions and processes emphasize cooperation, participation, and respect, focusing not on written laws but on social harmony and order.

For the rest of Latin America's population, community justice is a much newer experience. The broadest and most ambitious form of community justice is the Justicia de Paz, a network of neighborhood conflict-resolution forums. Previously, local and family disputes were usually handled by small-claims courts in the regular judiciary. But under the new projects, many governments have handed this power to neighborhood *jueces de paz*. Receiving little or no remuneration, and usually with no professional prerequisites, the *jueces de paz* are supposed to be known, trusted leaders chosen directly by citizens to resolve disputes in a way appropriate to the community and acceptable and understandable to each party. Since the 1980s, a formal Justicia de Paz has been implemented into law by Guatemala, Peru, Colombia, and Venezuela.[2] Most other Latin American countries are developing related kinds of community conflict resolution, either creating new forums from scratch or expanding a court-based Justicia de Paz previously limited to small-claims actions.

But even though they sidestep judicial disarray and executive power, community justice reforms do not escape from them. As new and independent bodies, they are vulnerable to manipulation from officials and agencies wary of anything out of their control. Many judges and lawyers see *jueces de paz* as professional interlopers, and many judicial administrators see them as competitors for financial opportunities. Political parties are also worried about the potential of justice forums to cut into their own influence. As party identification is a basis of patronage in public services, jobs, and other benefits, independent forms of activity can foul up carefully cultivated party controls. More generally, community justice also increases expectations that democracy might not be ready to meet. Local and national justice are inexorably linked, but citizens using the former as a channel to the latter are likely to be disappointed. Judicial and executive agencies threaten community justice not only through political meddling but also through their general weaknesses as well.

The Role of Community Justice in Democracy

Community justice provides fresh answers to the basic questions of judicial access. Above all, it expands the answer to the question "Access by whom?" by bringing in many of the individuals kept out of regular courts. Neighborhood forums have few if any of the bureaucratic, legal, educational, economic, and geographic barriers of the state judiciary. Their answers to the questions "Access to what?" and "Access for what?" are more limited but no less important. The system to which they provide access is more rudimentary than the regular courts yet more likely to satisfy the grievances being presented. Citizens emboldened by participation may then follow their claim to the state institution originally or additionally responsible. Although damages that these forums can grant are far more moderate than those in regular courts, they are more likely to form accurate and self-enforcing remedies of restitution and enjoinment. Community vigilance and cultural expectations are more effective enforcers of decisions than are coercive and distant institutions.

But community justice is more than just a better answer to the questions of judicial access. By breaking through traditional boundaries of conflict resolution, these parallel systems of justice provide overdue acknowledgment of separate legal norms that have long existed but rarely been legislated. Beyond a country's formal laws are distinct sets of "intuitive" or "living" rules on matters such as education and security that enjoy most people's principal allegiance (Podgorecki 1985). When intuitive laws drift away from official laws, the growing distance between them can undermine the rule of law as well as political order. Many countries have experienced such tension at some point in their history. Just as the demands of capitalism and nationalism once challenged the legal structures of European monarchs, the norms of poor, marginalized populations pose a challenge to contemporary democracies in Latin America. But even though the bourgeois and nationalist forces were able to gather the collective strength against decadent royals in the past, the poor populations that compose Latin America's majority may be too economically and politically fragmented to bring about similar shifts today.

Although it does not necessarily threaten the state's judicial structure, community justice does challenge its normative and structural foundations. The state's legal authority is based on specific provisions and the larger bodies of law containing them. Civil and commercial law—the bodies of laws that mediate disputes between parties—are distinguished from criminal law, where most prosecution takes place. When there are violations of state laws, the judiciary functions to prove and punish them. With its "necessity to attribute certain events to the action (or inaction) of a person" (Ietswaart 1982: 158), state justice focuses on objectively specifying the details of relevant actions, categorizing levels of responsibility, and squeezing all circumstances into a very narrow pattern of causality. Community justice, in contrast, does not distinguish between civil and criminal laws, between victims and victimizers, or between an incident and its societal context. Community justice considers the entire person and the entire community—and not just their relation to the incident—as relevant. Instead of narrowing down a case to objective facts, community justice is open to opinions, trends, and discussions of morality. Causes and responsibilities are placed not only on an individual but also on a social group, a problem like a lack of housing, or even the larger political system. Thus "guilt" involves people and conditions beyond the accused.

Such attributions of guilt beyond the responsible individuals test the legal and political boundaries of community justice. In the past, spontaneously developing community justice forums were not threatening to the state when they were limited to communities not well integrated into the larger political system. Forums in the rural areas of Brazil and the *favelas* of Rio de Janeiro during the 1970s were two examples. But when community justice forums are seen to be encroaching upon the judiciary, the state responds. In Chile, popular justice arose in many urban areas during the 1970–1973 Salvador Allende government, which tried to shut down the ones that became too popular. In April 1972, for example, some neighborhood leaders who carried out popular justice were charged with "usurpation of the judicial function" (Ietswaart 1982: 154). Clashes with the state also arise when forum cases become a basis for legal action against private enterprises and state agencies, or when a community conflict affects people outside the community. Indigenous law, for example, often comes into direct conflict with national law over indigenous tribunals' lack of predetermined punishments for specific crimes, sentences involving forced labor, use of collective punishments, and other normally illegal practices (Van Cott 2000: 215). Witchcraft, for example, is a grave matter among many Indian communities. But the tradition to punish it with death, often after trials based almost entirely on witnesses, does not sit well with the legal establishment. Such differences can put governments in political as well as legal binds. In Ecuador, organizing by indigenous communities led to popular victories against oil companies drilling in the Amazon region. But when one of the antidrilling indigenous leaders joined an unconstitutional revolt against the government in January 2000, a warrant went out for his arrest. The MP and other agencies would not carry out the arrest, however, knowing that it would trigger disruptive and potentially violent responses.

Community justice presents a more serious challenge to democracy when the sources of conflict are land, resources, health services, education, and other provisions that residents don't expect community law to provide. As in poor urban shantytowns, many conflicts arise over dwindling resources and services, sparking individual disputes that can grow into extralegal grievances against the state. Democracy itself does not create these deficiencies, of course, but democratic activity can increase the belief that democratic government is unable to meet basic needs. Through local justice forums, citizens get a clearer view of state neglect.

And when it comes to the issue of crime, communities themselves consciously abandon the positive side of community justice and the protection of individual rights inherent in constitutional democracy. Throughout urban Latin America, residents fed up with crime find themselves quickly exhausting the established means for fighting it. In most cases, they first turn to neighborhood councils, often called *juntas de vecinos*. But many of these councils are weak because the minimum size of membership requires those interested in forming a *junta de vecino* to go beyond their immediate neighborhood. Once a council is formed, competition and differing priorities often reduce active members to those from just one area—usually that of the original organizers—which limits the council's effectiveness. In middle-class areas, residents also form peaceful protest groups, such as Venezuela's Lights Against Crime movement, which organized marches where people would turn on their car headlights and wear yellow clothing. As a second, or complementary, step, residents appeal to the police, as discussed in Chapter 2. But even when police officers respond they focus on detaining individuals rather than trying to resolve the sources of criminal activity. The police may be called about armed youths who gather on an abandoned basketball court, but the police do not do much about preventing that court from attracting criminals in the first place.

The last but rapidly preferable resort is vigilantism. Like prison overcrowding and police violence, citizen vigilantism is a product of the tensions between limits and demands in a democracy. In many crime-ridden areas, vigilante groups have risen up to carry out a job that the state is seen as forfeiting. Most of the targets are individuals publicly accused of specific crimes, ranging from robbery to murder, but some targets are victims of rumors and circumstance. Nearly all of urban Latin America has experienced a surge of neighborhood vigilantism and lynching. In Guatemala, ninety lynchings were reported between January and September 1999, a sharp increase over the total of 182 over the three previous years combined (MINUGUA 2000). In Ecuador, lynchings have been documented in every region of the country, with sixteen confirmed deaths between January and September 1999 (State Department 1999). In the poor areas of Buenos Aires, since the early 1990s there has been an increase in violent conflicts between neighbors, most of which are instigated by youths (Ministerio de Justicia 1996: 249).

In Venezuela, official statistics are not recorded, but newspaper and police reports reveal an increase in lynchings from only a few during 1995 to one nearly every week since 1997.[3] The practice first came to public awareness in the early 1990s, when officials stepped up efforts to better document the different causes of the escalating death rate in the barrios.

Although most of the killings were the result of robberies and shootouts, many others seemed to be carried out by gangs organized for more than regular robberies and assaults. At around the same time, anonymous pamphlets began to appear, exhorting residents to "declare war" against crime and using language reminiscent of death squads such as the Black Hand from the 1970s.

The practice is most common in the poorest and most sprawling shantytowns, such as those of Catia, which spread over the western half of Caracas. As the once-distinct neighborhoods of Catia blend into each other and absorb new arrivals, each neighborhood has gradually lost its sense of identity and control. The growing number of robberies and murders personify this loss of power, to which vigilantism becomes a normal and easily justifiable response. More worrying is the rise in vigilantism in older and more established barrios such as La Vega and Las Brisas del Paraíso. Closer to downtown and with more services such as running water, these neighborhoods have a stronger sense of identity and more educated populations, presumably more aware of peaceful means of crime control. But these communities, too, have felt a loss of control and, in addition, have suffered the impact of a contracting state more directly than have the poorer areas. Even though most residents in Las Brisas del Paraíso say that they reject vigilantism, quickly organized meetings of so-called self-defense groups still attract sizable attendance.[4] And actually, this neighborhood may be less ambivalent than the country as a whole. In a 1995 nationwide poll, 57 percent of respondents said they favored the practice of lynchings.[5]

Even in the face of such practices, the government has developed few coherent responses. Its reaction to lynchings, in fact, exemplifies its larger lack of criminal policy. In early 1995, the justice minister criticized the lynchings even as the interior minister qualified this criticism by saying that the "community" is trying to act in its "own defense."[6] In 1995, the Interior Ministry met with the heads of self-defense groups as well as private security agencies, which were estimated to employ 18,000–20,000 personnel. Although the stated purpose of the meeting was to request the cooperation of these groups "to guarantee better security," the unintended result may have been to give approval to their activities.[7] With little reduction in crime, five years later the interior vice-minister said that although Venezuela is "a traditionally violent country," the government is still "making a big effort that [lynching] does not become a national problem."[8] But in a bad omen for judicial reform, much of the vigilantism has been blamed in the media since 1998 on a perception of increased tolerance for criminals under the new penal code. In June 2001, Caracas experienced the most tumultuous protests against the new code to date. And, as on other issues, the state's reflexive reaction has been to associate controls over it with a weakening of public order.

Community Justice Forums

Community justice forums such as the Justicia de Paz and mediation centers are a compromise between rigid national standards and unformed local ones. Not only do they relieve the courts of many potential cases; their approaches and solutions are almost always preferable for the parties involved. In cases from petty rivalries to acts of violence, forum procedures are seen not as zero-sum games with a clear winner and loser but as searches for the conflict's causes and for harmonious reconciliation.

Guatemala and Peru, whose extensive poverty and large indigenous populations were the main motivation for establishment of Justicia de Paz programs, substantiate much of this promise. With little preparation, most of these countries' *jueces de paz* have been able to customize justice to their own particular community norms. In Peru, the *jueces* are technically state officials, but most communities have reconfigured them to be more representative of the community by emphasizing harmony, responsibility, persuasion, and the use of state law only when necessary (Gálvez 1987: 243). The laws that create and regulate Peru's *jueces* have facilitated this successful application. As in other countries, Peruvian *jueces* do not have to be lawyers (about 70 percent are not; Brandt 1995: 93), and to maximize community support and minimize corruption, the *jueces* are elected, get only basic material support, and must step down from political-party positions. Although the *jueces* must comply with the law and are empowered to refer to the courts those cases that they cannot resolve, they do not have to base rulings on any legal code (article 66) and can take unconventional measures such as open-ended discussions. This approach has been effective: about 63 percent of minor cases in the country are resolved by *jueces de paz*, and 51 percent of Peruvians prefer them to formal courts in minor disputes (Brandt 1995: 95).

In Guatemala, the end of the civil war and the tiny percentage of indigenous judges in upper-level courts motivated the Guatemalan government to create that country's Juzgados de Paz Comunitarios (Community Peace Courts). The legislation was approved in September 1997, and following the first set of elections *jueces* began to serve in January 1998. The enacting law tries to tailor courts to local needs, placing them in areas without other judicial forums, that are predominantly Maya-speaking, and that have given their explicit approval. Recognizing the municipality's role among indigenous peoples as the "nucleus" of political unity and religious values (Carmack 1979: 306), in fact, preliminary government reports emphasized the *juzgados'* potential ability to address increasing levels of minor disputes as well as violent crimes.[9] Independent follow-up studies confirm these benefits, pointing out forums' use of more culturally appropriate sanctions, involvement by indigenous organizations, and, above all, increases in individual access to grievance resolution (Ordoñez 2000: 190).

Argentina

Like other institutions in Argentina, the Justicia de Paz has had an unstable history. In colonial and early independence eras, *jueces de paz* "served as a pre-delictual security measure for 'vagabonds and social outcasts' [by enforcing] obligatory military service, generally in the battle against indigenous peoples" (Zaffaroni 1994: 254). But in the late 1800s, some provinces formed *jueces de paz* on a limited basis for the poor, and national ones were incorporated into the civil and commercial court system under Law 18.809 of 1972. Through these measures, *jueces* came to specialize in small claims instead of providing a parallel system of justice.

But that latter function was reintroduced in the post-1983 democratic era. Many provinces have begun community justice forums, as has the national government in the Federal Capital. In February 1995, the Justice Ministry implemented its Social Program of Juridical Service, composed of community justice centers in seven of Buenos Aires's poorest neighborhoods. Emphasizing education and mediation, these centers have demonstrated the ability of citizen-controlled ADR mechanisms to address community disputes.[10] As their caseloads demonstrate, the centers reflect residents' most pressing concerns. In the working and poor areas of Argentina since the late 1980s, such concerns have revolved around unemployment, wages, social service cuts, and high prices resulting from currency parity with the U.S. dollar. Regular courts, occupied with issues such as privatization, business disputes, and executive decrees, have had little opportunity to handle individual grievances. In some cases, they have declared them outside of their judicial competence. But the community centers have not shied away from such cases and conflicts and have generally demonstrated high rates of success in their treatment of them.

A typical community justice center is that operating in the working-class Once neighborhood, located in the middle of the Federal Capital. Residences range from middle-class apartment buildings to shacks for the poor, and because many residents work in the service industry, they have directly felt the effects of national economic fluctuations. In Once's center, 92 percent of the cases that were accepted for mediation led to satisfactory resolutions.[11] The center has dealt with residents' most urgent concerns, which break down as follows: labor/work complaints (45 percent of cases between July and August 1996); family disputes (13 percent); neighbor conflicts (8 percent); rent conflicts (7 percent); contamination (5 percent); preventative measures (4 percent); specific incidents (3 percent); commer-

cial disputes (2 percent); administrative matters (2 percent); criminal matters (2 percent); and other issues (9 percent). The vast majority of these
cases would not have been resolved by the courts, allowing the center to
step in and become a key judicial agency.

Venezuela

Community justice in Venezuela has focused on the *jueces de paz*, which,
unlike ADR, have a history in that country. As discussed earlier, the Justicia
de Paz was first created upon independence but eventually fell out of use as
the state centralized. But in the 1980s, pressing judicial needs started to
build support to revive the Justicia de Paz as an entirely separate judicial
system. In the early 1990s, a group of lawyers, university professors,
Family Ministry officials, and some members of Congress from the leftist
Causa R party formulated legislation for a strong Justicia de Paz, promoting it as a way to relieve stress on the judiciary as well as a method of resolution appropriate to individual communities. The enacting organic law
(*Ley Orgánica de Tribunales y Procedimientos de Paz*) was approved in
September 1993.

By mandating a Justicia de Paz in each of the country's parochial districts, the law became a keystone of judicial decentralization as well as of
community justice. Attempting to cover all of the regular courts' weaknesses, the law requires community courts to exercise orality, simplicity, equality, efficiency, and transparency—and to be free. It allows judges to resolve
certain disputes in penal law, municipal family laws, neighborhood disputes, transit issues, and many kinds of material claims. In taking on such
conflicts, judges must avail themselves "of all possible routes of conciliation" that encourage the disputants to "consensually resolve their problems." They have wide leeway in using evidence and consulting specialists,
and the punishments they can impose include a range of fines and community services. Their rulings stand unless appealed by a disputant or by the
attorney general.

The law attempts to sift out unqualified and biased judges by requiring all candidates to "have serious recognized professional and moral
development, social sensitivity and recognition in family and local issues,
along with proven capacity for dialogue, sensitivity and respect for the
conditions of their fellow citizens." Once elected, *jueces de paz* must be
completely impartial. If compromised in a case because of personal connections, a *juez* must recuse himself or herself in favor of the first or second deputy judge (i.e., those who received the second and third highest
number of votes, respectively). Judges guilty of breaking the rules can be
suspended through a municipal council disciplinary process, or be

removed permanently through a referendum of the parochial or inter-parochial jurisdiction, which is conducted with the support of 20 percent of its population.

Elections of judges are organized by each parochial district. Although the organic law stipulates the basic framework of these elections, each municipality decides on election dates and can initiate efforts to drum up participation. Although bureaucracy and politics delayed elections for the first slate of judges until August 1995, more than 250 more *jueces* were elected in municipalities around the country in 1996, and more than seventy-three municipalities elected 1,600 *jueces* in 1997. The high levels of popular support for the *jueces* first became apparent when the first eighty-five *jueces* garnered two to three times the votes received by mayors and city council members in the same election cycle.

In the first year of functioning, the resolution of 3,500 disputes also showed an ability to tap into communities' concerns. In particular, the *jueces de paz* deal with Venezuela's two largest societal problems: violence and poverty.[12] The issues handled by the *jueces de paz* break down as follows: family violence (46.5 percent of cases); violence between neighbors (13.4 percent); bothersome noises (14 percent); problems concerning minors (12 percent); environmental problems (8.1 percent); solid wastes (3 percent); and consumer protection (3 percent).

More than in Argentina or other countries, the Justicia de Paz attempts to resolve some of the tensions that have given Venezuela Latin America's fourth highest murder rate. In Caracas alone, the number of homicides increased 500 percent in the 1990s. In one typical nationwide poll, 43 percent of respondents said that crime was the country's most serious problem, and only 18 percent cited unemployment and 15 percent the cost of basic goods.[13] Reflecting the lack of confidence in the state's crime-fighting ability, 69 percent of respondents in another poll said that it was probable that they would be assaulted or robbed within the following two months, with 65 percent of them believing it was probable that the attacker would be a police officer.[14] Yet people lack confidence not only in the police, as discussed earlier, but also in the armed forces, neighborhood associations, and private security firms (Hillman and Cardozo 1998). Without trust in any of these agencies, *jueces de paz* offer the alternative solution of minimizing or preventing violence in the first place by attempting to defuse disputes through peaceful cooperation.

Bolivia

Bolivia faces all of the problems that make a Justicia de Paz appropriate and useful: high rates of poverty, low education and literacy levels, large non–Spanish-speaking indigenous populations, and geographic fragmentation. Bolivia's community justice forums are also a natural outgrowth of strong indigenous legal norms. The Aymara, Quechua, and Guaraní peoples, who are the country's largest Indian populations, have retained much of their cultural and political identities. But amid the increasing economic problems and physical dispersion of these populations, community justice forums help form a stable foundation of authority and coherence. Recognizing this need, in the mid-1990s the Justice Ministry launched its Traditional Justice Project, with goals that included development of the Justicia de Paz to carry out traditional forms of conflict resolution. The project has systematically studied forms of authority and conflict resolution in each area of the country, bringing them together in legislation formulated by the Justice Ministry and Congress. Pilot forums, as part of this and other projects, have led to legislation establishing judges in at least 40 percent of the country's municipalities (World Bank 1995).

The many needs addressed by community justice can be seen in the areas surrounding the capital city of La Paz, where poor rural indigenous peoples have immigrated in massive numbers. Given the limited space in the valley that holds metropolitan La Paz, most migrants have settled in the high plateau above. Such settlements have all but created the city of El Alto, whose population of about 1 million almost equals that of La Paz proper. Many neighborhoods within El Alto have set up different types of community justice (*justicia comunitaria*) forums, ranging from highly structured disciplinary tribunals to *juntas de vecinos* with judicial functions. No matter what their structures or powers, these councils enjoy high levels of popular legitimacy and support. They are democratically elected, utilize the familiar and understandable customs originating in the rural areas from which residents have migrated, and apply mediation procedures well suited to the unfolding problems of newer communities. These approaches have generally been very effective, and studies report that more than 92 percent of council sanctions are obeyed (Ministerio de Justicia y Derechos Humanos 1998: 62).

More important, the councils are free and fast: of the 152 cases taken to a junta of the Villa Bolívar "D" neighborhood in El Alto, seventy-eight (51 percent) were resolved in a week or less and twenty-three (15 percent) in less than three weeks. If El Alto represents the demographic trends of Bolivia, Villa Bolívar "D" represents those of El Alto. More than 90 percent of residents came from rural indigenous areas, more than two-thirds are Aymara-speakers, and more than a third are under thirty years of age. The rate of unemployment is high, and many residents work in the informal economy. As in Argentina and Venezuela, the kinds of conflict taken to the council of Villa Bolívar "D" reflect the community's most common tensions and strains. Most conflicts involve physical altercations, robbery, and various forms of cheating. The majority of others tend to be interfamily disputes, ranging from domestic violence to cheating within extended families. The conflicts resolved by the Junto de Vecinos of Villa Bolívar "D" break down as follows: conflicts (fights, robbery, etc.) among community members (44.7 percent of cases); domestic conflicts (21.7 percent); conflicts among relatives (14.5 percent); immediate family conflicts (11.8 percent); and conflicts with others in the household (7.2 percent).

Despite their high level of activity, however, El Alto's community justice forums are limited. Above all, they do not have many effective sanctions or means of enforcement at their disposal. Their main penalties are to oblige the guilty party to present gifts, initiate reconciliation, or provide goods such as animals to the community at large. "Moral" punishments, such as expulsion from the community, were very severe in the residents' former rural areas, as it was difficult to survive in the forests or deserts or to be taken in by other communities, but in El Alto the defendant can easily move to another neighborhood. Some forums try to make up for these weaknesses by being more assertive. But when they do, residents complain that they become less sympathetic, dominated by cliques, and start to take actions outside their mandate, like seizing private property.[15] Such behavior risks the citizen support on which forums ultimately depend.

Because of these imbalances, many El Alto residents would like to see forums and *juntas de vecinos* combine with local courts to form a single body of dispute resolution and sanction. Such a combination, however, could dilute the spirit of community justice without necessarily avoiding conflicts with the judiciary. In most Bolivian neighborhoods with community justice forums, serious crimes such as rape and murder are reported to the PTJ, which in turn recognizes the community justice procedures to resolve them. But disputes erupt when a community tries to use indigenous methods of punishment—such as torture and the death penalty—that are illegal under national law. The distrust that ensues has made the police and courts increasingly reluctant to allow trials and to enforce their rulings. In many cases, citizens then end up paying a *fiscal* to initiate judicial proceedings. By that point, the coherence and self-sufficiency of community justice have been lost. For these and other reasons, the Traditional Justice Project got stalled by criticisms from the congressional commissions in charge of the bill as well as by a general lack of political will in Congress. Although the legality of traditional justice has been accepted, politics has blocked the legislation needed to make it happen.

For similar reasons, community justice remains limited throughout Latin America. These forums can be separate from state institutions but are not isolated from them. Part of the blame lies with the law and its implementation. One of the intended objectives of Venezuela's program is greater legal education for citizens, but the organic law contains no concrete provision to realize this goal or even to increase *jueces*' or citizens' access to existing sources of information. In Peru, the initial community support for *jueces de paz* has weakened in some areas because of judges' overuse of state laws and/or their lack of information and understanding regarding those laws.

Because the disputes dominating community justice forums are rooted in broad societal hardships, moreover, long-term resolution requires effective government policies and laws. Even institutionalized community justice can wind up being overwhelmed if government policies do not reduce urban crime, rural poverty, and other sources of conflict in poor communities. Residents are then more likely to turn to options such as vigilantism. In some El Alto neighborhoods, for example, residents want their community justice councils to deal with crime, yet they still use whistles to alert each other of a "criminal," who they then beat up or kill. National governments, for their part, have not done enough to remedy such problems. Although state officials should refrain from micromanaging these forums, their failure to follow up sometimes suggests a desire to see them fail.

Because of limited jurisdictions, community councils and *jueces de paz* need to be backed by clear judicial positions on the key constitutional questions that matter to ordinary citizens. Just as important for citizens as the resolution of minor issues is an overall belief that the judiciary supports basic rights. Anger and disputes among neighbors often spring out of a larger insecurity and frustration over the state's poor protection of rights and the judiciary's inconsistent rulings. Even disputes between two individuals usually involve legal questions or politics—originating somewhere far beyond their reach.

Community justice forums are also in danger of getting entangled in conflicts with state agencies. In the shantytowns of large cities like Caracas, Rio de Janeiro, Bogotá, and Mexico City, some of the community leaders who provide social services and physical protection are involved in organized crime like drug-trafficking. When they win forum elections, such individuals are then in positions of judicial authority and at odds with state officials and national law. Community justice forums are particularly likely to run up against the police. In the marginalized areas where most of Venezuela's *jueces de paz* operate, the police remain unaccountable for their abusive practices. In Buenos Aires, the directors of the Juridical Service admit that most of their clients' problems—but not the cases they bring—stem from confrontations with and abuses from officers.[16] On the rare occasion that citizens do challenge police policy or individual officers, it is unlikely the police agency will submit to the *jueces de paz* or to even to government-sponsored ADR mechanisms.

Finally, community justice forums will never be free of meddling by local officials. Unclear provisions, undeveloped practices, and informal procedures all make it hard for the Justicia de Paz to resist being pulled into local party politics. In Peru, in fact, many complain that nearly all *jueces de paz* begin as respected and independent community leaders, yet many do not continue that way because of outside influences. In Guatemala, community judges have gradually become more representative of the population since 1998, but in the first year of the reform only 5 percent of judges were fully indigenous. Many blame this poor representation on the use of outside money and on the low levels of effective organizing among indigenous communities.

In Venezuela, vociferous political opposition to the *jueces de paz* has increased the likelihood of such obstacles. The original bill's architects had to navigate years of negotiation to win approval in 1993, aided by the rare circumstance of a provisional president not beholden to either of the major political parties. In the course of the congressional debate, many ministers and members of Congress argued that nonlawyers should not be making judicial decisions, and the powerful minister of decentralization warned that *jueces de paz* may make good community leaders but lack the background to be good judges.[17] Regarding the bill's provision that *jueces de paz* receive compensation no smaller than that of a parochial council member, one congressman said that counterproductive rivalries and other problems would ensue.[18]

Executive-branch officials and their allies have proven to be an even bigger obstacle than legislators. Only months after the law's promulgation, many Venezuelan mayors rejected the new judges as an "unnecessary expense" and refused to cooperate without at least full executive funding of judges' elections and "maintenance."[19] In May 1994, an alliance of lawyers submitted a petition of unconstitutionality against the forums, arguing that they involved an unconstitutional transference to the municipalities of federal government function. The constitution clearly makes the national government responsible for administering and ensuring justice, and the law was seen as a way for it to shirk that obligation. Asserting that the Justicia de Paz did not and could not guarantee due process, critics also claimed that it violated the right to an adequate defense before a regular judge.[20] Editorials blasted the new law as a "politicization of justice at the municipal level" that destroys the stability of the courts and derails decentralization.[21]

Even if these political and legal obstacles can be overcome, the reasonable controls placed on the *jueces de paz* also open up room for manipulation. The high standard of qualifications, for one, can be a basis for a revoking referendum or at least for the threat of one against a judge. Requiring a judge to be knowledgeable about local issues, and with no connection to a case, could also be interpreted liberally and be the basis for disciplinary action by municipal councils controlled by a political party. Legal obligations to have forum hearings based simultaneously on orality, simplicity, equality, efficiency, and transparency are also potential justifications for sanctions on this overly demanding set of standards. Even the strict limits placed on elections can be abused. The law prohibits the campaign use of posters, placards, and media advertisements. But it does not restrict participation in radio and TV programs, interviews, and neighborhood meetings. Although not as vulnerable to abuse as paid media, community programs and centers are also used to tilt the playing field. No matter how many limits are placed on campaigning and expenditure, however, throwing a new institution into the mix of local party control and rivalry will inevitably cause abuses.

Conclusion

All of these pressures can destroy the community support and legal accommodations that allow the community justice to function. But in the long run, a lack of alternatives and the general distrust of the government should provide a sufficient foundation for its continuation. Thus far, forums in locales as different as Buenos Aires's working-class neighborhoods, Bolivia's migrant communities, and Venezuela's barrios have developed an institutionalization able to hold up against judicial disarray, executive power, and party influence. In Venezuela, renewed popular mobilization is likely to keep community justice on track, especially if President Chávez promotes citizen action as a permanent alternative to the discredited state judiciary. But it is hoped that community justice will complement instead of replace the judicial system, pushing it to better respond to society's needs. A working Justicia de Paz may not immediately create a surge of demand for better *defensores*, but it will boost specific judicial reforms like better ADR mechanisms, educate citizens on legal processes, and provoke citizens to demand improved assistance when they do need the courts. For democracy in general, these forums can help guide Latin American governments along the same path toward judicial access that occurred in the West during the 1800s and 1900s, in which access channels gradually reached society's most disadvantaged citizens. More than most other rule of law reforms, community justice embodies the citizen engagement necessary for a reform's effectiveness—and for giving society a stake in democracy.

Notes

1. Author interview, February 16, 1995.
2. The Justicia de Paz in Colombia was created in the 1991 constitution. Judges of the peace have been eliminated at the federal level in Argentina but are still used in some provinces. Although in most countries the judges of the peace do not have to have legal training, in Mexico and Uruguay they do.

3. *Ultimas Noticias,* 1995–2000, the newspaper with coverage of crime that is both detailed and accurage.

4. Author interviews, Catia, La Vega, and Las Brisas del Paraíso, 1990, 1992, 1995, and 1998.

5. *El Nacional* (Caracas), March 14, 1995; *El Diario de Caracas,* March 15, 1995, p. 2.

6. Based on broadcast news during May-July 1995.

7. "Escovar Salom se reunirá con empresas de vigilancia y grupos de autodefensa," *Ultimas Noticias,* February 2, 1995, p. 12.

8. Raúl Domínguez, Vice Minister of the Interior, author interview, June 29, 1998.

9. Presidencia del Organismo Judicial y de la Corte Suprema de Justicia: September 1987–January 1988. This study also defined *juzgados'* jurisdictions to be limited to misdemeanors committed in the community and to crimes whose punishments do not exceed one year or a fine of 1,000 *quetzales.*

10. Graciela Benin Chirico and Mario Carlos Tarrio, Program Directors, author interviews, December 2, 1994, and November 28, 1996.

11. Miguel Unamuno, Coordinator of the Once Centro Jurídico Comunitario, author interview, November 29, 1996.

12. According to the World Bank, the murder rates per 100,000 persons in Latin America break down as follows (the first figure is for the late 1970s–early 1980s, the second for the late 1980s–early 1990s): Colombia (20.5/89.5); Brazil (11.5/19.7); Mexico (18.2/17.8); Venezuela (11.7/15.2); Peru (2.4/11.5); Panama (2.1/10.9); Ecuador (6.4/10.3); United States (10.7/10.1); Argentina (3.9/4.8); Uruguay (2.6/4.4); Paraguay (5.1/4.0); Chile (2.6/3.0).

13. Marcanalisis 21, January 1990.

14. Consultores 21, Caracas, January 1990.

15. Author interviews, El Alto neighborhood council meetings, August 2000.

16. Graciela Benin Chirico and Mario Carlos Tarrio, Program Directors, author interviews, December 2, 1994, and November 28, 1996.

17. Transcript of the debate of the *Ley Orgánica de Tribunales y Procedimientos De Paz,* Congreso de la República, Cámara de Diputados, Comisión de Desarrollo Regional, 1993, p. 23.

18. Deputy José Antonio Adrián; ibid., p. 27.

19. "Gobierno central debe absorber gastos de los Jueces de Paz," *El Globo,* May 26, 1994.

20. "Solicitan nulidad de Ley de Jueces de Paz," *El Universal,* May 13, 1994.

21. "Jueces de paz o jueces políticos," *El Nacional,* June 30, 1994.

8

CONCLUSION:
RULE OF LAW REFORM AND
DEMOCRATIC CONSOLIDATION

BECAUSE THE RULE OF LAW reaches beyond the judiciary and deep into history, it is far simpler to define than to bring about. Centuries of executives with too much power, and of judiciaries with too little, have cast a long shadow over the few decades of democracy. Democracy does not automatically make the executive respect the courts, force state agencies to comply with the law, or swing open the doors of justice. But through reforms, democratization helps courts gain authority, creates channels of participation, makes officials answer for their actions, and institutionalizes oversight.

To be effective, each rule of law measure must address the practices and flaws of the executive and judicial branches. Reforms on the executive focus on making it more responsive to citizen needs, less authoritarian, or both. In particular, reforms must involve policies and accountability mechanisms that loosen executive control, improve administration, and allow for local-level innovation. Reforms on the judiciary focus on making it more efficient, more accessible, or both. Specific measures must draw a line on interference in the courts, provide consistent material support, and help citizen grievances be heard. The contemporary democracies of Latin America are all considering and enacting a wide range of such reforms. But the combination of pressing needs, vacillating commitments, and political impediments often breaks reform into piecemeal changes, heightening the risk that each one is subsumed by executive power and judicial disarray. Judicial councils may not be strong enough to reduce corruption, newly trained prison personnel may be overcome by inmate violence, and *Defensorías del Pueblo* may end up doing little more than relay complaints.

The obstacles to the rule of law embody the obstacles to the wider process of democratization. Progress between democratic transition and consolidation is difficult to recognize due to the breadth of democracy as well as the specific pressures on each regime. Consolidated democracy is

229

made up of many different characteristics, such as citizen participation in public affairs, free and fair elections, and civilian rule over reserve domains of power. Requirements such as electoral fairness are relatively easy to evaluate, but others, like control by reserve domains of power, are not. The rule of law gives substance to these more elusive characteristics. In this regard, the reforms that lead to a rule of law are parallel to the steps toward consolidated democracy. Practices such as corruption and intimidation undermine judicial rights just as they undermine all other democratic standards.

Historical patterns, discussed in the second sections of the book's chapters, and contemporary politics, discussed in the third sections, determine the general prospects for overcoming damaging practices. In Argentina, the brutality and later collapse of the *Proceso* created strong popular momentum for a rule of law as well as a political break that allowed reforms to be relatively free of partisan interests. On the other end of the spectrum, control over Venezuela's democratic transition by political parties injected partisan interests into nearly every policy. Over time, the corruption and inefficiency of the Venezuelan "partyocracy" led to support for reform and an even stronger demand for starting from scratch. Democratic structures are valued for their balance and access after an era of repression, but they are prone to be regarded as dysfunctional and abusive when controlled from above.

Argentina and Venezuela are at two ends of this spectrum, and most Latin American democracies fall in between. Compared to Argentina, the lower level of violence by the military regimes in Uruguay and Brazil dampened the push for wide-ranging reforms. In Chile, the support for reform created by the Pinochet regime's repression was tempered by the agreements of the 1989 transition and the continuing popularity of the right wing. In Mexico, the seventy-one-year rule of a dominant party created support for reform, but it was more measured than in Venezuela because of the still substantial political and bureaucratic power of the Partido Revolucionario Institutional. In countries such as Peru, Bolivia, Nicaragua, and Paraguay, popular support for reform has been checked by the even greater fear of uncertainty.

In addition to the legacies of an authoritarian past and the complications of transition from it, the difficulties of legislating and enforcing change in any democracy become additional breaks on reform. As the authoritarian past recedes, in fact, contemporary politics has an increasing impact on the rule of law. Economic problems and political threats can cause new regimes to take measures, such as human rights amnesties, that hinder the rule of law and democratic consolidation. This range of problems is constantly expanding and mutating. But putting them into the categories of executive power and judicial disarray help show how they obstruct both a rule of law and democratic consolidation. The executive branch, first of all, remains critical even without authoritarian controls. Its importance is demonstrated by the effects of most changes in presidential leadership during Latin America's current democratization. Whether occurring from peaceful transfers within a party or the rise of an independent populist, the contrasts between successive governments on rule of law reform have usually been sharp. A genuinely proreform president, motivated by recognition of the need to reign in state repression or to improve inefficiencies that stifle economic progress, is often the biggest boost the rule of law can receive. Argentina's Alfonsín in the 1980s, Bolivia's Gonzalo Sánchez de Lozada in the 1990s, and Mexico's Vicente Fox after 2000 are three examples. By the same token, an executive that blocks or dismantles reform, as in Venezuela and Honduras, can stop change in its tracks. In Peru, the ability of Fujimori to both strengthen and abolish the SIN (the National Intelligence Force) shows both sides of this executive power.

Judicial disarray, the second category of problems affecting reform, captures the underlying practices that undermine the rule of law on a daily basis. A democracy's legal standards may be clear and refined, but rarely so is the process of putting them into practice. Nearly every one of the rights spelled out in the constitution is abused in courtrooms, prisons, police stations, and the streets. Even comprehensive improvement of a lengthy judicial process can be reversed by a single official or bureaucratic loophole. Public defense laws mean little without public defenders; alternatives to incarceration mean little without cooperative agencies; and citizens will refrain from using courts that are not independent.

Many rule of law reforms are enacted during a country's first years of democracy, when most institutions and processes are in flux. New practices that become engrained or old ones that return are more difficult to alter, and reform must wait for another political shift and critical mass of support, which scares officials into supporting change. But when changes are too sudden, as in Argentina in the 1920s, they can debilitate governments, confuse policy, render state rule of law functions ineffective, and threaten the democratic regime itself. The sudden drop of support for Venezuelan President Pérez and for Argentine President Alfonsín in the 1980s nearly brought down democracy in those countries. Governments often try to wait out pressure for change or are constrained by politics and finances. When the dust settles, reforms tend to be introduced slowly. But a gradual approach brings the opposite problem: uneven patterns of legitimacy and institutionalization. Without comprehensive change, certain laws command respect while others are ignored; new trial procedures get overwhelmed; some agencies become legitimate while others stumble.

Most reforms, however, stand a good chance of being effective if they succeed in becoming institutionalized. Judicial councils can create a new power base with real effects on judicial independence; a new affiliation can help a police force cooperate with judges; and community justice forums can give citizens a real stake in the administration of justice. Such benefits usually extend beyond a reform's stated objectives. Judicial councils set an example for oversight of all state structures, a stronger MP can be a check on police abuses in the streets, and community justice promotes ADR mechanisms and better criminal policies. As new penal codes demonstrate, reform is most effective when it involves all relevant agencies and processes.

As a general rule, reforms prevail over obstacles when they focus on the standards of democracy that the rule of law supports. In most cases, it is premature to declare that a particular democracy is consolidated. Economic vulnerability, political rivalry, and government inefficiency prevent many democratic regimes from moving completely past the risk of breakdown. Thus, consolidation is usually defined with more general attributes, as when the public believes that a democracy is most appropriate for their country, when no significant actor expends significant resources to form a nondemocratic regime, and when both state and society are accountable to the law. After long periods of authoritarianism, of course, such beliefs and behaviors do not materialize quickly. They can be developed only through proactive measures that actually make the judiciary more independent, oblige state agencies to abide by the law, and open up channels of citizen access. In this way, rule of law reform becomes critical to democratic consolidation.

As discussed in Chapter 1, rule of law reforms help set the path toward consolidation by addressing the problem of accountability. Accountability is considered essential to democracy but, like democracy, is difficult to define, measure, and establish. Rule of law reform brings substance to accountability and roots out vulnerabilities by countering nondemocratic processes within democratic structures. Many agree that a transition will not move forward without elimination of "non-democratic components of the constitution," such as executive decree powers (Linz and Stepan 1996: 95–98). But just as problematic are unchecked undemocratic uses and interpretations of "democratic" components. Most constitutions prohibit the executive from exercising judicial functions, for example, but such prohibitions have been violated so routinely that courts often begin to justify such actions. Top officials, distracted by more pressing concerns or lacking "a normative commitment to democracy," may not check such practices.[1] The "virtuous institutionalization" of democratic standards and procedures (Mainwaring 1992), as a result, fails to take hold. This failure then allows nondemocratic powers such as the military to exercise "broad oversight of the government" (Valenzuela 1992: 62–64) and lower-level officials to take control of the daily administration of justice. Without the oversight and accountability the rule of law helps bring, actors and processes can keep democracies unconsolidated.

Democracies see the importance of this issue when economic crisis, societal grievances, or institutional fragility bring the system to the edge of breakdown. Governments try to fend off collapse by using emergency powers and pushing through laws, constitutional amendments, and decrees. Such responses occurred during the most destabilizing moments in contemporary Argentina and Venezuela. Severe economic problems combined with governmental weaknesses and the resentment of a segment of the armed forces to spark military rebellions in Argentina from 1987 to 1990 and two attempted coups in Venezuela in 1992. In both cases, the governments responded with amnesties, constitutional suspensions, executive decrees, and other legal manipulation. Instead of turning to a rule of law, the governments turned against it. But legal weaknesses, such as poor accountability of powerful officials in the executive and military, helped cause the crises in the first place.

Apart from disgruntled military factions, however, most actors refrain from creating nondemocratic alternatives because their interests are better served by *not* challenging governments or rules. Harmful patterns can then coexist and often overtake progressive patterns. A free press and free elections, for example, are negated by a judiciary that upholds censorship or fixed votes. The only way out is through accountability and related measures that draw and maintain the line between democratic and undemocratic practices. "The process of consolidation, or its derailment, thereby unfolds through precedent-setting political confrontations that either fortify constitutional standards or allow harmful practices to continue" (Valenzuela 1992: 71). Although many such confrontations occur over rule of law reform, they are not well examined in the literature that aims to explain democracy.

"Attitudinally," a democracy is consolidated "when a strong majority" of people believes "that democratic procedures and institutions are the most appropriate way to govern collective life in a country such as theirs" (Linz and Stepan 1996: 6). This support, of course, is for institutions that act democratically. But when citizenry feel that constitutional obligations are not being applied, the result can be widespread frustration with and a withdrawal from democratic processes. High abstention rates, the popularity of politicians unaffiliated with traditional parties, and low confidence in state institutions are some of the indications of such disillusion. In a 2000 poll of sixteen Latin American countries, 60 percent of respondents said that they preferred democracy as a form of government, but only 37 percent liked the way it functioned in practice.[2] The kind of "shallow" belief in the effectiveness and legitimacy of democratic institutions (Dahl 1971: 139), blamed for the chronic failure of democracy in the past, has not disappeared. Without a rule of law, the promise of accountability exists without the means to achieve it.

So even though democratic transition literature does look behind democracy's formal arrangements to identify obstacles to consolidation, it still must flesh out how such obstacles affect routine governance and how proposals to overcome obstacles are worn down by political interests. When democratic rules are hijacked by unseen and undemocratic processes, ranging from presidential pressure on supreme court justices to prohibitively expensive court fees, it is not the lack of good laws and intentions that prevents consolidation. Instead, politics and processes are the source of the problem—gutting the constitution, watering down citizenship, and weakening a carefully constructed legal apparatus without any actor ever being identified as "undemocratic." As explored throughout this book, the effectiveness of accountability mechanisms depends less on what they directly affect and more on whether they can redirect the attitudes, decisions, and interactions of daily government. The challenge is "not how to introduce public accountability where it had never previously been known, but rather how to redesign, focus, and render effective practices that have long been subject to manipulation and abuse" (Whitehead 2000: 4).

Along with accountability and attitudes, security is an essential but elusive part of democratization. To be consolidated, democracies need to provide an environment in which citizens can make plans and contest policies that affect their well-being. Citizens will resent a democracy that expects them to obey laws it does not itself obey. Reforms like the *Defensoría* help improve these state-society relations by allowing citizens to challenge and participate in state policy. Amid economic and political insecurity, a regime would have a hard time consolidating without such channels for popular frustration. Reforms thereby give people a stake in democracy and give substance to democratic rights, even if the democratic regime is weak or ineffective. "A situation in which one can vote freely and have one's vote counted fairly, but cannot expect proper treatment from the police or the courts ... severely curtail[s] citizenship" that is the foundation of liberal and durable democracy (O'Donnell 1993: 1361).

Part of citizen security is economic. This does not mean that democratic consolidation requires a welfare state, but that it at least forms a stable economic foundation. The relationship between democracy and economics, of course, depends on individual perspectives as well as on changing domestic conditions. One body of analysis examines why certain democratic regimes are able to weather painful economic measures. Past experiences, a lack of perceived alternatives, and tolerance for short-term sacrifice are some of the conditions determining such ability. The differing fates of previously untried economic policies in Ecuador, Mexico, Peru, Argentina, and Venezuela are evidence of these influences.

Another body of analysis looks at the contribution of democracy to economic growth. An overview of twenty studies of this relationship reported that two of the studies found a negative contribution, ten found no relationship, five found a conditional relationship, and just three found a positive relationship (Weder 1997). In other words, democracy was not seen as a contributor to macroeconomic growth. Such skepticism is rooted in perceptions that burdens such as external debt lead governments to adopt popular but economically rash measures and that promarket reforms cannot coexist with greater popular access.[3] International disapproval of some of the economic measures taken by the beleaguered government of Argentine President de la Rúa is one example of this condition.

Beneath these various analyses, however, awareness is growing over how undemocratic patterns and "a weak legal system" are "prime obstacles to economic development and growth."[4] Claiming that Latin America rates just above Africa on rule of law issues, one multinational report calculated that a weak rule of law, corruption, and ineffective public administration accounted for nearly 60 percent of the income gap between Latin America and high-income regions like Southern Europe (World Bank 2000). On one level, practices like clientelism and police violence limit individual freedom and movement necessary to many economic interactions. More generally, the rule of law fosters economic stability and acceptance of economic policy by all sizes of businesses. To maximize competitiveness needed for growth in an interdependent world, governments must attract investment, business must adapt foreign-based technology, and both must put together schemes such as joint ventures and free-trade zones.

All of this requires stable banking, contract and investment laws, as well as government policies that stimulate business without controlling it. Asked about obstacles to investment, most entrepreneurs interviewed in one report stressed the harms of discretionary state action. Specifically, they blamed poor economic performance and low investment on arbitrary enforcement of rules and laws by bureaucrats, the "large, unpredictable swings in these rules" and policies; and "uncertainties about judiciary enforcement" (Weder 1997: 4). Increasing numbers of individuals, companies, and small businesses enter contracts that require legal enforcement, which, if not forthcoming, can weaken the economic system. In 1991, for example, a Venezuelan publisher began putting out a magazine entitled *¡Hola!*, with the same format and themes as a popular internationally distributed Spanish magazine by the same name. The original *¡Hola!* sued, but the courts, influenced by those running Venezuela's version, ruled against it.[5] Throughout Latin America, in fact, "private economic activity ... is not responding as fast as expected" to economic rules, partly because "reforms are not being properly implemented" or are not seen as "credible" (Sherwood et al. 1994).

But many of the needs articulated by international businesses are disconnected from basic democratic norms. Elections, for example, were not considered a necessity in the Weder study. Many interviewees decried the arbitrary actions of elected Latin American governments but valued the legal predictability provided by authoritarian Asian governments. In respondents' evaluation of the effects on economic growth by different variables, the variable of "political credibility" accounted for 50 percent of expectations of growth; judges' impartiality explained 23 percent. The variable of "democracy," in contrast, actually had a negative relationship. Such expectations can be a self-fulfilling prophecy, as seen in the early flight of international capital from Chávez's Venezuela. Many businesses rely on predictions of government action, and they anticipated in Chávez a future of harmful populist economics. Although investment in unstable countries can yield big profits, such investments are usually concentrated in raw materials, with extraction being far from the major population centers. And even those investments require an outlay that large multinational corporations are reluctant to spend. In violent countries, foreign firms must spend more than 5 percent of their budgets on security, along with more for personnel relocation incentives.[6]

The divergence between popular and business interests can be huge. As the states of Latin America and other regions reduce spending and ownership, and as inequality grows amid massive wealth creation, the economic experiences of ordinary citizens take on added political importance. Most people do not have the property or assets to soften the impacts of neoliberalism and the world economy. Whether they accept a government's economic approach, however, depends partly on the rule of law. On one level, for reforms to be popular they must be designed to bring greater security to small businesses, students, and others living day to day. The immense popularity of anti-inflation policies is testament to the importance of such stability. But on another level, they must also be seen to address general demands for justice and equal opportunity. Popular support for a democratic regime gives it valuable time to implement difficult policies and help those policies reach the poor. But increasing inequality, inefficiency, and corruption will erode support and increase the likelihood of violence, demonstrations, and promotion of alternatives that may be less democratic but more responsive to the poor's immediate needs. In such a scenario, carefully constructed reforms can be swept away by a single election or presidential decree. The experiences of Venezuela, Peru, and Colombia may well be repeated throughout the region.

The best way to balance the macroeconomic demands of the international economy with the microeconomic needs of a poor population is through the channels and institutions that rule of law reform helps create. This is done, above all, through "well-specified and enforced property rights" (North 1992: 13). Such rights, supported by well-designed laws and unbiased courts, help existing businesses by guaranteeing investments and applications of expertise, facilitating entry and exit (as through investment and bankruptcy), and resolving conflicts. Each "successful case of law enforcement and dispute resolution [then] creates a demonstration effect that builds overall trust in the legal process" (Gray 1997: 4). Such enforcement is especially needed by newer and smaller businesses, which are an engine for growth and distribution in Latin America's undeveloped economies. Without adequate enforcement, capital becomes concentrated because of the greater security of transactions within than between firms (Williamson 1985) and because business transactions become based on reputation and personal contacts (Stone et al. 1992). Because economic activity expands through interactions, firms fearing weak enforcement are unlikely to engage in contracts with other firms or, in a dispute, are more likely to abandon a contract than endure unpredictable, costly procedures. Poor enforcement dries up loans as well, which undermines needed commercial lending and risk-taking. Contracts with the state also decrease, as businesses believe they have little recourse against government favoritism.

The biggest beneficiaries of secure property rights, however, are the poor. New guarantees and reforms increase court impartiality on economic disputes, help ensure that the police will take action against violence intended to inflict economic harm, and establish procedures for economic complaints against officials. They also help citizens make decisions and investments that provide a way out of poverty. With many people lacking ownership of land and structures they have long occupied, a more democratic and equitable system of property rights for rural land and urban housing gives the poor a political and economic stake in the system. In most of Latin America's big cities, most of the poor are unable to improve their lot because they buy or rent plots of land but cannot obtain title to them. But they often prefer precarious ownership and lack of services to public housing, where they own nothing and have to put up with gangs and drug traffickers. In more and more cases, people fed up with this terrible choice take over abandoned property. In São Paulo, the Movement of the Roofless has sprung up to organize takeovers of vacated downtown buildings. In Caracas, about 30,000 people invaded empty buildings in the months after Chávez's election.

Such actions scare business and violate laws, yet they are an expression of the popular needs and principles discussed above. Without secure employment, many people try to raise capital to fund small businesses but cannot do so without title to their property. Even those who have lived on a plot for generations cannot prove ownership. But with new and well-enforced property rights, people can use their modest assets as collateral to obtain loans, credit, and services such as electricity and telephones (de Soto

1989). Registration of ownership also makes it easier for economic interactions to take place, because records and documentation provide security in contracts and even in purchases at the community market. Because people in poor areas do not have access to or confidence in local businesses, they often do all of their tasks themselves. In Caracas's Catia barrios, for example, residents must painstakingly locate the materials to build and rebuild houses rather than rely on local suppliers or contractors. More secure property rights not only are democratic, as the majority of people support them, but also give poor economies an essential foundation. In one study of eighty countries where overall annual per capita income rose by at least 2 percent, in fact, a broader distribution of wealth was attributed in part to the law's defense of basic property rights (Dollar and Karay 2000).

Conclusion

Struggles with rule of law reform are unfolding in countries throughout the world. Most of those countries face even sharper societal divisions and more powerful nondemocratic forces compared to Latin America. Economic problems have blunted judicial access measures in Eastern Europe, for example, and ethnic tensions in Africa (Hedley et al. 1997) have prevented application of constitutional standards in many countries there. In troubled Asian democracies like Malaysia and Indonesia, powerful executives have effectively blocked even the consideration of many court reforms.

But as in Latin America, new democracies in those regions are still managing to enact rule of law reforms. Democratizing countries in Africa and Eastern Europe, for example, have set up independent ombudsmen agencies at the national, provincial, and local levels. Among those countries are Tanzania, Gabon, Mauritania, Senegal, Ghana, Nigeria, Namibia, South Africa, Poland, Hungary, Lithuania, Slovenia, and the Philippines. Other countries, particularly in Eastern Europe, have also set up judicial councils and constitutional courts. Penal law reform and prison restructuring have also become increasingly common around the world.

Because the rule of law is important to any democracy and because reforms follow similar paths, this book's approach can be applied to these other world regions. Just as a democratic constitution is *most* needed during a crisis, rule of law reforms are most needed by more fragile democracies. Historical analysis underscores the need to incorporate each country's own experiences of executive authority and judicial functioning. Similarly, nonjudicial agencies and citizen beliefs demonstrate the importance of incorporating a country's entire societal context. Because judicial independence, a law-abiding state, and judicial access are requirements for any rule of law in every contemporary state, each can be "unpacked" under any political circumstances. Doing so reveals the obstacles to a reform's enactment and effectiveness. Judicial structures vary widely among countries but always need freedom from undue interference by executive officials; states have vastly different capacities but always require oversight mechanisms; judicial access is defined very differently among countries but always requires equality among citizens. Providing specific measures on these issues is how, in the end, rule of law reform lays out a roadmap between political realities and democratic ideals.

Notes

1. Dankwart Rustow (1970: 357). Scott Mainwaring adds that many leaders lack "a normative commitment to" democracy. He adds (1992: 308) that others (Huntington 1984; Karl 1986c) concur with this assessment.

2. Latinobarometro, Santiago de Chile, poll conducted between January and March 2000.

3. The relationship between macroeconomic policy, microeconomic conditions, and democracy also depends a great deal on political timing. Countries respond in a variety of ways to economic crises, even the same ones (Little et al. 1993; Stallings 1990), complicating the picture. The spectrum of responses is exemplified by Argentina and Venezuela. Whereas initial neoliberal reforms enacted by Pérez in 1989 precipitated a threat to Venezuelan democracy, similar reforms enacted by President Caldera six years later were met with milder reactions. Pérez had just been elected by harkening back to the flush economic times of his first administration; Caldera, however, turned to some neoliberal solutions as part of a muddled retraction from an ineffective populist approach that left society more resigned than angry. In Argentina, Menem's neoliberal program was accepted partly because of his success at taming inflation. At the end of the Menem presidency, those same policies were part of an electoral rejection of Menem's party because of high unemployment as well as a sense of corruption and privilege in the government. Poor results grow not out of policies implemented by democracies but rather policies implemented badly by any government.

4. Beatrice Weder (1997: 3), referring to studies of Peru, Equatorial New Guinea, and Brazil.

5. When the government changed in 1994, the law was changed to allow the Spanish version of the magazine ¡Hola! back in over the Venezuelan version. The magazine had also been involved in defamation suits in the 1980s.

6. "Business in Difficult Places," *The Economist,* May 20, 2000, p. 86.

GLOSSARY

alcaldes de crimen   Officials responsible for much of law enforcement in colonial Latin America, often acting as criminal judges.

alcaldes ordinarios   Municipal officials in colonial Venezuela in charge of judicial matters.

alguacil   Bailiff/constable of the court in Latin America.

amparo   A legal recourse against most illegal actions by the state.

audiencias   In Spanish colonial Latin America, *audiencias* were regional centers, hierarchically beneath the viceroyalties, which served as the link between local settlements and the viceroyalties. In addition to having legislative powers, the *audiencias* were the highest judicial agencies.

averiguación de antecedentes   Police detention in order to check a person's police record.

bolívar   The form of Venezuelan currency, named after Simón Bolívar, the country's founder.

cabildos   In Spanish colonial Latin America, *cabildos* were the governments of the local settlements. In isolated regions such as the southern cone, they developed with little outside influence, controlled by officials who enjoyed strong citizen loyalty and established a sort of populist authoritarianism.

Cámara de Diputados or **Representantes**   The lower house of Congress in most Latin American countries.

Cámaras Federal de Apelaciones and **Cortes de Casación**   A common name for superior appellate courts in Latin America.

Caracazo   The mass riots that engulfed Venezuela at the end of February and the beginning of March 1989, set off by unexpected austerity measures involving a rise in gasoline prices and transportation fares.

casación/recursos de casación   Appeals in Latin American courts.

241

caudillos   Regional leaders with strong executive powers and control over their area.

Código de Enjuiciamiento Criminal   The common name for a Latin American trial code.

comisario   The chief (commissioner) of a police station.

concursos públicos   Public forums to debate the records of nominees to the courts.

Consejo de la Judicatura or **de la Magistradura**   Judicial councils responsible for most of the selection and discipline of judges, as well as administration of judicial finances.

Consejo de Indias or **Real y Supremo Consejo de Indias**   The Spanish colonial agency in charge of colonial administration. Legal appeals could be made against an *audiencia*'s ruling to the Consejo.

contravenciones (often also *edictos* or *faltas*)   Infractions or misdemeanors, less serious than crimes (cf. *delitos*).

corregimientos   Colonial Latin American committees with judicial powers.

Cuerpo Técnico de Policía Judicial (PTJ)   Venezuela's judicial police.

customary law   Unwritten law that is enforceable because it expresses legal standards and practices validated by continuation through long periods of time.

Defensor General de la Nación   The head of the public defense agency in Argentina.

defensores volantes   A new kind of public defender in Argentina, whose function is to coordinate the work of defenders working in different court levels.

Defensorías del Pueblo   National, regional, or local ombudsmen in Latin America, which are independent agencies that receive complaints of the state's violation of constitutional rights.

delitos   Crimes, as opposed to misdemeanors or infractions (cf. *contravenciones*).

derecho real   The area of law regulating rights over property.

Dirección Ejecutiva de la Magistratura   The Executive Judicial Office, an agency within the high court, created by the 1999 Venezuela constitution to be in charge of court discipline.

Dirty War (Guerra Sucia)   The campaign of killing and torture of suspected leftists by Argentina's 1976–1983 dictatorship.

escabinos   Nonjudge citizens who preside and rule in certain trials.

escraches   Popularized by children of the "disappeared" between 1976 and 1983, this is a form of protest in which charges are read aloud in front of the homes of officials believed to have been responsible for Dirty War crimes in Argentina.

escuelas de la judicatura   Training schools for judges and other judicial personnel.

favelas   Shantytowns in Brazil.

fiscal   A public prosecutor from the Attorney General's Office.

Fiscal General   Attorney General.

Fiscalía General   Attorney General/government attorney/comptroller or auditor's office.

gatillo fácil   Literally, "trigger happy." Used to refer to questionable shootings by police.

hacienda   A large plantation common in precolonial and nineteenth-century Latin America.

intendencias   To dilute some of the power of local authorities, in its Latin American colonies Castile created the *intendencias*, an administrative agency between the *cabildos* and the *audiencias*.

jefe de gabinete   A presidentially appointed minister in Argentina who coordinates the ministries' work and is their congressional liaison.

jueces capitulares   Colonial Latin American officials who oversaw many regular criminal and civil judicial affairs.

juntas de vecinos   Neighborhood councils set up or elected to serve specific community needs, such as, in Bolivia, for resolving minor disputes.

jurado de enjuiciamiento   A special jury in Argentina to formally try judges after they have been investigated and accused of violations by the judicial council.

justicia comunitaria   Literally, "community justice," referring to different forums used to resolve community conflicts.

Juzgados de Paz Comunitarios   The Community Peace Courts of Guatemala.

ley orgánica   Directly below the constitution in Latin America's legal hierarchy, "organic laws" set out the general outlines of an area or institution of the law.

magistrado   A top-level judge or judicial official serving on the Supreme Court, Constitutional Court, or judicial council.

Ministerio Público   The Justice Department or Attorney General's Office, responsible for prosecuting cases on behalf of the state.

Proceso or *Proceso de Reorganización Nacional*   Literally, the process of national reorganization, the self-styled name of Argentina's 1976–1983 dictatorship.

Procurador General   The head of both *fiscales* and *defensores* in Argentina until the 1994 constitutional reforms created the *Defensor General*.

quetzal   The form of Guatemalan currency, named after the national bird.

Seguridad Nacional   The repressive and powerful national police force functioning in Venezuela in the 1940s and 1950s.

Siete Partidas   The main document of Iberian Law, which specified the roles of judges and lawyers and outlined colonial judicial processes.

stare decisis   A doctrine holding that a court, once it has laid down a principle of law as applicable to a certain set of facts, will adhere to that principle and apply it to all future cases in which the facts are substantially the same.

tribus   Literally, "tribes," this term refers to powerful alliances of law firms and lawmakers with influence in the judiciary.

Trienio   The three-year democratic regime in Venezuela, led by the Acción Democrática party from 1945 to 1948.

U.S. Agency for International Development   The U.S. state agency designing and funding programs for development and democratization abroad.

viceroy (*virrey*) and viceroyalties   The colonial official in Latin America heading each of the four viceroyalties.

vocal   Voting member of a council or board (aside from the president, treasurer, etc.).

writ of certiorari   An order used by an appellate court when the court has discretion whether or not to hear an appeal; this allows the court itself to determine some of the cases that come before it.

BIBLIOGRAPHY

Alberdi, Juan Batista. 1886. *Obras Completas*. Buenos Aires: La Tribunal Nacional.
Alterini, Atilio Aníbal. 1992. *La Inseguridad Jurídica*. Buenos Aires: Abeledo-Perrot.
Altamira, Pedro Guillermo. 1963. *Policía y Poder de Policía*. Buenos Aires: Abeledo Perrot.
Alvarez, Gladys Stella. 1995. "Alternative Dispute Resolution Mechanisms: Lessons of the Argentine Experience." In World Bank, *Judicial Reform in Latin America and the Caribbean*, Technical Paper 280. Washington, D.C.: World Bank.
Amnesty International. 1988. *Memorandum al Gobierno de Venezuela*. London: AI Press.
———. 1987. *El Poder Judicial en la reforma del estado venezolano*. Caracas: Monte Avila.
Aranguren Córdova, Jesús, et al. 1994. *Descentralización del Poder Judicial: Importancia del Juez de Paz*. Maracaibo: Ediciones Instituto Municipal de Capacitación y Educación Ciudadana.
Arano, María Laura. 1997. *El Ombudsman y su Recepción Constitucional*, Buenos Aires: Editorial Belgrano.
Araujo, O. 1968. *Violencia violenta*. Caracas: Herpérides.
Aristotle. 1984. *The Politics*. Cambridge: Cambridge University Press.
Asociación Venezolana de Derecho Tributario. 1985. *La Corrupción en Venezuela*. Caracas: Vadell Hermanos.
Badeni, Gregorio. 1994. *Reforma Constitucional e Instituciones Políticas*. Buenos Aires: AD-HOC S.R.L.
Baizan, Mario. 1993. "La Justicia en la Picota: Conversaciones con Carlos Saúl Menem." Revista *Administración Pública*. Buenos Aires, September: 4–10.
Baker, Richard D. 1971. *Judicial Review in Mexico*. Austin: University of Texas.
Baragli, Néstor, and María Poli. 1996. *Consejo de la Magistratura: Guia de Debate*. Buenos Aires: Conciencia y Fundación Poder Ciudadano.
Barceló, Javier Malagón. 1966. *Estudios de Historia y Derecho*. Xalapa, Mexico: Universidad Veracruzana.
Barker, R. 1988. S. "Consitutionalism in the Americas: A Bicentenial Perspective." *University of Pittsburgh Law Review* 49, no. 3: 891–914.
Barroso, Manuel. 1990. *Autoestima del Venezolano: Democracia o Marginalidad*. Caracas: Editorial Galac.

Bayley, David H. 1985. *Patterns of Policing: A Comparative International Analysis.* New Brunswick, N.J.: Rutgers University Press.

Bergalli, Roberto. 1974. "La política criminal en la República Argentina." *Nuevo Pensamiento Penal* 3 (Enero-Diciembre): 19–32.

Berizonce, R. 1987. *Efectivo Acceso a la Justicia.* La Plata: Librería Editorial Platense SLC.

Berthelemy, H. 1923. *Traité Élémentairs: Droit Aministratif,* Paris: Librairie Arthur Rousseau.

Bidart Campos, German. 1963. *Derecho Constitucional, Tomo.* Buenos Aires: Edior.

———. *Derecho de Amparo.* 1961. Buenos Aires: A. S. Editores.

Bickel, Alexander M. 1986. *The Least Dangerous Branch.* New Haven: Yale University Press.

Bielsa, Rafael. 1993. *Transformación del Derecho en Justicia.* Buenos Aires: La Ley.

———. 1950. *Régimen Jurídico de Policía.* Buenos Aires: La Ley.

Bielsa, Rafael. 1990. "La Justicia y las deudas de la soberanía." *La Ley,* 55 (230).

Bierbrauer, Günter, et al. 1978. "Conflict and Its Settlement." In M. Cappelletti, ed., *Access to Justice,* vol. 2, book 1. Milan: Guiffrè.

Binder, Alberto. 1993. "Balance y Perspective de la Reforma Judicial en Latinoamérica." In Management Science for Development MSD/Bolivia, *Primer Seminario de Reforma Judicial.* Sucre: Consejo de la Judicatura and Corte Supreme de Justicia.

Black, Donald. 1973. "The Mobilization of Law." *Journal of Legal Studies* 2: 125–129.

Blackwelder, Julia Kirk, and Lyman L. Johnson. 1982. "Changing Criminal Patterns in Buenos Aires, 1890 to 1914." *Journal of Latin American Studies* 14, pt. 2 (November): 359–379.

Blair, Harry. 1994. *A Strategic Assessment of Legal Systems' Development in Uruguay and Argentina.* Washington, D.C.: U.S. Agency for International Development.

Bouzón de Terzano, Emilia, and J. Carlos García Basalo. 1985. *Realidad Penitenciaria Argentina, 1974 y 1983, Tomo I.* Buenos Aires: Instituto de Estudios Criminológicos.

Brading, D. 1991. A. *The First America.* Cambridge: Cambridge University Press.

Brandt, Hans-Jürgen. 1995. "The Justice of the Peace as an Alternative: Experiences with Conciliation in Perú." Technical Paper No. 280. Washington, D.C.: World Bank.

———. 1990. *In the Name of Communal Peace: An Analysis of the Justice of the Peace of Peru.* Lima: Friedrich Naumann Foundation, Center for Judicial Studies of the Supreme Court of the Republic.

———. 1987. *Justicia Popular.* Lima: Friedrich Naumann Foundation, Center for Judicial Studies of the Supreme Court of the Republic.

Bravo Lira, Bernardino. 1989. *Derecho Común y Derecho Propia en El Nuevo Mundo.* Santiago de Chile: Editorial Jurídica de Chile.

Bravo Oliveros, José Ignacio. 1977. *Simposio Sobre Sistemas de Tratamiento y Capacitación Personal en América Latina: El Tratamiento al Delincuente en Venezuela.* San José: ILANUD.

Brewer-Carias, Allan R. 1982. *El Estado, Crisis Y Reforma.* Caracas: Biblioteca de la Academia de Ciencias Políticas y Sociales.

———. 1980. *Estudios sobre la reforma administrativa.* Caracas: Universidad Central de Venezuela.

————. 1979. *Política estado y administración pública*. Caracas: Editorial Ateneo de Caracas.

————. 1975. *Cambio Político y reforma del estado en Venezuela*. Madrid: Editorial Tecnos.

Brewer-Carias, Allan R., and Carlos M. 1991. Ayala Corao. *Ley Orgánica de Amparo Sobre Derechos y Garantias Constitucionales*. Caracas: Editorial Jurídica Venezolana.

Briceño Vivas, Gustavo. 1993. *El Defensor del Pueblo en Venezuela: La Figura del Ombudsman*. Caracas: Editorial Kinesis.

Brysk, Alison. 1994. *The Politics of Human Rights in Argentina: Protest, Change, and Democratization*. Stanford: Stanford University Press.

Busaniche, José Luis. 1965. *Historia Agentina*. Buenos Aires: Ediciones Solar.

Buscaglia, Edgardo. 1995. "Judicial Reform in Latin America: The Obstacles Ahead." *Journal of Latin American Affairs 4* (Fall/Winter): 1–16.

Buscaglia, Edgardo, and Maria Dakolis. 1996. "Judicial Reform in Latin American Courts: The Experience in Argentina and Ecuador." Washington, D.C.: World Bank.

Buscaglia, Edgardo, Maria Dakolis, and William Ratliff. 1995. *Judicial Reform in Latin America: A Framework for National Development*. Stanford: Hoover Institution.

Búvinic, M., and A. Morrison. 1999. "Notas técnics sobre la violencia." Washington, D.C.: Inter-American Development Bank.

Cadenas Madariaga, Mario A., and Cadenas Madariaga, Mario A. (h). 1990. "El Poder Judicial de la Nación." *La Ley*, 1990-E, pp. 1000–1006.

Calcaño de Temeltas, Josefina. 1982. "La responsabilidad de los jueces en Venezuela." Caracas *El Universal*, April 13.

Callaghy, Thomas. 1984. *The State-Society Struggle: Zaire in Comparative Perspective*. New York: Columbia University Press.

Cámara de Diputados de la Provincia de Buenos Aires, Secretaria Legislativa. 1987. *Instituciones de Derecho Parlamento*. La Plata: Cámara de Diputados de la Provincia de Buenos Aires.

Cappelletti, Mauro. 1971. *Judicial Review in the Contemporary World*. New York: Bobbs-Merrill.

Cappelletti, Mauro, and Bryant Garth. 1978. "Access to Justice: The Worldwide Movement to Make Rights Effective." In Mauro Cappelletti, ed., *Access to Justice,* book 1. Milano: Dott. A. Giùffre Editores.

Carballo de Cilley, Marita. 1987. *¿Qué pensamos los argentinos?* Buenos Aires: Ediciones El Cronitas América.

Cardenas, Eduardo J., and Carlos M. Paya. 1985. *En Camino a la Democracia Política: 1904–1910*. Buenos Aires: Astrea.

Carías, Germán. 1979. *Crimen, C.A.* Caracas: Editorial Ateneo de Caracas.

Carmack, Robert M. 1979. *Historia Social de los Quichés*. Guatemala: Seminario de Integración Social No. 38.

Carrera Damas, Germán. 1983. *Una nación llamada Venezuela*. Caracas: Monte Avila Editores.

Carrió, Alejandro D. 1994. *Garantías constitucionales en el Proceso Penal*. Buenos Aires: Editorial Hammurabi.

————. 1987. *The Criminal Justice System of Argentina*. Baton Rouge: Louisiana State University.

Catacora, Manuel. 1991. "Ministerio Público, Administración de Justicia y Derechos Constitucionales." In Diego García-Sayán, ed., *Poder Judicial y Democracia*. Lima: Comisión Andina de Juristas.

Cavagna Martínez, M. A., R. A. Bielsa, and E. R. Graña. 1994. *El Poder Judicial de la Nación.* Buenos Aires: La Ley.

Centro de Estudios Judiciales de la República Argentina. 1994. *Estudio de Opinión Acerca de la Administración de Justicia.* Buenos Aires: Instituto Gallup de Argentina.

Centro de Estudios Legales y Sociales (CELS). 1996a. *Informe anual obre la situación de los Derechos Humanos en la Argentina.* Buenos Aires: CELS.

———. 1996b. *Programa: Violencia institucional, seguridad cuidadana y derechos humanos.* Buenos Aires: CELS.

Centro de Estudios Legales y Sociales and Americas Watch. 1991a. *Verdad y Justicia en la Argentina: Actualización.* Buenos Aires: Paz Producciones.

———. 1991b. *Police Violence in Argentina.* Buenos Aires: CELS.

Chaffee, Wilbur. 1992. *The Economics of Violence in Latin America.* New York: Praeger.

Chaudhry, Kirin Aziz. 1989. "The Price of Wealth: Business and State in Labor Remittance and Oil Economies." *International Organization* 43: 101–145.

Chayes, Abram. 1976. "The Role of the Judge in Public Law Litigation." *Harvard Law Review* 89, no. 7: 1281–1316.

Chevigny, Paul. 1995. *Edge of the Knife: Police Violence in the Americas.* New York: The New Press.

Chiosone, Tulio. 1967. *Derecho Procesal Penal.* Caracas: Monte Avila.

Ciria, Alberto. 1974. *Parties and Power in Modern Argentina, 1930–1946.* Albany: State University of New York Press.

Ciudad de Buenos Aires. 1996. *Constitución de la Cuidad de Buenos Aires.* Buenos Aires: Ciudad de Buenos Aires.

Clagett, Helen L. 1952. *The Administration of Justice in Latin America.* New York: Oceana Publications.

Coase, Ronald. 1960. "The Problem of Social Cost." *Journal of Law and Economics* (October): 1–44.

Código Procesal Penal. 1992. Buenos Aires: Ghaem Editorial.

Colegio de Abogados del Distrito Federal. 1983. *Conferencia de los Jueces de Instrucción de Venezuela.* Caracas: Colegio de Abogados del Distrito Federal.

Combellas, Ricardo. 1990. *Estado de Derecho.* Caracas: Editorial Jurídica Venezolana.

Comisión Andina de Juristas. 1992. *Venezuela: Administración de Justicia y Crisis Institucional.* Lima: Comisión Andina de Juristas.

Comisión Bicameral para la Revisión de la Constitución. 1992. *Proyecto de Reforma General de la Constitución de 1961, Con Exposición de Motivos.* Caracas: Congreso de la República.

Comisión Presidencial para la Reforma del Estado (COPRE). 1994. *La Reforma del Estado: Proyecto Nacional de Nuestro Tiempo: Memoria y Prospectiva.* Caracas: COPRE.

———. 1990. *Constitución y Reforma.* Caracas: Grafisistem C.A.

———. 1987. *Reformas Inmediatas al subsistema Penal-Penitenciario,* Caracas: COPRE.

Conferencia Iberoamericana Sobre Reforma de la Justicia Penal. *Memoria de la II Conferencia sobre Reformade la Justicia Penal.* Centro de Investigaciones y Capacitación del Proyecto de Reforma Judicial.

Congreso de la República, Cámara de Diputados, Comisión de Desarrollo Regional. 1993. *Debate sobre la Ley Orgánica de Tribunales y Procedimientos de Paz.* Caracas: Congreso de la República.

Consejo Consultivo de la Presidencia de la República. 1993. *Informe*. Caracas: Imprenta Nacional.

Consejo de la Judicatura, Dirección de Planificación. 1994. *Memoria y Cuenta del Consejo de la Judicatura*. Caracas: Consejo de la Judicatura.

Consejo de la Judicatura, República de Bolivia. February 2000. "Carta al Jorge Ramírez, Presidente del H. Congreso Nacional." Sucre: Consejo de la Judicatura.

Consejo Para la Consolidación de la Democracia. 1989. *Hacia una Nueva Justicia Penal, Tomo II*. Buenos Aires: Presidencia de la Nación.

———. 1986. *Reforma Constitucional: Dictamen preliminar del Consejo para la Consolidación de la Democracia*. Buenos Aires: Eudeba, November.

Controlaria General de la República, Dirección General de Control de Estados y Municipios. 1989. *Evaluación Integral de las Policías Uniformadas*. Caracas: Controlaria de la República.

Corrales, Javier. 1997–1998. "Do Economic Crises Contribute to Economic Reform? Argentina and Venezuela in the 1990s." *Political Science Quarterly* (Winter): 617–644.

Correa Sutil, Jorge. 1994. *Diagnóstico de Los Poderes Judicial y Legislativo del Sistema Federal Argentina: DRAFT*. Santiago de Chile: Informe de Consultoría para el Banco Interamericano de Desarrollo.

———. 1993. "The Judiciary and the Political System in Chile." In Irwin P. Stotzky, ed., *The Transition to Democracy in Latin America: The Role of the Judiciary*. Boulder: Westview Press.

Corte Suprema de Justicia. 1997. *Cartelera Informativa* 5. Caracas: Corte Suprema de Justicia.

Crahan, Margaret E. 1982. *Human Rights and Basic Needs in the Americas*. Washington, D.C.: Georgetown University Press.

———. 1974. "Spanish and American Counterpoint: Problems and Possibilities in Spanish Colonial Administrative History." In Richard Graham and Peter H. Smith, eds., *New Approaches to Latin American History*. Austin: University of Texas Press.

Cupolo, Marco. 1989. *Un Análisis del Consejo del Municipio Autonomo Miranda (Calbaza, Estado Guárico)*. Caracas: Ministerio de Descentralización.

Dahl, Robert A. 1971. *Polyarchy*. New Haven: Yale University Press.

Dakolias, Maria. 1996. "The Judicial Sector in Latin America and the Caribbean: Elements of Reform." Washington, D.C.: World Bank.

Damaska, Mirjan. 1975. "Structures of Authority and Comparative Criminal Proceedings." *Yale Law Journal* 84, no. 3 (January): 480–554.

Das, Dilip K. 1994. *Police Practices: An International Review*. London: Scarecrow Press.

Davis, Daniel, et al. 1994. "Decentralization by Default: Local Governance and the View from the Village in the Gambia." In *Public Administration and Development* 14, no. 3: 253–269.

Dealy, Glen. 1968. "Prologemena on the Spanish American Political Tradition." *HAHR*, XLVIII.

de la Cruz, Rafael, ed. 1992. *Decentralization, Gobernabilidad y Democracia*. Caracas: Nueva Sociedad.

del Olmo, Rosa. 1981. *América Latina Y Su Criminología*. Mexico City: Siglo Veintiuno Editores.

Defensoría del Pueblo. 1998. *Primer Informe del Defensor del Pueblo al Congreso de la República*. Lima: Defensoría del Pueblo.

Delgado Rosales, Francisco Javier. 1988. *Inseguridad Ciudadana en Venezuela.* Maracaibo: Universidad de Zulia, Facultad de Derecho.

de Soto, Hernando. 1989. *The Other Path: The Invisible Revolution in the Third World.* New York: Harper and Row.

Deutsch, Karl W. 1981. "The Crisis of the State." *Government and Opposition* 16, no. 3(Summer): 331343.

DeVries, Henry P., and José Rodriguez-Novás. 1965. *The Law of the Americas.* New York: Columbia University.

Diamond, Larry, et al. 1989. *Democracy in Developing Countries, volume 4: Latin America.* Boulder: Lynne Rienner.

Diez, Francisco, ed. 1994. *La Justicia en La Argentina.* Buenos Aires: Poder Ciudadano.

Dirección de Asistencia Jurídica, Municipalidad de Buenos Aires. 1972. *Report: July 20, 1972.* Buenos Aires.

Dobbs, Dan B. 1993. *Law of Remedies: Second Edition.* St.Paul, Minn.: West Publishing Company.

Dogan, Mattei. 1995. "Testing the Concepts of Legitimacy and Trust." In H. E. Chehabi and Alfred Stepan, eds., *Politics, Society, and Democracy: Essays in Honor of Juan Linz.* Boulder: Westview Press.

Dollar, David, and Aart Karay. 2000. "Growth Is Good for the Poor." Washington, D.C.: World Bank.

Donna, Edgarda A. 1974. "La crisis del pensamiento penal y su superación." *Nuevo Pensamiento Penal* 3 (Enero-Diciembre): 67–80.

Dromi, José Roberto. 1985. *Policía y Derecho.* Buenos Aires: Ediciones UNSTA.

———. 1982. *El Poder Judicial.* Buenos Aires: Ediciones UNSTA.

Duguit, León. 1907. *Manuel de droit constitucionnel: theorie general,* Paris: Ancienne Librairie Thorin et Fils.

Dworkin, Ronald. 1985. *A Matter of Principle.* Cambridge, Mass.: Harvard University Press.

Echeverría, Juan Martín. "Preguntas a la Justicia." *El Universal,* March 19, 1995.

Editorial Nacional. 1956. *Enciclopedia de la Historia Latinoamericana.* Madrid: Editorial Nacional.

Elia de Molina, Alexandra. 1992. "Medidas Alternativas a la Reclusión." *Policía Científica* 1, no. 4 (October): 9–13.

Elichiguerra, Javier. 1978. "Juez Natural y Tribunales Militares." In *Casación Penal (Jurisprudencia).* Caracas: Instituto de Ciencias Penales y Criminológicas, Universidad Central de Venezuela, pp. 187–193.

Elster, Jon, and Ruth Slagstad, eds. 1988. *Constitutionalism and Democracy,* Cambridge: Cambridge University Press.

Escobar, Arturo, and Alvarez, Sonia E. 1992. *The Making of Social Movements in Latin America.* Boulder: Westview Press.

Evans, Peter B., Dietrich Rueschmeyer, and Theda Scocpol, eds. 1985. *Bringing the State Back In.* Cambridge: Cambridge University Press.

Ewell, Judith. 1989. "Debt and Politics in Venezuela." In *Current History* 88, no 536: 121–149.

———. 1984. *Venezuela: A Century of Change.* Stanford: Stanford University Press.

Farer, Tom. 1989. "Reinforcing Democracy in Latin America: Notes Toward an Appropriate Legal Framework." *Human Rights Quarterly* 11, no. 3: 434–451.

Fayt, Carlos S. 1994. *Supremacía Constitucional e Independencia de los Jueces.* Buenos Aires: Depalma.

Febres Cordero, Adan, et al. 1990. *Conferencias y Conclusiones del Gran Foro: Problematica de la Administración de Justicia en Venezuela.* Caracas: Editorial Argonca.

Fernández, Fernando M. 1993. *Independencia judicial y control disciplinario de los jueces en Venezuela.* Caracas: El Colegio de Abogados del Distrito Federal.

Fernández, Gerardo V. 1992. *Los Decretos-Leyes (La facultad extraordinaria del Artículo 190, ordinal 8º de la Constitución.* Caracas: Editorial Jurídica Venezolana.

Ferre, Y., et al. 1989. *La Comunidad Marabina y su Reacción Ante las Acciones Policiales (1987–1988).* Maracaibo: Facultad de Ciencias Económicas y Sociales, Universidad de Zulia.

Fiscalía General, República de Venezuela. 1971. *Report of the Fiscal General to the Congress, 1971.* Caracas: Fiscalía General.

Fiss, Owen M. 1993. "The Right Degree of Independence." In Irwin P. Stotzky, *Transition to Democracy in Latin America: The Role of the Judiciary.* Boulder: Westview Press.

Fix-Zamudio, Héctor. 1977. *Función del poder judicial en los sistemas constitucionales latinoamericanas.* Mexico: Instituto de Investigaciones Jurídicas.

Font, Miguel Angel, comp. 1996. *Compendio de Leyes Administrativas,* Buenos Aires: Editorial Estudio.

Foro de Estudios sobre la Administración de Justicia (FORES). 1985. *Definitivamente...Nunca Más (La otra cara del informe de la CONADEP).* Buenos Aires: FORES.

Foucault, Michel. 1979. *The Birth of the Prison.* New York: Random House.

Freytes, Esteban Agudo. 1991. "La Policía Técnica Judicial." Caracas: CPTJ.

Frías, Pedro J. 1991. "La descentralización anunciada." *La Ley,* Tomo 1991-C, pp. 1117–1118.

Friedman, Lawrence M. 1978. "Access to Justice: Social and Historical Context." In Mauro Cappelletti, ed. *Access to Justice, vol. 2, book 1.* Milan: Guiffrè.

Fuller, Lon. 1964. *The Morality of Law.* New Haven: Yale University Press.

Fundación de Investigaciones Económicas Latinoamericanas. 1996. "La Reforma del Poder Judicial en la Argentina." Buenos Aires: Fundación de Investigaciones Económicas Latinoamericanas.

Gabaldón, Luis Gerardo. 1996. "La Policía y el Uso de la Fuerza Física en Venezuela." In Peter Waldmann, ed., *Justicia en la Calle.* Medellín: Biblioteca Jurídica Diké.

Gabaldón, Luis Gerardo, and Daniela Bettiol. 1988. "Presencia Policial en Zonas Residenciales Urbanas." Mérida, Venezuela: Universidad de los Andes.

Gabaldón, Luis Gerardo, et al. 1996. "La Policía Judicial en Venezuela: Organización y Desempeño en la Averiguación Penal." In Peter Waldmann, ed., *Justicia en la Calle.* Medellín: Biblioteca Jurídica Diké.

Gálvez, Modesto. 1987. "El Derecho en el Campesino Andino del Peru." In Comisión Andina de Juristas, *Derechos Humanos y Servicios Legales en el Campo.* Lima: CAJ.

Gamarra, Eduardo. 1991. "The System of Justice in Bolivia: An Institutional Analysis." Miami: Center for the Administration of Justice, Florida International University.

García Lema, Alberto Manuel. 1994. *La Reforma por Dentro.* Buenos Aires: Editorial Planeta Argentina.

Garcia-Gallo, Alfonso. 1972. *Estudios de Historia del Derecho Indiano.* Madrid: Instituto Nacional de Estudios Jurídicos.

Geddes, Barbara. 1994. *Politician's Dilemma: Building State Capacity in Latin America*. Berkeley: University of California Press.

Geller, William A., and Hans Toch. 1996. *Police Violence*. New Haven: Yale University Press.

Gentili, Rafael Amadeo. 1995. *Me va a tener que acompañar: una visión crítica sobre los Edictos Policiales*. Buenos Aires: El Naranjo Ediciones.

Gibson, Charles. 1966. *Spain in America*. New York: Harper.

Giles, Michael W., and T. Lancaster. 1989. "Political Transition, Social Development, and Legal Mobilization in Spain." *American Political Science Review* 83, no. 3 (September): 817–833.

Gil Fortoul, José. 1963. "Historia Constitucional de Venezuela." In Gil Fortoul, *Obras Completas*. Caracas: Ministerio de Educación, Dirección de Cultura y Bellas Artes.

Gil Yepes, José Antonio. 1981. *The Challenge of Venezuelan Democracy*. New Brunswick, N.J.: Transaction Books.

Gómez Calcaño, Luis, and Margarita López Maya. 1990. *El Tejido de Penélope: La Reforma del Estado en Venezuela, 1984–1988*. Caracas: CENDES.

Gómez Grillo, Elio. 1995. "Sumario Histórico de la Delincuencia en Venezuela." In *Policía Científica* No. 37. Caracas: Cuerpo Técnico de Policía Judicial, February.

———. 1988. *Las Penas y Las Cárceles*. Caracas: Empresa el Cojo.

———. 1988. *Perfil Humano, Profesional y Socio-Económico de la Policía Metropolitana*. Caracas: Instituto de Instituto de Ciencias Penales y Criminológicas.

Gonzalez-Casanova, Pablo. 1965. *Democracy in Mexico*. México: Ediciones ERA.

Goodman, Louis, et al. 1995. *Lessons of the Venezuelan Experience*. Washington, D.C.: Woodrow Wilson Center Press.

Government of Argentina. 1966. "Estatuto de la Revolución Argentina." *Anales de Legislación Argentina*. Buenos Aires: La Ley.

———. 1950. *Presupuesto Nacional*. Buenos Aires: La Ley.

———. 1879. *Registro Oficial: Volumen 1*. Buenos Aires: Government of Argentina.

———. 1863. *Colección de Leyes y Decretos sobre Justicia Nacional, Publicación Oficial*. La Plata: Imprenta del "Comercio del Plata."

Government of Venezuela. 1973. *Gaceta Forense, 3 Etapa*, Enero-Marzo, No. 79.

———. 1967. *Gaceta Forense, 2 Etapa*, Julio-Septiembre No. 57.

———. 1950. Bulletin of the National Codification Commission, No. 44. Caracas: Government of Venezuela.

———. 1949. *Gaceta Oficial* No. 22.952, June 23.

———. 1939. *Recopilación de Leyes y Decretos de Venezuela*, vol. 59. Caracas: Imprenta Nacional.

———. 1855. *Colección de Leyes de Procedimiento*. Caracas: Imprenta Nacional.

Gray, Cheryl. 1997. "Reforming Legal Systems in Developing Countries." Washington, D.C.: World Bank.

Greenfield, Gerald Michael. 1994. *Latin American Urbanization*. Westport, Conn.: Greenwood Press.

Griffin, Charles C. 1992. "The Enlightenment and Latin American Independence." In Arthur Whitaker, ed., *Latin America and the Enlightenment*. New York: Appleton-Century Company.

Groisman, Enrique I., ed. 1990. *El Derecho en la transición de la dictadura a la democracia: La experiencia en América Latina/2*. Buenos Aires: Biblioteca Política Argentina.

Groves, Roderick. 1965. "Administrative Reform in Venezuela, 1958–1963." Ph.D. diss. University of Wisconsin.

Guevara, Pedro. 1989. *Concertación y Conflicto*. Caracas: Universidad Central de Venezuela.

Günter, Bierbrauer, et al. 1978. "Conflict and its Settlement." In Mauro Cappelletti, ed., *Access to Justice, vol. 2, book 1*. Milan: Guiffrè.

Gurr, Ted. 1970. *Why Men Rebel*. Princeton: Princeton University Press.

Habermas, Jurgen. 1996. *Between Facts and Norms*. Cambridge, Mass.: MIT Press.

Haggard, Stephan, and Robert R. 1995. Kaufman. *The Political Economy of Democratic Transitions*. Princeton: Princeton University Press.

Hammergren, Linn. 1998. *The Politics of Justice and Judicial Reform: Peru in Comparative Perspective*. Boulder: Westview Press.

Hardoy, Jorge Enrique, ed. 1969. *El Proceso de urbanización en América desde sus orígenes hasta nuestros días*. Buenos Aires: Editorial del Instituto, Instituto Torcuato di Tella.

Hardy, José Toro. 1992. *Venezuela: 55 Años de Política Económica*. Caracas: Editorial Panapo.

Hart, H. L. A. 1961. *The Concept of Law*. Oxford: Clarendon Press.

Hauriou, Maurice. 1914. *Precis de droit administratif et de droit public*. Paris: Librairie de la Société de Recueil Sirey.

Hayek, F. A. 1973–1976. *Law, Legislation, and Liberty*. London: Routeledge and Kegan Paul.

Heller, Agnes. 1988. "On Formal Democracy." In John Keane, ed., *Civil Society and the State*. Verso: London.

Herman, Donald L. 1988. *Democracy in Latin America: Colombia and Venezuela*. New York: Praeger.

Hermoso González, Andrés. 1994. *Crónicas de la Justicia Imposible: Confesiones de un juez*. Caracas: Fondo Editorial Predios.

Hernández, Tosca. 1986. "Los Operativos Policiales 'Extraordinarios' en Venezuela." In *Anuario del Instituto de Ciencias Penales y Criminológicas*. Caracas: Universidad Central de Venezuela, no. 9.

Herrera Luque, Francisco. 1970. *Los Viajeros de Indias*. Caracas: Monte Avila Editores.

Hillman, Richard S. 1994. *Democracy for the Privileged: Crisis and Transition in Venezuela*. Boulder: Lynne Rienner.

Hillman, Richard S., and Elsa Cardozo de Da Silva. 1998. "Venezuelan Political Culture and Democracy: 1996 and 1997 Survey Results." Paper presented at the annual meeting of the Carribean Studies Association, Antigua.

Howard, Rhoda E. 1995. *Human Rights and the Search for Community*. Boulder: Westview Press.

Huggins, Martha, ed. 1991. *Vigilantism and the State in Modern Latin America*. New York: Praeger.

Human Rights Watch/Americas. 1993. *Human Rights in Venezuela*. New York: Human Rights Watch.

Huntington, Samuel. 1968. *Political Order in Changing Societies*. New Haven: Yale University Press.

Ietswaart, Heleen F.P. 1982. "The Discourse of Summary Justice and the Discourse of Popular Justice: An Analysis of Legal Rhetoric in Argentina." In Richard L. Abel, *The Politics of Informal Justice*. New York: Academic Press.

Igartua Salaverria, Juan. 1987. *Los Jueces en una Sociedad Democrática*. Oñatí: Instituto Vasco de Administración Pública.

Iñigo Carrera, Hector J. 1985. *La Experiencia Radical: 1916–1922*. Buenos Aires: Astrea.

Inspector General de Cárceles. 1999. *Informe Anual.* Caracas: Ministerio de Justicia.

Institucion Interamericano de Derechos Humanos. 1984. *Sistemas Penales y Derechos Humanos en América Latina.* Buenos Aires: Ediciones Depalma.

Instituto Municipal de Capacitación y Educación Ciudadana. 1994. *Importancia del Juez de Paz.* Maracaibo: Ediciones Astro Data S.A.

Instituto Nacional de Estadísticas y Censos (INDEC). 1994. *Estadísticas Sociodemográficas del INDEC.* Buenos Aires: Sociedad Argentian de Estadística.

Inter-American Bar Association. 1994. *Estudio de Investigación Sobre Justicia Comunitaria en 4 Villas de la Ciudad de El Alto.* La Paz: Consejo de la Judicatura.

Izard, Miguel. 1970. *Estadisticas para la historia de Venezuela.* Mérida: Universidad de los Andes.

Jelín, Elizabeth. 1989. *Los nuevos movimientos sociales.* Buenos Aires: Centro Editor de América Latina.

Jiménez A., María Angélica. 1992. "Sistema penal y medidas alternativas." *Capítulo Criminológico,* Instituto de Criminología de la Universidad de Zulia, No. 20: 123–137.

Johnson, Lyman L., ed. 1990. *The Problem of Order in Changing Societies: Essays on Crime and Policing in Argentina and Uruguay, 1750–1940.* Albuquerque: University of New Mexico Press.

Jurisprudencia Argentina. 1825–1995. Buenos Aires: Jurisprudencia Argentina.

Karl, Terry. 1995. "The Venezuelan Petro-State and the Crisis of 'Its' Democracy." In Jennifer McCoy et al., *Venezuelan Democracy under Stress.* Miami: North-South Center, University of Miami.

———. 1990. "Dilemmas of Democratization in Latin America." *Comparative Politics* 23, no. 1 (October): 1–21.

———. 1986. "Petroleum and Political Pacts: The Transition to Democracy in Venezuela." In Guillermo O'Donnell et al., eds., *Transitions from Authoritarianism: Latin America.* Baltimore: Johns Hopkins University Press.

Karl, Terry, and Philippe C. Schmitter. 1991. "Modes of Transition and Types of Democracy in Latin America, Southern and Eastern Europe." *International Social Science Journal,* no 128: 269–289.

Karst, Kenneth, and Keith Rosenn. 1975. *Law and Development in Latin America.* Berkeley: University of California Press.

Karst, Kenneth, et al. 1973. *The Evolution of Law in the Barrios of Caracas.* Los Angeles: UCLA.

Kazancigil, Ali, ed. 1986. *The State in Global Perspective,* Brookfield, Vt.: Gower.

Kelsen, Hans. 1992. *An Introduction to the Problems of Legal Theory.* Oxford: Clarendon Press.

Keane, John. 1988. *Democracy and Civil Society.* London: Verso.

Kohli, Atul, and Vivienne Shue. 1994. "State Power and Social Forces: On Political Contention and Accommodation in the Third World." In Joel S. Migdal et al., eds., *State Power and Social Forces: Domination and Transformation in the Third World.* Princeton: Princeton University Press.

Kornblith, Miriam. 1991. "The Politics of Constitution Making: Constitutions and Democracy in Venezuela." *Journal of Latin American Studies* 23, no. 1.

La Roche, Humberto J. 1984. *Institucioneds Constitucionales del Estado Venezolano, 9ta Edición.* Maracaibo: Editorial Mesas.

Labarca P., Domingo A. 1979. "Las fuentes del Derecho en la Constitución de 1961." *Estudios Sobre la Constitución, Tomo I.* Caracas: Universidad Central de Venezuela, Facultad de Ciencias Jurídicas y Políticas.

Langbein, John, and Lloyd Weinreb. 1978. "Continental Criminal Procedure: 'Myth' and Reality." *Yale Law Journal* 87, no. 8 (July): 1549–1569..

Laserna, Roberto. 1994. "Las Drogas y La Justicia en Cochabamba: Los 'Narocos en el País de Culpables." 18th International Congress of the Latin American Studies Association, March 10.

Lauder, Stella, and A. Morris. 1994. *Decentralization in Latin America*, New York: Praeger.

Lawson, Stephanie. 1993. "Conceptual Issues in the Comparative Study of Regime Change and Democratization." *Comparative Politics* 25, no. 2 (January): 183–205.

Lawyers Committee for Human Rights and Programa Venezolano de Educación-Acción en Derechos Humanos (PROVEA). 1996. *Halfway to Reform: The World Bank and the Venezuelan Justice System.* New York: Lawyers Committee for Human Rights.

Levene, Ricardo. 1950. *El Proceso Histórico de Lavalle a Rosas.* La Plata: Archivo Histórico de la Provincia.

———. 1936. *Historia de la Nación Argentina.* Buenos Aires: Academia Nacional de la Historia.

Levine, Daniel H. 1973. *Conflict and Political Change in Venezuela.* Princeton: Princeton University Press.

Lijphart, Arend. 1968. "Typologies of Democratic Systems." *Comparative Political Studies* 1 (April): 3–44.

Lijphart, Arend, and Carlos H. Waisman. 1996. *Institutional Design in New Democracies: Eastern Europe and Latin America.* Boulder: Westview Press.

Linares Quintana, Segundo V. 1960. *Acción de Amparo.* Buenos Aires: Editorial Bibliográfica Argentina.

Linz, Juan. 1978. *Crisis, Breakdown, and Reequilibration.* Baltimore: Johns Hopkins University Press.

Linz, Juan, and Alfred Stepan. 1996. *Problems of Democratic Transition and Consolidation: Southern Europe, South America, and Eastern Europe,* Baltimore: Johns Hopkins University Press.

———, eds. 1978. *Breakdown of Democratic Regimes: Latin America.* Baltimore: Johns Hopkins University Press.

Little, I.M.D., et al. 1993. *Boom, Crisis, and Adjustment: The Macroeconomic Experience of Developing Countries.* New York: Oxford University Press.

Lynch, Dennis O. 1948. *Legal Roles in Colombia.* Uppsala: Scandinavia Institute of African Studies, International Center for Law and Development.

Lynch, John. 1981. *Argentine Dictator: Juan Manuel de Rosas, 1828–1852.* Oxford: Clarendon Press.

Maier, Julio Bernardo, Martín Abregú, and Sofía Tiscornia. 1996. "El Papel de la Policía en la Argentina y su Situación Actual." In Peter Waldmann, ed., *Justicia en la Calle.* Medellín: Biblioteca Jurídica Diké.

Mainwaring, Scott. 1992. "Transitions to Demoracy and Democratic Consolidation: Theoretical and Comparative Issues." In *Issues in Democratic Consolidation: The New South American Democracies in Comparative Perspective.* Notre Dame, Ind.: University of Notre Dame Press.

Malagón Barceló, Javier. 1966. *Estudios de Historia y Derecho.* Mexico: Universidad Veracruzana Xalapa.

Malamud-Goti, Jaime. 1996. *Game Without End: State Terror and the Politics of Justice.* Norman: University of Oklahoma Press.

Mann, Michael. 1984. "The Autonomous Power of the State." *Archives Européens de Sociologies* 25, no. 2.

Mantellini González, Pedro J. 1983. "La Vigencia del Ministerio Público." In Tomas Enrique Carrillo Batalla, ed., *Contribución al Estudio de las Ciencias Jurídicas y Sociales: Ciclo Ordinario de Conferencias de la Acaemia, Años 1981–1983.* Caracas: Universidad Central de Venezuela.

Manzini, Vincenzo. 1926. *Trattato di diritto penale italiano.* Torino: Unione tep. editrice torinse.

Marshall, T. H. 1992. "Citizenship and Social Class." In T.H. Marshall and Tom Bottomore, *Citizenship and Social Class.* London: Pluto Press.

Marshall, T. H., and Tom Bottomore. 1992. *Citizenship and Social Class.* London: Pluto Press.

Martz, John. 1966. *Acción Democrática: Evolution of a Modern Political Party in Venezuela.* Princeton: Princeton University Press.

Martz, John, and David Myers. 1986. *Venezuela: The Democratic Experience.* New York: Praeger.

Mattarollo, Rodolfo. 1992. *El Problema de la Violación de los Derechos Humanos por Agentes no Estatales Frente al Derechos Internacional.* San José: Instituto Interamericano de Derechos Humanos.

Mawhood, Phillip. 1987. "Decentralization and the Third World in the 1980s." *Planning and Administration* 14, no. 1: 20–33.

Mayer, E. G. 1947. *Leitfaden Für Polizeibaemte.* Munich: Städtischer Rechstat.

McCoy, Jennifer, et al. 1995. *Venezuelan Democracy under Stress.* Miami: University of Miami.

Méndez, José Augustín. 1976. "El Recurso de Casación." Revista *Proceso,* nos. 24/25 (May/June).

Mendoza, José Rafael. 1940. "De la Suspención de las Faltas en el Código Penal y en el de Enjuiciamiento Criminal." Caracas: Vargas.

Mendoza, T. 1975. "El Cuerpo Técnico de Policía Judicial." In *Revista del Ministerio de Justicia* (Enero-Diciembre). Caracas: Ministerio de Justicia de la Nación.

Merryman, John Henry, et al. 1979. *Law and Social Change in Mediterranean Europe and Latin America.* Stanford: Stanford University Law School.

Migdal, Joel S. 1988. *Strong Societies and Weak States: State-Society Relations and State Capabilities in the Third World.* Princeton: Princeton University Press.

Migdal, Joel S., Atul Kohli, and Vivienne Shue. 1994. *State Power and Social Forces: Domination and Transformation in theThird World.* Princeton: Princeton University Press.

Mignone, Emilio. 1990. *Derechos Humanos y Sociedad: El Caso Argentino.* Buenos Aires: Ediciones del Pensamiento Nacional.

Miller, Jonathan, and María Angélica Gelli. 1987. *Constitución Y Poder Político.* Buenos Aires: Editorial Astrea.

Miller, Jonathan, María Angélica Gelli, and Susana Cayuso. 1991. *Constitución y derechos humanos, Tomo I y II.* Buenos Aires: Astrea.

Ministerio de Justicia, Inspector General del Sistema Penitenciaría. 1994. *Informe Anual, 1994.* Caracas: Ministerio de Justicia.

Ministerio de Justicia de la Nación, Secretaría de Justicia, Dirección de Política Criminal. 1996. *Hacia un Plan de Política Criminal.* Buenos Aires: Ministerio de Justicia.

Ministerio de Justicia de la Nación, Secretaría de Política Penitenciaria y de Readapción Social. 1994. *Plan Director de la Política Penitenciaria Nacional.* Buenos Aires: Ministerio de Justicia.

Ministerio de Justicia de la Nación, Registro Nacional de Reincidencia y Estadística Criminal. 1993. *Estadística Criminal, Año 1992.* Buenos Aires: Ministerio de Justicia.

Ministerio de Justicia y Derechos Humanos, República de Bolivia y Centro de Asesoramiento Social y Desarrollo Legal. 1998. *Justicia Comunitaria, Vol.4: Las Zonas Urbano Marginales de la Paz y Cochabamba.* La Paz: Ministerio de Juticia y Derechos Humanos.

Ministerio de la Familia, República de Venezuela. 1995. *Venezuela ante la Cumbre Mundial Sobre Desarrollo Social.* Caracas: Ministerio de la Familia, March.

Ministerio Público, República de Venezuela, Fiscal General de la República. 1995–1966. *Informe al Congreso de la República, Tomo I, II, y III.* Caracas: Imprenta Nacional.

————. 1990. "Fiscal General de la República Presentara Anteproyecto de Ley de Seguridad Ciudadana." Caracas: Ministerio Público.

Ministerio Público de la Nación, Fiscalía General de la República de Bolivia. 1996. *Informe del Fiscal General de la República: Gestiones 1994–1995.* Sucre, Bolivia: Editorial Judicial.

MINUGUA (United Nations Mission for the Verification of Human Rights and Compliance with the Commitment of the Comprehensive Agreement on Human Rights in Guatemala). 2000. *Funcionamiento del sistem de justicia en Guatemala.* Guatemala: MINUGUA.

Mitchell, Timothy. 1991. "The Limits of the State: Beyond Statist Approaches and Their Critics." *American Political Science Review* 85, no. 1 (March): 77–96.

Monsalve Casado, Ezequiel. 1986. *La Reforma de la Administración de Justicia.* Caracas: Biblioteca de la Academia de Ciencias Políticas y Sociales.

Montesquieu, Charles de Secondat. 1869. *De l'esprit des lois.* Paris: Garnier Freres.

Morello, Augusto Mario. 1991. *La Reforma de la Justicia.* La Plata: Adelado-Perrot, Libreria Editora Platense.

Morello, Augusto Mario, and Calros Vallefín. 1992. *El amparo, régimen procesal.* La Plata: Libreria Editora Platense.

Moreno, Mariano. 1943. *Escritos.* Buenos Aires: Ediciones Estrada.

Moreno Ocampo, Luis. 1993. *En Defensa Propia.* Buenos Aires: Editorial Sudamericana.

Morón, Guillermo. 1964. *A History of Venezuela.* London: George Allen and Unwin.

Morris, Arthur, and Stella Lowder, eds. 1991. *Decentralization in Latin America.* New York: Praeger.

Navarro, Juan Carlos, and Rogelio Pérez Perdomo, eds. 1991. *Seguridad Personal: un Asalto al Tema.* Caracas: Ediciones IESA.

Needler, Martin C. 1965. *Latin American Politics in Perspective.* Princeton: Van Nostrand.

Nettl, J. P. 1967–1968. "The State as Conceptual Variable." *World Politics* 20, no 4 (July): 559–592.

Nieves, David. 1979. *La tortura y el crimen político.* Caracas: Poseidon.

Nikken, Pedro, ed. 1990. *Agenda Para La Consolidación de la Democracia en América Latina.* San José, Costa Rica: Instituto Interamericano de Derechos Humanos.

Nino, Carlos Santiago. 1992. *Fundamentos de derecho constitucional.* Buenos Aires: Astrea.

———. 1992. *Un País al Margen de la Ley,* Buenos Aires: Emecé.

———. 1985. "The Human Rights Policy of the Argentine Constitutional Government." *Yale Journal of International Law,* Vol. 11-217.

Nonet, M., and J. Selznick. 1978. *Law and Society in Transition.* New York: Harper and Row.

Nordlinger, Eric. 1987. "Taking the State Seriously." In Samuel Huntington, ed., *Understanding Political Development,* Cambridge, Mass.: Harvard University Press.

North, Douglass. 1994. "Transaction Costs, Institutions, and Economic Performance." Occasional Papers No. 30, International Center for Economic Growth.

Oberto, Luis Enrique. 1999. *Justicia y Gobernabilidad.* Caracas: Nueva Sociedad.

———. 1998. "El Código Orgánico Procesal Penal." Washington, D.C.: Inter-American Development Bank.

Oblitas Poblete, Enrique. 1979. *Recurso De Amparo Constitucional.* La Paz: Ediciones Populare Camarlinghi.

Observatoire International des Prisons. 1995. *Rapport 1995.* Lyon: Observatoire International des Prisons.

O'Donnell, Guillermo. 1994. "Delegative Democracy," *Journal of Democracy* 5, no. 1 (January): 55–69.

———. 1993. "On the State, Democratization, and Some Conceptual Problems: A Latin American View with Glances at Some Postcommunist Countries." *World Development* 21, no. 8: 1355–1369.

O'Donnell, Guillermo, and Philippe C. Schmitter. 1986. *Transitions from Authoritarian Rule: Tentative Conclusions About Uncertain Democracies, Southern Europe, and Comparative Perspectives.* Princeton: Woodrow Wilson Center.

O'Donnell, Guillermo, Philippe C. Schmitter, and Lawrence Whitehead, eds. 1986. *Transitions from Authoritarian Rule.* Princeton: The Wilson Center, 1986.

Offe, Claus. 1984. *Contradictions of the Welfare State.* London: Hutchinson.

Oficina Central de Estadística e Información (OCEI), República de Venezuela, Presidencia de la República. 1993. *Annuario Estadístico de Venezuela.* Caracas: OCEI.

———. 1993. *Mapa de la Pobreza.* Caracas: OCEI.

Ojeda, William. 1995. *Cúanto Vale un Juez.* Caracas: Vadell Hermanos.

Olbrich, Gudrun. 1989. *Historia del Derecho Penal Venezolano.* Caracas: Universidad Central de Venezuela.

Ordenanza de Policía Urbana y Rural del Distrio Federal. 1936. Caracas: Edición Oficial, Editorial Bolívar.

Ordoñez, Aylín. 2000. "Investigación Sobre Acceso a la Justicia en la República de Guatemala." In Banco Interamiricano de Desarrollo (BID) and Instituto Interamericano de Derechos Humanos (IIDH), *Acceso a la Justicia y Equidad.* San José de Costa Rica: BID and IIDH.

Organización Revista Jurisprudencia. 1990. *Conferencia y Conclusiones del Gran Foro: Problematica de la Administración de Justicia en Venezuela.* Caracas: Editorial Argonca C.A.

Oropeza, Ambrosio. 1985. *Evolución Constitucional de Nuestra República y otros textos.* Caracas: Biblioteca de la Academia de Ciencias Políticas y Sociales, Serie Estudios.

Oteiza, Eduardo. 1994. *La Corte Suprema.* La Plata: Libreria Editora Platense S.R.L.

Ots y Capdequi, José María. 1969. *Historia del Derecho Español en América y del Derecho Indiano.* Madrid: Aguilar, S.A. de Ediciones.

Paolini de Palm, María R. 1993. *La Presunción de Inocencia.* Valencia: Universidad de Carabobo.

Parker, Kellis. 1975. *Modern Judicial Remedies.* Boston: Little, Brown.

Parry, J. H. 1940. *The Spanish Theory of Empire in the Sixteenth Century.* Cambridge: Cambridge University Press.

Peña, Alfredo, ed. 1978. *Democracia y Reforma del Estado.* Caracas: Editorial Jurídica Venezolana.

Pérez, Francisco de Sales. 1985. *Policía Judicial.* Caracas: Instituto Jurídico de Estudios Superiores.

Pérez Guilhou, Dardo. 1989. *La Corte Suprema de Justicia y los gobiernos de facto, 1861–1983.* Buenos Aires: Depalma.

Pérez Perdomo, Rogelio. 1987a. "Acceso a La Justicia en la Sociedad contemporánea." In *Justicia y Pobreza en Venezuela.* Caracas: Monte Avila Editores, C.A..

———. "Asistencia Jurídica y Acceso a la Justicia." 1987b. In *Justicia y Pobreza en Venezuela.* Caracas: Monte Avila Editores, C.A.

Petkoff, Teodoro. 1983. *Más Democracia: Propuestas para la Reforma del Estado Venezolano.* Caracas: Centro Nacional de Capacitación y Estudios Municipales.

Pimentel, O. "Víctimas y Victimarios." *El Diario de Caracas,* June 4, 1989, p. 20.

Pinheiro, Paulo Sergio. 1991. "Police and Political Crisis: The Case of the Military Police." In Martha Huggins, ed., *Vigilantism and the State in Modern Latin America.* New York: Praeger.

Pinto, Jose Machillanda. 1988. *Poder Político Y Poder Militar en Venezuela.* Caracas: Ediciones Centauro.

Poder Ciudadano. 1994. "¿Más Fuerza que Seguridad?" Revista *Poder Cuidadano* 4, no. 38 (November): 2–4.

Podgorecki, Adam, et al., eds. 1985. *Legal Systems and Social Systems.* London: Croon Helm.

Policía Federal Argentina. 1935. *Historia de la Policía de la Ciudad de Buenos Aires.* Buenos Aires: Policía Federal Argentina.

Policía Metropolitana. 1981. *Plan Unión Uno.* Caracas: Departamento de Estadística de la República.

Potash, Robert. 1969. *The Army and Politics in Argentina, 1928–1945.* Stanford: Stanford University Press.

Poulantzas, Nicos. 1968. *Pouvoir Politique et classes sociales,* Paris: Librairie François Maspero.

Presidencia del Organismo Judicial y de la Corte Suprema de Justicia, República de Guatemala. 1987–1988. "Dictamen para la Regionalización de los Juzgados de Paz de la República de Guatemala." Guatemala: Corte Suprema de Justicia, September 1987–January 1988.

Prillaman, William C. 2000. *The Judiciary and Democratic Decay in Latin America.* Westport, Conn.: Praeger.

Programa Venezolano de Educación-Acción en Derechos Humanos (PROVEA). 1996. *Informe Annual 1995.* Caracas.

———. 1989–1995. *Situación de los Derechos Humnanos en Venezuela: Informe Annual.* Caracas: PROVEA.

———. 1989–1991. *Referencias.* Caracas: PROVEA.

Przeworski, Adam. 1991. *Democracy and the Market.* New York: Cambridge University Press.

Quadri Castillo, Mario. 1986. *La Argentina Descentralizada.* Buenos Aires: Editorial Universitaria de Buenos Aires.

Quintero, Mariolga. 1988. *Justicia y Realidad.* Caracas: Universidad Central de Venezuela.

Rafanelli, Horacio Alberto. 1993. "Justicia de Paz en la Provincia de Buenos Aires: Propuestas para su reforma." *Revista del Colegio de Abogados de La Plata* 33, no. 53 (March-December).

Rawls, John. 1971. *A Theory of Justice.* Cambridge, Mass.: Harvard University Press.

Ré, Juan. 1937. *El Problema de la mendicidad en Buenos Aires,* Buenos Aires: Editorial Policial.

Registro Nacional de Reincidencia y Estadística Criminal. 1992. *Estadística Criminal, Año 1992.* Buenos Aires: Ministerio de Justicia de la Nación, República Argentina.

Rico, José M. 1985. *Crimen y Justicia en América Latina, 3ra ed.* Mexico City: Siglo Veintiuno Editores.

Rock, David. 1987. *Argentina, 1516–1987.* Berkeley: University of California Press.

Rodríguez Molas, R. 1985. *Historia de la tortura y el orden represivo en la Argentina.* Buenos Aires: Eudeba.

Rodríguez Torres, José Gregorio. 1988. *La Averiguación de Nudo Hecho.* Caracas: Ediciones Orley.

Rojas Pellerano, Hector. 1967. "Diferencia entre delitos y contravenciones." In *Jurisprudencia Argentina,* Vol. 1967-IV: 70–80.

Romero, José Luis. 1965. *El Desarrollo de las Ideas en la Sociedad Argentina del Siglo XX.* Mexico City: Fondo de Cultura Económica.

Rondinelli, Dennis. 1981. "Government Decentralization in Comparative Perspective." *International Review of Administrative Science* 47, no. 2: 133–145.

Rosenn, Keith. 1987. "The Protection of Judicial Independence in Latin America." *Inter-American Law Review* 19, no. 1.

Ruiz Gutiérrez, Urbano. 1952. "Algunas ideas sobre el origen del Ministerio Público en España." *Revista de Derecho Procesal,* no. 3 (July-September): 407–420.

Rustow, Dankwart. 1970. "Transitions Toward Democracy: Toward A Dynamic Model." *Comparative Politics* 2, no. 3 (April): 337–363.

Saenz, Jimena. 1985. *Entre Dos Centenarios, 1910–1916.* Buenos Aires: Astrea.

Sagárzazu, Luis. 1904. *La Constitución de 1901 y la reforma.* Caracas: Universidad Central de Venezuela.

Sagüés, Néstor Pedro. 1986. "Reforma Constitucional (II): El Poder Judicial." In *Reforma Constitucaional: Dictamen Preliminar del Consejo para la Consolidación de la Democracia.* Buenos Aires: EUDEBA, 165–178.

Salvioli, Fabián. 1995. *La Constitución de la Nación Argentina y los derechos humanos.* Buenos Aires: Movimiento Ecuménico por los Derechos Humanos.

Sanguinetti, Esteban Adolfo. 1992. "Evolución Histórica de la Policía." *Mundo Policial* 22, no. 71 (Buenos Aires: Policía Federal Argentina, February-March).

Santos, Boaventura de Sousa. 1977. "The Law and the Oppressed: the Construction and Reproduction of Legaltiy in Pasagarda." *Law and Society Review* 12, no. 5 (Fall): 5–126.

Santos Alvins, Thamara. 1992. *Violencia Criminal y Violencia Policial en Venezuela.* Maracaibo: Instituto de Criminologia de la Universidad de Zulia.

Sargent, Charles S. 1994. "Argentina." In Gerald Michael Greenfield, ed., *Latin American Urbanization*. Westport, Conn.: Greenwood Press.

Sarmiento, Domingo Faustino. 1929. *Facundo*. Buenos Aires: Libreria La Caculto.

Schedler, Andreas, Larry Diamond, and Marc F. Plattner, eds. 1999. *The Self-Restraining State*. Boulder: Lynne Rienner Publishers.

Schumpeter, Joseph. 1950. *Capitalism, Socialism, and Democracy*. New York: Harper and Row.

Sherwood, Robert M., et al. 1994. "Judicial Systems and Economic Performance." Washington, D.C.: World Bank, Feburary.

Seligman, A. 1992. *The Idea of Civil Society*. New York: Mexwell Macmillan International.

Serra, Maria Mercedes. "Poder Judicial: Su Presupuesto." *La Ley*, 1985-C: 1230–1235.

Shane, Paul. 1980. *Police and People: A Comparison of Five Countries*. St. Louis: C.U. Mosby.

Shumway, Nicolas. 1991. *The Invention of Argentina*. California: University of California Press.

Slatta, Richard W., and Karla Robinson. 1990. "Continuity in Crime and Punishment: Buenos Aires, 1820–50." In Lyman L. Johnson, ed., *The Problem of Order in Changing Societies*. Albuquerque: University of New Mexico Press.

Snow, Peter G. 1979. "Argentina: Politics in a Conflictual Society." In Howard J. Wiarda and Harvey F. Kline, eds., *Latin American Politics and Development*. Boulder: Westview Press.

Stallings, Barbara. 1990. "Political and Economic Crisis: A Comparatives Study of Chile, Peru, and Colombia." In Joan Nelson, ed., *Economic Crisis and Policy Choice: The Politics of Adjustment in the Third World*. Princeton: Princeton University Press.

Stambouli, Andrés. 1990. "Déficit Democrática y Gobernabilidad del sistema políti-ca Venezolano." In *Venezuela del siglo XXI: un proyecto para constitucionali-dad*. Carlos Blanco, Caracas: Nueva Sociedad.

Stebbings, Robert Y. 1975. *Pueblo y Justicia: Ayuda Jurídica Gratuita en la Argentina*. Buenos Aires: Depalma.

Stein, Stanley J., and Barbara H. Stein. 1970. *The Colonial Heritage of Latin America*. New York: Oxford University Press.

Stepan, Alfred. 1988. *Rethinking Military Politics*. Princeton: Princeton University Press.

———. 1978. *The State and Society: Peru in Comparative Perspective*. Princeton: Princeton University Press.

Stinchcombe, Arthur L. 1963. "Institutions of Privacy in the Determination of Police Administrative Practice." *American Journal of Sociology* 69: 150–160.

Stone, Andrew, et al. 1992. "Public Institutions and Private Transactions: The Legal and Regulatory Environment for Business Transactions in Brazil and Chile." Washington, D.C.: World Bank, Policy Research Working Paper WPS 891.

Stotzky, Irwin P. 1993. *Transition to Democracy in Latin America: The Role of the Judiciary*. Boulder: Westview Press.

de Sucre, Antonio José. 1918. *Cartas del general Antonio José de Sucre*. La Paz: Litografia e Imprenta Moderna.

Terez Sadek, María, and Rogerio Bastos Arantes. 1994. "The Crisis of the Brazilian

Judiciary: The Judges' Perspective." 16th World Congress, International Political Science Association, August.

Thome, Joseph. 2000. "Heading South but Looking North." Paper presented at the annual meeting of the Latin American Studies Association, Miami, March 16–18.

Thompson, Kenneth W. 1991. *The U.S. Constitution and the Constitutions of Latin America.* Lanham, Md.: University Press of America.

Tilly, Charles. 1992. *Coercion, Capital, and European States AD 990–1992.* Cambridge, Mass.: Blackwell.

————. 1978. *From Mobilization to Revolution.* Reading, Mass.: Addison-Wesley.

Tizón, Alejandro. 1993. *Defensoría del Pueblo.* Santa Fé, Argentina: Editorial Panamericana.

Toharia, José Juan. 1974. *Cambio Social y Vida Jurídica en España.* Madrid: Edicusa.

Tomaselli, Michele. 1951. *Proyecto de Ley sobre Policía Judicial.* Caracas: Universidad Central de Venezuela.

Toro Hardy, José. 1992. *Venezuela: 55 Años de Política Económia.* Caracas: Editorial Panapo.

Torres, Arístedes. 1987. "Los Pobres y la Justicia Penal." In Rogelio Pérez Perdomo, ed., *Justicia y Pobreza en Venezuela.* Caracas: Monte Avila Editores, C.A.

Trubek, David M. 1978. "Unequal Protection: Thoughts on Legal Services, Social Welfare, and Income Distribution in Latin America." *Texas International Law Journal* 13, no. 2: 243–262.

Truman, David B. 1951. *The Government Process: Political Interests and Public Opinion.* New York: Knopf.

Tudela y Bueso, Juan Pérez. 1998. *Obras Clásicas para la historia de Iberoamérica.* Madrid: Fundación Histórica Tavera Digibis.

Tulchin, Joseph S., ed. 1993. *Venezuela in the Wake of Radical Reform.* Boulder: Lynne Rienner.

Unger, Roberto Mangabeira. 1976. *Law in Modern Society.* New York: Free Press.

United Nations. 1979. Resolution 1963: *Code of Conduct for Officers in Charge of Law Enforcement.* New York: United Nations.

United States Department of State. 1983–1996. *Country Human Rights Practices, 1983–1999.* Washington, D.C.: U.S. Department of State, Bureau of Democracy, Human Rights, and Labor.

Universidad Nacional Autonoma de México. 1988. *El Constitucionalismo en las postrimerias del siglo XX.* Mexico City: Universidad Nacional Autonoma de México.

Valenzuela, J. Samuel. 1992. "Consolidation in Post-Transitional Settings: Notion, Process, and Facilitating Conditions." In Scott Mainwaring et al., *Issues in Democratic Consolidation: The New South American Democracies in Comparative Perspective.* Notre Dame, Ind.: University of Notre Dame Press.

Valero Briceño, Hidalgo. 1993. *Crisis Penal y Fenómeno Delictivo en Venezuela.* Caracas: Hidalgo Valero Briceño.

Van Cott, Donna Lee. 2000. "Legal Pluralism in Bolivia and Colombia." *Journal of Latin American Studies* 32, pt. 1 (February): 207–234.

Van Groningen, Karin. 1980. *Desigualdad social y aplicación de la ley penal.* Caracas: Editorial Jurídica Venezolana.

Vanossi, Jorge R. 1988. *Reforma de la Constitucion.* Buenos Aires: Emece Editores.

Vásquez, Néstor. 1993. "Institucionalización de las Escuelas Judiciales dentro de las Garantías Constitucionales." *Revista del Colegio de Abogados de La Plata,* no. 53.

Velásquez, Ramón J., et al. 1992. *Cúando se Jodió Venezuela.* Caracas: Consorcio de Ediciones Capriles.

Velázquez, Efrain J. 1991. *El Deficit Público y La Política Fiscal en Venezuela, 1980–1990.* Caracas: Banco Central de Venezuela.

Veliz, Claudio. 1978. *The Centralist Tradition of Latin America.* Princeton: Princeton University Press.

Vera Delgado, Ricardo. 1983. "Aspectos Fundamentales Sobre el Funcionamiento de la DISIP." In *Conferencias de los Jueces de Venezuela.* Caracas: Colegio de Abogados del Distrito Federal.

Verbitsky, Horacio. 1993. *Hacer la Corte.* Buenos Aires: Espejo de la Argentina.

Verner, Joel. 1984. "The Independence of Supreme Courts in Latin America: A Review of the Literature." *Journal of Latin American Studies* 16, pt. 2 (November): 463–506.

Vives Heredia, Pedro. 1972. "Patrocinio Jurídico a los necesitados, a cargo de la comuna de Buenos Aires." Revista *El Derecho* (January): 186–195.

Waldmann, Peter, ed. 1996. *Justicia en la Calle.* Medellín: Biblioteca Jurídica Diké.

Weber, Max. 1947. *The Theory of Social and Economic Organization.* New York: Oxford University Press.

Weder, Beatrice. 1997. "Legal Systems and Economic Performance: The Empirical Evidence." Washington, D.C.: World Bank.

Wheaton, Henry. 1827. *Reports of Cases Argued and Adjudged in the Supreme Court of the United States.* January Term, 1827, vol. 13. New York: R. Donalson.

Whitehead, Laurence. 2000. "Institutional Design and Accountability in Latin America." Paper presented at the annual meeting of the Latin American Studies Association, Miami, March 16–18.

Wilson, James Q. 1968. *Varieties of Police Behavior: The Management of Law and Order in 8 Communities.* Cambridge, Mass.: Harvard University Press.

Wise, George. 1951. *Caudillo: A Portrait of Antonio Guzmán Blanco.* New York: Columbia University Press.

World Bank (International Bank of Reconstruction and Development). 2000. "Development Beyond Economics." Washington, D.C.: World Bank.

———. 1995. *Staff Appraisal Report: Bolivia Judicial Reform Project.* Washington, D.C.: World Bank.

———. 1994a. *Ecuador: Judicial Sector Assessment,* Washington, D.C.: World Bank.

———. 1994b. *Encuentro Sobre Reforma de la Administración de la Justicia.* Buenos Aires: World Bank.

Wróblewski, Jerzy. 1987. "Theoretical and Ideological Problems of Judicial Independence." In Juan Salaverria, ed., *Los Jueces en Una Sociedad Democráticam.* Onatí: Herri-Arduralaritzaren Euskal Erak Undea.

Zaffaroni, Eugenio. 1994. *Estructuras Judiciales.* Buenos Aires: Sociedad Anónima Editora.

Zafra, J. 1961. "Posición del Ministerio Público en el futuro." *Revista de Derecho Procesal,* no. 4: 753–843.

Zemans, Frances Kahn. 1983. "Legal Mobilization: The Neglected Role of the Law in the Political System." *American Political Science Review* 77, no. 3 (September): 690-703.

INDEX

ABOUT THE BOOK

Elusive Reform explores one of the Latin American countries' biggest challenges: establishing a rule of law. Based on a close examination of historical patterns, it demonstrates how executive power and judicial disarray thwart progress toward judicial independence, state accountability, and citizen access to effective means of conflict resolution.

Ungar critiques the wide spectrum of agencies responsible for enforcing the law, from the police and prisons to provincial governors, the attorney general, and the judiciary itself. He similarly analyzes the region's most recent reform innovations, among them judicial councils, national ombudsmen, and community justice forums. Although his focus is on Argentina and Venezuela, he presents valuable material on other Latin American countries, particularly Bolivia.

Exposing many overlooked vulnerabilities of Latin America's democratic institutions, *Elusive Reform* broadens our understanding of democracy itself.

Mark Ungar is assistant professor of political science at Brooklyn College, City University of New York.

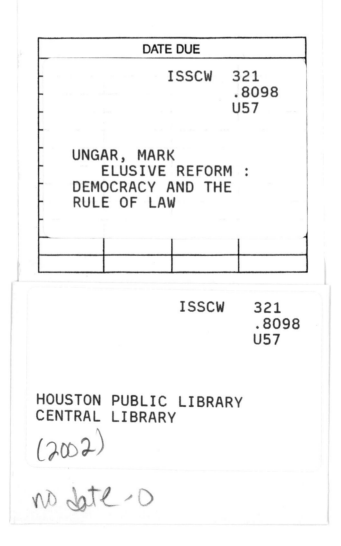